Radio Free Europe and Radio Liberty

Radio Free Europe and Radio Liberty

The CIA Years and Beyond

A. Ross Johnson

Woodrow Wilson Center Press
Washington, D.C.

Stanford University Press
Stanford, California

EDITORIAL OFFICES

Woodrow Wilson Center Press
Woodrow Wilson International Center for Scholars
One Woodrow Wilson Plaza
1300 Pennsylvania Avenue, N.W.
Washington, D.C. 20004-3027
Telephone: 202-691-4029
www.wilsoncenter.org

ORDER FROM

Stanford University Press
Chicago Distribution Center
11030 South Langley Avenue
Chicago, IL 60628
Telephone: 1-800-621-2736; 773-568-1550
www.sup.com

2 4 6 8 9 7 5 3 1

Library of Congress Cataloging-in-Publication Data

Johnson, A. Ross.
   Radio Free Europe and Radio Liberty : the CIA years and beyond /
A. Ross Johnson.
      p.   cm.
   Includes bibliographical references and index.
   ISBN 978-0-8047-7356-0 (hbk.)
   1. Radio Free Europe—History.   2. Radio Liberty—History.   3. United States.
Central Intelligence Agency—History.   4. International broadcasting—Europe,
Eastern—History.   5. International broadcasting—United States—History.
6. Radio in propaganda—Europe, Eastern—History.   7. United States—Foreign
relations—Europe, Eastern.   I. Title.
HE8697.45.E852J64 2010
384.54094—dc22

                                                                      2010031873

Woodrow Wilson
International
Center
for Scholars

The Woodrow Wilson International Center for Scholars is the national, living U.S. memorial honoring President Woodrow Wilson. In providing an essential link between the worlds of ideas and public policy, the Center addresses current and emerging challenges confronting the United States and the world. The Center promotes policy-relevant research and dialogue to increase understanding and enhance the capabilities and knowledge of leaders, citizens, and institutions worldwide. Created by an act of Congress in 1968, the Center is a nonpartisan institution headquartered in Washington, D.C., and supported by both public and private funds.

Conclusions or opinions expressed in Center publications and programs are those of the authors and speakers and do not necessarily reflect the views of the Center staff, fellows, trustees, advisory groups, or any individuals or organizations that provide financial support to the Center.

The Center is the publisher of *The Wilson Quarterly* and home of Woodrow Wilson Center Press and *dialogue* television and radio. For more information about the Center's activities and publications, including the monthly newsletter "Centerpoint," please visit us on the Web at www.wilsoncenter.org.

Lee H. Hamilton, President and Director

The activities and ramifications of our original organization have grown like a great oak tree whose steadily developing branches now reach out in many directions. But oaks spring from acorns; they have a beginning, and it is not without interest to remember the beginning of this whole movement.

—Joseph C. Grew, first chairman of the Free Europe Committee, 1954

Contents

Preface

This study of Radio Free Europe and Radio Liberty is based on research in a number of archives and utilizes information from a number of primary sources. The first major source is the Radio Free Europe / Radio Liberty (RFE/RL) Corporate Records Collection, which is deposited in the Hoover Archives at the Hoover Institution on War, Revolution, and Peace at Stanford University.[1] I have supplemented this corporate documentary record with the memoirs of, and my own interviews with, a number of former RFE and RL executives. I have had access to the RFE/RL historical security and personnel files, which remain closed at RFE/RL. I have also utilized the Sig Mickelson and other collections at the Hoover Archives that include RFE/RL materials, the transcriptions of RFE's Hungarian broadcasts during the 1956 Revolution made by the National Széchényi Library in Budapest, and the Robert F. Kelley Papers deposited in the Georgetown University Library, which contain key documents from the early years of Radio Liberty.

The second major source for this book is the extensive collection of records of the Central Intelligence Agency (CIA) and other U.S. government

---

1. RFE and RL were separate organizations until 1976, when they were merged as RFE/RL, Inc. They remained separate operating divisions of RFE/RL until 1994,when they were merged as one broadcasting division. RFE, RL, and RFE/RL records—cited in the footnotes as documents of the Free Europe Committee (FEC), American Committee for Liberation (AMCOMLIB), Radio Liberty Committee (RLC), RFE, and RL— are unclassified in their entirety and are part of the RFE/RL Collection, Hoover Archives. As private, nonprofit corporations, the organizations had no U.S. government authority to classify documents. Some documents bear markings such as "Strictly Confidential" and "RL Confidential"; these are corporate proprietary categories and not U.S. government classifications.

agencies retained at the CIA's All-Agency Records Center. I have also utilized declassified U.S. government documents, which are variously available on the CIA Web site (www.cia.gov), published in the State Department's *Foreign Relations of the United States* series, included in Gale's
Declassified Documents Reference Service database, or available at the National Archives and Records Administration.[2]

The CIA made available for my research extensive project files and other
internal records related to RFE and RL. Many of these records that I consulted remain classified and are referenced obliquely in the text. Others have
been declassified in whole or in part or are still being reviewed for possible
declassification at my request. All the CIA and other U.S. government documents that were declassified for this book are being deposited in the Vir-
tual Archive of the Cold War International History Project of the Woodrow
Wilson International Center for Scholars (www.cwihp.org).

The discussion of RFE/RL's German context draws on declassified German government archives available at the Political Archive of the German
Foreign Office in Berlin and the Bavarian State Archive in Munich. For
chapter 7, I utilized records from several Eastern European Communist
Party, intelligence, and security service archives, especially the East German Interior Ministry (Stasi) records at the Office of the Federal Commissioner (BStU) in Berlin, the Polish Interior Ministry records at the Institute
of National Remembrance in Warsaw, and the Polish Communist Party
records at the Archive of Contemporary History of the Polish State Archives
in Warsaw.

This book could not have been written without the encouragement and
support of many institutions and individuals. The Hoover Institution, where
I am a research fellow, and the Woodrow Wilson International Center for
Scholars, where I was a public policy scholar and am now a senior scholar,
supported my research. The Hoover Archives made available the RFE/RL
corporate records. The CIA's Review Panel approved my request for access
to records on RFE/RL under the provisions of Executive Order 12958. The
Center for the Study of Intelligence provided office space and research support. CIA information review officers provided access to classified records
under their jurisdiction and facilitated the document declassification
process. And the Archivists at the Political Archive of the German Foreign

---

2. As a general rule, the earlier the release of U.S. government documents, the
greater the redaction of references to RFE and RL before 1971, and thus the larger their
propensity to distort by omission the role of RFE and RL in U.S. policy.

Office in Berlin helped me locate and use declassified German government records on RFE/RL.

Former RFE and RL officials Arthur Brew, James Critchlow, Paul Henze, Robert Hutchings, John Leich, Gene Mater, Gene Parta, Arch Puddington, William Rademaekers, John Richardson Jr., Edward Van Der Rhoer, Gene Sosin, Robert Tuck, and Ralph Walter shared their experiences in publications, interviews, and written communications. Several of them read the manuscript and provided helpful suggestions, as did Robert Gillette and Csaba Békés. Paul Henze also made available his private correspondence as RFE deputy political adviser between 1952 and 1958. I draw on my own experience as RFE policy assistant for Poland between 1966 and 1969 and as RFE director from 1988 to 1991.

In granting me access to classified CIA records for historical research, the CIA stipulated that the resulting publication be submitted to its Publications Review Board to ensure that it contained no classified information. The board had no objection to any part of my manuscript, providing the following disclaimer:

> All statements of fact, opinion, or analysis expressed are those of the author and do not reflect the official positions or views of the CIA or any other U.S. government agency. Nothing in the contents should be construed as asserting or implying U.S. government authentication of information or Agency endorsement of the author's views. This material has been reviewed by the CIA to prevent the disclosure of classified information.

In addition to the individuals cited above, I am indebted to the following for support of and help with this book project: at the Hoover Institution, Director John Raisian, Elena Danielson, Charles Palm, Blanka Pasternak, Anatol Shmelev, Maciej Siekierski, and Richard Sousa; at the Woodrow Wilson Center, Director Lee Hamilton, Michael van Dusen, Mircea Munteanu, Christian Ostermann, and Samuel Wells; at the CIA, Herb Briick, Nicholas Djumovic, Mark Elcessor, Ben Fischer, Woodrow Kuhns, David Robarge, Scott Koch, and Michael Warner; and at the National Széchényi Library, Gábor Hanák and Bea Lukács. Priscilla Roberts generously shared with me her research on Frank Altschul in the Lehman Collection at Columbia University. None of them bears any responsibility whatsoever for the citations, exposition, and judgments in this book; that is mine alone.

Abbreviations and Acronyms

AMCOMLIB	American Committee for Liberation (renamed the Radio Liberty Committee, RLC, in 1964)
BBC	British Broadcasting Corporation
CIA	Central Intelligence Agency
CRBP	Committee on Radio Broadcasting Policy
DCI	Director of Central Intelligence
DDRS	Declassified Document Reference System (Gale–Cengage Learning)
FEC	Free Europe Committee
FRUS	*Foreign Relations of the United States* series of documents (U.S. Department of State)
IOD	International Organizations Division of the CIA
NARA	National Archives and Records Administration
NSC	National Security Council
NTS	Narodno-Trudovoy Soyuz (National Alliance of Russian Solidarists)
OPC	Office of Policy Coordination
RFE	Radio Free Europe
RIAS	Radio in the American Sector, Berlin
RL	Radio Liberty (until 1959, Radio Liberation)
RLC	Radio Liberty Committee
USIA	U.S. Information Agency
VOA	Voice of America

Radio Free Europe and Radio Liberty

Introduction: Radio as Soft Power

We are engaged in a difficult, complex task, partly private but predominantly governmental; many persons, nations, states, governments and U.S. government agencies are involved; our chance to do something useful for our country is unique; opportunities for misunderstandings and causes for feelings of frustration abound. For these reasons, we consider a continuation of our close cooperation and consultation is essential.

> —Frank G. Wisner, director of the Office of Policy Coordination, to DeWitt Poole, first president of the Free Europe Committee, 1949[1]

Since the fall of the Berlin Wall in 1989 and the dissolution of the Soviet Union in 1991, Radio Free Europe (RFE) and Radio Liberty (RL) have been widely praised in both the East and the West as contributing to the end of Communism in Europe and Eurasia. Asked in 1990 if RFE had contributed to the triumph of Solidarity in Poland, Lech Wałęsa responded rhetorically, "Is the Sun important for the Earth?" These Cold War "Radios" (as RFE and RL collectively came to be known) are praised in a series of documentary films—*Voice of Hope* (Poland), *Cold Waves* (Romania), *Waves of Liberty* (Spain), and *To Russia with Love* (Germany), all featuring testimonials of praise from listeners. The Radios are discussed, usually sympathetically, in the books listed in the bibliography. American officials and commentators today often invoke the experience of RFE (always better known than RL) in suggesting how "soft power" can be used to "win hearts and minds" today in the Muslim world and elsewhere.

1. Free Europe Committee letter to DeWitt Poole from Frank Wisner, August 1, 1949.

1

If we are to consider the relevance of this experience today, we must understand both how RFE and RL functioned during the Cold War and RFE/RL's record since the end of the Cold War in providing independent information to major parts of the former Communist Eurasian world. It is the Cold War experience that is the subject of this book; the aftermath awaits a chronicler.

Scope of the Book

This is not the first book on RFE and RL. Much of the existing literature focuses on the workings of the Radios as institutions, and on the operations and personalities in the Radios' broadcasting centers in Munich. Arch Puddington's *Broadcasting Freedom* (2000) and Sig Mickelson's *America's Other Voice* (1983) provide comprehensive overviews, and these and other useful books and articles are listed in the bibliography. A smaller body of literature, especially Gene Parta's *Discovering the Hidden Listener* (2007), focuses on the audience for the Radios' broadcasts.[2]

This book examines the role of RFE and RL as instruments of U.S. foreign and security policy during the first two decades of the Cold War. It is focused on the Radios' relationship with Washington—the source of most of their funds, their transmitter frequencies, and their ability to operate in Germany, Portugal, Spain, and Taiwan. It provides the first documented account of the origins of both Radios and their evolution into full-service substitute national broadcasters, later termed "surrogate" broadcasters. The book sets the record straight on the one RFE story that never dies—its broadcasts during the 1956 Hungarian Revolution—and on the neglected stories of RFE's performance during the Polish crisis of 1956 and RFE and RL's performance during the Soviet occupation of Czechoslovakia in 1968. It traces steps taken by the Communist regimes to counter the flow of uncensored information from the West that threatened their rule. It considers the nature of the public-private partnership between the Office of Policy Coordination and the Central Intelligence Agency (CIA) and the Radios they founded, funded, and oversaw for two decades. It addresses the question that puzzles more than troubles many former Eastern European and Soviet

---

2. Full information for the works mentioned in this paragraph, and for the other works mentioned in this introduction, is given in the bibliography and throughout the book, where they are cited in detail.

listeners: If the Radios were public broadcasters, why was the CIA involved at all?

I set out to write a book about both Radios during the entire Cold War period, concerned that I would lack sufficient documentation. "Be careful what you wish for." The volume of documentary material available at the Hoover Archives and other public archives and the extensive CIA records on the subject made available to me resulted in a focus on the first two decades, the CIA period. It was only later, during the 1970s and 1980s after all CIA involvement had ended, that the Radios truly proved their effectiveness. This had nothing to do with the change of funding and oversight, which became the responsibility of a new, openly funded executive branch agency, the Board for International Broadcasting. It had everything to do with the emergence of individual dissent and then organized opposition in the broadcast region that RFE and RL were able to reinforce. (The last section of chapter 8, "Life after the CIA," gives highlights of this period and provides references to the existing literature, especially Arch Puddington's book *Broadcasting Freedom*). But the Radios could not have played the important role they did in the 1970s and 1980s had not the institutions been shaped, and their policy and editorial course set, under the CIA in the 1950s and 1960s.

A further caveat is in order. This book deals with the Voice of America (VOA) and the British Broadcasting Corporation (BBC) World Service only to the extent that they affected RFE and RL history. Both major broadcasters, and other smaller national broadcasters, also played an important role in providing independent information to the Soviet orbit during the Cold War. VOA's Cold War role is examined in Alan Heil's *Voice of America* (2003), while the BBC World Service broadcasts to the Soviet orbit await a full history. The programs of these major international broadcasters were intended to be and largely were complementary and not duplicative. Each was ascribed a distinct mission at the outset, and while these missions converged over time, they never merged.

Words and Concepts

Contemporary literature on Cold War international information programs is bedeviled by three terms—"propaganda," "political and psychological warfare," and "covert operations." Today these terms usually grate and are often used pejoratively—but are rarely defined. As conceived in the late 1940s and early 1950s, political warfare was envisaged by George Kennan and others as a positive alternative to military conflict with an implacable enemy possessing nuclear weapons. Today, most prefer the term "soft power." Psychological warfare referred to the use of information in this context. Today, most prefer the phrase "communicating to unfree societies." Covert operations were seen by policymakers and analysts as a necessary modality for conducting certain foreign programs judged to be in the national interest that if conducted openly would have been thwarted by other countries or particular domestic constituencies. Today, the American democracy has little tolerance for covert operations and little ability to keep them covert. The term itself obfuscated vast differences between such secret U.S. government activities as mounting a paramilitary operation, supporting a coup, helping noncommunists win an election, "keeping Tito afloat," subsidizing an anticommunist publication, or starting RFE and RL.

"Propaganda" is the Cold War word most relevant to this book. Though a neutral term in many languages, "propaganda" has taken on a negative connotation in the English-speaking world and become a synonym for "spin," for biased, nonobjective, counterfactual, dishonest journalism or, worse, the deliberately misleading, manipulative pseudojournalism known as disinformation. In reading early Cold War documents, the reader should understand that "propaganda" ("any organized or concerted group, effort, or movement to spread particular doctrines, information, and so on—*Webster's New Collegiate Dictionary,* 1956) was a positive term for all international broadcasters. It may be translated into the current political vernacular as "information with a purpose," with no negative connotation. U.S. Cold War international information programs, whether overt or covert, were funded not for their own sake but "to disseminate abroad a spectrum of stories, news, interpretation and commentary which, it was hoped, would advance American interests and undermine those of its adversary."[3] Those programs sought (in the words of a 1950 Senate resolution) to counter Communist propaganda in the "contest for the minds of loyalties of men" through the "international propagation of the democratic creed," through a "Marshall Plan in the field of ideas."[4]

3. James M. Murphy, review of Hugh Wilford's *The Mighty Wurlitzer: How the CIA Played America* (Cambridge, Mass.: Harvard University Press, 2008), *Times Literary Supplement,* July 2, 2008.

4. U.S. Department of State, ed., *Foreign Relations of the United States* (Washington, D.C.: U.S. Government Printing Office, various years), 1950, IV, 315.

For RFE and RL, that purpose was, broadly stated, broadcasting freedom —as Arch Puddington aptly titled his book on the subject. Promoting freedom had nothing to do with propagating falsehoods. As RFE and RL quickly learned, if their message was to have any effect, it had to be fact based, balanced, and credible to an often skeptical audience. It had to cover the bad along with the good about the United States. It had to cover noncommunist socialist as well as more conservative approaches to public policy. Of course, there were "red lines" that could not have been crossed without violating democratic values. Of course, judgments had to be made daily about selection, emphasis, and tone. And of course, not all these judgments were wise— as is true with every group of editors in every practice of journalism.

This book examines the particular "red lines" and specific editorial policies adopted during the first two decades of the Radios' broadcasts. Some underlying assumptions are recorded in a 1954 Free Europe Committee memorandum.[5] The contemporary reader will better understand these assumptions if the text below from this 1954 memorandum is read with "information" substituted for "propaganda" throughout:

> It should be clearly established that RFE propaganda is neither white nor black, neither official nor clandestine. It is home service propaganda. One cannot say, therefore, that certain programs are "propaganda" and others by inference merely entertainment or "non-propaganda." The entire operation of Radio Free Europe, even its station identification repeated throughout the day, is propaganda.
>
> The semantics of propaganda have become involved since totalitarian techniques and the employment of the big lie came into existence. But exasperation with opposing uses of propaganda should not alter or guide our own. The basis of persuasion to a point of view, to a cause, is the hypothesis of propaganda thought and action and ours can be largely incorporated in one word, "freedom," together with the principles of conduct we believe to be part of that concept.
>
> Since there is no standard procedure for propaganda content analysis, one must rely on credibility of content and acceptability of method. Home service broadcasting, as method, needs no defense. Through this service cultural propaganda, which can state a good case, is often more effective than political propaganda. No one can say whether the broad

5. Free Europe Committee memorandum, "Analysis of Radio Free Europe's New York Programs," no author given, December 1954, 3–5.

base of propaganda is less important than its sharp point. Inspirational religious broadcasts may be *as* effective in any audience area as the speedy announcement of [Soviet prosecutor and foreign minister Andrei] Vishinsky's death or disclosures by [Polish secret police defector Józef] Światło. . . .

RFE does not attempt to be doctrinal or propagandistic, to employ propaganda for the sake of propaganda. It *can* attribute much of its program success to fluidity and diversity. Propaganda is not only policy but morality and humanity, and in this respect its techniques must serve the idea and not vice versa. Because RFE's idea is "freedom," special care must be taken in its presentation.

The intent of RFE and RL was to provide listeners with an intellectual bridge to Western Europe and the United States and a factual basis for comprehending their own lives and the world around them, so as to preserve the independent thinking that the controlled domestic media sought to prevent or suppress. The underlying premise of the Radios' programming was that preserving this capacity for independent thought and, at least on a limited basis, discussion would prevent the authoritarian governments in the Soviet sphere from fully consolidating their power over the societies they ruled. This premise would prove to be correct.

Chapter 1

Present at the Creation

Books on Radio Free Europe and Radio Liberty, many listed in the bibliography, usually describe the establishment of both Radios as part of an American effort to utilize World War II refugees from the USSR and Eastern Europe to communicate anticommunist messages to their homelands. Histories written after the early 1970s, while acknowledging funding from the Central Intelligence Agency and the initial contribution of such U.S. government officials as George Kennan and Frank Wisner, generally portray the founding of the Radios as largely private initiatives and minimize subsequent CIA and U.S. government involvement.

CIA and other U.S. government records reviewed for this book, and other declassified U.S. government records now available, tell a more nuanced story—on two scores. The Radios were not the beginning but the culmination of efforts in the late 1940s and early 1950s to harness the talents of recent émigrés from the Soviet Union and Soviet-controlled Eastern Europe to promote the United States' national interests in the aftermath of World War II. This process focused initially on supporting émigrés financially and preparing them for a role in restoring freedom to their homelands in peace or war, rather than putting them to work as communicators.

And though the Radios enjoyed a perhaps surprising degree of autonomy in their operations, given oversight and funding by a government intelligence organization, they would not have emerged without the initiative and backing of the Department of State and the organizational efforts of the Office of Policy Coordination and the CIA, of which it was a loose part. Moreover—to preview a thesis developed in this book—the Radios would have been emasculated or closed down at several points throughout the first two decades of their history had it not been for the supporting hidden hand of

7

the CIA, especially the responsible CIA offices in the then–Directorate of Plans (that is, operations)—first the International Organizations Division, and later the Covert Action Staff.

Planning for what would become the Radios began in 1947, when deteriorating Soviet-American relations and tightening Soviet control over Eastern Europe led influential Americans both inside and outside the government to consider how Soviet and Eastern European émigrés might be utilized to help the United States confront what it saw as an emerging Soviet challenge. Present at the creation of several émigré projects were, most notably, George Kennan and Frank Wisner, by mid-1947 both in Washington at the State Department and with past service in the USSR and Eastern Europe, respectively, and Allen Dulles, then in private law practice in New York but with close Washington ties and past service as chief of the Office of Strategic Services (OSS) in Switzerland. Official sanction for these early efforts was provided by National Security Council (NSC) Directive 4/A of December 1947, which authorized the CIA to conduct "covert psychological operations designed to counteract Soviet and Soviet-inspired activities which constitute a threat to world peace and security."[1]

Following a tour of displaced persons' camps in occupied Germany in the fall of 1947, in his capacity as deputy assistant secretary of state for occupied areas, Wisner drafted a paper on how those refugees—of which perhaps a half million remained after millions were forcibly repatriated under the terms of the Potsdam Agreement—might help advance American interests. Kennan addressed the same issue in a Policy Planning Staff paper that called on the CIA to recommend whether the mass of refugees "can be effectively utilized to further U.S. interests in the current struggle with the U.S.S.R."[2] In March 1948, Wisner convened an ad hoc interagency committee to consider (drawing on Kennan's paper) how to utilize refugees "to fill the gaps in our current official intelligence, in public information, and

---

1. "NSC 4A, December 17, 1947," reproduced by Michael Warner, ed., *CIA Cold War Records: The CIA under Harry Truman* (Washington, D.C.: Center for the Study of Intelligence, 1994), 173–75. Kennan, as first head of the State Department's Policy Planning Staff, participated in interagency discussions that resulted in the directive, urged that the State Department approval be required for any covert operation, and received one of three copies of the document. See U.S. Department of State, *Foreign Relations of the United States* (hereafter, *FRUS*) (Washington, D.C.: U.S. Government Printing Office, various years), 1945–50, *The Emergence of the Intelligence Establishment,* 615–52.

2. Policy Planning Staff paper 22/1, "Utilization of Refugees from the Soviet Union in U.S. National Interest," March 11, 1948, in *The Department of State Policy Planning Papers 1948* (New York: Garland, 1983), vol. II, 88–102.

in our politico-psychological operations."[3] Kennan took the next step, and in May 1948 he submitted to the NSC a paper titled "The Inauguration of Organized Political Warfare" that proposed support of émigré liberation committees, underground activities behind the Iron Curtain, and indigenous anticommunist forces in threatened countries of the Free World. Kennan specifically suggested formation of a public American organization, working closely with government, "enabling selected refugee leaders to keep alive as public figures with access to printing presses and microphones [but] not engage in underground activities." All such covert activities were to be coordinated by the Department of State and conducted by a new political warfare organization separate from the CIA.[4]

International tension increased in 1948 following the Communist takeover in Czechoslovakia in February and the emerging Berlin crisis. In this atmosphere, lobbying by Wisner was instrumental in turning Kennan's draft into American policy in the form of NSC Directive 10/2 of June 1948 (superseding NSC 4/A). NSC 10/2 established the Office of Policy Coordination (OPC; first called the Office of Special Projects) as a "new agency" loosely connected with the new CIA for "quarters and rations" but responsible to the secretaries of state and defense "to plan and conduct covert operations" to counter Communist activities directed against U.S. interests. Such operations, including "assistance to refugee liberation groups," along with "propaganda" and "subversion against hostile states," were to be so conducted "that any U.S. Government responsibility for them is not evident to unauthorized persons and that if uncovered the U.S. Government can plausibly deny any responsibility for them."[5] Overt foreign information programs "designed to influence attitudes in foreign countries in a direction

3. State-Army-Navy-Air Force Coordinating Committee 395, "Utilization of Refugees from the Soviet Union in U.S. National Interest, " March 17, 1948, State-War-Navy Coordinating Committee case files 382-402, March 1947–June 1949, NARA.

4. "Policy Planning Staff Memorandum," May 4, 1948, document 269, in *FRUS, Emergence of the Intelligence Establishment.* The final draft of this memorandum, dated April 30, 1948, was released under the Freedom of Information Act with fewer redactions to Douglas Selvage, who kindly made a copy available to the author.

5. NSC 10/2, June 18, 1948, copy reproduced by Warner, *CIA Cold War Records,* 213–16. For details of this history see *FRUS, Emergence of the Intelligence Establishment,* 615–21; Warner, *CIA Cold War Records,* xviii–xxi; and Evan Thomas, *The Very Best Men* (New York: Simon & Schuster, 1995), 24–31. The OPC retained substantial autonomy until January 1952, when it and the CIA's Office of Special Operations, responsible for espionage, were merged into the new CIA Directorate of Plans (later renamed the Directorate of Operations and now the National Clandestine Service).

favorable to the attainment of U.S. objectives and to counter effects of anti-U.S. propaganda" had earlier been made the responsibility of the Department of State (and after 1953 would become the responsibility of the United States Information Agency [USIA] until its disbandment in 1998).[6]

Origins of the Free Europe Committee

Before the establishment of the OPC in mid-1948, covert psychological operations were the responsibility under NSC 4/A of the Special Procedures Group within the emerging CIA Office of Special Operations (the clandestine espionage service). In early 1948, the Special Procedures Group had begun preparing broadcast and print facilities in Europe for use by émigrés against both the USSR and its satellites, designated Project UMPIRE. The OPC inherited this planning effort.[7] Following calls by influential private citizens for enhanced psychological warfare capabilities to supplement the armed forces,[8] and approval by President Harry Truman of NSC 10/2 that established the OPC, an interagency working group convened in August 1948 to put into practice the political warfare measures outlined in Kennan's May paper. According to an OPC memorandum, the working group suggested using covert U.S. government funds to establish "a democratic philanthropic organization in New York under some such name as the American Committee for Free Europe which in turn would organize a committee of responsible foreign language groups now in the western zones of Germany and provide them with facilities for communication with their homelands."[9] The plan assumed that "the offer of this opportunity to communicate with their homelands would serve as the catalytic agent in creat-

6. "NSC 4, December 17, 1947," document 252, in *FRUS, Emergence of the Intelligence Establishment.*

7. "Memorandum from the Assistant Director for Policy Coordination (Wisner) to Director of Central Intelligence Hillenkoetter," document 306, in *FRUS, Emergence of the Intelligence Establishment.*

8. E.g., John Foster Dulles' speech "In Defense of Freedom" to the Bond Club, New York City, May 6, 1948, where he called for the creation of a Cabinet-level federal agency, termed by the *New York Times* (May 7, 1948) a "Department of Non-Military Defense," that would use radio and print media to "bring out the facts" of Communist rule and also provide support to exile leaders.

9. The Free Europe Committee was incorporated in New York as the Committee for Free Europe, Inc., a nonprofit corporation, on April 29, 1949. The name was changed on May 15, 1949, to National Committee for Free Europe, Inc.; changed again to National Committee for a Free Europe, Inc. on April 11, 1950; changed to Free Europe Commit-

ing unity among the presently disunited refugee foreign nationality groups in W. Germany."[10]

The August 1948 plan specified that the New York committee was to approach General Lucius Clay, commanding general of American Occupation Forces in Germany, to request permission for foreign language groups to broadcast to their homelands, with the understanding that the committee had offered facilities for this purpose. The real preparations occurred behind the scenes. Shortly after the August 1948 meeting, a member of Wisner's staff drafted a statement of principles for the new committee. In October 1948, OPC officer Maynard Barnes visited General Clay and obtained his support for the project. Wisner himself followed up with the U.S. high commissioner for Germany, John J. McCloy, in May 1949.[11]

In early 1949, the OPC moved to put the émigré support plan into operation, but with an altered émigré and geographic focus. The project now focused on Eastern European and not Soviet émigrés and envisaged a key role for the various U.S.-based émigré organizations grouped into national councils instead of European émigré organizations. This shift to a U.S.-based operation focused on Eastern Europe is explained by two factors. First, at that time General Clay feared increased Soviet pressure on Germany if anti-Soviet émigré organizations were to openly operate there.[12] Second, the State Department wished to free itself from the burden of daily dealings with the Eastern European émigré groups in Washington. Reflecting later on the origins of the Free Europe Committee (FEC), Kennan wrote:

The Department of State was beginning to be troubled, by 1949, with frequent visits from various well-known and worthy individuals who were refugees or voluntary exiles from the iron curtain countries. What these

---

tee, Inc., on March 5, 1952, and to Free Europe, Inc. on November 15, 1965. Throughout, this book usually refers to the "Free Europe Committee," or FEC.

10. OPC, memorandum of conversation, August 26, 1948, released to the author in March 2009. The meeting was attended by Wisner and his OPC deputies, Director of Central Intelligence Hillenkoetter, and representatives of the Office of Special Operations / SPG, the State Department Policy Planning Staff, and the Joint Chiefs of Staff.

11. "Memorandum from the Assistant Director for Policy Coordination, Central Intelligence Agency (Wisner) to Members of His Staff, June 1, 1949," document 310, in *FRUS, Emergence of the Intelligence Establishment.*

12. Earlier, Clay had objected strongly to a 1946 State Department plan for the Voice of America to broadcast to the USSR from Germany as violating the spirit of the Quadripartite Government for Germany. This was well before any planning for Radio Liberty. See *FRUS,* 1946, vol. 5, 687–89; Jean D. Smith, *Lucius D. Clay: An American Life* (New York: Henry Holt, 1990), 285 (which misidentifies the project as RL).

people wanted . . . was mostly sympathy, understanding, and support for their efforts . . . [to ignite] the spark of hope for a better future in their respective countries. All this they deserved, . . . but it seemed clear to me that the Department of State was not the proper place for them to receive it. . . . I did not think it proper that geographic desk officers, in particular, who were charged with the responsibility of communication with the official representatives of those governments, should also be entertaining relations with people interested only in the overthrow of the regime in question.[13]

Kennan, Wisner, and Llewellyn E. Thompson Jr. (a State Department Soviet expert) agreed on the revised OPC plan on February 21.[14] Kennan and Wisner jointly recommended the project to Secretary of State Dean Acheson, who endorsed it on March 1, 1949. Kennan subsequently reendorsed the project to Acheson as of "vital importance" and "one of the principal instrumentalities for accomplishing a number of our most important policy objectives." Wisner met with Federal Bureau of Investigation director J. Edgar Hoover in April to obtain his blessing for the U.S.-based project.[15] Wisner approved the committee project on April 26, 1949. The OPC, as the responsible U.S. government agency, began preparations to rent office space in New York and provide for covert funding.

In the fall of 1948, Wisner and Kennan had begun to reach out to prominent Americans outside the government to include in the project. Wisner first consulted with Mark F. Etheridge (a confidant of President Truman, and one drafter of the "Truman Doctrine"), who was at the time chairman of the U.S. Advisory Committee on Information, which oversaw State Department information programs, including Voice of America. Not only did Wisner obtain Etheridge's endorsement, he enlisted him as a founding member of the FEC. Wisner then contacted other prospective FEC members, most

13. FEC letter to Joseph C. Grew from George Kennan, November 4, 1954. Tom Braden later commented: "The problem was with the refugees. . . . They were eating up everyone's time. And they were high-level people, like former prime ministers. . . . There had to be some way to keep them in a blue suit. I always figured that was what it was really about." Braden interview, May 5, 1982, Mickelson Collection.

14. OPC memorandum to Wisner, "Notes on Discussion of New York Committee with Mr. George Kennan, February 18, 1949," released to the author in March 2009. The memorandum is signed by Kennan, Wisner, and Thompson.

15. OPC memorandum for the files, April 19, 1949, released to the author in March 2009.

important, Allen Dulles (then with his New York law firm, Sullivan & Cromwell, but chairing an NSC study group on intelligence), Charles Spofford (New York lawyer and World War II general), John C. Hughes (textile magnate and OSS officer), Harry Harper, and General Marshall; the first three agreed to join. By early 1949, Allen Dulles was actively involved in the effort from New York, reaching out to several of his former OSS associates to enlist their participation while reworking the statement of principles originally drafted by the OPC "to embody some ideas from my brother and from one or two other confidential sources [Hamilton Fish Armstrong was one], as well as certain of my own thoughts on the subject."[16] Kennan remained actively involved in recruiting FEC members. Although he failed to enlist Henry Stimson to serve as FEC chairman,[17] he did persuade Joseph C. Grew (former undersecretary of state and ambassador to Japan, earlier an officer in the U.S. Embassy to Tsarist Russia) to take the position. DeWitt C. Poole (who headed the State Department's Russia Division in the early 1920s and was later chief of the OSS Foreign Nationalities Branch) agreed to serve as executive director (a post soon renamed president). Other eminent Americans and many former senior officials, including Dwight D. Eisenhower, agreed to join the FEC. The first board of directors included, in addition to Dulles, Grew, and Spofford, Frank Altschul (secretary of the Council on Foreign Relations), Fred Dolbeare (a prominent lawyer who had served with Dulles in the State Department and the OSS), retired general Hugh A. Drum, Arthur W. Page (an AT&T public relations executive), and Gregory Thomas (a business executive and former OSS chief for Iberia), Most FEC directors had World War II backgrounds in intelligence, covert operations, or psychological warfare. Seven of the thirteen FEC directors who served in 1949 and 1950 were OSS veterans, while others had served in military psychological warfare units.[18]

16. Dulles wrote to an unnamed correspondent (probably Fred Dolbeare) on February 17, 1949, that "a possible opening for interesting and constructive work somewhat along the lines of the work we did together in the war days may open up rather shortly." He corresponded on March 21 with DeWitt Poole and Maynard Ruddock (Wisner's deputy) on the committee charter; Letters in RFE/RL Collection, Hoover Archives. The final statement of principles issued by the Free Europe Committee on June 1 was essentially Dulles' reworked draft.

17. Kennan to Bohlen, April 18, 1949, Records of Charles E. Bohlen, box 1, record group 59, NARA, as cited by Michael Wala, *The Council on Foreign Relations and American Foreign Policy in the Early Cold War* (Providence: Bergham Books, 1994), 215.

18. The FEC was legally a membership corporation, with members (initially forty-one as of early 1950), a board of directors, and an executive committee of that board.

The FEC was launched with great fanfare (initially as the National Committee for Free Europe) on June 1, 1949. In a press conference that day, Ambassador Grew listed its three objectives: "to find suitable occupations for those democratic exiles who have come to us from Eastern Europe"; "to put the voices of these exiled leaders on the air, addressed to their own peoples back in Europe, in their own languages, in the familiar tones [and] to get their messages back by the printed word"; and to experience democracy in action in the U.S. and convey that message to their homelands.[19] At Kennan's request, Secretary of State Acheson informed State Department missions abroad of State's "unofficial approval" and publicly endorsed the project at a June 23 press conference: "Yes, the State Department is very happy to see the formation of this group, such a distinguished group. It thinks that the purpose of the organization is excellent and is glad to welcome its entrance into this field and gives it its hearty endorsement."[20]

As the FEC directors held their first meetings, Wisner met privately with Poole and Dulles (who became chairman of the FEC's Executive Committee) on the task of soliciting private contributions, an activity seen from the outset by Dulles and other FEC directors more as a way to gain public support for the FEC's efforts and provide a cover for covert U.S. government funding than as a significant source of revenue.[21] This was the origin of the Crusade for Freedom, publicly launched on April 26, 1950, under the chairmanship of now-retired General Clay and overseen by FEC director Arthur Page.[22] General Eisenhower endorsed the start-up of the crusade in a nationwide radio address on September 4. The crusade quickly developed a national network of local outreach and fundraising activities, centered first on

19. FEC memorandum, "Portions of Introductory Statement by Joseph C. Grew, June 1, 1949"; also, FEC, "Declaration of Policy, June 1949," in NCFE Handbook, May 1950.

20. Department of State airgram, June 21, 1949, excerpt in RFE/RL Collection; press conference of Secretary of State Dean Acheson, June 23, 1949, printed in *American Foreign Service Journal,* September 1949.

21. After the meeting, Wisner quoted Dulles as saying: "Only by the solicitation of sizeable contributions from individuals will their interest, attention and support be evoked. This is needed in order to make of the Committee the really important instrument which it is designed to be. In addition to this, there is the necessity of creating cover for the governmental funds which are used."

22. Noel L. Griese, *Arthur W. Page: Publisher, Public Relations Pioneer, Patriot* (Atlanta: Anvil, 2001), 345ff. Also see Richard H. Cummings, *Radio Free Europe's "Crusade for Freedom": Rallying Americans Behind Cold War Broadcasting, 1950–1960* (Jefferson, N.C.: McFarland & Co., 2010).

the Freedom Bell, a replica of the Liberty Bell, to be placed in West Berlin. It organized a National Crusade for Freedom Council; one early member was Senator J. William Fulbright, who was later to become an archenemy of the Radios.[23] The crusade soon took on a life of its own. Separately incorporated as a nonprofit corporation in October 1950, it sometimes competed for resources and public attention with the FEC it was supposed to support. Its net financial contribution to RFE was only $500,000 in the first three years.[24]

The Crusade for Freedom would become more successful during the Eisenhower administration's two terms, when it was managed by the American Heritage Foundation and raised about $3 million a year at a cost of $1 million, netting $2 million yearly for the FEC.[25] This reinvigoration of the crusade was a consequence of both the stronger "liberation" rhetoric of the first Eisenhower term about Eastern Europe and regular White House dinners or luncheons for large corporate donors, which were first hosted by Eisenhower in September 1953 and continued into the Lyndon Johnson administration. These corporate contributions from executives who knew or suspected the U.S. government's if not the CIA's role in funding the FEC constituted the bulk of crusade revenue, not "Truth Dollars" from unwitting individual citizens. The International Organizations Division sounded the alarm to the director of central intelligence about this focus on corporate gifts in early 1955, arguing for a return to the original concept, described as establishing and maintaining "cover" of the FEC as an official instrument and generating grassroots support in the United States for FEC operations. Corporate gifts nonetheless continued to provide the bulk of the revenue.

The FEC itself, during its first months of operation, focused on finding useful work for talented émigrés. By the end of 1949, it was supporting more than a hundred exiles in various study projects,[26] which would in time expand to include the Free Europe Press, the Mid-European Studies Center, the Free European University in Exile in Strasbourg, and many other activities. Inevitably, the FEC quickly became enmeshed in émigré politics —so much so that the OPC evidently became concerned that it was slow off the mark in organizing radio communications to Eastern Europe from Germany and devoting too much time and energy to the various émigré national councils under its auspices.

---

23. FEC document, Crusade for Freedom, Campaign Letter No. One, May 1, 1950.
24. Griese, *Arthur W. Page.*
25. Ibid. The FEC's total budget in those years was around $16 million.
26. FEC memorandum, "Progress Report—January 1950."

The OPC's concerns were exaggerated, for however much time FEC officials spent on émigré issues, they did not neglect preparations for broadcasts. By the spring of 1950, the FEC was preparing for the first broadcasts of RFE, to be taped in New York and aired on a 7.5-kilowatt shortwave transmitter near Frankfurt made available by the OPC. This approach was viewed from the outset as a stopgap measure, and it was assumed that powerful European-based shortwave transmitters would follow. Planning for radio broadcasts was the responsibility of the FEC's radio policy subcommittee headed by Frank Altschul. The subcommittee comprised, apart from Altschul, six renowned journalists and public figures—Edward R. Murrow, Arthur Schlesinger Jr., Jay Lovestone, C. D. Jackson, Paul Kesten, and Edgar Ansell Mowrer—who began in mid-1949 to plan for radio broadcasts.[27]

Altschul hired Robert Lang, another former OSS officer then at General Mills, to get radio broadcasts on the air. Lang spent December 1949 in Europe, unsuccessfully attempting to lease time on existing European transmitters (including those of the BBC, which declined to provide such a channel for émigré views),[28] and then exploring alternatives with High Commissioner John J. McCloy and his aide Forrest McCluney. It was on that trip that Lang became acquainted with Radio in the American Sector (RIAS) in Berlin and concluded that its full-service substitute home radio (later termed "surrogate") concept for Eastern Germany was the model for future RFE broadcasts. The FEC received the same message from General Clay, an enthusiastic supporter of RIAS, who joined the FEC after retiring from his European command.[29]

27. Altschul outlined programming, informational, and technical challenges that a radio operation would need to master in a memorandum to Poole, July 12, 1949, Lehman Collection, Columbia University Library. I am indebted to Priscilla Roberts for generously sharing her research on Altschul in the Lehman Collection. A good discussion of the issues confronting the radio committee a year later is contained in an FEC memorandum to Allen Dulles from Frank Altschul, August 21, 1950.

28. "The BBC's function is to reflect British opinion on affairs and the views of exiles are closely subordinated in our broadcasts to that end." Letter to Charles E. Dewey Jr. from J. B. Clark, Director of External Broadcasting, BBC, July 10, 1953, RFE/RL Collection.

29. Clay interview, in Smith, *Lucius D. Clay,* 565–66. Clay viewed RIAS as "independent from the government," notwithstanding its open financing by the Military Government. RIAS broadcasts notwithstanding, FEC directors evidently also explored the possibility of broadcasting to East Germany. "Memorandum by Mr. Robert P. Joyce of the Policy Planning Staff to the Deputy Assistant Secretary of State for European Affairs (Thompson)," in *FRUS,* 1950, IV, 945–46.

RFE's first broadcasts, in Czech/Slovak[30] and Romanian, were aired on July 4, 1950, and were followed over the next two months by New York–produced broadcasts in Polish, Hungarian, and Bulgarian, and on June 1, 1951, in Albanian. Broadcasts in the languages of the Baltic states were planned (but never started because of State Department opposition). Broadcasts to Yugoslavia were also originally envisaged, but they were abandoned as the Tito-Stalin conflict worsened and Yugoslavia's relations with the West improved. These first RFE broadcasts, however brief and however weak their signal, had some immediate resonance, as indicated by negative references by a Polish Communist leader and Soviet official A. I. Zharov and a positive report from the U.S. Embassy in Prague.[31]

Branded as "Voice of Free Czechoslovakia," "Voice of Free Poland," and similarly for the other Eastern European countries, RFE broadcasts were presented as communications from émigrés enjoying in the West freedoms now abolished in their homelands. But which émigrés? In the spring of 1950, Altschul posed the crucial question: "To what extent is Radio Free Europe the voice of the émigré groups, rather than the voice of American citizens using émigré groups to the maximum advantage?"[32] The initial answer of the State Department and OPC was that RFE was the voice of émigrés, as represented by the various national councils supported by the FEC: "the National Councils should be afforded Radio facilities in order that they

---

30. In 1954, the Czechoslovak Service also broadcast a daily five-minute program in Carpatho-Ruthenian for the minority in eastern Slovakia, but also reaching Ukraine.

31. Zharov report, document 43, given in *Cold War Broadcasting: Impact on the Soviet Union and Eastern Europe—A Collection of Studies and Documents,* ed. A. Ross Johnson and R. Eugene Parta (Budapest: Central European University Press, 2010), document 43; Department of State Prague dispatch, September 5, 1950, sanitized copy enclosed with FEC letter to Fred Dolbeare from OPC, September 6, 1950, W-493, RFE/RL Collection. The RFE/RL Collection includes unclassified communications between FEC and AMCOMLIB/RLC and CIA. The FEC correspondence used pseudonyms before 1959, and thereafter was conducted between the "President" of the Free Europe Committee and the "Executive Committee" [not to be confused with the FEC directors' own executive committee], i.e., the CIA. References to "Advisory Council" in this correspondence mean the Department of State. The AMCOMLIB/RLC correspondence was conducted between the "President" of the committee and the "Advisory Board" or the "Board of Trustees," i.e., the CIA.

32. "Memorandum Regarding Organization of Radio Free Europe" [by Frank Altschul], June 12, 1950, Altschul papers, Lehman Collection. Writing to Allen Dulles in August, Altschul added that "to a considerable extent these Councils represent the past, and in measure the unpalatable past, of the peoples whom we wish to influence." FEC Letter to Dulles from Altschul, August 21, 1950.

may communicate with their fellow countrymen behind the Iron Curtain."[33] This was the principle reflected in FEC president Jackson's oft-quoted declaration to émigré staff at the dedication of the Munich English Garden building in 1951: "I am turning over to you the keys to this building which is yours to operate as you see fit."[34] It was the principle reflected in FEC president Harold Miller's remarks on the occasion of the first RFE Polish broadcasts originating from Munich in 1952: "Captain [Jan] Nowak . . . I present to you this new station, Radio Free Europe, the Voice of Free Poland."[35]

Such words, however welcome to émigrés, were hyperbole. The original notion of RFE broadcasts as communications of unified national emigrations operating in the freedom of the West with acknowledged leaders and represented by national councils was never implemented in practice and was, as a principle, soon confronted with the reality of émigré disarray and infighting. Thus, Robert Joyce of the State Department's Policy Planning Staff lamented in the fall of 1950 to Frank Wisner:

> It appeared to me incredible that the various individuals in the refugee groups should be quarrelling over issues such as the boundary between Croatia and Serbia, Slovak separatism, the percentage of the votes obtained by the Hungarian Small Holders Party in 1945, whether or not G. Hitrov was the authentic leader of the Bulgarian peasant party, etc., etc., rather than agreeing as patriotic citizens of their respective countries on fundamental issues such as self-determination, the reestablishment of basic human freedoms and democratic processes in their respective countries.

It was the incredulity of Joyce, former OSS intelligence chief for the Balkans, that was incredible, given his recent exposure to Balkan ethnic politics and the history of conflict within all political emigrations from time immemorial. The condition of sixteenth-century English refugees in Holland

---

33. "Principles Governing Relations of National Council for a Free Europe with the National Councils of Refugee Political Leaders from Eastern Europe," no author indicated, n.d. [1949], Kelley Papers, box 5, folder 3; FEC Letter to DeWitt Poole from OPC, W-6581, October 27, 1950.

34. Quoted by Sig Mickelson, *America's Other Voice: The Story of Radio Free Europe and Radio Liberty* (New York: Praeger, 1983), 42.

35. Recording of May 3, 1952, inauguration of the Polish Service in Munich, RFE/RL Collection.

was not much different.[36] This was not the first time that a government would attempt to base a national security policy on the illusion of united national emigrations able to speak for their fellow citizens at home—nor the last. As FEC official John Foster Leich saw it:

> Political exile is a sui generis condition, with its attendant frustrations, problems, and discouragements. In the absence of an elected mandate, the political exile can only emphasize his differences with the fellow exiles; and he begins to see victory in terms of favors or concessions he has extracted from the protecting powers.[37]

In the early 1950s, the OPC and then the CIA were much quicker than the State Department to face up to the reality of émigré squabbling and the impracticality of broadcasts organized by and representing émigré organizations. This realism was one factor motivating the OPC to argue for distancing RFE physically from American émigré politics and moving most production and therefore staffing of RFE radio programs to Europe. Other factors behind the shift to Europe were the desire to avoid excessive news focus on the United States, viewed as duplicative of the Voice of America; the ability to recruit fresh talent from the larger pools of émigrés in Europe; and the possibility of providing more timely information to the broadcast countries from a base in the same time zone, essential for RIAS-like home service broadcasting.

By late 1950, the FEC concluded that its (never implemented) "original plan of permitting exiles, through their loosely organized Councils or Committees, to wholly develop, manage, and control RFE broadcasting" was unworkable.[38] It began to plan for the production as well as transmission of broadcasts in Europe. Reviewing the situation at the end of 1950, Wisner concluded that the choice was either to expand the RFE effort and base it in Europe or to close it down. Remaining in the United States, he said, would mean "too heavy Americana and there will be a tendency to be influenced by professional political refugees of ancient vintage and no particular meaning within the target areas." FEC director Allen Dulles had expressed this

36. Tom Braden, in his interview with Sig Mickelson, recalled Macaulay's account in his *History of England from the Accession of James II.*

37. John Foster Leich, "Great Expectations: The National Councils in Exile, 1950–1960," *Polish Review* 35, nos. 3–4 (1990): 195.

38. FEC memorandum, "RFE Exile Personnel Selection," n.d. [late 1950].

same view in early November 1950. After joining the CIA later that month, he was in a position on January 11, 1951, to endorse Wisner's (and his own) recommendation for RFE's expansion and relocation to Europe.[39]

Once authorized, work on European facilities for RFE proceeded rapidly. Construction of a studio facility on the edge of Munich's English Garden was approved in January 1951; the building was partly in operation four months later and fully operational in November. The first broadcasts, by the Czechoslovak Service, were carried on a mobile transmitter near the Czechoslovak border provided by the OPC, but this mobile transmitter was replaced in May by a powerful newly constructed medium-wave (AM) transmitter at Holzkirchen near Munich.[40] By November 1951, four short-wave transmitters were in operation at Biblis, near Frankfurt (including the original transmitter moved from nearby Lampertheim, vacated for use by RL). These transmitter sites could be made available without delay because all were former German military bases now controlled by the American military occupation authorities. Austrian stations interfered with the Holzkirchen medium-wave transmitter frequency, so the FEC negotiated with the government of still-occupied Austria for it to vacate the frequency (719 kilocycles) in exchange for financial and technical assistance for Austrian stations operating on a different wavelength.[41]

The physics of shortwave broadcasting required transmitters located at a greater distance from Eastern Europe than Germany, and Portugal was an early candidate. Following State Department approval in December 1950

39. CIA memorandum to DCI from Wisner, November 22, 1950, with concurrence of Assistant Secretary of State for Public Affairs Edward Barrett, released to the author in October 2004; CIA memorandum to Dulles from Wisner, January 11, 1951, released to the author in October 2004. Barrett was an FEC member before joining the State Department. His support for RFE is indicated in his memoirs; Edward W. Barrett, *Truth Is Our Weapon* (New York: Funk & Wagnalls, 1953), 96. Although he resigned his FEC management positions upon joining the CIA, Dulles remained a member of the FEC corporation until he was appointed DCI in early 1953.

40. A management consultant gave the FEC high marks in mid-1951 for creating a far-flung operating organization in a few months. Westinghouse Electric International Company, Survey Report on Radio Free Europe, by R. G. Duffield, special consultant. Munich was evidently chosen as the locale for RFE's European headquarters because it was the second-largest city in the U.S. Occupation Zone, distant from the U.S. High Commission in Frankfurt, and a center of many émigré-related activities. See Mickelson, *America's Other Voice,* 31–32.

41. FEC document, "Agreement between Representatives of the Austrian Government and the National Committee for a Free Europe, Inc., New York, N.Y." [October 30, 1951].

of the FEC's negotiations with Portugal on a shortwave transmitter facility, the American ambassador broached the issue with Portuguese leader Antonio Salazar, and within twelve months, under the auspices of a Portuguese subsidiary (RARET), a powerful RFE shortwave transmitter facility was operating from what had been an inaccessible cork plantation. The key to this rapid success in Portugal was the personal relationship between the American negotiator, FEC director Gregory Thomas, who had served in Portugal as OSS chief for Iberia, and Salazar, no defender of free speech, who viewed hosting an anticommunist American facility as a way to strengthen Portugal's position in NATO and the Atlantic Community.[42]

On May 1, 1951, RFE broadcast from Munich its first European-produced program, in Czech/Slovak, expanding weekly broadcast hours from 10 to 145, and now carried on medium wave (that is, AM) as well as shortwave. The initial broadcasts met with a positive response in interested Western European circles. The Swiss paper *Gazette de Lausanne* published a front-page article by its chief editor on May 23 welcoming the RFE Czechoslovak service, while cautioning that it would need to remain objective to be effective. Expanded RFE Hungarian broadcasts from Europe soon followed, and full-service Polish broadcasts were launched on May 3, Polish National Day, in 1952.

The FEC originally envisaged that Bulgarian (and later Romanian) broadcasts would be produced at and transmitted on medium wave not from Munich but from a second RFE overseas facility located in Turkey.[43] The U.S. government authorized the FEC in June 1954 to negotiate with the Turkish government, and the FEC proposed to Ankara a Turkish subsidiary modeled on RARET in Portugal, with the important difference that it would be responsible for original program production facilities as well as the operation of a million-watt medium-wave transmitter station. Negotiations dragged on for two years but ultimately proved unsuccessful as projected costs mounted, the Turkish government insisted on excessive control, and the country's political stability was questioned in Washington.[44] In retrospect, it is fortunate

42. Thomas summarized his activities in Lisbon in early 1951 in an FEC memorandum dated March 9, 1955, with appended copies of his 1951 progress reports, and in an extensive interview with Sig Mickelson, Mickelson Collection, Hoover Archives. See also Mickelson, *America's Other Voice*, 43–50.
43. FEC memorandum, "Basic Policy Paper; Istanbul Project" [January 1954].
44. FEC's proposal to the Turkish government is summarized in an undated 1954 memorandum, copy in DDRS. Paul Henze (then deputy policy adviser in Munich), who participated in the negotiations, described their failure in an informal memorandum,

that the negotiations with Turkey failed. Had they succeeded, two separate RFEs—one for the Northern Tier and one for the Southern Tier—would have evolved, with great potential for bureaucratic, funding, and policy conflicts between them. This did not happen, and expanded Bulgarian and Romanian broadcast production was also centered in Munich, albeit on a smaller scale than for Czechoslovakia, Hungary, and Poland.

RFE's rapid expansion in 1951 led, no doubt inevitably, to bureaucratic conflict with the Voice of America, then part of the State Department, which had barely survived the post–World War II demobilization but was now expanding with the outbreak of the Korean War. Although the FEC and OPC had outlined a mission for RFE different from and seen as supplementing that of VOA, VOA officials saw matters differently. They viewed RFE European-based programming as duplicating the work of VOA's own large Munich Programming Center. RFE's Eastern European broadcasts were already a fact of life, so VOA officials focused on heading off RFE's planned Baltic broadcasts, arguing that they would duplicate just-started VOA broadcasts in Estonian, Latvian, and Lithuanian. VOA management also understandably resented the Crusade for Freedom's exclusive focus on RFE (and the short-lived Radio Free Asia of the day) as threatening political and budgetary support for VOA in the U.S. Congress and among the American public.

FEC and State Department officials attempted unsuccessfully in mid-1951 to agree on a division of labor.[45] Matters came to a head in a State Department–CIA "summit" in November 1951 involving Allen Dulles (now CIA deputy director), Frank Wisner, Edward Barrett (assistant secretary of state for public affairs), Foy Kohler (VOA director), and Robert Joyce (of the State Department's Policy Planning Staff).[46] Given State's strong opposition, Dulles agreed to postpone any decision on RFE Baltic broadcasts and

---

"Notes on Demise of RFE Istanbul Project and State of Affairs in Munich," September 30, 1955, Henze Correspondence.

45. In a letter to VOA director Foy Kohler dated June 12, 1951, Altschul suggested that "the Voice is essentially a propaganda arm of the United States government" whereas "Radio Free Europe . . . is a citizens adventure in the field of psychological warfare." In a reply dated June 19, 1951, Kohler (who had managed VOA Russian broadcasts after service in the Moscow Embassy before becoming VOA director) objected that "your memorandum reflected very little information about what VOA does" and suggested alternative language. Letters in Lehman Collection.

46. "Memorandum for the Files, November 23, 1951," document 94, in *FRUS, The Intelligence Community,* reporting on a November 20 meeting. Some of the same group had reviewed the issues, without reaching agreement, in a previous meeting on November 15.

to tone down the Crusade for Freedom's exclusive focus on RFE. In a follow-up meeting in January 1952 that also included FEC directors C. D. Jackson and Abbott Washburn, it was agreed to continue but reduce the scale of the crusade in 1952.[47] That decision—which in fact had little impact on crusade operations—led Jackson to resign in protest from the FEC—the first of many such resignations and, like later protests, one he soon withdrew. The postponement of RFE broadcasts to the Baltic states led to protest by Baltic émigré groups in the United States[48]—the first of many such protests that finally led to the initiation of RFE/RL Baltic broadcasts in 1975.

The year 1951 brought some clarification of the relationship between RFE and the various Eastern European émigré organizations in the United States. The State Department had continued to view RFE broadcasts as properly the emanations of émigré national councils under the purview of the FEC, and urged that as a first step the Hungarian National Council (the best organized) be given full responsibility for RFE broadcasts.[49] By then, the OPC had come to view this approach as unworkable, because the national councils were internally divided and poorly led. It viewed the Romanian Council, with its own source of funds (prewar Romanian gold), as particularly troublesome and noted that the divided Polish emigration could not even agree on constituting a council. Wisner underlined this state of affairs to the State Department in April 1952, arguing that the original concept of national council–sponsored broadcasts was no longer useful. Though the State Department subsequently and reluctantly accepted the OPC/CIA concept of RFE broadcasting, which was endorsed by the Jackson Committee in 1953,[50] it continued to insist that the FEC remain responsible for various émigré matters (including welfare).

47. "Memorandum of Conversation, January 17, 1952," document 100, in *FRUS, The Intelligence Community.*

48. For the protest to the State Department by heads of the Lithuanian and Estonian government-in-exile legations, see "Memorandum of Conversation, by Willard Allan of the Office of Eastern European Affairs, December 18, 1951," document 657, in *FRUS, 1951, IV.*

49. FEC copy of State Department / Office of Eastern European Affairs memorandum, "The Functions of NCFE and RFE," January 22, 1952, copy also in Kelley Papers, box 5, folder 3.

50. "The Report of the President's Committee on International Information Activities, June 30, 1953," in *FRUS, 1952–54, National Security Affairs,* vol. 2, part 2, 1831–34; "Memorandum for the National Security Council," October 1, 1953, in *FRUS, 1952–54,* vol. 2, part 2, 1898–99, quoting Jackson Committee Recommendation 11: "[FEC] should devote primary attention to RFE. The other activities of [FEC] should be

Just as the State Department had sought to shift responsibility for most émigré matters to the FEC so that it could concentrate on official relations with the Eastern European countries, the FEC now organized the Assembly of Captive European Nations in September 1954 to separate (and partly distance) émigré affairs from RFE. The assembly remained dependent on the FEC for funding but took on a life of its own. It came to vocally oppose the U.S. "bridge-building policy" of the 1960s and thus put itself at odds with both U.S. foreign policy and RFE broadcasting guidelines.[51]

Although the OPC played a crucial role in the birth of the FEC, the FEC enjoyed substantial autonomy from the outset—partly by OPC design, partly by FEC self-assertion, and partly because both organizations were working out the ground rules of an unprecedented public-private enterprise as they went along. As an internal CIA review later noted, "The Agency had not formally conceived of subsidy and proprietary projects as types of activities within the broad sphere of Agency operations. At that time there was no general Agency policy and there were no provisions in Agency regulations by which the formal conception of a project of this nature could be governed." The OPC envisaged from the outset, as an early 1949 memorandum from the director of central intelligence (DCI) stated, that the FEC "would not be a simple cut-out for money and direction but would have the greatest possible freedom of action . . . consistent with general government practices with respect to the disbursement and accountability of such funds." Yet it should have come as no surprise to Wisner and his OPC associates that prominent directors of the FEC, many with OSS backgrounds

---

subjected to review by CIA." The FRUS documents are heavily redacted; in February 2008, the CIA released an almost complete copy of the Jackson Committee Report as part of the Richard Helms Collection.

51. FEC directors expressed concern in early 1964 about Assembly of Captive European Nations (ACEN) statements "causing on occasion considerable embarrassment to our government"; FEC directors Executive Committee minutes, January 9, 1964. ACEN expressed "reservations" about Secretary of State Dean Rusk's speech of February 25, 1964, on selective U.S. engagement in Eastern Europe, arguing that the "much vaunted changes" only served to strengthen the regimes and "undermine further the spirit of resistance of the vast majority of non-Communists." "ACEN's Reaction to Dean Rusk's Speech," *ACEN News,* April–May, 1964, 21, 22. ACEN's budget was cut in half in 1965. See Anna Mazurkiewicz, " 'The Voice of the Silenced Peoples': The Assembly of Captive European Nations," in *Anti-Communist Minorities in the U.S.: Political Activism of Ethnic Refugees,* ed. Ieva Zake (New York: Palgrave Macmillan, 2009), chap. 8; also see Arnold Beichman, "European Exiles in a Squabble," *New York Herald Tribune,* October 10, 1965; Leich interview with the author.

like his own and some with far more experience in psychological warfare than his, had their own ideas about the project and welcomed U.S. government funds far more than U.S. government guidance. Symptomatic of the FEC's self-assertiveness were its decisions to incorporate without telling the OPC in advance and to add William J. Donovan to its roster of members,[52] notwithstanding OPC reservations about placing the former OSS chief in such a high-profile role. As Wisner reported to DCI Roscoe H. Hillenkoetter in May 1949, even in the planning stage "a difficulty was posed by the insistence of the committee on having complete autonomy for their actions, and the stated responsibility of the DCI for certification as to the use of funds." One FEC director, perceiving efforts by the OPC to increase its control over the operation, wrote to Alan Dulles in the fall of 1949: "Frank [Wisner] and the [FEC] are in substance equal contributors and in equal working partnership. . . . He has a bear by the tail."[53]

The FEC-OPC partnership was formalized in a memorandum of understanding in October 1949. The memorandum reaffirmed the purpose of the FEC as outlined in its June 1949 Declaration of Policy and described it as a public organization incorporating a high degree of government interest, as "autonomous" but having "due regard for the source of its funds," that is, the OPC, as the U.S. government body providing funds, requiring certain administrative procedures, and serving as the channel for policy guidance from the State Department.[54] A second memorandum of understanding, dated August 4, 1952, stipulated that the FEC would submit its program and budget proposals yearly by May 1, that the CIA would provide security clearances for appropriate FEC employees, that FEC directors could continue to deal directly with the DCI on major issues (thus bypassing the CIA liaison office), that the CIA would provide the FEC with appropriate policy guidance, and that the FEC would ensure that its activities were conducted in a manner consistent with U.S. government policy.[55]

52. CIA general counsel Lawrence Houston interview, October 12, 1982, Mickelson Collection, tape 3.

53. "To turn the private agency now back into something more nearly an official agency is to lose much of what it has been sought to gain." FEC Letter to Dulles [from an unnamed FEC Director], September 8, 1949.

54. The October 1949 memorandum of understanding is discussed in an FEC letter to Allen Dulles from DeWitt C. Poole, September 28, 1950, CIA copy released in June 1999, available at www.foia.cia.gov.

55. This two-page document imposed fewer restrictions on the FEC than the eleven-page draft originally proposed by the CIA. FEC vice president Spencer Phenix outlined

It is further testimony to the partnership that, apart from subsequent security agreements, these were the only such memoranda of understanding ever agreed to between the CIA and the FEC in twenty-two years of CIA oversight. Their substance testified to the unique CIA-FEC relationship, which recognized the autonomous prerogatives of the FEC. Radio Liberty, discussed in the next section, was launched on a quite different basis. Yet in time it would come to enjoy much the same degree of autonomy as RFE.

Origins of the American Committee for Liberation

With the FEC launched in mid-1949 and focused on Eastern Europe, George Kennan and Frank Wisner, along with other State Department and OPC officials, returned to the question of Soviet refugees in Europe, drawing on a May 1949 paper, "Utilization of Russian Political Refugees in Germany and Austria," by Robert F. Kelley, a senior Foreign Service Soviet expert and mentor to Kennan who had joined OPC in the spring of 1949.[56] A Soviet émigré project was endorsed at a State Department–OPC meeting in July 1949 that included Kennan, Wisner, and State Department Soviet experts Charles E. Bohlen and Llewellyn E. Thompson Jr. The project was authorized in a memorandum to Wisner from Kennan in September. It envisaged a central organization in Germany, with branches in New York and Paris, controlled and funded by the OPC and focused initially on émigré welfare until the operation could become effective enough to be used for political warfare. It was not to involve the FEC, which was told to exclude

---

objections to the original draft in an FEC memorandum to President Miller dated June 13, 1952.

56. Kelley headed State's Division of Eastern European Affairs from 1926 to 1937, where he worked with Allen Dulles and mentored George Kennan, Chip Bohlen, and other Soviet experts. An opponent of recognition of the USSR, he was "exiled" to the American Embassy in Turkey during World War II and then joined OPC in early 1949. See Frederic L. Propas, "Creating a Hard Line toward Russia: The Training of State Department Soviet Experts, 1927–1939," *Diplomatic History* 8, no. 3 (July 1984): 209–26 (the citation here is on 225); Foy D. Kohler and Mose L. Harvey, *The Soviet Union: Yesterday, Today, Tomorrow—A Colloquy of American Long Timers in Moscow* (Miami: University of Miami Center for Advanced International Studies, 1985), 30, 164; and Kelley Papers, box 2, folder 1. Kelley joined AMCOMLIB in September 1953 and was its senior representative in Europe until his retirement in 1967. He maintained contact with Kennan and at least once quietly hosted Kennan at Radio Liberty; communication from James Critchlow, March 5, 2009.

Russians from its purview and remain focused on Eastern Europe (including the Baltic states).[57]

The first step toward the Soviet émigré project was a survey of Soviet émigrés in Europe, a task Wisner authorized in December 1949. Kelley was dispatched to Europe to conduct the survey, and his initial report concluded optimistically that "the dominant trend of the political strivings of the Russian emigrants is toward unity and not towards the creation of irrevocably opposed groupings."[58] Based on this conclusion, Kelley recommended that the OPC encourage the emergence of an anticommunist united front embracing all worthwhile elements of the Russian emigration, establish a separate directing "bureau" for the unified émigré organization, begin radio broadcasts to the USSR and support émigré publications, and establish a cover organization in the United States to conceal the role of the U.S. government.

Kelley's report was the basis for discussion among Kennan, Wisner, and their associates during the summer of 1950. Prominent émigrés provided inputs directly. The Menshevik leader Boris Nikolaevsky advocated to the OPC a Russian and not American organization that would promote anticommunist dissent in the USSR by radio broadcasts and the printed word.[59] The outcome was a project, code named QKACTIVE,[60] approved by the OPC on September 28, 1950.

As a first step in carrying out the project, the American Committee for Liberation from Bolshevism (AMCOMLIB) was launched in February

57. Department of State memorandum to Wisner from Kennan, September 13, 1949, released to the author in March 2009. A State Department memorandum—"Political Warfare against the USSR, October 21, 1949"—and an OPC response by Kelley—November 7, 1949, Kelley Papers, box 5, folder 1—were further contributions to defining the Soviet émigré project.

58. "Survey of Russian Emigration," by Robert F. Kelley, April 26, 1950, 128, Kelley Papers, box 5, folder 14; excerpts also in Lebed archives, Harvard Ukrainian Research Institute, box 1, file 12. Kelley wrote two updates to the basic study, "Supplement (Covering 1950–1951) to Survey of the Russian Emigration," December 1951, and "Composition of the Coordinating Center of Anti-Bolshevik Struggle and Question of its Expansion," January 1, 1953, Kelley Papers, box 5, folder 14a.

59. Letter to [OPC official] Carmel Offie from Nikolaevsky, April 10, 1950, with enclosure "Russian Action and Its Tasks," Kelley Papers, box 5, folder 1.

60. The project name is given in declassified RG 263 documents at NARA. The origins of AMCOMLIB are traced in an OPC memorandum to Dulles from Wisner, "History of Project," August 21, 1951, released to the author in March 2009, and elliptically in "RLC Memorandum to The President from Donald C. Dunham, March 31, 1960," Annex 1, "The Chronological Development of the American Committee as a Propaganda Instrument in Political Warfare."

1951 (initially, as the American Committee for Freedom for the Peoples of the USSR), with the aim "to encourage the establishment in Western Germany by the refugees from every part of the Soviet Union of a central organization embracing all democratic elements."[61] Just as for the FEC, George Kennan helped recruit the initial trustees (as AMCOMLIB directors were called), whose roster would include Eugene Lyons (former Moscow correspondent and *Reader's Digest* editor, who became AMCOMLIB president); Reginald T. Townsend, who became executive director; William Henry Chamberlin (a writer for *Wall Street Journal* and *New Leader* and author of a history of the Russian Revolution), Allen Grover (vice president of *Time*), William Y. Elliot of Harvard, William L. White (a journalist and publisher), Charles Edison (a former governor of New Jersey), and the Russian-born journalist and author Isaac Don Levine. Kennan's interest was personal as well as professional; some of the impetus came from knowledge of the "Committee of American Friends of Russian Freedom" established by his great uncle and namesake in the late 1800s.[62] The project envisaged the establishment of a cover committee, a central organization uniting all democratic émigrés, and various publicity and welfare functions—but at the outset not broadcasting.[63] An initial OPC plan for a full-blown radio operation targeted at the USSR was rejected by DCI Walter Bedell Smith in August 1951 on the grounds that expected benefits did not justify the costs. The OPC then fell back on a more modest approach, planning radio broadcasts only for Soviet forces in East Germany over RFE transmitters (with the possibility envisaged—but never implemented—of RFE itself producing Russian programming until the new committee could take it over). The State De-

61. AMCOMLIB press release, March 7, 1951. The American Committee for Liberation was originally incorporated in Delaware in March 1951 as the American Committee for Freedom for the Peoples of the USSR, Inc., a nonprofit corporation. The name was changed to American Committee for Liberation of the Peoples of Russia, Inc., in June 1951; to American Committee for Liberation from Bolshevism, Inc., in April 1953; to American Committee for Liberation, Inc., in September 1956; and to Radio Liberty Committee, Inc., in January 1964. The multiple changes of name reflected the Committee's dilemma in dealing with the Soviet nationality issue. Throughout, this book refers to the American Committee for Liberation, AMCOMLIB, or the Radio Liberty Committee, RLC.

62. OPC memorandum, "Cinderella Discussion with Mr. Kennan of 21 August 1950," August 21, 1950, released to the author in March 2009; Kennan interview with Robert T. Holt, *Radio Free Europe* (Minneapolis: University of Minnesota Press, 1958), 233.

63. AMCOMLIB press release, March 7, 1951.

partment's priorities for the project, as recorded in a 1951 memorandum by Franklin Lindsay, were first, supporting an émigré newspaper; second, organizing broadcasts to Soviet occupation forces in Germany; and only third, envisaging broadcasts to the USSR itself.[64]

Early operational planning nonetheless assumed that RL would eventually broadcast to the USSR itself. An August 1951 engineering survey identified Biblis, Germany, and Barcelona as optimal transmitter sites for shortwave broadcasts to European Russia.[65] The U.S. high commissioner for Germany reserved radio frequencies, studios were planned for Paris, and a basic mission statement was drafted sharply differentiating the planned broadcasts from those of VOA.[66] All this echoed the preparatory steps for RFE broadcasts in 1949 and 1950. Yet the negative experience of the FEC notwithstanding, the OPC/CIA and AMCOMLIB efforts in 1952 were devoted not to starting radio broadcasts but to attempting to unify the Soviet emigration. This was seen as the priority by all who were involved in the project—George Kennan in (temporary) retirement (who was consulted regularly by OPC and CIA officers), Foy Kohler at VOA (who continued to have a negative view of the initial RFE and Radio Free Asia broadcasts and perhaps saw this approach as a tactic to delay additional non-VOA broadcasts), AMCOMLIB, and the OPC/CIA. AMCOMLIB planning assumed that an organization representing the united emigration would be responsible for program content, delegating day-to-day responsibility to émigré program directors, with AMCOMLIB limiting itself to overall supervision and financial and technical support.[67] AMCOMLIB trustee Isaac Don Levine outlined this perspective (in language echoing that used by C. D. Jackson in Munich a year earlier) to émigré representatives assembled in Germany in June 1952: "The radio must be built on the basis of the principle: a radio from the emigration—for the peoples behind the iron curtain. . . . We will

64. OPC memorandum for the record, "Subject: Development of Russian Political Center" [discussion among senior OPA/CIA and State Department officials], September 6, 1951, released to the author in March 2009.

65. "Short Wave Transmitter Locations for Serving Russia," A. D. Ring & Co., Washington, August 10, 1951. RFE/RL Collection.

66. AMCOMLIB letter to Lyons from General Thomas T. Handy, commander in chief, U.S. Armed Forces in Europe, February 28, 1952.

67. AMCOMLIB executive committee meeting minutes, July 18, 1952. An AMCOMLIB release of August 1952 highlighted the role of the Russian émigré organization "through which [AMCOMLIB] will channel such material aid and friendly guidance as it can muster." Kelley Papers, box 5, folder 1, p. 6.

give you [émigrés] an excellent and powerful radio station." In the words of an internal AMCOMLIB history: "Although certain controls and restrictions might have to be imposed by the Committee for reasons of policy or from budgetary considerations, the initiative and thereby the spirit of its activity would spring from the emigration."[68]

Doubts about the feasibility of a unified émigré organization sponsoring broadcasts gradually set in.[69] AMCOMLIB trustee Levine organized three meetings of émigré groups in Germany in 1951 and two more meetings in 1952. At the fifth meeting, held in Munich in October 1952, four Russian groups (with the most active group, the National Alliance of Russian Solidarists, Narodno-Trudovoy Soyuz, abstaining) and five primarily Caucasus nationality groups (but, of particular importance, not the Ukrainian group) agreed to form a "Coordinating Center for the Anti-Bolshevik Struggle" that would produce broadcasts under a program director named by the center. AMCOMLIB signed an agreement with the Coordinating Center in November 1952 that limited its role in radio programming to "special rights of inspection." The Coordinating Center's Central Bureau and AMCOMLIB officials signed an additional agreement in January 1953 on the management of RL that confirmed a primary role for the Coordinating Center.[70]

Two more meetings of émigré organizations were held under AMCOMLIB auspices in 1953; at the seventh meeting, held at Tegernsee in May, whatever common ground had been reached earlier dissipated and the "Coordinating Center" split into two parts, one Russian and the second the non-Russian Soviet nationalities (the League for the Liberation of the Peoples of the USSR, the so-called Paris Bloc). Broadcasting in Russian and other

68. AMCOMLIB memorandum, "Negotiations for an Effective Partnership: A Study of the Negotiations between the American Committee for Liberation from Bolshevism and Leaders of the Emigration from the USSR to Create a Central Émigré Organization for Anti-Bolshevik Activity" [probable author: Wil Cates], June 30, 1956; copy also in Kelley Papers, box 5, folder 2, pp. 3, 87; "Brief History of the Munich Organizational Activities of the American Committee for the Liberation from Bolshevism," draft, November 11, 1953, Kelley Papers, box 5, folder 1.

69. Dissent from the assumption that the Soviet emigration could be unified was expressed within the OPC and the CIA from the outset. Reacting to the Kelley report, another OPC officer argued in mid-1950 that "conditions essential for a reasonably cohesive united front organization do not exist."

70. "Negotiations for an Effective Partnership"; Harry Schwartz, "Russian Émigrés Form Single Unit," *New York Times,* November 5, 1952; AMCOMLIB memorandum, "Basic Principles Concerning the Management of the Radio Station," April 8, 1953.

languages began at the urging of AMCOMLIB president Admiral (Retired) Leslie Stevens, and with the CIA's blessing on March 1, 1953, nominally under the sponsorship of the short-lived Coordinating Center.[71] But the center had been unable to identify a suitable program director, and in late 1952 AMCOMLIB itself (in the person of radio adviser Manning Williams, another former Foreign Service Soviet expert, assisted by Boris Shub from AMCOMLIB in New York, who had worked at RIAS) began to assemble the team of broadcasters that produced the first RL programs. AMCOMLIB itself also planned the Coordinating Center's newspaper.[72]

In the course of 1952, the CIA (which had by now had fully assimilated the OPC) realized the difficulty of uniting various Russian émigré groups and the impossibility of uniting Russians and non-Russians. An internal CIA project reviewer concluded in late 1952 that the sooner radio operations could be removed from the Coordinating Center's political control, the sooner it would be possible to put a radio program on the air.

The FEC's directors were, if anything, ahead of the OPC/CIA in realizing that émigré organizations could not effectively carry out broadcasting to Eastern Europe in the U.S. interest. The opposite was the case at AMCOMLIB. The CIA's view was resisted by AMCOMLIB president Stevens, who continued to affirm the importance of programming produced by and in the name of a united emigration.[73] Internal CIA reviews in early 1953 highlighted the differences between Stevens' continued espousal of broadcasting sponsored by émigré organizations and the CIA's disenchantment with that

71. The list of initial RL broadcast services was determined by participation of émigré organizations in the Coordinating Center: Russian, Georgian, Azerbaijanian, Armenian, Turkestanian, and North Caucasian. AMCOMLIB later reached separate agreements with Belorussian and Ukrainian émigré organizations and established those language services in 1954. See RLC memorandum [by Kelley], [1955].

72. AMCOMLIB memorandum, "Guidance on Projected Newspaper for Coordinating Center," by L. S. Stevens, March 6, 1953.

73. Stevens (who succeeded the first AMCOMLIB president, Admiral [Retired] Alan G. Kirk, a former ambassador to the USSR) was himself a Russia expert. He had served as naval attaché in Moscow between 1947 and 1950, was a key figure on Truman's Psychological Strategy Board, and authored a book on Russia. He was no Pollyanna about the prospects of émigré unification, but believed that working together on limited projects such as radio broadcasting and a newspaper with American encouragement and support could mitigate émigré divisions. AMCOMLIB memoranda by Stevens: "The Role of the Soviet Emigration" [December 1952], "Additional Note 'On the Role of the Soviet Emigration,'" n.d. [late 1952 or early 1953], and "Guidance on Projected Newspaper for Coordinating Center," March 6, 1953.

approach. The reviews concluded that the Coordinating Center had no value as an instrument for unifying the emigration, that the center's sponsorship of RL was actually inimical to practical radio operations, and that control had to be firmly in American hands because RL was designed to serve U.S. interests. The Soviet Russia Division of the Directorate of Plans had taken over from the OPC responsibility for AMCOMLIB and RL in 1952, and division chief Dana Durand endorsed these views to Frank Wisner. Lamenting that to date project QKACTIVE had focused on émigrés rather than on the peoples of the Soviet Union and that it would prove impossible to operate the radio effectively as long as the center projected its political quarrels into the station, Durand concluded that the radio had to be independent of the center. The 1953 Jackson Committee report likewise recommended less attention to the émigré coordinating center, stating that AMCOMLIB should focus its attention on radio broadcasting, not émigré affairs.[74]

Meanwhile, Radio Liberation (as it would be known until 1959) was on the air. Its broadcasts that began on March 1, 1953, a few days before Stalin's death, consisted of a half-hour Russian program and several fifteen-minute programs in non-Russian languages daily, repeated several times. They were aired to European Russia on shortwave transmitters from Lampertheim (near Biblis, taken over from RFE) and to the Soviet Maritime Provinces from transmitters leased on Taiwan from 1954 to 1971 (when the lease was ended for budgetary reasons). In 1954 the State Department approved AMCOMLIB approaches to Spain and Pakistan for transmitter sites, and AMCOMLIB president Howland Sargeant began talks with the Spanish government in June 1955 with assistance from Ambassador John Davis Lodge. AMCOMLIB's negotiations with Spain proceeded more slowly than had the FEC negotiations with Portugal, a consequence of a temporary hold on the project in the wake of the Hungarian Revolution and the absence of a direct personal tie to Spanish leader Francisco Franco comparable to Gregory Thomas's connection with Salazar in Portugal. It was four years after initial project approval before RL transmissions began from Playa de Pals, near Barcelona, increasing by 1964

---

74. "The Report of the President's Committee on International Information Activities, June 30, 1953," in *FRUS, 1952–54, National Security Affairs,* vol. 2, part 2, 1829–31; "Memorandum for the National Security Council," October 1, 1953, in *FRUS, 1952–54,* vol. 2, part 2, 1898–99, quoting Jackson Committee Recommendation No. 10: "[AMCOMLIB] should concentrate on the improvement of Radio Liberation and reduce expenditures on the émigré coordinating center"; also available in the February 2008 version of the report released by CIA as part of the Richard Helms Collection.

to 1.3 million watts of shortwave transmitter power.[75] The Spanish facility complemented what became 340 kilowatts of shortwave transmitter power at Lampertheim in Germany and 160 kilowatts of leased transmitter time on Taiwan, for a combined RL transmitter power of 1.8 million watts.

With the first RL broadcasts on the air, the policy dispute about the role of émigré organizations in RL broadcasting came to a head in mid-1953. AMCOMLIB president Stevens staunchly defended the original concept of the broadcasts as the voice of the Soviet emigration, while the Soviet Russia Division and other CIA units concluded that the Russian emigration—let alone the Ukrainian and other Soviet nationalities—would never be united enough to take responsibility for the broadcasts. By then George Kennan, too, had given up on uniting the emigration and in consequence downplayed the importance of the broadcasts, which he thought could be conducted by RFE and might serve a later purpose as a bargaining chip with the USSR. When Stevens continued to dissent, the CIA forced his replacement by former assistant secretary of state for public affairs Howland Sargeant in October 1954.[76]

Controversy about the role of émigré organizations in AMCOMLIB broadcasting—now split between an all-Russian "Coordinating Center for the Liberation of the Peoples of Russia" and the "Paris Bloc" of non-Russian émigré organizations—would continue. But even early enthusiasts for the cause of émigré unity had become disenchanted; Isaac Don Levine, who had devoted 1951 and 1952 to that effort in Europe, now wrote: "First, the quest for a fairly broad political front in the emigration is a chimera and a delusion. . . . Second, the chasm between the majority of the Great Russians and of the non-Russian nationalities is beyond bridging."[77] AMCOMLIB would continue to work with individual émigré organizations, and a Council of Editors comprising émigré broadcast service directors would participate in policy discussions. But the concept of émigré organization sponsorship for RL broadcasts was abandoned as a precept incompatible with

75. The Playa de Pals story is well told in Mickelson, *America's Other Voice,* chap. 8, "Franco Pays Off" and in the documentary film *Waves of Liberty,* Canal Paradis, Barcelona, 2007.

76. CIA dissatisfaction with Stevens was magnified by his pretensions to define U.S. foreign policy toward the USSR and by his insistence on living in Annapolis and commuting to New York City.

77. AMCOMLIB memorandum by Isaac Don Levine, "New Policy for AMCOMLIB," December 15, 1954.

effective radio broadcasting. Accordingly, CIA project planning for fiscal year 1955 defined RL broadcasts as overt anti-Soviet efforts organized by the U.S. government aimed at weakening Soviet power and prestige "with such cooperation as is obtainable from moderate elements in the emigration." This shift away from émigré projects in general and from broadcasting managed by a united émigré organization in particular was made clear in the first sentence of the April 1954 AMCOMLIB mission statement: "To conduct overt anti-Soviet activities designed to weaken the prestige and power of the Soviet dictatorship, primarily within the USSR, and thereby to reduce its threat to world security, with such cooperation as is obtainable from moderate elements in the emigration from the USSR which are willing to work together in this task."[78] Thomas W. Braden (by then responsible for the project at the CIA) added in mid-1954 that, with the dissolving of the Coordinating Center,

> Radio Liberation was freed from interference and control of émigré politics and politicians. Full control is firmly in the hands of the American staff. Nevertheless, the voice of Radio Liberation remains true to its basic concept. The programming staff is composed largely of recent Soviet escapees who write and articulate all of the radio's output. It is this staff which enables Radio Liberation to speak in a voice and from a point of view which is most understandable to the peoples within the USSR.

The change in mission statement effectively closed the chapter on émigré sponsorship of RL broadcasts, just as it had been closed in 1950 for RFE broadcasts. It left open the question of the provenance of RL broadcasts— the question Frank Altschul had asked about FEC broadcasts in 1950. Who produced RL broadcasts; for whom did they speak? Though RFE broadcasts were plausibly presented as the émigré voice of the prestigious and highly visible FEC, AMCOMLIB assumed no such public countenance, for bureaucratic and not policy reasons. That invisibility was to both help and harm RL in the years to come.[79]

The OPC's efforts to organize what would become the American Committee for Liberation and Radio Liberty followed and drew lessons from its

78. "American Committee for Liberation from Bolshevism, Mission and Objectives, April 21, 1954," released to the author in October 2004.
79. Some of this AMCOMLIB and RL history was discussed by William Henry Chamberlin (without disclosing his role in helping to establish the organization) in an article in *Russian Review*, April 1954.

initial experience with the Free Europe Committee. By mid-1950, Frank Wisner had become frustrated with what he saw as the extensive autonomy of the FEC, the "bear by the tail." The OPC designed its Soviet émigré project differently, forgoing a prestigious activist board of directors, avoiding outside fund-raising and publicity, and generally seeking tighter control. It sought to avoid being a clone of the FEC, where (as one disgruntled OPC officer viewed matters in mid-1950):

> The Executive Secretary's [President's] semi-autonomous position as the representative of a semi-autonomous committee is one of the basic difficulties in the whole project and the cause of a great number of our worst headaches. OPC has not had adequate control of this key figure. . . . In [AMCOMLIB] there must be no question of whom he is working for. He must get his orders from OPC, and . . . policy guidance from State through OPC. The semi-autonomous cover committee is the other major difficulty connected with the NCFE [National Committee for a Free Europe] which we wish to avoid this time.

This was an understandable, if shortsighted, bureaucratic lesson learned. Less understandable was the OPC's failure to draw lessons from its negative experience with Eastern European émigré organizations and the OPC/CIA's continued insistence until 1953 that broadcasts to the Soviet Union be produced by and transmitted in the name of a unified émigré organization.

These different approaches to the FEC and AMCOMLIB were also attributable in part to the fact that initially different departments within first the OPC and then the CIA Directorate of Plans were responsible for the two committees at the working level. The FEC was the responsibility (after the fall of 1951) of the International Organizations unit, headed first by Tom Braden and later by Cord Meyer. AMCOMLIB, after the fall of 1951, was the responsibility of the Soviet Russia Division (and was transferred to the International Organizations unit only in October 1953). The CIA's different approaches to the FEC and AMCOMLIB were also attributable in part to the person of Allen Dulles, who before joining the CIA had been one of the three "founding fathers" of the FEC and retained a special interest in the operation he had helped start and trust in the former associates he had helped recruit. Reflecting on his last day in office in November 1961, he admitted that he had always been prejudiced in favor of RFE. It was indicative of Dulles' personal interest that Cord Meyer regularly addressed his memoranda on RFE issues to Dulles, rather than simply to Frank Wisner as deputy director for plans, to whom he was formally subordinate. Indeed, once RFE was up and running, Wisner seems to have paid very little attention to its operations. He paid even less attention to the start-up of AMCOMLIB, leaving that to his deputies Franklin Lindsay and Dana Durand.[80]

Fathers of Success

Success always has many putative fathers. John C. Hughes, a founding FEC director who was chairman in 1964, recalled that the "FEC was conceived of and started, not by the [Central Intelligence] Agency but by a group of prominent American businessmen and Government officials, to do a job which could not be done by an official organization." George Kennan claimed that "the initial impulse to this undertaking came from myself."[81] According to Frank Wisner, writing in late 1954, "but for the enormous labors of this [Central Intelligence] Agency, the Committee for Free Europe would never have come into being in the first place, and moreover its activities would have amounted to very little. We took the germ of George Kennan's idea and literally built the house ourselves. I know this was so because I was one of the architects and carpenters. It fell to us to do all of the original explaining, selling, and recruiting of the members and directors and even of Mr. Grew himself, with only an occasional assist from State."

The documentary record makes clear that Kennan's inspiration and support from 1947 to 1949 were crucial to the start-up of the FEC and planning for AMCOMLIB. Kennan had written in his (then-anonymous) July 1947 *Foreign Affairs* article that Soviet pressure against the West could be "contained by the adroit and vigilant application of counter-force at a series of constantly shifting geographical and political points." He later regretted he had not included in his "X" article the discussion of Soviet vulnerabilities in Eastern Europe about which he had written from Moscow in May 1945.[82]

80. Sig Mickelson's description of this early history based on his interviews (deposited in the Hoover Archives) with several of the responsible U.S. government and CIA officials including Lindsay is largely confirmed by CIA records reviewed for this book. Sig Mickelson, *America's Other Voice,* 59–75.

81. Letter to Grew from Kennan, November 4, 1954.

82. George F. Kennan, *Memoirs. 1925–1950* (Boston: Little, Brown, 1969), 357; Kennan, "Russia's International Position at the Close of the War with Germany," reprinted in ibid., 532–46.

Kennan explained the rationale for his (then-undisclosed) initiative to organize covert operations that led to NSC 4/A and NSC 10/2 in a December 1947 lecture at the National War College:

> Our objective is to remove Russian influence throughout Europe to an extent which would make it possible for all the European countries to lead again an independent national existence. . . . We are dealing here in the political field, and I can only say that the weapons we have for conducting this type of operation, short of war, are pathetically weak and rudimentary. Political warfare is foreign to our tradition. . . . Take a look at our [weak propaganda apparatus] as it exists today. . . . You can not operate on . . . a shoestring if we are ever going to build up a real [foreign] information service.[83]

Because Kennan was skeptical about the utility of traditional military forces for either side, he viewed political warfare as an important "counterforce" against Soviet pressure. He wrote in January 1949 that "every day makes more evident the importance of the role which will have to be played by covert operations if our national interests are to be adequately protected."[84] He would soon become disenchanted with what he saw as the militarization of U.S. foreign policy and leave the State Department to take up residence in Princeton. Though CIA officials continued to consult him, he played no role in the start-up of RL or the operations of either Radio. The start-up of the Radios was the responsibility of Frank Wisner and his associates, and the record supports Wisner's claim that he and his OPC staff were "architects and carpenters." But they did not build alone. Once the foundations had been laid, construction was in the hands of a group of prominent Americans who were outside the government but part of a homogenous national security elite. It was these prominent leaders of the American Establishment—relying on covert government funds, enjoying great autonomy in a public-private partnership, and effectively employing

83. George F. Kennan, "What Is Policy: Lecture to the National War College, December 18, 1947," in *Measures Short of War: The George F. Kennan Lectures at the National War College, 1946–1947* (Washington, D.C.: National Defense University Press, 1991). Also see Nicholas Thompson, *The Hawk and the Dove: Paul Nitze, George Kennan, and the History of the Cold War* (New York: Henry Holt, 2009), 62ff.
84. "Memorandum to Frank Wisner, January 6, 1949," document 308, in *FRUS, Emergence of the Intelligence Establishment*.

individual talented émigrés—who turned the Radios into effective instruments of American national security policy. By 1953, it was clear to all those involved that united emigrations of any nationality were a chimera and that that émigré organizations could not produce the desired broadcasts. Rather, the challenge was to effectively employ talented émigrés in a derivative partnership between American managers and émigré broadcasters. And this was the challenge that RFE and RL tackled and largely mastered in the early 1950s.

Chapter 2

Birth Pangs in the Early 1950s

By the end of 1953, both the FEC and AMCOMLIB had in practice abandoned earlier notions that organizations of unified national emigrations could themselves assume responsibility for broadcasts to Eastern Europe and the USSR. Both Radios continued to focus on their target countries in an émigré context—Poles speaking to Poland, Russians speaking to Russia—that would differentiate RFE and RL from VOA and the BBC. FEC president DeWitt C. Poole, describing planned RFE broadcasts, had said: "The programs will not be marked by a distinctive Americanism. We shall seek to have them seem Hungarian to the Hungarians, Polish to the Poles, and so forth."[1] RFE director Robert Lang told *The New Yorker* at the time, "We don't want to sound like Americans broadcasting to East Europeans."[2] An OPC draft of mid-1951 outlined for RL "a program of Russians speaking to Russians, not the U.S. government speaking to the Russians and other nationalities of the Soviet Union." A June 1952 OPC document described the envisaged RL broadcasts as

> Russian broadcasts, not American broadcasts; they are to serve the interests of the Russian liberation movement, not the United States (indirectly, the broadcasts will serve American interests to a very high degree [by] weakening the Soviet state). Consequently, they will not explain or defend American policies, propagate American ideas, extol the American way of life, build up American prestige, play American jazz, or otherwise encroach upon the field of activity of VOA. . . . As the broad-

1. "Progress Report—January 1950," NCFE Handbook, May 1950.
2. Rex Lardner, "Plenty of Bite," *The New Yorker,* July 22, 1950.

casts are Russian broadcasts, it is important that all material be presented from the point of view of the peoples of the Soviet Union.[3]

Both RFE and RL broadcasts began with this émigré focus, but with little thought as to the organization and actual content of the broadcasts. As FEC director Howard Chapin observed in May 1952, "a superb method and facility was evolved before we knew what the strategy or plan or aim was."[4]

From RFE "Poison Factory" to Surrogate Broadcasting

The first RFE broadcasts from New York were short and negative, denouncing Communist perfidy and exposing purported Communist collaborators. In Frank Altschul's words, "We are unhampered by the amenities of diplomatic discourse, we enter this fight with bare fists. . . . We identify Communist collaborators by name. We give their addresses and an account of their misdeeds. And sometimes . . . we add: 'This is the sort of man to whom an accident might happen on a dark night.' "[5] Altschul's technical adviser, Peter Mero, referred to those early RFE broadcasts as Altschul's "poison factory." The FEC, the OPC, and the State Department all agreed that the broadcasts should be harder hitting than those of VOA because they were "freed of diplomatic limitations" and could utilize " certain types of material not permissible on the Voice of America, since they do not openly reflect government policy."[6] Editorial policy guidelines ("guidances" in FEC terminology) for Polish broadcasts during this early period, for example, emphasized exposing the Bierut regime's "national front" as a Communist tool, reporting peasant resistance to collectivization, highlighting

3. OPC memorandum to Joyce, Department of State, June 2, 1952, requesting comments on proposed policy paper for RL broadcasts, released to the author in March 2009.

4. FEC memorandum, "Princeton Meeting on Political Warfare, May 10–11, 1952," 22; copy in DDRS.

5. Letter to C. D. Jackson from Altschul, June 2, 1951, Lehman Collection.

6. "NCFE Press Release, July 3, 1950," and "Department of State Policy Statement Poland, November 27, 1950," in *Foreign Relations of the United States,* ed. U.S. Department of State (hereafter, *FRUS*) (Washington, D.C.: U.S. Government Printing Office, various years), 1950, IV, 1040ff, 1051; "Record of the Undersecretary's Meeting, February 2, 1951," document 611, in *FRUS,* 1951, IV, part 2, quoting Edward Barrett. A 1952 CIA memorandum argued that "neither [VOA or RFE] can be wholly effective by itself. The violins and cellos do not constitute a complete orchestra. The brasses and kettle drums [i.e., RFE] are equally indispensable."

regime anti-American propaganda, and denouncing regime officials and informers.[7] Altschul's subcommittee was transformed into the FEC Radio Committee to oversee broadcasts, and Altschul, Robert Lang, and others in FEC management reviewed broadcast texts in advance and wrote some of the programs themselves.

There were many critics of this early negativism. An FEC official in Paris reported views among émigrés there that "RFE broadcasts rub . . . most listeners the wrong way, or simply bore them."[8] An FEC internal review pointed out the pitfalls: "It is possible that these scripts serve to re-emphasize feelings of impotence and helplessness."[9] A team from the BBC Central European Service, visiting Munich just after the start of operations, lauded the enthusiasm of RFE broadcasters but criticized their programs for mixing opinion with fact in newscasts, denouncing Communist collaborators with little evidence, and ignoring policy restraints on content and tone of presentation. The BBC would keep its distance. "We concluded from our visit that while we could give Radio Free Europe technical assistance whenever practicable as to an ally using different weapons in a war which is in part our war, we should avoid any form of association in public."[10]

It was with the shift of most RFE programming from New York to Munich that the concept of what would become known as "surrogate broadcasting" took shape and what was in fact a second RFE was born. The model, as noted in chapter 1, was RIAS, which had evolved from the voice of the American occupation authorities in Berlin to a de facto free home service for East Germany. RFE director Lang had been impressed by the RIAS approach during his visit to Berlin in late 1949, and Lucius Clay remained an advocate.[11] William E. Griffith, RFE's Munich policy adviser

7. FEC Polish guidances for 1950 and 1951.

8. Memorandum to DeWitt Poole from Royal Tyler, December 6, 1950, Arthur W. Page Papers, as cited by Noel L. Griese, *Arthur W. Page: Publisher, Public Relations Pioneer, Patriot* (Atlanta: Anvil, 2001), 357.

9. FEC memorandum, "Review of RFE Production for Period January 31, 1952 through February 13, 1952," February 19, 1952.

10. BBC memorandum, "Report on Radio Free Europe" [by three members of the BBC Central European Service], July 16, 1951, RFE/RL Collection.

11. Sig Mickelson, *America's Other Voice: The Story of Radio Free Europe and Radio Liberty* (New York: Praeger, 1983), 25; Robert Lang interview, Mickelson Collection. An overview of RIAS's concept and operations is Donald R. Browne, "Radio in the American Sector, RIAS Berlin," in *Western Broadcasting Over the Iron Curtain*, ed. K. R. M. Short (New York, St. Martin's Press, 1986). Memoirs of RIAS officials and broadcasters are contained in *Radio–Reminiszenzen: Erinnerungen an RIAS Berlin*, ed. by Manfred Rexin (Berlin: Vistas Verlag, 2002).

from 1952 to 1958, first formulated the concept of "surrogate broadcasting" in 1952, specifying four essential elements: (1) a saturation "home service" —"Radio Prague and Radio Budapest as they would still be were Eastern Europe free and democratic"; (2) a nimble Front Line operation, able to monitor Communist media quickly, interview refugees, and imbue a sense of morale and élan among the broadcasters; (3) avoidance of exile politics, allowing professional broadcasters to set forth both conservative and liberal democratic perspectives; and (4) empowerment of exile broadcasters, treated by American management as equal partners "who know more about how to talk to their own people than do the Americans themselves."[12] According to this conception, RFE itself was not a broadcaster; rather, it was a management and policy structure for five national broadcasting stations, the largest of which were the Voice of Free Poland, the Voice of Free Czechoslovakia, and the Voice of Free Hungary. In Frank Wisner's words at the time, their aim was "to compete within each country as an indigenous national station."

It was also with the shift of most RFE programming production from New York to Munich that American oversight of émigré-produced programming shifted from prebroadcast approval to postbroadcast review. That change was dictated in part by the sheer volume of full-service substitute home service broadcasting. It was also dictated by the concept of American-exile partnership outlined in Griffith's 1952 memorandum, which assumed that detailed control of scripts before broadcast resulted in poor émigré staff morale and less effective programming.[13]

Effective surrogate broadcasting also assumed comprehensive information about developments within the broadcast countries. Initial planning for RFE operations assumed, quite simplistically, that intelligence information could be provided to RFE in sanitized form and used for broadcasts—a plan that quickly proved impractical because of the dearth of information more than difficulties of sanitization. Altschul concluded as the first broadcasts were being prepared that "the amount of covert material reaching Radio

---

12. FEC memorandum by William E. Griffith, "RFE: Four Essential Ingredients of Its Success," February 15, 1952. Griffith outlined indirect mechanisms of policy control in a supplementary FEC memorandum, "Techniques of Control—RFE, Munich," July 11, 1952. Brutus Coste had earlier previewed some of Griffith's ideas; see Brutus Coste, "Propaganda to Eastern Europe," *Public Opinion Quarterly* 14, no. 4 (Winter 1950–51): 639–66.

13. FEC memorandum, "Policy Implementation and Script Control in RFE," n.d.

Free Europe is woefully inadequate."[14] Much of the material the OPC delivered to New York in fact consisted of Eastern European regime publications. A CIA/IOD officer commented in early 1952, "Today, RFE, on its own, gets almost all the news available to government sources. We can give them very little they can't get themselves."

But RFE needed a lot more information to be effective and developed a vast information-gathering system for that purpose. Starting in August 1951, it monitored Communist broadcasts at its Schleissheim facility just north of Munich and transcribed them in the original languages (some 250,000 words daily, with key items in real time) for RFE broadcasters. By 1960, RFE was monitoring seventy-four Communist radio stations and teletype services. It subscribed, often through third parties in the West, to hundreds of Eastern European publications. It established a network of news and information bureaus (fifteen at their peak) around Western Europe, which were utilized to report on Western European developments and interview Eastern European travelers and refugees.[15] Interviews with travelers would become a major source of both topical and background information on domestic developments. In 1969, RFE bureaus submitted 2,705 information reports, and 1992 of these were considered useful enough for internal distribution as information "items."[16] RFE organized a research department to process and evaluate what soon became a flood of information. Although the rationale for this effort was to support surrogate broadcasting, in the process RFE became the premier Western center for the analysis of current Eastern European developments. RL developed a similar monitoring and research capability. The CIA early became a consumer of rather than the source for this information, and the CIA's Directorate of Intelligence analysts were assigned to Munich to draw on it directly.[17]

14. Memorandum to Poole from Altschul, "Subject: Information," May 23, 1950, Lehman Collection.

15. RFE attempted to establish a bureau in Belgrade as well, but Yugoslav regime interest faded as Soviet-Yugoslav relations improved in 1955. Interviewers gathered news, background material, and human interest stories from Soviet Bloc travelers. FEC memorandum, "Guide for Interviewers," by Russell Hill, Vienna News Bureau, March 24, 1953; FEC memorandum, "Radio Free Europe; Overseas Information Offices," February 8, 1954.

16. RFE memorandum to Ralph E. Walter from J. F. Brown, "An Inquiry into Information Reporting," March 2, 1970. This thirty-one-page memorandum provides a comprehensive history of the activity.

17. Paul B. Henze, "RFE's Early Years: Evolution of Broadcast Policy and Evidence

Both RFE and RL also developed capabilities to gather information on listenership—"quantitative" research on numbers of listeners and "qualitative" research on listener reactions to specific programs and listener views on broader social, political, and economic issues. This was necessarily "surrogate" audience research. In the 1950s, it was limited to an analysis of listener mail (some of which evaded censorship by being posted to an ever-changing set of forwarding addresses around the world) and a limited number of interviews with visitors and refugees. As East-West contacts expanded in the 1960s, RFE and RL audience research also expanded to include surveys among Communist Bloc travelers (who were viewed as more representative of the audience than refugees) conducted by Western European polling institutes under contract. It is testimony to the seriousness of the effort that RFE and RL together commissioned some 150,000 such audience research interviews between 1960 and 1990.[18]

Recasting RFE's Message: From Denunciation to Liberalization

Operating as substitute free home radio services, it was the mission of RFE and RL (in the words of a 1950 State Department policy document on Eastern Europe) to break through Communist regimes' information monopoly "in order to maintain the morale of the people and to hinder efforts to establish full Soviet control in these nations, *although [broadcasts] should not promise imminent liberation or encourage active revolt.*"[19]

Another State Department guidance of late 1950 was devoted to Hungary but applied generally to Eastern Europe:

> The Free Hungarian Radio should seek to keep alive the aspirations of the Hungarian people for a democratic, free, and independent existence.

---

of Broadcast Impact," in *Cold War Broadcasting: Impact on the Soviet Union and Eastern Europe—A Collection of Studies and Documents,* ed. A. Ross Johnson and R. Eugene Parta (Budapest: Central European University Press, 2010), chap. 1.

18. R. Eugene Parta, *Discovering the Hidden Listener: An Assessment of Radio Liberty and Western Broadcasting to the USSR During the Cold War* (Stanford, Calif.: Hoover Institution Press, 2007); Aigner interview, RFE/RL Collection. Helmut Aigner organized RFE traveler surveys in Vienna for three decades.

19. "Policy toward Soviet Satellites in Eastern Europe," April 11, 1950," in *FRUS,* 1950, IV, 14–17. In May OPC provided the FEC with a minor revision of this document dated April 26 and with the emphasized words added.

While avoiding any incitation of the Hungarian people to rash and overt acts of defiance, the Free Radio should endeavor to maintain and strengthen their passive resistance to the Communist regime and ideology. It should encourage in the Hungarian people a sober yet confident hope of ultimate liberation from Communist oppression and growing assurance of the eventual failure and collapse of international Communism.[20]

As these and countless other U.S. government documents demonstrate, RFE (and RL) did not function in a policy vacuum. In public statements, they were presented as "a private undertaking not influenced by government," operating "in consonance with the established views of our government in world and human affairs."[21] In fact, both Radios operated within broad policy guidelines set at the State Department (initially coordinated by Robert Joyce of the Policy Planning Staff) and transmitted through the CIA, albeit generally discussed and agreed on in advance by representatives of State, the CIA, and the FEC (or AMCOMLIB).[22] FEC formulations on RFE's purpose generally reflected this consensus. Altschul saw as RFE's purpose:

> To keep hope alive among our friends, and to confuse, divide and undermine our enemies within the satellite states. . . . We seek to convey to our audience our firm and continuing belief in their ultimate liberation. While avoiding any suggestion of early intervention, we try to demonstrate the economic and potential military strength of the West. We seek to convince our friends of our intimate, day-by-day understanding of the tragic situation in which they find themselves. . . . We attack every aspect of the Communist regime, both directly and by satire and ridicule.[23]

Reacting to a *New York Times* article purportedly (in fact erroneously) reflecting State Department thinking that "in the satellite states . . . an uprising plainly would be in [the satellite peoples'] own interest," Altschul wrote: "Our view in Radio Free Europe has been that in the present phase

20. FEC letter to Poole from OPC, W-701, December 29, 1950, forwarding a political guidance "prepared by our friends" [Department of State].

21. NCFE Handbook, May 1950 (Declaration and President's Report).

22. "Memorandum of Conversation, by Mr. Claiborne Pell of the Office of East European Affairs, May 4, 1950," in *FRUS,* 1950, IV, 19–20; FEC memorandum to Shepardson from Galantiere, "State Department and FEC," August 10, 1954.

23. Memorandum, "The Present Orientation of Radio Free Europe," by Frank Altschul, November 6, 1950, Lehman Collection.

of the cold war to invite uprising in the prisoner states would be equivalent to inviting the mass suicide of our best friends in these countries."[24]

In these early years, while there was a general consensus on policy goals, there was contention within and among the FEC, AMCOMLIB, and the U.S. government on how best to realize them. Debate about mission was not a one-way street; many policy suggestions originated with the Radios and their sponsoring committees and were endorsed by the CIA and the State Department. FEC officials were, for example, equal participants along with those of State and the CIA at a May 1952 discussion of psychological operations held in Princeton at C. D. Jackson's initiative.[25] Indeed, as the State official responsible for such matters complained in 1954, although the FEC and RFE are powerful instruments "controlled by the [Central Intelligence] Agency and . . . supposed to operate under policy guidance from the [State] Department; . . . decisions involving matters of policy consequence are frequently taken by FEC and RFE without reference to the Department through the Agency."[26] FEC officials—Jackson especially—often made public statements positing far-reaching U.S. foreign policy aims.

In evaluating such statements then and later, it is important for the contemporary observer and historian to distinguish hortatory declarations of prominent Americans intended for Western audiences from the internal editorial policies of the Radios and from the content of broadcasts. As FEC counselor Lewis Galantiere noted in 1956, "We have handicapped ourselves by yielding to the Crusade [for Freedom] line of appeal which oversimplified the whole business by presenting us as fighters against the evil of communism and nothing else. . . . We ought to be reformulating our line

24. *New York Times,* May 27, 1951, reporting Acheson's appeal to Georgians on VOA's Georgian Service; letter to C. D. Jackson from Altschul, May 28, 1951, Lehman Collection. Also see FEC document, *Radio Free Europe Policy Handbook,* November 30, 1951.

25. FEC memorandum to C. D. Jackson from Galantiere, June 6, 1952, enclosing meeting summary; copy also in DDRS; full transcript enclosed with FEC memorandum to Tom [Braden] from C. D. Jackson, May 20, 1952. The resulting U.S. government document was restrained, pledging support short of war for the entry of Eastern European countries dominated by the Soviet Union into the "family of friendly [European] nations" "as soon as their national liberties are restored" and was intended "to provide current psychological operations in Eastern Europe with needed support without implying any more ambitious programs there." Psychological Strategy Board memorandum, "Princeton Statement," July 16, 1952, released to the author by the CIA in March 2009.

26. "Memorandum from the Deputy Operations Coordinator in the Office of the Under Secretary of State (Hulick) to the Under Secretary of State (Hoover), August 23, 1954," document 188, in *FRUS, The Intelligence Community.*

in public relations to make it follow more closely what we are actually doing."[27] While Jackson and other FEC directors spoke expansively in the early 1950s of "creat[ing] conditions of inner turmoil," "creating chaos," and "keeping the pot boiling" in Eastern Europe,[28] FEC and RFE officials (Americans and émigrés alike) with responsibility for broadcasts objected to such formulations.[29]

Early broadcasts were in fact far more pedestrian, consisting of short newscasts, commentary, religious programs, voices of exile leaders, satire, and verbal denunciations of "Bolshevik intruders and quislings."[30] With the start-up of full-service surrogate broadcasting in Munich (with eighteen hours of programming daily broadcast to Czechoslovakia, Hungary, and Poland; and five hours daily to Bulgaria and Romania), denunciation was moderated and much airtime was devoted to the national history, literature, and culture of the Eastern European countries and to the coverage of international events. By the 1960s, RFE broadcasts included news (24 percent of total airtime), press reviews (7 percent), commentary (25 percent), features (13 percent), sports (4 percent), music (12 percent), entertainment (6 percent), and culture (9 percent).[31] Regular programs of the Polish Service included the following:[32]

Newscasts of ten minutes at the top of every hour (obligatory for every RFE broadcast service)

Letter for Communists—raising questions about Communist precepts and recalling the officially suppressed chapters of Polish Communist history

Tea Time at the Microphone—political satire

Behind the Kremlin Walls—developments in the Communist world

27. FEC letter to "Dick" [Richard Condon] from Galantiere, May 12, 1956.
28. FEC president C. D. Jackson, quoted in the *New York Times,* November 25, 1951; Jackson memorandum, n.d., as cited by Arch Puddington, *Broadcasting Freedom: The Cold War Triumph of Radio Free Europe and Radio Liberty* (Lexington: University Press of Kentucky, 2000), 15.
29. FEC memorandum to Jackson from Galantiere, November 26, 1951, objecting to Jackson's words on creating turmoil.
30. FEC, "President's Report for the Year 1950."
31. FEC memorandum, "RFE Programming," July 1965.
32. Jolanta Hajdasz, *Szczekaczka czylii Rozgłośnia Polska Radia Wolna Europa* (Poznań: Media Rodzina, 2006), 69–72.

Emigration Leaders Address the Country—talks by prominent Poles in exile

No Curtain Divides Us—a program for workers

On the Red Index—serialized readings of books banned in Poland

Roaming Reporter—reportage from Western cities

"Rendezvous at 6:10"—morning music program featuring Western popular music

Forbidden Songs—of earlier Polish insurrections, of the Home Army, and (in the 1980s) of the Solidarity movement

Facts and Views—the flagship half-hour daily political program of news and commentary

Panorama of the Day—a radio magazine of current events

RFE broadcast content was forced into focus by two events in 1953—the inauguration of the Dwight D. Eisenhower administration in January and the abortive East German uprising in June. The 1952 American presidential election campaign had generated rhetoric from the Republican Party accusing presidents Franklin D. Roosevelt and Harry S. Truman of perfidy in "selling out Eastern Europe" at Yalta.[33] It took a leaf from James Burnham's book, *Containment or Liberation,* including his phrase "what can be made to happen in Eastern Europe" and John Foster Dulles' *Life* magazine article, "A Policy of Boldness," including his call for America to make known "that it wants and expects liberation to occur," albeit by peaceful separation from Moscow and not by "a series of bloody uprisings and reprisals."[34]

RFE could hardly ignore the attention to Eastern Europe in the 1952 American electoral campaign, although it downplayed the strongest "liberation" rhetoric. A policy memorandum dated September 2, 1952, cautioned

33. Bennett Kovrig pointed out both the policy continuity and rhetorical hyperbole of "liberation." His book *The Myth of Liberation* remains a useful corrective to works postulating a discontinuity of policy content between "containment" and "liberation." See Bennett Kovrig, *The Myth of Liberation: East Central Europe in U.S. Diplomacy and Politics since 1941* (Baltimore: Johns Hopkins University Press, 1973).

34. James Burnham, *Containment or Liberation* (New York: The John Day Company, 1953), 108; *Life* magazine, May 19, 1952. Dulles had emphasized "liberation" in a 1950 memorandum and in his 1950 book, *War or Peace*. See Townsend Hoopes, *The Devil and John Foster Dulles* (Boston: Little, Brown, 1973), 83–85, 115–16, 126–28.

against enthusiastic comment on Eisenhower's and Dulles' campaign language about liberation:

> To do so would be to deceive our listeners by inspiring in them exaggerated hope of a Western intervention. . . . No one word in these statements can be used to encourage militant anti-communists to go over from passive to active resistance in the expectation that such resistance will be supported by Western elements. . . . It would be cruelly dangerous to our listeners if speakers in RFE were to allow their hearts to run away with their heads in their comments upon these American expressions of concern for the fate of our peoples.[35]

Thus RFE did not carry a controversial October 1952 campaign speech by Dulles on liberation because, as Tom Braden noted at the time, it might be misinterpreted behind the Iron Curtain.

After President Eisenhower assumed office in January 1953, the administration quickly turned its attention to expanded international information ("psychological warfare") programs. C. D. Jackson moved to the White House and spearheaded this effort as Eisenhower's adviser on foreign information activities. He played a key role in the committee established by Eisenhower and chaired by William H. Jackson (deputy CIA director in 1950–51) to recommend improvements in foreign information programs.[36] The new administration issued various public statements on the cause of freedom in Eastern Europe, beginning with speeches by Eisenhower and Dulles in April. It also issued internal directives calling for an expansion of psychological warfare and encouragement of opposition forces in Eastern Europe.[37] At the time, a number of State Department and CIA officials cau-

35. FEC "Special Guidance [no. 4] for Broadcasts on Liberation," September 2, 1952.

36. *The Report of the President's Committee on International Information Activities,* June 30, 1953. A heavily redacted version was published in *FRUS,* 1952–54, National Security Affairs, vol. 2, part 2, 1785ff. A nearly complete text was released by the CIA in February 2008, Helms Collection.

37. NSC 158, "United States Objectives and Actions to Exploit Unrest in the Satellite States," June 29, 1953 [incorporating recommendations of Psychological Strategy Board report, as approved by Eisenhower on June 26 with the caveat that "more emphasis be placed on passive resistance"], reprinted in *Uprising in East Germany, 1953,* ed. Christian F. Ostermann (Budapest: Central European University Press, 2001), document 74. This directive viewed the 1953 unrest in Eastern Europe as creating new opportunities "to nourish throughout the European satellites, particularly in Czechoslova-

tioned about the pitfalls of such a policy. State Department Soviet expert Charles E. Bohlen, in testimony to the Jackson Committee, cautioned that propaganda could only have limited effect and pointed to the danger of proclaiming Eastern European liberation a policy objective, rather than working quietly to that end.[38] Franklin Lindsay concluded as he prepared to retire from the CIA that spring that the West had little capability to reduce Soviet power within the Soviet Bloc and no possibility of organizing clandestine resistance.[39] Tracy Barnes, then head of the CIA's Political and Psychological Warfare Division, cautioned against encouraging active opposition in Eastern Europe unless the United States was prepared to support it militarily, noting that it could only result in resentment of America if revolt broke out spontaneously and was crushed.[40]

The FEC (most of whose key officials were Republicans) welcomed the new administration and its new tone on Eastern Europe. Jackson, now in the White House, was joined on the Jackson Committee by FEC director John C. Hughes, while its executive secretary was Abbott Washburn, formerly FEC director of public relations. The FEC viewed President Eisenhower's foreign policy address of April 16, 1953, as "the end of the American policy of 'containment'; it is the beginning of the Eisenhower policy of liberation. . . . The U.S.A. will not sell out our listeners for an unjust peace with the Kremlin."[41] An FEC policy guidance asked broadcasters to quote repeatedly Secretary of State Dulles' words in his address of April 18, 1953: "We should make clear to the captive peoples that we do not accept their captivity as a 'permanent fact of history.'" The author of that guidance added:

kia, the spirit of active resistance to communist oppression" and focused on discrediting the Communist regimes while pressuring them for specific reforms. The Operations Coordinating Board replaced the Psychological Strategy Board in September 1953 and continued the planning efforts.

38. Bohlen's testimony to the Jackson Committee staff, February 24, 1953, document 24, in *FRUS, 1952–54*, vol. 8.

39. "A Program for the Development of Cold War Instruments," March 3, 1953, DDRS; excerpt from an October 1952 draft of the memorandum quoted by Peter Grose, *Operation Rollback: America's Secret War behind the Iron Curtain* (Boston: Houghton Mifflin, 2000), 188.

40. CIA memorandum to special assistant to the director from C. Tracy Barnes, November 18, 1953, released to the author in September 2007. Barnes was responding to a memorandum to Allen Dulles from C. D. Jackson regarding opportunities for exploiting what he saw as an upcoming "winter of discontent" in Eastern Europe.

41. FEC "Special Guidance No. 8 on President Eisenhower's Speech of April 16, 1953," April 16, 1953.

"What RFE has so long prayed for has now come to pass—a Government at Washington which boldly announces that peace without freedom is not enough; which boldly declares that the strength of the West is greater than that of the Kremlin; which speaks directly to our peoples and says to them 'The status quo is not good enough for us; we do not accept your captivity as a condition of peace with Moscow.'"[42]

Echoing such Eisenhower administration rhetoric, many FEC policy statements in 1953 focused on "liberation." One such statement declared it was the mission of the FEC "to give the peoples of the captive countries reason to hope for liberation."[43] Looking back in 1956, an FEC policy official noted that broadcasts had treated "liberation" with caution in the context of the American election campaign and American public opinion, but added:

Nevertheless, the impact of the proclamation of the liberation policy was considerable. Since the statements came from authoritative quarters and since they were carried by every radio station on Earth, they could not be played down; at the same time they inspired RFE's [broadcasters] who were given basic policy directives to the effect that the United States meant what it said, even though it would not necessarily go to war in order to accomplish it.[44]

"The Opening of a New Phase," as a June 1953 FEC policy memorandum was titled, seemed to portend a more aggressive broadcast strategy conforming to the administration's emphasis on psychological warfare: "The time has come to call Moscow's bluff and to force the hands of the stooges who claim to be the government . . . by increasing passive resistance and by taking all positive steps of which fighters for freedom are capable." A related policy memorandum of June 29 said that, in the wake of demonstrations in Pilzen in early June, it was RFE's task "to rouse [the Czechoslovak workers'] anger by keeping alive his burning resentment against the regime and its Muscovite masters."[45]

42. FEC "Special Guidance No. 9 on the J. F. Dulles Speech, April 18," April 20, 1953.
43. FEC document, "NCFE Policy," March 25, 1953.
44. FEC memorandum, "Radio Free Europe Policies, 1950–1956," by R. S. N. [Rubin S. Nathan], n.d.
45. FEC "Special Guidance No. 12-A: The Opening of a New Phase, " June 19, 1953; FEC "Czechoslovakia: Guidance No. 10," June 29, 1953.

Such language from FEC officials in New York met with immediate resistance by RFE executives with direct responsibility for broadcasts. RFE director Lang (who threatened to resign) and other RFE officials quickly dissented, on grounds similar to those of dissenters within the administration cited above. As Lang saw it, RFE was a "long-term instrument" that could not usefully "toughen up more than we are" and would be harmed by "the stupidity of tricks."[46] Polish Service director Jan Nowak protested that RFE broadcasts had to avoid advice and instructions that would create false hopes; rather, they should inform listeners about facts and events that the regimes wanted to keep hidden and present regime concessions as gains for society.[47] When asked, at a July 1953 FEC meeting, "Why don't we advocate sabotage to Poland?" Griffith (temporarily in New York) replied that the Americans and émigrés at RFE would not do it. Paul Henze privately vented to Griffith his frustration at the "stupid" "hare-brained" advice of U.S. government and FEC "psy-warriors," agreeing that "our exiles here will never carry out the kind of orders the PW-boys want to give."[48] The RFE antiliberation policy "dissidents" prevailed in the months following the abortive East German uprising. The Eisenhower administration concluded that it was powerless to quickly or radically limit Soviet control over Eastern Europe, and broadcasts continued to aim (in the words of an NSC directive of January 1955 cited below) "for evolutionary rather than revolutionary changes."

RIAS broadcasts, by all accounts, played an important role in the spreading of demonstrations in East Berlin in June 1953 to revolt throughout much of East Germany. Before June, RIAS broadcasts (covering East Germany on FM as well as AM transmitters) had encouraged labor unrest and passive resistance and were acknowledged secretly by the East German Communist Party as an alternative public opinion. With the outbreak of demonstrations in East Berlin on June 15, RIAS confronted the daunting challenge of reporting on revolutionary developments without inciting—the challenge that would face RFE and RL in 1956, 1968, 1981, 1989, and 1991. RIAS fully covered the East German unrest, including voices calling for

46. FEC teletype to Spencer Phenix from Lang (then in Munich), June 18, 1953. Lang subsequently joined C. D. Jackson and other FEC directors in a meeting with Allen Dulles at which the hard line was (temporarily) confirmed. C. D. Jackson log, as cited by Jan Nowak, "War on the Airwaves: A Frontline Report," unpublished manuscript, 247.

47. Comments to Czechoslovak Guidance No. 10, July 3, 1953, copy in *Wojna w eterze,* by Jan Nowak-Jeziorański (Kraków: Znak, 2000), 122–24.

48. Griffith to Henze, July 23, 1953, Henze to Griffith, August 1, 1953, Henze Correspondence.

more demonstrations and free elections, but (in a decision first made locally by RIAS political director Gordon Ewing) refused to turn over its microphones to worker delegations from East Berlin. In the following days, RIAS programs became more supportive of the uprising, and one commentary by program director Eberhard Schütz urged listeners to side with the demonstrators. But, as senior Soviet officials in East Berlin acknowledged, RIAS broadcasts also urged listeners to avoid clashes with Soviet forces. Once the uprising had been suppressed, RIAS heavily publicized the U.S. food assistance program that provided more than 5 million food parcels, picked up in West Berlin, to East Germans.[49]

Soviet suppression of the East German uprising in June 1953 dashed any hope of any early end to Soviet hegemony in Eastern Europe. Thereafter, the U.S. government set more limited policy aims, focusing on immediate issues and working to keep alive hope of what came to be seen as eventual self-liberation.[50] National Security Council Directive 162/2 of October 1953 concluded: "The ability of the USSR to exercise effective control over, and to exploit the resources of, the European satellites has not been appreciably reduced and is not likely to be so long as the USSR maintains adequate military forces in the area. The detachment of any major European satellite from the Soviet bloc does not now seem feasible except by Soviet acquiescence or war."[51]

It was in this spirit that NSC Directive 174 of December 1953 focused on how the United States could exploit tensions and fissures within the Communist world and maintain Eastern Europeans' faith in the eventual restoration of freedom, "while avoiding premature revolts and any commitments regarding when and how these people may be liberated."[52] An Operations Coordinating Board report of December 1954 acknowledged the limited capability of the United States to affect Eastern European developments and viewed as unlikely the detaching of any Eastern European state from the Soviet orbit short of war.[53] NSC Directive 5505/1, "Ex-

49. This account of RIAS's role is taken from *Uprising in East Germany, 1953,* ed. Ostermann.

50. As John Foster Dulles wrote to Henry Ford II on March 24, 1954, as cited by Kovrig, *Myth of Liberation,* 149.

51. NSC 162/2, October 30, 1953, DDRS.

52. NSC 174, "United States Policy toward the Soviet Satellites in Eastern Europe," December 11, 1953, reprinted in *Uprising in East Germany, 1953,* ed. Ostermann, document 95.

53. Operations Coordinating Board, "Analysis of the Situation with Respect to Possible Detachment of a Major European Soviet Satellite," December 30, 1954, DDRS.

ploitation of Soviet and European Satellite Vulnerability," issued in January 1955, declared that U.S. policy should "continue basic opposition to the Soviet system . . . but stress evolutionary rather than revolutionary change."[54]

The FEC remained dedicated to the cause of restoring Eastern Europe to what would later be called "a Europe whole and free," but acknowledged that it could not offer a plausible scenario for this to occur. As Free Europe Press director Samuel Walker wrote in November 1955, "we are totally unable to specify the nature and the timing of the 'confluence of events' which, nevertheless, remains the only realistic theory of liberation."[55] In other words, liberation was a long-term aspiration, never a policy that guided RFE broadcasts. Nowak had said the same thing more poetically in his inaugural radio commentary to Polish listeners in May 1952:

> The struggle is being waged not in the forests, streets, or in the underground but in Polish souls—within the four walls of a Polish home. It is this struggle we wish to join here on the airwaves of Radio Free Europe. . . . We will tell you the truth, . . . which the Soviet regime wants to hide from you in order to kill the remnants of hope in your minds. . . . We will battle Russification. . . . We will counter the attempts to falsify our history and traditions. The day will come when the dawn of freedom will light up the Warsaw sky. It will be a day of triumph, your triumph.

"Liberation" was American political rhetoric, never U.S. foreign policy. It was essentially an American election campaign football, a by-product of the breakdown of foreign policy bipartisanship in the early 1950s. The "sellout" of Eastern Europe at Yalta and thereafter attributed by the Republican Party to the Truman administration was worse than caricature. Truman and his secretary of state, Dean Acheson, had never condoned Soviet hegemony over Eastern Europe and had initiated what were in retrospect overly ambitious programs of covert political and psychological warfare in an effort to undermine or at least weaken that hegemony short of war and without encouraging suicidal revolt. The aim of the Eisenhower administration's concept of "liberation"—peaceful restoration of free Eastern European countries to a free Europe—was no different. What was different

54. "National Security Council Report, January 31, 1955," document 4, in *FRUS, 1953–57, XXIV.*

55. FEC memorandum to Howard S. Weaver from Samuel S. Walker Jr., November 18, 1955.

were the rhetoric and the policy context. "Liberation" was overblown rhetoric launched just at the moment (unknown publicly at the time) when covert action programs of the Truman administration intended to support the anticommunist underground in the Soviet Bloc had failed dramatically.[56] And however qualified to exclude Western military support, the rhetoric of liberation contained what the historian Bennett Kovrig aptly termed a "perilous optimism," exaggerating the potential of information programs ("propaganda") and sometimes suggesting a concrete timetable, such as the five to ten years mentioned by Dulles in his *Life* magazine article. As *The Economist* wrote in early 1953, "belief in the powers of psychological warfare" spawned "the myth that there was a new secret weapon" overlooked by the Truman administration to weaken the Soviet monolith.[57] (In fact, only the public rhetoric was new; many in the Truman administration also saw "propaganda as a sort of magic weapon to perform miracles which cannot be accomplished by other means."[58]) Townsend Hoopes aptly concluded in his biography of Dulles that "this call to 'moral offensive' . . . was intellectually thin and politically mischievous."[59] More culpable in this regard than the administration were conservative legislators such as Representative Charles Kersten (R-Wis.) and Senator Alexander Wiley (R-Wis.), whose rhetoric was stronger than that of Dulles and who inspired budget appropriations (never spent by the Eisenhower administration) for the establishment of émigré "liberation" armies.

It seems indisputable (as Kovrig concluded) that the liberation doctrine "frightened America's allies, and nurtured false assumptions about U.S. foreign policy in the halls of Congress and among the grass roots."[60] Did it also, as Kovrig and others have contended, "arouse . . . false hopes among East Europeans"? There is no way to gauge the impact of the liberation rhetoric of American leaders on Eastern European audiences; that would require both a detailed reconstruction of what was actually broadcast in newscasts

56. Most dramatically, exposure by the Polish Communist regime in December 1952 of the Freedom and Independence underground movement (WiN) as regime controlled. See Grosse, *Operation Rollback,* 164–89.

57. Issue of March 21, 1953, as cited by Nicholas J. Cull, *The Cold War and the United States Information Agency: American Propaganda and Public Diplomacy, 1945–1989* (Cambridge: Cambridge University Press, 2008), 79 n. 225.

58. "Paper Prepared in the Office of the Assistant Secretary of State for Public Affairs, 'U.S. Views on Capturing Initiative in Psychological Field,'" n.d., in *FRUS,* 1950, IV, 297.

59. Hoopes, *Devil and John Foster Dulles,* 85.

60. Kovrig, *Myth of Liberation,* 121.

(or otherwise conveyed to Eastern Europeans) and how it was perceived. Anecdotal evidence from 1950 and 1951 suggests that listeners reacted negatively in disbelief to broadcasts suggesting "freedom soon" as only lowering morale and increasing feelings of despair. Subsequent anecdotal evidence suggests that the American talk of liberation was perceived through the prisms of different recent historical experience in various countries. East German rebels in 1953[61] and Polish rebels in 1956 evidently did not count on Western help. Hungarian revolutionaries in 1956 evidently did, even though the liberation rhetoric of American politicians had largely disappeared by then.[62]

The year 1953 was the turning point for RFE broadcast policy. The U.S. government and FEC policy context for RFE broadcasts reverted to the status quo ante Dulles-liberation rhetoric. It corresponded to the conclusions of some twenty different studies and analyses of the Soviet orbit conducted within or commissioned by the U.S. government during both the Truman and Eisenhower administrations, which concluded that Soviet control was a fact of life, that the United States could at best try to prevent the complete Sovietization of Eastern Europe and keep the spirit of resistance alive, but that "liberation" (meaning an end to Soviet control and Communist rule) was a long-term aspiration.[63] All this predated 1956, often viewed as the turning point in American policy toward Eastern Europe and RFE broadcasting policy, by three years.

If the events of 1953 demonstrated Soviet resolve to maintain control over Eastern Europe by force, they also indicated Soviet willingness to introduce certain concessions in order to maintain that control. This "New Course" in Hungary, for example, involved deemphasizing heavy industry,

61. CIA officials in Berlin did believe that Dulles' rhetoric, transmitted over RIAS, contributed to the East German uprising. See Bayard Stockton, *Flawed Patriot: The Rise and Fall of CIA Legend Bill Harvey* (Dulles, Va.: Potomac Books, 2006), 46.

62. E.g., Eisenhower's Christmas Message of 1955, broadcast over RFE, which read in full: "During the Christmas season, I want you to know that the American people recognize the trials under which you are suffering, join you in your concern for the restoration of individual freedoms and political liberty, and share your faith that right in the end will prevail to bring you once again among the free nations of the world." The message did not conclude with a sentence, wrongly recalled later by Griffith, that "if any East European shows a visible opposition to the Soviet oppression, it can count on our help." Message published in *New York Herald Tribune,* December 31, 1955; Griffith quoted by Puddington, *Broadcasting Freedom,* 113.

63. Jim Marchio, "Resistance Potential and Rollback: US Intelligence and the Eisenhower Administration's Policies toward Eastern Europe, 1953–1956," *Intelligence and National Security* 10, no. 2 (April 1995): 219–41; the citation here is on 229.

relaxing agricultural collectivization, lowering consumer prices, limiting police coercion and releasing political prisoners, and creating a new "popular front" to limit low-level Communist Party control.[64] RFE saw an opportunity to expand those concessions by devoting continued publicity to Communist repression while urging popular pressure on weakened regimes.[65] Revelations of terror by and also within the Polish Communist Party from Józef Światło, a senior Polish secret police official who defected to the West in December 1953, were conveyed to Polish audiences in a series of radio broadcasts in late 1954 and early 1955 and leaflets delivered by balloon and postal mail (termed Project Spotlight). Światło's revelations had an enormous impact (arguably more impact than any other set of Western broadcasts during the Cold War), leading to the dismissal of Minister of Internal Affairs Stanisław Radkiewicz and a shakeup of the entire secret police apparatus.[66]

These twin features of 1953—Soviet crackdown and Soviet concessions—spawned an ambitious FEC program to encourage not "liberation" but creeping "self-liberation." The FEC now aimed at fostering the emergence of internal oppositions within Eastern European countries that would challenge the Communist Party's authority with nonviolent means at the lowest levels of the system and turn the Communists' own instruments of control—the mass "People's Front," trade unions in the state economic enterprises, and local government councils—against them. At the State Department, Christian M. Ravndal, heading the American Legation in Budapest, recommended conciliatory U.S. government gestures toward the Hungarian government and urged that RFE and VOA efforts "be directed at continuing to nudge regime further in present direction."[67] The FEC's self-liberation strategy for Hungary took a different tack, outlined by FEC counselor Galantiere:

64. Csaba Békés, Malcolm Byrne, and János M. Rainer, *The 1956 Hungarian Revolution: A History in Documents* (Budapest: Central European University Press, 2002), 4–8.

65. FEC memorandum, "Guidance on Nagy Speech of July 11," July 13, 1953; also FEC memorandum, "The 'New Course' and Its Aims," by Paul B. Henze, January 28, 1954. Hungarian broadcasts at that time suggested sabotage of forced agricultural deliveries to the state, e.g., the program "Farmer Balant Says," July 16, 1953.

66. See Puddington, *Broadcasting Freedom*, 33–35; FEC memorandum, "Operation Spotlight," November 9, 1954; FEC memorandum to Condon and Griffith from Henze, "The Światło Affair," October 28, 1954; FEC memorandum, "The Światło Story: Its Impact on Poland," n.d. [1955]; Andrzej Paczkowski, *Trzy twarze Józefa Światły* (Warsaw: Prószyński Media, 2009); A. Ross Johnson, "Origins of the Światło Broadcasts on RFE," February 2010, http://wolnaeuropa.org/history%20forum/content/view/17/1/.

67. Department of State Budapest Telegram No. 187, October 20, 1954, document 58, in *FRUS, 1952–54*, VIII.

Our primary purpose is to focus the attention of the Hungarian people upon certain means by which they can continue to baffle, thwart, and wrench concessions from the regime, . . . to make the people aware that they constitute, spiritually through not organizationally, a National Opposition Movement, and that the present aim of that movement is to obtain satisfaction of . . . Twelve Demands.[68]

In this FEC conception, opposition currents assumed to exist in nascent form were to be emboldened to nonviolent political action through targeted radio broadcasts and leaflets—some mailed to elites in what proved to be the justified calculation that a certain number would elude postal censors, but most dropped from high-altitude balloons. This was the rationale that underlay "VETO" and "FOCUS," the two such multimedia campaigns, launched in 1954 with State Department, CIA, and Operations Coordinating Board concurrence. Looking back in 1957, Samuel Walker, head of the printed-word programs, described the FEC strategy from 1953 to 1956 that he had helped formulate: "Our contribution was to introduce the notion of demands (not necessarily the specific demands which we formulated, but the *concept* that people could even *think* about making realistic demands upon a totalitarian regime—and sometimes succeed). We proposed this in 1954 as a sensible alternative to illusions about 'liberation' and Western military assistance."[69]

FEC balloon-leaflets with more general messages had been dispatched eastward since August 1951 as the Winds of Freedom, Prospero, and other campaigns. VETO, launched for Czechoslovakia with fanfare in April 1954,[70] now propagated "Ten Demands" of the "People's Opposition," including reduced work quotas, less bureaucratic interference, and more free time for workers. As originally drafted, VETO also included suggestions about particular Communist candidates who, it would be suggested, did not deserve to be elected to workplace committees; that provision was deleted at State Department insistence (after the leaflets had carried that demand for six weeks, a consequence of FEC officials Galantiere and Lang either misunderstanding or ignoring State-CIA guidance).[71]

68. FEC "Hungarian Guidance No. 15 on Operation Focus," by Lewis Galantiere, September 16, 1954.
69. FEC memorandum to Crittenberger from Walker, February 26, 1957; emphasis in the original.
70. Edward R. Murrow covered it in a CBS Radio newscast on May 27, 1954.
71. FEC "Czechoslovak Guidance No. 13: The 1954 Czechoslovak Electoral Cam-

FOCUS was launched for Hungary in October 1954 and was keyed to Nagy's New Course, which envisaged a role for a revived "popular front" as a mass organization also encompassing noncommunists. The FOCUS campaign publicized "Twelve Demands" of the "National Opposition Movement," with an approach similar to that of VETO. The "Demands" included "Real Autonomy for the Local Councils," "Free Speech, Free Assembly," and "Services to the People in the Hands of the People [that is, the privatization of retail services]."[72] As characterized by Cord Meyer in mid-1954, "This operation is predicated on the theory that liberation is not likely to come through war or even coup d'état but is more likely to be a gradual process in which the popular will of the people gradually asserts itself through mass action and an organized state of mind."[73]

The FEC strategy that gave rise to VETO and FOCUS was offensive rather than defensive, in that it sought to encourage internal dissent from outside rather than react to regime actions. It was responsible, in that it encouraged Eastern Europeans to harness peacefully low-level Communist-controlled institutions for democratic purposes. "Their success would clarify to individual anti-communists in Czechoslovakia and in Hungary that they did not stand alone, that they were part and parcel of a popular movement that was bound to assert considerable though gradual influence on communist policies."[74]

This post-1953 moderation made the FEC (as analogous moderate RL broadcasts made AMCOMLIB) a target for conservative American anti-

---

paigns," January 25, 1954, as modified by FEC teletype NYC 29, June 8, 1954, directing (at the CIA's insistence) that "RFE should not . . . tell listeners now to conduct their balloting in any way." CIA/IOD reported this change to the State Department in a memorandum to Lampton Berry from Braden, June 10, 1954, released to the author in March 2009. A September 1954 guidance was more emphatic: "We shall not attempt to influence the selection of candidates [for shop council elections], we shall not instruct workers in how they are to vote, and will drop entirely the notion of 'infiltrating' or 'capturing' the councils"; FEC "Czechoslovak Guidance No. 14 for the Autumn Elections, 1954," September 14, 1954. Also see FEC letter to CBS Radio from Rita Whearty, undated [1954]; FEC "Czechoslovak Guidance No. 16 and Hungarian Guidance No. 16, Continuation of Operations Veto and Focus, January and March 1955," January 5, 1955.

72. FEC FOCUS leaflet in Hungarian, "National Opposition Movement; Twelve Demands."

73. FEC memorandum, "Operation Focus: Basic Strategy October–December 1954," October 22, 1954; Kovrig, *Myth of Liberation,* 149–51; Robert T. Holt, *Radio Free Europe* (Minneapolis: University of Minnesota Press, 1958), 153–69.

74. FEC memorandum, "Radio Free Europe Policies; 1950–1956."

communists who espoused a harder line. Geographic distance, covert funding, and the CIA bureaucracy protected RFE and RL from the wave of McCarthyism that purged VOA and other Washington agencies. Criticism of RFE "softness" nevertheless continued in émigré circles and conservative media.

Dissent from the moderate strategy also developed within the FEC (and AMCOMLIB). Lawrence de Neufville, an FEC official in New York, and Bernard Yarrow, an FEC vice president who had served with Allen Dulles in the Office of Strategic Services, pushed for a tougher line (even suggesting at one point that that Griffith, Lang, and others had become at least unwitting Soviet agents). De Neufville remonstrated to Lang that "the regimes represent professional revolutionary movements that cannot be removed by unplanned popular opposition and resentment but only by an expertly planned revolutionary campaign" (the specifics of which were never stated) targeted on the regime apparatus of repression itself—the army and police.[75] DeNeufville and Yarrow took their complaint directly to Allen Dulles. Frank Altschul, having left the FEC by then, expressed regret to Dulles that the FEC and RFE had poor leadership, were weakened by bureaucratic conflict, and had marginalized exile leaders.[76] Although Dulles did not intervene and the Lang-Griffith line generally prevailed, Lang cited disregard for Polish émigré criticism of the Światło broadcasts and leaflets, neglect of RFE New York concerns vis-à-vis those of RFE Munich, CIA interference, and general unhappiness with FEC management as the basis for his resignation as RFE director in the spring of 1955.[77] He was replaced by a former USIA official, W. J. Conerey Egan.

Projects VETO and FOCUS have frequently been criticized (and sometimes mocked) in histories of the Cold War. Most of this criticism misses the point. It focuses on one medium—leaflets delivered by balloon—of what were multimedia campaigns using both saturation radio and the printed

75. FEC memorandum to Lang from de Neufville, June 1, 1954.
76. Letter to Dulles from Altschul, May 20, 1955, Lehman Collection.
77. FEC memorandum to the FEC Executive Committee from Robert E. Lang, March 4, 1955, copy with references to Dulles redacted in DDRS; full text at the Dwight D. Eisenhower Presidential Library, released by NARA, May 16, 1997. Lang read his resignation statement to the FEC Executive Committee, joined by Allen Dulles, on March 4. Earlier, Lang registered his dissatisfactions (including his view that RFE had retreated from its original concept of partnership with émigrés) in an FEC memorandum to Shepardson, June 28, 1954. He continued to work for the FEC in Turkey until late 1955; Lang interview, Mickelson Collection.

word. Balloon delivery of leaflets, taking advantage of prevailing high-altitude winds blowing from West to East, was used by many organizations in the early Cold War as different politically as the Russian émigré organization the National Alliance of Russian Solidarists (Narodno-Trudovoy Soyuz, NTS) and the West German Social Democratic Party. It was an effective delivery vehicle under the circumstances, conveying some 20 million leaflets a month in early 1955 to Czechoslovakia and Hungary (and millions more to Poland). As mentioned above, leaflets were also mailed, in the realistic expectation that some percentage would make it through regime postal censorship.

VETO and FOCUS are better criticized on other grounds. The FEC strategy of attempting from outside to encourage nonviolent actions that would give birth to an opposition was, in the context of the times, an offensive, responsible, moderate strategy aimed at promoting evolutionary change. But it was ineffective[78]—a reasonable but fundamentally unsuccessful and (at least with hindsight) misconceived experiment with lessons applicable far beyond Eastern Europe in the 1950s. The approach was responsible, in the sense that it neither promoted violence nor needlessly exposed individuals to retaliation. But it overestimated the strength of popular self-confidence and seriously underestimated the effectiveness of the control apparatus consolidated by the Communist regimes over the previous eight years.[79] More fundamentally, it misjudged the relationship between internal and external factors of political change, overestimating the potential of the latter. It sought to provide from outside programmatic demands for political change—VETO's "Ten Demands of the People's Opposition" and FOCUS's "Twelve Demands of the National Opposition Movement"—that reflected domestic sentiments but had not yet been articulated by any individuals, let alone any groups. It sought to encourage from outside the coalescence of existing dissatisfactions into "movements" that did not yet exist. In the late 1960s and the 1970s, indigenous dissent, opposition voices, and eventually movements would arise in Eastern Europe and the USSR, and RFE and RL

78. This was a point made by U.S. Embassy representatives in Eastern Europe at the 1955 "Schramm conference," reporting that they had no indication of resonance to the "Ten Demands" or "Twelve Conditions." This was one of a series of annual conferences chaired by the Stanford University communications specialist Wilbur Schramm, which in the 1950s brought together in Europe representatives of VOA, RFE, RL, RIAS, the State Department, and the CIA.

79. That optimistic analysis was reflected in FEC Special Guidance No. 19, "The Turn of the Tide, June–July 1953," May 25, 1954.

would come into their own, not attempting to create but to amplify and strengthen indigenous dissent. But those conditions did not exist in the 1950s. The lesson of the FEC experiment represented by the VETO and FOCUS projects was that, no mater how massive the resources and however clever the tactics, external actors could only amplify, not induce, indigenous forces of change.

The VETO and FOCUS projects had short lives, as Soviet reversal of the New Course in spring 1955 made clearer the obstacles to effectively utilizing lower-level regime institutions for oppositional purposes. State-CIA-FEC discussions on the issue concluded with a decision to end on March 31, 1955, these specific projects that aspired to encourage "movements" and instead utilize leaflets as a kind of opposition press similar to RFE broadcasts while avoiding any hint of outside direction of passive resistance.[80] Some 100 million mini-newspaper leaflets of this kind were dropped on Czechoslovakia, Poland, and Hungary between April and September 1955. By April 1956, a half million balloons had carried 257 million copies of eighty-six different leaflet issues, amounting to two and a half billion page-sides delivered to those three countries.[81]

International developments in 1955 also had an impact on RFE (and RL) operations. The four-power Geneva summit led RFE to stress that only Soviet tactics had changed, not Soviet intentions, and to assure Eastern European audiences (and RFE and RL émigré broadcasters) that they were not being "sold out" to Moscow.[82] Khrushchev's apologetic visit to Belgrade in May 1955 and John Foster Dulles' meeting with Marshal Tito on Brioni in December focused some RFE and RL programming on the possibilities of "national Communism." Perhaps most important, the Austrian State Treaty of May 1955 was seen as a precedent for Soviet withdrawal from other European countries. By then, the targeted efforts in the VETO and FOCUS campaigns to encourage passive resistance had ended, and both radio broadcasts and leaflets were devoted to general encouragement of evolutionary change. But extensive RFE reporting on the Soviet withdrawal

80. FEC letter from CIA/IOD, W(OM) 5767, March 17, 1955.
81. FEC memoranda, "Free Europe Press: Changes in Editorial Formula," August 29, 1955; and "Effectiveness of FEC Leaflet Operations: A Summary Evaluation" [April 1956], summarizing anecdotal audience response and regime media attacks. Hungarian refugee accounts of balloon-dropped leaflets were reported in Vienna Embassy dispatch 1086, March 24, 1955, given by Békés, Byrne, and Rainer, *1956 Hungarian Revolution,* document 6.
82. FEC "Special Guidance No. 22 on the Four-Power Conference," May 31, 1955.

from Austria would contribute to overoptimistic hopes in 1956 that Hungary might be able to follow the same path.

The Evolution of Radio Liberty's Policy and Programs

Radio Liberty's broadcast policy, like that of RFE, evolved from a preoccupation with the Soviet émigré community to focus on the Soviet audience. This shift away from émigré projects and broadcasting managed by a united émigré organization was made clear in the phrase *"with such cooperation as is obtainable* from moderate elements in the emigration from the USSR which are willing to work together in this task" in the first sentence of the April 1954 AMCOMLIB mission statement. This policy document was a revision by the State Department and CIA of an original draft by AMCOMLIB president Leslie Stevens still focused more on émigré affairs than broadcasting. As the history of this key mission statement indicates, State Department and CIA officers were involved in RL policy discussions from the outset more intimately than was true in the case of RFE. AMCOMLIB's weekly management meetings were regularly attended by State Department and CIA representatives, a consequence of AMCOMLIB's less autonomous and less public position in its early years.

When Howland Sargeant replaced Leslie Stevens as AMCOMLIB president in October 1954, he could draw on his knowledge of the organization's early history from his service as assistant secretary of state for public affairs and on the Psychological Strategy Board to expand AMCOMLIB's autonomy. Although his plea for some counterpart to the Crusade for Freedom to raise the organization's public profile fell on deaf ears at the CIA, Sargeant nonetheless continued to press for greater autonomy, and in time he was able to secure for AMCOMLIB much of the same freedom of action that the FEC had enjoyed from its outset. He would exercise that authority in October 1956 when, against the advice of his Munich staff and some CIA officials, he (briefly) banned any original RL commentary on the Hungarian Revolution as potentially inciting.

Early RL programs suffered from the same problems of abstract anticommunist invective that beset the initial year of RFE broadcasts. RL's first broadcast called for "overthrow of the Soviet system and the liquidation of Bolshevism."[83] When unrest broke out in East Germany in June 1953, RL

83. Quoted by Gene Sosin, *Sparks of Liberty: An Insider's Memoir of Radio Liberty* (University Park: Pennsylvania State University Press, 1999), 17.

Munich officials on their own initiative sought to organize loudspeaker appeals to Soviet forces in Berlin and to carry German-language interviews intended for the East German population. The Office of the High Commissioner for Germany put a stop to both initiatives, which it viewed as needlessly provocative, before they could materialize. A review of the first six months of RL Russian broadcasts flagged problems that would only gradually be reduced—"special pleading for American power-political objectives, or for émigré ambitions that can only be achieved with the aid of foreign military intervention," "broad, vague verbal labels," failure "to speak to the audience as an equal addressing equals," and use of "violent, emotional language" instead of "sensible discourse on concrete problems which the Communist dictatorship is incapable of solving."[84] By mid-1954, CIA reviewers saw a marked improvement in programming; one reviewer saw "great improvement in the past few months. Near hysteria is no longer in evidence. The tone of the speakers is expressive, but moderate. The features have also improved." But for all the verbal bombast, RL programming in these early years was in some respects more cautious than the first RFE broadcasts. RL (if only because it lacked specific allegations) did not try to expose crimes of named low-level functionaries. An early RL policy paper of February 1953 cautioned against incitement to violent overthrow of the Soviet government while suggesting "liberation" as a positive concept around which the émigré community and Soviet listeners could rally. This had nothing to do with revolution or Western military intervention. "It is positive in seeking amelioration of a specific evil, or groups of evils, yet it does not constitute a direct challenge to the regime nor automatically inspire listeners to make useless sacrifices."[85] Information from the USSR was scarcer than from Eastern Europe, early newscasts drew primarily on a variety of Western sources, and conflicts about policy continued within as well as among the various émigré groups of broadcasters—and all these factors worked against any clear-cut editorial line.[86] AMCOMLIB's 1954 policy guidelines described the purpose of RL broadcasts as to "keep alive the spirit of resistance within the USSR," encourage dissension within the regime, and present democratic alternatives to Communist dictatorship—

84. AMCOMLIB memorandum from Stevens, October 15, 1953, enclosing a paper by an unnamed reviewer, "Improving the Effectiveness of Radio Liberation."
85. AMCOMLIB memorandum, "General Guidance for American Radio Advisory Personnel," February 11, 1953.
86. Mickelson, *America's Other Voice,* 105 ff.

moderate objectives that could have been outlined in the same words in the 1960s or the 1980s.[87]

As was the case with RFE, this moderate RL line had its critics. Early RL programming was criticized by some in the Russian and Ukrainian emigrations as pro-Marxist. CIA officers reviewing the programs thought they were vulnerable to such charges. AMCOMLIB president Stevens rejected such criticism and, like the FEC, stoutly defended the use of anticommunist ex-Marxists or Marxists in RL broadcasts: "Denunciations of Communism in theory and in Soviet practice will have the greatest effect on the Soviet audience if they come not from people accepted as 'right guard,' conservative, or even 'Western,' but from persons known to have been brilliant sympathizers and supporters at one time, and who therefore, in Soviet eyes, have a high degree of understanding."[88]

Reviewing RL broadcasts in mid-1955, Wilbur Schramm, a professor of communications and journalism at Stanford University and a regular consultant on Radio projects, concluded that it was too early to judge whether they could be effective. He nevertheless argued for strengthening RL's broadcast staff and transmitter power (RL was then still inaudible in the Moscow area):

The objective of Radio Liberation, . . . as it appears from the recent documents of [AMCOMLIB], is much more modest than that of Radio Free Europe. It is essentially to plant the seeds of doubt in the minds of Russians who have previously never heard more than one side of political questions, to make a beginning toward restoring the art of political thought to a culture where people have been invited to agree rather than to eval-

87. "American Committee for Liberation from Bolshevism: Mission and Objectives, " April 21, 1954, released to the author in October 2004. This policy statement was a CIA / State Department revision of AMCOMLIB president Stevens' draft, which described the mission as "to weaken and eventually disintegrate the power and influence of the Soviet dictatorship." Reviewing this somewhat pedestrian paper, one CIA official commented: "I am delighted to see that this Committee is going to be in favor of good and against evil." RL's mission and policy were further defined in RL Basic Guidance No. 1, December 10, 1953, and April 1, 1954; RL Basic Guidance No. 2, January 8, 1954; and AMCOMLIB "Statement of Mission, Operating Objectives, and Policy Guides, " September 1, 1954, a derivative of the once-classified April 1954 paper.
88. Letter to AMCOMLIB from CIA, "Radlib Scripts Which Provoke Pro-Marxist Charges," May 24, 1954; and AMCOMLIB memorandum by L. C. Stevens in response, n.d.

uate, and, in a very small way, to keep the isolated and walled-in Soviet peoples in touch with the world outside the [Iron] Curtain.[89]

RL's realistic mission, Schramm concluded, was smaller than its name, Radio Liberation, might indicate. RL management preferred a broader statement of purpose: "to supply Soviet citizens who are isolated from the outside world and denied free discussion at home with ideas and information which will give them a more conscious desire and a stronger will to achieve a democratic regime in place of the present totalitarian Communist regime."[90]

Like RFE, RL devoted many hours and multiple frequencies to broadcasting initial reports on and then, in June 1956, the full text of Khrushchev's Secret Speech delivered at the Twentieth Soviet Party Congress in February in which he denounced Stalin's crimes (see chapter 3). The Secret Speech caused many Communists to question Soviet ideology, and RL covered the bitter reactions to it by Natalia Sedova (Trotsky's widow), Howard Fast, and other prominent opponents of Stalinism and disillusioned Communists.[91] In the wake of the Secret Speech and on the eve of the "Polish October" and the Hungarian Revolution, Sargeant emphasized the importance of RL programs that offered alternatives to the Communist system and provided examples in various fields demonstrating fallacies of Marxism. The 1956 update of the RL policy manual (dated June 29) specifically renounced encouragement of overt or violent resistance to the Soviet regime and pledged that RL "will make no promises which it cannot itself fulfill, and will never indicate that freedom and democracy will be achieved except through the will and endeavors of the peoples of the USSR themselves."

By 1956 and well before the Hungarian Revolution, then, RL and RFE both had abandoned their original policy statements that seemed to envisage the end of Communist regimes in the Soviet orbit in some foreseeable future. Both sought at the policy level to encourage challenges to Communist orthodoxies within the regimes and among the populations without encouraging suicidal revolt. RFE programs had moderated much original ver-

89. Quoted in AMCOMLIB memorandum, "Comments on Schramm Report" [by Kelley], February 1, 1956.
90. AMCOMLIB draft policy memorandum, October 14, 1955, quoted in "Comments on Schramm Report." AMCOMLIB memorandum, "Radio Liberation Programming Staff Comment on the [Schramm Report]," June 29, 1956; AMCOMLIB memorandum by Sargeant, May 11, 1956.
91. Sosin, *Sparks of Liberty,* 55–65.

bal bombast; RL, on the air for only three years, was still in the process of attempting to do that.

The German Context

RFE and RL were both launched in American-occupied Germany. They would not have gotten off the ground elsewhere. Successive commanding generals of American occupation forces in Germany and U.S. high commissioners were personally involved in making occupied German military facilities available for transmitter sites, expediting leases of a section of Munich's central park for the RFE building and the former Munich airport administration building for RL, allocating radio frequencies under Allied High Commission Law No. 5 (which gave the Allies exclusive control over media) over the opposition of many countries represented in the International Telecommunications Union, and providing support services to the RFE and RL staffs (including access to military schools and commissaries). The U.S. military openly supported the FEC's balloon-leaflet projects, providing hydrogen containers and weather data, and launching site security patrols.

Occupied West Germany became the sovereign Federal Republic of Germany in May 1955. RFE and RL operated there for the next forty years, and any full history of the Radios requires attention to the German context. Even before restoration of sovereignty, German foreign and internal security policies and domestic politics influenced both Radios and constrained some of their operations.

The German government operating under the occupation regime resented the FEC's initial RFE broadcasts and leaflet-balloon launchings, over which it had no control. As State Secretary Franz Thedieck told the German cabinet in 1951, "The appropriate German authorities have been informed but they themselves have no influence on the operations."[92] Bavarian minister-president Wilhelm Högner responded to complaints about RFE from Bavarian parliament members that "the Bavarian government has had no influence on the program and no ability to check people."[93] During an April 1952 meeting of the High Commission, Chancellor Konrad Adenauer complained

92. Cabinet meeting of August 19, 1951, *Die Kabinettsprotokolle der Bundesregierung,* band 4, 1951 (Boppard am Rhein: Boldt Verlag, n.d.), 595–96.
93. Meeting with Landtag deputies on October 10, 1951, Minn 97578, Bayerische Staatsarchiv.

that RFE's "propaganda" from Munich was "for us very unwelcome."[94] Addressing the Bundestag that same month, the Social Democratic Party (Sozialdemokratische Partei Deutschlands, SPD) leader Herbert Wehner objected to RFE Czechoslovak broadcasts as violating German interests.[95]

However unwelcome the German authorities found RFE broadcasts and FEC balloon-delivered leaflets at the outset, they were powerless to stop them during the occupation regime and so focused on regularizing their operations. They formally recognized the legal status of RFE and RL as foreign nonprofit organizations operating in Germany and approved registration of the Institute for the Study of the USSR as an association (*Verein*) under German law.[96] Anticipating in 1952 an early restoration of German sovereignty in conjunction with the birth of the abortive European Defense Community, which was ultimately vetoed by France in 1954, the FEC (with State Department backing) negotiated with the German government a contingent broadcast license agreement, to enter into force upon the restoration of German sovereignty. AMCOMLIB made a similar arrangement. The contingent agreements licensed the transmission of RFE and RL broadcasts from Germany for a term of five years, stipulated that they not contain material contradicting German national interests, required the Radios to retain recordings of all broadcasts for one month and make them available to the German government for review on demand, and stated that the German government reserved its right to demand immediate cessation of any transmissions that, in its judgment, violated German policies. The German government made these terms a matter of public record in response to a formal inquiry (*kleine Anfrage*) from SPD parliamentary deputies in November 1952,[97] and it restated them after the licenses were granted in 1955.[98] The FEC and AMCOMLIB formally accepted these obligations and restric-

94. Session of April 21, 1952, *Akten zur auswärtigen Politik der Bundesrepublik Deutschland, Bd. 2. Adenauer und die Höhen Kommissare 1952* (Munich: R. Oldenbourg Verlag, 1990), 84.

95. Deutsche Bundestag-204th Session, April 3–4, 1952, 8755.

96. Decree of the Minister of Internal Affairs, May 5, 1953, recognizing AMCOMLIB, Minn 87575, Bayerische Staatsarchiv,.

97. FEC letter from State Secretary Hallstein, May 30, 1952; AMCOMLIB letter from Foreign Office, March 14, 1952; Foreign Office document 454-08 II 14984/52, Deutscher Bundestag, 1. Wahlperiode 1949, Foreign Office Political Archive [FOPA] B12, band 302. An FEC document, "German Broadcast Permission," n.d. [1969], compiled in translation many of the relevant German permissions.

98. Foreign Minister Brentano response to SPD Bundestag Deputy Reitener, November 23, 1955, *Süddeutsche Zeitung*, August 24, 1955.

tions.[99] The major if unstated consequence of the "German national interests" caveat was that RFE could not take an editorial position or provide full reporting on the issue of Poland's western border, which still was formally provisional under the terms of the Potsdam Agreement, a condition resented by all Poles (this issue is discussed further in chapter 4). It also meant that RFE was constrained from programming on the mass expulsion of Germans from the Sudetenland without the right of return, a provision of the Potsdam Agreement defended by almost all Czechs.

German domestic politics also intruded. RFE and RL were based in Bavaria, where in the early 1950s nearly a fourth of the electorate were German expellees from Czechoslovak Sudetenland and elsewhere well represented in the Bavarian parliament. The Sudeten expellee organizations viewed the RFE Czechoslovak Service with great suspicion, especially because many Czech broadcasters—including the director, Ferdinand Peroutka—had been associated with President Edvard Beneš, who was responsible in their eyes for the mass expulsions. They sought to influence RFE broadcasting policies and personnel, proposing the formation of a Sudeten advisory council and the inclusion of German-language programs in RFE Czechoslovak Service broadcasts. Slovak nationalists and German expellees from Silesia and East Prussia, now part of Poland, also sought to influence RFE's operations. The expellee causes were regularly taken up by deputies in the Bavarian parliament and by the Bavarian press.[100] The Sudeten leader and Bavarian parliament member Franz Gaksach was a constant critic in the parliament and press.[101] His personal attacks on Czechoslovak Service broadcasters were picked up by all-German media (resulting in a lawsuit for slander and eventually a retraction by the respected weekly *Die Zeit*).[102]

99. FEC letter to Hallstein from Spencer Phenix, September 2, 1952; FEC letter to the German government from Condon, July 7, 1955. RFE and RL's Portuguese and Spanish broadcasting licenses also contained a provision that as-broadcast tapes be retained for a month and be available for review; the Portuguese and Spanish governments never exercised that right.

100. FEC memorandum, "The German Assault on Radio Free Europe," July 15, 1955.

101. Gaksach called for the expulsion from Germany of many of the Czechoslovak Service broadcasters who allegedly shared responsibility for the expulsion of the Sudeten Germans; Bayerischer Landtag, 31 Sitzung, Donnerstag, den 4, August 1955. Five years later, he took a different tack: "We do not know how many salon Communists, Titoists, and radical leftist intellectuals work in the Radio"; *Tages-Anzeiger,* Regensburg, December 14, 1960.

102. "Sender der Unbelehrbaren" [Radio Station of the Incorrigible], *Die Zeit,* May 26, 1955; retraction, July 18, 1958. *Der Stern* published a similar retraction.

The anti-RFE campaign mounted by expellees in West Germany was echoed in the United States by conservative and nationalist (especially Slovak nationalist) émigré organizations critical of the FEC. These organizations had the support of several congressional staffers—most prominently Kurt Glaser, a counsel for the House Committee on Communist Aggression (known as the Kersten Committee). Hearings of the committee held in Munich in June 1954 (adroitly managed by RFE and the German government) eased the concerns of some committee members about RFE's personnel and policies.[103]

Pressure on RFE from German émigré groups increased following the restoration of German sovereignty in May 1955. The Czechoslovak regime's "redefection campaign" (described in chapter 7) resulted in the return to Prague with fanfare of several individuals connected with RFE. This gave *Der Stern* and other popular nationalist media an excuse to attack RFE as an American-imposed organization harboring Communist sympathizers. A Slovak adversary (a former official of the Nazi-satellite Slovak Republic during World War II) was assassinated in Munich, and *Der Stern* (on July 17) insinuated that RFE employees were involved. Criticism of RFE continued in the Bavarian parliament.

The FEC was able to deflect these expellee pressures, thanks in no small part to the intimate knowledge of German and expellee matters and the Bavarian and all-German connections of two RFE officials who earlier had played key roles in the American occupation administration in Bavaria—political adviser William E. Griffith (who had been in charge of de-Nazification) and German affairs adviser Ernst Langendorf (a German-American who had been responsible for the media). By 1953 Griffith had come to believe that some public German participation in RFE would be necessary, but that expellee concerns could be mitigated by incorporating their representatives in a European-wide ("Umbrella") "consultative body of private persons."[104]

Conversely, efforts to reduce expellee concerns through broadcasts acknowledging their grievances were counterproductive. Czechoslovak Service director Peroutka sought to defuse tensions in a commentary broadcast

103. At the insistence of the German government, Sudeten German expellees and Slovak nationalists did not testify, and those émigrés who did appear were supportive of RFE.

104. FEC memorandum, "NCFE and the German Problem: After Ratification of the Contractual Agreements," by Condon and Griffith, April 6, 1953.

on October 7, 1951, acknowledging that, horrendous crimes committed by the Nazis notwithstanding, Czechs had also committed atrocities against Czechoslovak Germans in 1945. Peroutka's commentary was a classic case of too much and too little, only making matters worse and illustrating RFE's dilemma in dealing with the expellee issue. The commentary was too weak to satisfy the Sudeten expellee organizations yet (as pointed out by U.S. ambassador Ellis O. Briggs in Prague) too strong for the Czechoslovak audience and implicitly at odds with U.S. policy based on the Potsdam Agreement, which regarded the mass expulsion of Germans from Eastern Europe as legitimate and a closed book. The only practical solution for RFE was to say as little as possible on the subject. Meanwhile, Griffith and Langendorf cultivated ties with the German media and officialdom. One important tool was *Osteuropäische Rundschau,* a German edition (edited by Langendorf) of the FEC publication *News from Behind the Iron Curtain,* later retitled *East Europe.*

The German government was always more concerned about RFE than RL, given the border and expellee issues, and its attention to RFE increased with the restoration of German sovereignty in 1955. The previous year, U.S. government and FEC officials so feared the consequences of that approaching date that they concluded that RFE would have to find a new home in another European country.[105] Mid-level German Foreign Office officials suggested that the German government should have a voice in RFE operations. The first secretary of the new West German Embassy in Washington, Wilhelm Turnwald, himself a Sudeten German, was particularly hostile to RFE. The Bavarian Interior Ministry internally questioned why the Radios, which it asserted were funded by American intelligence agencies, should operate independently on German territory.[106] In the end, the conservative Adenauer government and its successors found it to West Germany's advantage to have the Radios operate from German soil in the service of common anti-communist goals without having to assume responsibility for them, so long

105. "It is hard to see how RFE can have more than another year of life in Germany," FEC memorandum, "Germany and FEC" [no author listed, evidently drafted by Griffith], August 17, 1954, DDRS. FEC and State Department officials meeting on December 10, 1954, were pessimistic about RFE's future in Germany. FEC "Memorandum of Conversation on Meeting of Department of State on Friday Afternoon, December 10, 1954," by Griffith, n.d.; FEC memorandum from Galantiere, December 13, 1954.

106. Communications between the German Embassy in Washington and the Foreign Office, 1955–56, FOPA, B12, band 302; Bavarian Interior Ministry memorandum, August 13, 1957, FOPA, B12, band 386.

as they respected key German interests.[107] They found the RFE research reports invaluable for understanding Eastern European developments. It was the private status of the Radios that made this arrangement possible. Few German officials could have had any doubt about the U.S. government's role behind the scenes, but it was in the interest of the German government as well as the U.S. government never to raise the issue. "Don't ask, don't tell" worked well for both countries.

Official German acceptance of RFE and RL broadcasting after 1955 did not extend to FEC balloon-delivered leaflets. Even during the occupation regime, the German government had objected to "an extremely worrisome violation of airspace sovereignty from the territory of the Federal Republic."[108] The FEC was, as noted above, hardly the only organization to take advantage of prevailing Western winds to launch leaflets to the East in the early 1950s. The SPD Ostbüro in Berlin, the NTS, and other organizations were in the balloon-leaflet business as well. But the FEC program, highly publicized by the Crusade for Freedom, was the most visible. FEC lobbying in Washington and Bonn to continue the program was undercut by a series of incidents, including an unfounded Czechoslovak government complaint to the International Civil Aviation Organization that an FEC balloon had caused an airliner crash,[109] an NTS deception leaflet reaching the USSR wrongly attributed to the FEC that embarrassed Chancellor Adenauer during his 1955 Moscow visit, and a household fire in Wilfersdorf, Austria, indirectly caused by a balloon malfunction.[110] Though the program found little support from State Department officers stationed in Eastern Europe,[111] German reservations were decisive. The Bavarian government registered its unhappiness with the program to the Foreign Office,[112] whose

107. *Süddeutsche Zeitung*, August 24, 1955, reporting information from the German Foreign Office; FO memorandum by Friedensburg (following talks with RFE and RL), 200-454-09 bzw. 08/8354/55, FOPA, B12, band 384.

108. Cabinet meeting, August 21, 1951.

109. Preparing a defense for the ICAO, the FEC ran an airborne experiment with a DC3 aircraft to see if the balloons they were using could somehow damage the plane. They could not.

110. The balloon fell with its load of leaflets on the farmhouse, causing little damage but frightening the housewife, who upset a cooking burner in the kitchen, which set part of the house on fire. The FEC compensated the farmers for the damage.

111. FEC letter to Weaver from Walker, October 14, 1955 (on the NTS leaflet); FEC memorandum to Michie from G. E. R. Gedye, April 11, 1956 (on Austrian protests); FEC memorandum to Galantiere from Griffith, September 28, 1956 (on State Department views expressed at the 1956 "Schramm conference").

112. Letter of March 3, 1956, FOPA, B12, band 302.

representatives suggested to RFE Munich management in February 1956 that the program be ended.[113] The Federal Republic of Germany's Washington embassy and Foreign Office officials, including State Secretary Walter Hallstein, in a meeting with FEC president Whitney H. Shepardson and Ambassador James Conant, requested in early 1956 that the balloon-leaflet program be terminated.[114] The State Department concurred, and all FEC leaflet-by-balloon activity ended at the beginning of the Polish and Hungarian crises in October. The German objection was to the method—balloon delivery—and not the printed-word message, and the Foreign Office looked favorably on the FEC's follow-on effort to deliver printed materials to Eastern Europe by mail and travelers.[115]

The apprehensiveness of FEC and U.S. government officials about the future of the Radios in a sovereign West Germany proved to be exaggerated, as Griffith acknowledged at the end of 1955,[116] and the Radios were able to operate for a decade and a half after 1955 without challenge from the German government to their broadcast policies, let alone to their existence. This was the case because the German government had an interest in their continuation as effective anticommunist instruments and because RFE and RL respected the "rules of the game" and (as their U.S. government policy guidelines stipulated) downplayed coverage of German border and expellee issues. Only once in the period from 1955 to 1970, after RFE's broadcasts during the Hungarian Revolution had become controversial in the German media, did the German government exercise its prerogative to review broadcast tapes (discussed in chapter 3). Notwithstanding concerns that motivated Allen Dulles to raise the broadcast license issue personally with Chancellor Adenauer,[117] RFE's and RL's broadcast licenses were re-

113. FO memorandum on a February 15, 1956 meeting with RFE management, FOPA, B13, band 183.

114. FO minutes of an April 27, 1956 meeting, FOPA, B12, band 302. The NTS and other organizations continued to send leaflets via balloon to the East after 1956, much to the dismay of the FEC; "translations of some of these leaflets show instances of the crassest violation of 'propaganda ethics,' including direct appeals to violence," FEC letter to the CIA, NW-7078, February 20, 1957.

115. FEC letter to Dirk Onken, German Foreign Office, from Matthews, November 26, 1957, FOPA, B13, band 184.

116. FEC memorandum to Galantiere from Griffith, "FEC Position in Germany," December 23, 1955.

117. "Mr. Dulles said that while RFE was a private station, it supported the interests of the Free World, Germany, and at the present moment the American position in Berlin." Dispatch from the German Embassy, Washington, to the Foreign Office on the Dulles-Adenauer exchange, Pol. 702-86.60/521/60 VS-NfD, March 30, 1960, FOPA, B12, band 387.

newed routinely after 1960. In extending the licenses, Foreign Office officials made a point of encouraging RFE to follow RL's example of keeping a very low public profile in Germany, while expressing continued concern about some of its Oder-Neisse coverage.[118] In 1967, overruling reservations of the Ministry of Post and Communications about allowing RFE and RL to increase transmitter power and frequency use, the Foreign Office said it was in the Federal Republic of Germany's interest that the Radios remain in Germany.[119] Only in 1970, following the election of Willy Brandt as chancellor and the launching of a new Eastern European policy, would the German government raise the issue of RFE and RL broadcast policies and continued operation from German territory.

If the restoration of German sovereignty had little impact on RFE and RL at the policy level, as providers of uncensored information to Eastern Europe and the Soviet Union, it had two major consequences for the Radios as employers. First, the German government asserted its sovereign prerogative to require RFE and RL non-German staff members to obtain German residence and work permits contingent on approval by the Bundesamt für Verfassungsschutz (Office for Protection of the Constitution, BfV, the domestic security organization).[120] Though under no illusion about the U.S. government's connections to the Radios, the BfV's Bavarian branch (Landesamt für Verfassungsschutz, LfV) maintained continuous direct liaison with Radio security officers on these matters. FEC records of contacts with the LfV indicate that the Bavarian organization remained well informed from its own sources about internal matters at RFE, and the same was doubtless true of RL.[121] LfV played a role, along with the CIA and the Radio

118. In the early 1950s, German officials sometimes confused RL with Radio Free Russia, an NTS station operating from occupied Germany. They were concerned that publicity on the bombing of the NTS building near Frankfurt in June 1958 would complicate the status of RFE and RL. Ministry of Post and Communications press release, July 28, 1958.

119. Letter to the Foreign Office from the Ministry of Post and Communications, March 29, 1967; response from the Foreign Office, May 9, 1967, FOPA, B40, band 148, fiche 148-1.

120. "RFE management is obligated not to employ any persons who are disapproved by the Bavarian Land Security Office." Foreign Office memorandum 200-87-20/5 to FEC from Oncken, January 30, 1958; FEC memorandum to Haselhoff from Rinker, June 10, 1958. The Foreign Office memorandum was in response to complaints from the Bavarian Interior Ministry that while earlier the LfV had objected to the continued employment of seventy-nine RFE personnel, only eight had been dismissed.

121. FEC memorandum for the record, "Meeting with Bavarian LfV," by Hans Fischer, December 20, 1960. This liaison continued after CIA oversight of the Radios

managements, in personnel matters and occasionally barred from Germany individuals the Radios sought to hire.

Second, both Radios now had to operate as private employers in the German labor market, where "co-determination" (giving workers a voice in management), trade union prerogatives, and job protection were fundamentals of the "social market economy" anchored in constitutional law. The Radios now had to pay German customs duties on imports. Radio employees now had to pay German taxes (albeit at concessionary rates for many years). They lost military commissary and most base privileges (because the Radios were not covered by the Status of Forces Agreement that replaced the occupation regime). In the following decades, German works councils and trade unions, supported by the Bavarian government and courts, asserted themselves on issues of jurisdiction (denying standing to the New York Guild, which represented journalists at RFE in New York and tried to organize in Munich), collective bargaining (salaries were determined by a collective bargaining agreement), job security, mandatory retirement age (applicability of German law was confirmed in a lawsuit that reached the U.S. Supreme Court), and other personnel issues. On some of these matters, RFE and RL managements did not push back as strongly as managements of German firms might have done. This was viewed by the Radios' managements (and their overseers) as the price they had to pay in order to keep the Radios out of the German media and domestic politics. One consequence was that over the years, Radio jobs provided better salaries and benefits than comparable media positions in Bavaria. Yet these high personnel costs and stringent labor regulations would foredoom efforts to continue operations in Germany with post–Cold War U.S. public funding.

Nonradio Activities

Although Radio Free Europe and Radio Liberty were the major projects of the FEC and AMCOMLIB and are the subject of this book, both committees were established originally to support émigré activities, and through the 1960s both committees continued to finance émigré-oriented publica-

ended. As RFE/RL security officer in Munich from 1980 to 1995, Richard Cummings maintained regular contact with the LfV, as had his predecessor in the 1970s. Personal communication from Cummings to the author; interview with LfV official by the author, September 11, 2001.

tion, educational, influence, and welfare activities. Though detailed treatment of these other projects cannot be undertaken here, a brief summary
will indicate their continuing importance in FEC and AMCOMLIB operations. As of mid-1952, the FEC Division of Exile Relations (formerly the
National Councils Division) worked with six national and four international
exile organizations and still aimed at creating united Romanian, Bulgarian,
and Polish national committees. A Research and Publications Service initially both organized the flow of information to Radio Free Europe and issued *News from Behind the Iron Curtain* and other publications for Western readers. The Division of Intellectual Cooperation supported exile
research projects, such as those of the Mid-European Studies Center (focused on "the structure of a liberated Eastern Europe"), the East European
Inquiry (focused on the Danubian area), the Mid-European Law Project,
and the East European Accessions List. The Free European University in
Exile in Strasbourg trained young émigrés.[122] Although the 1953 Jackson
Committee report had recommended that both committees give priority to
their radio operations, and although the CIA/IOD continued to encourage
the FEC to scale back its non-RFE operations, by 1955 some forty-five émi-
gré organizations were connected directly or indirectly to the FEC.[123]
Through the 1960s, both the FEC and AMCOMLIB (after 1964, the Radio
Liberty Committee) were much more than simply the Radios they operated.
Indeed, in 1964 the FEC still extended support to some thirty émigré or
other anticommunist organizations and a variety of publications, and in the
late 1960s non-RFE activities still accounted for nearly a quarter of the
FEC's budget.[124]

The other major FEC influence project was the Free Europe Press, an
FEC division parallel to the RFE Division, which was responsible for the
delivery of millions of leaflets by mail and balloon. With the end of its leaflet
program in 1956, the Free Europe Press (renamed the Publications and Special Projects Division) turned its energies to the distribution of mostly non-
political Western publications to Eastern Europe through the regular mail

122. FEC memorandum, "Primary NCFE Program Items for Fiscal Year 1952–53,"
n.d.
123. FEC letter from CIA (W (EJ) 5865), June 6, 1955.
124. FEC letter to CIA, "Updating List of Organizations Supported by FEC," FC-
2319, June 19, 1964. FEC FY 1965 expenditures were $13.2 million for RFE and $2.9
million for non-RFE projects (and $1 million overhead), totaling $17.3 million. FEC FY
1967 budget presentation.

and using travelers, a project usually known as the "book program."[125] It was conceived as "a rifle rather than a shotgun approach and is aimed at managers, intellectuals, and various other elites in the target countries, without any attribution to FEC."[126] The FEC book program and a counterpart RLC program together distributed two and one-half million books and periodicals to the USSR and Eastern Europe from the late 1950s to the late 1960s.[127] The FEC continued to provide financial support to hundreds of "worthy" émigrés, termed "stipendiaries"—a support function imposed by the Department of State that the FEC tried to minimize,[128] and then (in the late 1960s) end, so that more of its budget could be devoted to broadcasts and printed matter for Eastern Europe.

AMCOMLIB supported the Institute for the Study of the USSR, originally an outgrowth of the Harvard Refugee Interview Project, which employed émigré scholars and published a variety of émigré publications. It supported other émigré support activities, and a Western publications dis-

125. John P. Matthews, "The West's Secret Marshall Plan for the Mind," *Journal of Intelligence and Counterintelligence* 16, no. 3 (2003): 409–27; Alfred Reisch, *Hot Books in the Cold War: The West's Secret Book Distribution Program behind the Iron Curtain* (forthcoming); John Richardson Jr., *A New Vision for America: Toward Human Solidarity through Global Democracy—a Memoir* (New York: Ruder Finn Press, 2006), 96–97; John Richardson Jr., Oral History Interview, February 9, 1999, Foreign Affairs Oral History Collection of the Association for Diplomatic Studies and Training, Library of Congress, available at http://memory.loc.gov; FEC letter to Crittenberger from Walker, February 26, 1957, enclosing FEC memorandum, "Free Europe Press Editorial Program." Jan Nowak, citing the thanks of a Polish recipient of a scientific book, commented: "This activity deserves tribute not only to the Free Europe Committee, but also to the American people. I am sure that the time will come when this moving story can be told and will gain for America the gratitude and appreciation of the Captive Peoples"; FEC letter to Walker from Nowak, December 7, 1957. George C. Minden directed the program; his obituary appeared in the *New York Times* on April 23, 2006.

126. FEC Board of Directors meeting minutes, November 27, 1956.

127. "Report Prepared by the Central Intelligence Agency, March 30, 1970," document 149, in *FRUS,* 1969–76, XII, 463.

128. The State Department and the CIA were more involved in the FEC's émigré activities than its radio project. FEC official John Leich met regularly with State and CIA officials in Washington on émigré matters. For his report of an April 9, 1952 meeting, see his FEC memorandum of that date. Julius Fleischmann, heir of the yeast and gin magnate and another veteran of the Office of Strategic Services, served as the FEC's nonpublic representative in Washington to coordinate such liaisons; Leich interview. John Foster Leich discussed his experience with the émigré National Councils in "Great Expectations: The National Councils in Exile, 1950–1960, *Polish Review* 35, no. 3 (1990): 183–96.

tribution project ("book program") modeled on that of RFE.[129] Though these may have all been useful projects, by the 1960s—the "book programs" aside—they were no longer core mission requirements for either the FEC or the RLC. They absorbed resources that arguably would have been put to more productive use had they been reprogrammed into expanded broadcasting—for example, to begin broadcasts to the Baltic states or increase broadcasts to Ukraine.[130] It was only the transition from CIA oversight to public funding at the end of the 1960s that forced the FEC and the RLC to end all émigré-support activities and focus on their primary mission of broadcasting to Eastern Europe and the USSR.

129. Isaac Patch, *Closing the Circle: A Buckalino Journey Around Our Time* (privately printed, Wellesley College Printing Services, Wellesley, Mass., 1996), 356ff; James Critchlow, *Radio Hole-in-the-Head: Radio Liberty—An Insider's Story of Cold War Broadcasting* (Washington, D.C.: American University Press, 1995), 135; Yale Richmond, *Cultural Exchange and the Cold War: Raising the Iron Curtain* (University Park: Pennsylvania State University Press, 2003), chap. 13, "Hot Books in the Cold War"; RLC letter to Patch from Jack Stewart [his European deputy], March 16, 1965, enclosing the monthly situation report of the Special Projects Division for February 1965; RLC memorandum to Board of Trustees [CIA] from Patch, October 14, 1966; RLC memorandum, "Basic Briefing on Three Key Programs of the Radio Liberty Committee," from Sargeant, April 17, 1967.

130. The FEC spent $76.6 million on non-RFE projects through June 30, 1971, out of total expenditures listed in chapter 8 of $369 million. FEC memorandum to CIA, February 15, 1972.

Chapter 3

Two Octobers in 1956

The year 1956 was one of ferment throughout the Communist world. RFE and RL, in line with U.S. government policy, covered that ferment comprehensively in all broadcast languages and in so doing sought to help it spread. In February, Khrushchev caused an earthquake when he denounced Stalin at a closed session of the Twentieth Soviet Party Congress. As the content of this historic "Secret Speech" became known, it sent shock waves around the Communist world that caused many party members to question the role of the Soviet Union and their belief in communism. RFE and RL contributed to the dissemination of the "Secret Speech," first reporting in March initial Western press accounts. In June the Radios repeatedly broadcast in all their languages the full text of the speech as published in the *New York Times.* RFE devoted extensive coverage to the Poznań riots in Poland in June and the aftermath leading to the change in Communist Party leadership and partial liberalization of the system—the "Polish October"—in the fall. It reported the developing ferment in Hungary in the summer and fall of 1956, including discussions in the reformist Petőfi Circle (based in part on the reports of the *Time* magazine journalist Simon Bourgin, who observed the meetings and privately briefed RFE about them) and the October 16 protest meeting in Győr in western Hungary.[1] RFE had continued to

1. Bourgin later published his briefing notes in *The New Hungarian Quarterly* 37, nos. 142–43 (Summer–Fall, 1996). It should be noted that the Győr meeting articulated demands for fundamental system change before the outbreak of violence in Budapest on October 23, including calls for public trial of the head of the secret police, introduction of a multiparty system, a free press, and the withdrawal of Soviet forces. "Telegram from the Legation in Hungary to the Department of State," document 97, in *Foreign Relations of the United States,* ed. U.S. Department of State (hereafter, *FRUS*) (Washington, D.C.: U.S. Government Printing Office, various years), 1955–57, XXV.

report on developments in Austria after Hungary's neighbor regained its sovereignty and freedom in 1955.

RFE's basic approach to ferment in the Communist world in 1956 was outlined in several internal policy memoranda issued in the first half of the year. Special Guidance No. 26 of March 27, addressing the emerging unrest, cautioned, "There is no likelihood of military action by the West to liberate [the Eastern European] peoples." Special Guidance No. 27 of July 9 foresaw gradual, in-system change:

> We must expect . . . that no reforms can take place . . . except under the aegis of the [Communist] party in power and under the guise of the new "benevolence" announced by the 20th CPSU [Communist Party of the Soviet Union] Congress. . . . While national communism cannot be our goal, we ignore the label attached to a successful movement for reforms ("Titoist," "national communist," etc.); we judge the specific instance accordingly as it does or does not lighten our people's burden, and takes them along the path to democracy.

Drawing on this basic guidance in a policy memorandum dated September 26, 1956, policy adviser William E. Griffith defined RFE's task as "assist[ing] and prolonging and extending the thaw" and promoting liberalization even under conditions of continued Communist rule.[2]

These RFE guidances conformed to U.S. government policy at the time on conveying information to the Soviet orbit. The Operations Coordinating Board's Special Working Group on Stalinism, an interagency staff committee, in May defined the aim of U.S. policy and the task of "unattributable propaganda," that is, RFE and RL, as "a loosening of the ties binding the satellites to Moscow and creation of conditions that will permit the satellites to evolve toward independence of Moscow."[3] A draft NSC policy state-

---

2. As cited by Arch Puddington, *Broadcasting Freedom: The Cold War Triumph of Radio Free Europe and Radio Liberty* (Lexington: University Press of Kentucky, 2000), 97. These guidances drafted by FEC counselor Galantiere and Griffith implicitly contradicted parts of a vacuous policy memo issued by RFE director Egan on June 15 titled "Radio Free Europe's Opportunities versus a Moving Target." Egan issued this memorandum, which minimized the importance of regime concessions and discussed RFE's task in vague generalities, notwithstanding pointed critiques of his draft by Galantiere (FEC memorandum to Egan from Galantiere, May 26, 1956), Griffith (FEC Munich telex, May 25, 1956), and CIA IOD.

3. "Summary of U.S. Policy Guidance and Actions Taken to Exploit the [Anti-Stalin] Campaign," May 17, 1956, document 44, in *FRUS, 1955–57*, XXIV.

ment of early June, while noting that "Soviet domination of the East European satellites remained firm," viewed ferment in the Communist world as providing the United States with new opportunities to counter Soviet control of the region.[4] An NSC staff annex to the draft was more specific. Viewing as negligible the chance that "an anti-Soviet faction could seize or hold power in a satellite and bring about its detachment from the Soviet bloc," it recommended "promoting and encouraging evolutionary change toward the weakening of Soviet controls and the attainment of national independence." It defined the task of "our propaganda facilities"—that is, USIA, VOA, RIAS, RFE, and RL—as "avoiding, on the one hand, any commitments regarding the time and means of achieving freedom from Soviet domination and any incitement to premature revolt, and, on the other hand, seeking to maintain faith in the eventual restoration of freedom."[5] Following NSC discussion,[6] President Eisenhower approved a minor modification of the policy draft as NSC 5608/1. This updated basic statement of U.S. policy (replacing NSC 174 of December 1953) focused on "encouragement of evolutionary change resulting in the weakening of Soviet controls and the attainment of national independence by the countries concerned, even though there may be no change in their internal political structure." It provided no specific guidance for "propaganda" (USIA and the Radios), apart from implying that U.S. foreign information programs would be modified "as Communist controls and obstruction of communications are relaxed."[7]

4. "Draft Statement of Policy by the National Security Council on Policy toward the Soviet Satellites in Eastern Europe," document 73, in *FRUS*, XXV, 191–94 (redacted version); NARA release of October 28, 2009, provided to the author by Malcolm Byrne of the National Security Archive (full text).

5. "National Security Council Staff Study: Annex to NSC 5608, U.S. Policy toward the Soviet Satellites in Eastern Europe, July 6, 1956," document 76, in *FRUS*, XXV, 208–9 (redacted version); Csaba Békés, Malcolm Byrne, and János M. Rainer, *The 1956 Hungarian Revolution: A History in Documents* (Budapest: Central European University Press, 2002), document 12, 119–28 (full text).

6. "Memorandum of Discussion at the 290th Meeting of the National Security Council, Washington, July 12, 1956," document 79, in *FRUS*, XXV, 212–16 (redacted version); Békés, Byrne, and Rainer, *1956 Hungarian Revolution*, document 13, 129–35 (less redacted version); NARA release of February 17, 2004, provided to the author by Malcolm Byrne of the National Security Archive (full text).

7. An appendix to NSC 5608/1 declared that the United States would "assist nationalists in any form, where conducive to independence from Soviet domination." The July 12 NSC discussion indicates that this was an indirect reference to future Titoist regimes, moved to the appendix to limit dissemination of the politically sensitive prospect of backing national Communist regimes. The appendix also stated that the United States would

The importance of attention in broadcasts to evolutionary forces within Communist regimes, as well as the traditional emphasis on popular opposition to Communist rule, was reemphasized at the third annual "Schramm conference" on U.S. international broadcasting, held in Munich in August 1956 with representatives of the State Department, the CIA, and all the U.S. broadcasters attending.[8]

But just as in mid-1953, Western analyses and policies were quickly outpaced by events in Eastern Europe that would test RFE's ability to function as an effective, responsible surrogate broadcaster. In the case of Hungary, RFE must be judged to have failed that test in October 1956. In the arguably more important but little-discussed case of broadcasting to Poland, on the brink of conflagration that same month, RFE passed that test with flying colors.

---

not "discourage, by public utterances or otherwise, spontaneous manifestations of discontent and opposition to the Communist regime, despite risk to individuals, when their net results will exert pressures for release from Soviet domination. Authorizations which might lead to local violence will be authorized only by the Secretary of State with the approval of the President." This was compromise language attempting to reflect both John Foster Dulles' views at the July 12 NSC meeting that the more fluid situation in Eastern Europe argued for more active U.S. efforts there to counter Soviet power, even if these resulted in local violence ("it might be quite useful for the United States to have some violent outbursts in the satellite countries. Moreover, we shouldn't necessarily be appalled by the fact that if such uprising occurred a certain number of people would be killed. After all, one cannot defend or regain liberty without some inevitable loss of life") and the contrary views of National Security Advisor Dillon Anderson and special assistant to the president William Jackson. In any case, there is no evidence that this discussion changed U.S. policy. It had no evident effect on the deliberations of the interagency Special Committee on Soviet and Related Problems (as the Working Group on Stalinism had been renamed). It did not alter FEC and AMCOMLIB operations. Indeed, there is no trace of this emphasis in CIA guidance or RFE and RL policy documents in the summer and fall of 1956 quoted above. For emphasis on Dulles's views, and similar remarks of Vice President Nixon that violence in Eastern Europe might sometimes serve U.S. interests, see Békés, Byrne, and Rainer, *1956 Hungarian Revolution,* comment on document 13, 129. For an interpretation that after Stalin's death "the leaders and staff of RFE undoubtedly *listened* to all of Washington's signals but *heard* only those it wanted to hear—the calls for confrontation," see Charles Gati, *Failed Illusions: Moscow, Washington, Budapest, and the 1956 Hungarian Revolt* (Washington, D.C., and Stanford, Calif.: Woodrow Wilson Center Press and Stanford University Press, 2006), 100.

8. "Report on the Third Annual Conference on U.S. Broadcasting to the Soviet Orbit," Munich 1956, USIA Special Reports, S-31-56, as cited by Gary D. Rawnsley, *Radio Diplomacy and Propaganda: The BBC and VOA in International Politics* (New York: St. Martin's Press, 1996), 80 n. 66.

RFE and the Polish October

Józef Światło's revelation of abuses and crimes by the Polish Communist regime contributed to a limited political thaw in 1955 and early 1956. A peaceful demonstration by Poznań workers in June 1956 for better economic conditions immediately turned into political protest ("we want bread . . . we demand free elections") and escalated into anticommunist revolt. Rioters captured the party headquarters and destroyed a radio jamming station (a key instrument of Communist information control, as discussed in chapter 7). While the secret police and army quickly regained control, violent suppression of the Poznań protests only strengthened reform currents within the Polish Communist Party that had emerged as part of a "thaw" in 1955 involving eased police repression and surfacing of intellectual dissent.

It was the consensus of Washington officials, FEC and RFE managements, and the RFE Polish Service leadership that RFE broadcasts to Poland should provide comprehensive information on the protests in Poznań and related developments elsewhere in Poland, convey international reaction, but avoid programming that might contribute to increased bloodshed. In contrast to controlled domestic Polish media, the RFE Polish Service was able to obtain eyewitness accounts of the crackdown from Western visitors to the Poznań Trade Fair then under way. It provided regular international press reviews. And it went one step beyond simply avoiding inflammatory rhetoric by appealing to protesters as well as the authorities for restraint. The Polish Service director, Jan Nowak (whose views were shaped by his personal experience in the doomed 1944 Warsaw Uprising), broadcast one such appeal on June 29:

> Incidents like [the Poznań revolt] play into the hands of . . . [the] Stalinist clique, who want the return of terror and oppression. The struggle for freedom must end in victory, for no regime based on repression can last. But in that struggle prudence is necessary. And therefore in the name of the ardent desire, common to us all, for Poland's freedom, we must call on the people to preserve calm and refrain from acts of despair.[9]

In the following three months, RFE Polish broadcasts focused attention on the fate of those arrested for purportedly organizing the Poznań revolt.

9. Jan Nowak-Jeziorański, *Wojna w eterze* (Kraków: Znak, 2000), 241–42. A policy guidance at the time contained similar language; FEC memorandum to Shepardson from Egan on RFE's response to the Poznań riots, July 6, 1956.

The accused were in the end able to present a public defense, covered on RFE, and received light sentences. Broadcasts also covered conflict within the Communist Party between reformers and Stalinists, drawing on detailed reporting and private communications from Warsaw of Western journalists with good regime connections, including Sidney Gruson of the *New York Times* and Philippe Ben of *Le Monde*. In the dramatic days of mid-October, when a Soviet delegation headed by Khrushchev arrived unannounced in Warsaw on October 19 to back Polish Stalinists in their (unsuccessful) effort to prevent the return of Władysław Gomułka as party chief, RFE Polish Service commentary (like statements from Stefan Cardinal Wyszyński after his release from house imprisonment) again urged moderation. In so doing, RFE in effect supported Gomułka at that moment as the "lesser evil" to the national catastrophe of Soviet military intervention. An FEC guidance on October 20 cautioned against any broadcasts that might incite violence. RFE political adviser Griffith concluded that same day that Gomułka was consolidating his power with popular support, that only his reform Communist regime offered Poles hope of a measure of internal relaxation and independence from the USSR, but that Polish Stalinists and the Soviets might provoke violent protests as an excuse for Soviet intervention.[10] Polish Service broadcasts were guided by these assumptions. It was the approach taken by Nowak in a series of commentaries at the time:

> We have information that a group of Stalinists . . . is . . . trying to increase the boiling atmosphere, in order to justify the necessity of Soviet intervention from the outside. In this connection there arises the most important question: Will the community let itself be provoked or will it keep the necessary calm? The development in the next few days will depend first and foremost on whether the [Gomułka leadership] will be able to get the situation in hand, calm the atmosphere. (October 20)

> The Communist program will never be our Polish program. . . . [But] whoever acts to defend the independence of his country will have the support of the entire society, without regard to his political outlook or party affiliation. (October 23)

10. As cited by Robert T. Holt, *Radio Free Europe* (Minneapolis: University of Minnesota Press, 1958), 181–82. The potential for mass anti-Soviet protest is documented by Paweł Machcewicz, *Rebellious Satellite: Poland 1956* (Washington, D.C., and Stanford, Calif.: Woodrow Wilson Center Press and Stanford University Press, 2009), utilizing Polish secret police archives.

Poland remains in the Soviet embrace. . . . Russia with its enormous military might is near, and the United States is too far away to effectively protect Poland from Soviet attack. (November 9)[11]

The performance of the Polish Service during the dramatic days of October 1956 received high marks in RFE internal reviews conducted at the end of the year. The principal review concluded, after examining 200 program texts in translation and another 55 in the original: "Programs show constant evidence of skillful, imaginative, and effective policy implementation. The Voice of Free Poland responded to the crisis with discipline, reserve, and a soundly intelligent approach that reflects the highest credit on the desk as a whole."[12]

Published references to RFE in 1956 are generally limited to criticism of its Hungarian broadcasts. But RFE had five radio stations, and RFE broadcasting to Poland in October 1956 was a success story. That positive record is explained by the situation within Poland and inside RFE. In Poland, the Poznań revolt did not trigger a wave of violent protests. Power remained in the hands of the Communist Party and the government, not in the streets. Impetus for reform was concentrated within the party itself. RFE had excellent information about the situation in Poland, including details of the intraparty controversies, both from Western journalists in Warsaw that it cultivated and from its own Polish sources. It was able to influence developments within the party, for by publicizing the controversy between party reformers and Stalinists, it helped the reformers advance and promoted their cause of gradual change.[13]

Within RFE, the Polish Service was predisposed to restraint, and would have remained so even had the "Polish October" ended in violence. Seasoned veterans of the Home Army and the Warsaw Uprising, Nowak and his team

---

11. Nowak-Jeziorański, *Wojna w eterze,* 264, 290; Puddington, *Broadcasting Freedom,* 93; Holt, *Radio Free Europe,* 185. Transmitter recordings of these programs as broadcast reviewed by the author confirm the authenticity of the cited texts.

12. RFE memorandum to Richard Condon from William E. Griffith, "Policy Review of Voice of Free Poland Programming–1 October–30 November 1956," December 8, 1956.

13. Polish party officials then and later acknowledged RFE's positive role in Poland in the fall of 1956. As one said at the time, "Had RFE not told our people to be calm, I am not sure whether we alone would have managed to cope with the situation." As quoted by Allan A. Michie, *Voices through the Iron Curtain: The Radio Free Europe Story* (New York, Dodd, Mead, 1963), 191.

sought above all else to avoid another catastrophic foreign military suppression of Poland. Nowak later wrote:

> My own very painful war experience taught me the fine distinction between hope which sustains more and hope which thrusts people into action. I saw with my own eyes how the inflated, completely unsubstantiated hope in the Allies pushed Poles into the Warsaw Uprising. I had fresh memories of the devastation of Poland's capital and the death of over 200,000 of its inhabitants. I saw how easily false hopes changed into self-igniting explosives. We winced at the very thought that a similar misfortune might occur in our lifetimes.[14]

Many Polish broadcasters were also veteran prewar or wartime journalists and thus capable professional communicators. On both scores, they were a disciplined team, able to remain calm in a crisis and provide informed reporting on the dramatic developments in Poland while avoiding inflammatory tone or content.[15]

The performance of the Polish Service in October 1956 demonstrated that the RFE management principle of American-exile "partnership" that devolved most editorial decisions to émigré broadcasters on the assumption (in Griffith's words) that they "know more about how to talk to their own people than do the Americans themselves" could produce effective and responsible surrogate broadcasting. RFE broadcasting to Hungary in 1956 was quite a different story.

The Hungarian Revolution

On the eve of the Hungarian Revolution, RFE broadcasting to Hungary followed the same approach as RFE broadcasting to Poland, emphasizing the evolution of the Communist system. Examples of such broadcasts in the months before the Revolution (all objective and dispassionate by any standard) are a July 3 program directed to Hungarian Communists on anti-Stalin

---

14. Jan Nowak, "War on the Airwaves: A Frontline Report," unpublished manuscript, 170–71.

15. Of the forty-five Polish Service broadcasters in 1956, more than half had served in the Home Army or Polish Forces in the West and more than a third had been prewar journalists. Personal communication in 2009 from Lechosław Gawlikowski, who is completing a study of RFE Polish broadcasters.

ferment in the CPSU;[16] an August 10 program suggesting that the Hungarian Communist leadership study lessons drawn by the Polish Communists after the Poznań uprising about the need for reform;[17] an October 6 program stressing the need for an independent judiciary;[18] and an October 11 program devoted to the initial purges in the secret police.[19] Contrary to accusations leveled against RFE that it had somehow incited the Revolution,[20] a review of Hungarian broadcast scripts through October 22, 1956, indicates that no RFE broadcast before the outbreak of the Revolution called for insurrection, urged violent confrontation of the Communist authorities, or advocated a maximalist anticommunist platform. On the contrary, RFE Hungarian broadcasts in the months leading up to mid-October 1956 were generally dispassionate and espoused gradual reform. They promoted not "liberation" but "liberalization."

The U.S. Government and RFE Broadcast Policy

Encouraged by ferment in Poland that was reported selectively in controlled domestic Hungarian media and fully in Western broadcasts by RFE, VOA, and the BBC, Budapest students demonstrated peacefully on October 23. The regime response was a bitter denunciation by Communist Party leader Erno Gerő, use of live ammunition by the AVO (the internal security force), and then, as violence spread, employment of the Soviet army—which only escalated the violence.

The U.S. government believed that RFE, along with VOA, was one of the few instruments available to try to influence this course of events. The

16. Calling Communists No. C-291, "About the Consequences of the Personality Cult," by Sándor Korosi-Krizsán, July 3, 1956, original and translation on microfilm reel 147. All program texts (scripts) so cited are located in the RFE/RL Collection, Hoover Archives. Copies are also available at the National Széchényi Library in Budapest.

17. Reflector No. C-381, "Ochab, Gerő, and the Poznań Events," by Andrew Kazinczy, August 10, 1956, original and translation on microfilm reel 180. This program is labeled "Reflector No. C-381; either the label is wrong or Imre Mikes was the real author. I am indebted to Gábor Hanák of the National Széchényi Library for this correction and for general advice on the programs.

18. Reflector C-430, "On the Independence of Judges," by Imre Mikes, October 6, 1956, original and translation on microfilm reel 180.

19. Reflector No. C-434, "The State Security Department in its Own Shackles," by Imre Mikes, October 11, 1956, original and translation on microfilm reel 180.

20. E.g., "We are convinced that . . . RFE's aggressive propaganda is responsible to a large extent for the blood-bath which has occurred in Hungary." *Freies Wort* (organ of the West German Free Democratic Party), November 9, 1956.

CIA/IOD counseled restraint in a policy guidance for RFE New York on October 24. That guidance suggested that RFE quote extensively from President Eisenhower's speech of October 23 (which had been devoted primarily to Poland), especially his words that "a people which has once known freedom cannot be deprived for always of its national independence and its personal liberty." The CIA/IOD cautioned: "Do not prejudge the action of Nagy and Gomułka. We must know more about their actual policies," while noting that the Imre Nagy government would have to live down calling in Soviet troops to restore order, which it could only do by "establishing a climate of real freedom and material satisfaction."[21]

These points were expanded in an internal CIA/IOD memorandum of October 25, which noted the dilemma faced by RFE in supporting the revolutionaries without providing the Soviets with an excuse to stamp out the rebellion. The memorandum recommended several themes for RFE Hungarian broadcasts: support for Hungarian demands for withdrawal of the Soviet army, including coverage of President Eisenhower's remarks on the subject that day; sympathy and admiration for the courage and spirit of the embattled rebels; support for the rebels' demands for freedom; and coverage of Secretary of State Dulles' remarks on the anniversary of Austria's regaining its independence and ending foreign military occupation as an implicit example for Hungary to follow. The memorandum posed without answering the question as to whether RFE should provide direct suggestions to the Hungarian people, such as calls to cut off food and supplies to the Soviet army. It noted new information attributed to RFE Munich that Gerő and not Nagy had originally requested Soviet intervention. Even though Nagy had not asked the Soviet army to cease and desist, "it would seem appropriate for RFE to be very cautious about launching any major attacks against Imre Nagy until we have more facts."[22] This CIA guidance for RFE conformed to the State Department policy of not taking a position on Nagy one way or another in what was seen as an unclear and ambiguous situation.[23]

21. CIA/IOD memorandum for the record, "RFE Guidance, October 24, 1956, for Hungarian Developments," October 25, 1956, released to the author in March 2007. The U.S. Legation in Budapest similarly urged VOA and RFE "to avoid taking any kind of stand on Imre Nagy for time being"; see "Telegram from the Legation in Hungary to the Department of State, October 23, 1956–midnight," document 98, in *FRUS, 1955–57*, XXV.

22. CIA/IOD memorandum for the record, "Hungarian Conflict and FEC Action," October 25, 1956, released to the author in November 2006.

23. "Circular Telegram from the State Department to All Diplomatic Missions, October 30, 1956," document 143, in *FRUS, 1955–57*, XXV.

Viewing the insurgents as authentic representatives of the Hungarian people, the U.S. government specifically authorized RFE to serve as a "communications center" for the emerging independent media in Hungary and to rebroadcast reports aired by the "Freedom Radios" (local regime radio stations taken over by the insurgents) around Hungary. This was one policy issue discussed on October 26 at the interagency Special Committee chaired by Jacob Beam of the State Department.[24] Three days later, the Special Committee, addressing an issue raised in the October 25 IOD memorandum, cautioned against any tactical advice in RFE Hungarian broadcasts.[25]

All FEC and RFE guidances from New York conformed to this U.S. government policy. The Daily Guidance of October 23 drew parallels between Nagy and Gomułka. The Daily Guidance of October 24 said "the fact that Nagy called upon foreign troops to restore 'order' [which was not the case, but was believed by all observers at the time][26] is a fact he will have to live down. He will live it down by keeping his promises [for reform]." A New York guidance of October 28 stated that it was up to Hungarian revolutionary groups to decide on their leaders: "Radio Free Europe will avoid to the utmost extent any explicit or implicit support of individual personalities in a temporary government—especially of communist personalities such as Imre Nagy or [János] Kádár. . . . It will be for the patriot groups (many of whom seem to believe that Imre Nagy can and will further their wishes) to decide whether any individual should stay or go, under developing conditions."[27] RFE Munich agreed in a teletype response: "Concur entirely RFE avoiding support individual personalities."[28]

24. "Notes on the 39th meeting of the Special Committee on Soviet and Related Problems, October 26, 1956," document 117, in *FRUS, 1955–57*, XXV. A subsequent CIA document stated that RFE had been specifically authorized on October 25 to cover the Freedom Radios and also to broadcast in Russian to Soviet troops; CIA/IOD, memorandum for the record, "Radio Free Europe," November 19, 1956, released to the author in November 2006.

25. "Notes on the 40th Meeting of the Special Committee on Soviet and Related Problems, Washington, October 29, 1956," document 132, in *FRUS, 1955–57*, XXV. The meeting summary includes this dialogue: Cox (CIA): "Should we tell the rebels not to demobilize?" McKisson (State): "We should report that there is no evidence that the Soviets are moving out, but we should not be in the position of telling the insurgents what to do." Ernst (DOD): "What do we say to the insurgents?" Beam (State): "We keep them informed. That is about as far as you can go."

26. John Matthews, then a junior official in Munich, recalled questioning the assumption. John P. C. Matthews, *Explosion: The Hungarian Revolution of 1956* (New York: Hippocrene Books, 2007), 150.

27. FEC New York telex PREB 15, October 28, 1956.

28. FEC Munich telex MUN 292, October 29, 1956. Then, as later, some U.S. gov-

With the Revolution under way, RFE policy officials, like leading Hungarian insurgents, envisaged the consolidation of a postcommunist system tolerated by the Soviet Union. The RFE New York guidance of October 28 defined RFE's task as associating itself with the far-reaching demands of "patriot groups" in order to promote democratic freedoms and help avert Communist counterrevolution. By October 31, policy adviser Griffith saw as likely (albeit not inevitable) continued withdrawal of Soviet forces and the "establishment [of a] Western-type democracy, with Hungary either neutral like Austria (or at worst, from our viewpoint) a Finnish-type solution. . . . [The] Nagy 'government' [is] surely more and more in [the] hands of [the] Revolutionary Council, which must have the real power in its hands by now."[29] Reflecting this optimism, by that early date RFE Munich management raised the possibility that, once free elections were held and a free government established, the "essential mission of RFE in respect to Hungary will be completed."[30]

By November 3, with new reports of Soviet troops advancing on Budapest, this heady optimism seemed misplaced. Occasioned in part by concerns about negative treatment of Nagy in RFE Hungarian broadcasts that violated policy, an authoritative CIA–State Department guidance directed that RFE broadcasts "should say *nothing* which would provide an excuse for Soviet military repression and a resulting bloodbath or provide a pretext for a Soviet charge of U.S. intervention." RFE was enjoined against offering tactical advice and against taking a position for or against the government or the various patriot groups. Rather, it was told to "emphasize the need for the preservation of order and the need for unity among the Patriots in working in support of an interim caretaker government until genuinely free elections can be held." It was nonetheless RFE's role "to support the major objectives being proclaimed by the present Hungarian Government: the withdrawal of Soviet troops and UN action against the maintenance of Soviet troops in Hungary; free elections participated in by all political parties; the freedom of the press; dissolution of the AVH [the

---

ernment and RFE officials evidently had a lower opinion of Nagy than Gomułka. "Gomułka was a skilled, ruthless apparatchik, while Nagy was a naïve populist utopian, even worse at realpolitik than Dubček in 1968." William E. Griffith, "Interview with László Ribansky of RFE/RL, Bonn, May 13, 1986," RFE/RL Collection.

29. FEC memorandum, RFE Munich Office of the Political Advisor, Daily Analyses of Developments in Hungary, October 31, Part I; FEC memorandum by Griffith, "Analysis of Satellite Developments (Hungary) as of 1300 Hours, October 31, 1956."

30. FEC Munich telex MUN 330, October 31, 1956.

secret police]; the withdrawal of Hungary from the Warsaw Pact." RFE was told to "fully report the support of the free world for the Hungarian people's fight for freedom," including the statements of Eisenhower and Dulles, the offer of food and economic assistance, action in the UN, "guarantee of Hungary's neutrality," and the solidarity of groups around the world with their Hungarian counterparts.[31]

RFE Hungarian Broadcasts

It is difficult to fault these policy directives as either irresponsible or out of touch with rapidly unfolding developments in Hungary, which by then had far exceeded those in Poland.[32] But what did RFE actually broadcast to Hungary during these dramatic days?

The vast literature on RFE's Hungarian-language broadcasts after the outbreak of the Revolution on October 23 is, almost without exception, highly critical.[33] Principal charges are that RFE urged Hungarians to fight the Soviet army and promised the insurgents Western assistance that was never in prospect,[34] that RFE broadcasts hastened a Soviet decision to crush the Revolution,[35] that RFE undermined the position of Nagy, a Communist

31. CIA/IOD, "Suggested Guidance," November 3, 1956, retyped November 13, 1956; emphasis in the original. Released to the author in March 2007. A handwritten annotation indicates that the guidance was approved by Allen Dulles and Robert Murphy and phoned to RFE New York at 3:15 p.m. on November 3. Updated versions were then sent to the FEC on November 16 as "Proposed Interim Guidance for FEC" (CIA document released to the author in August 2007) and "Interim Guidance, November 20, 1956, RFE/RL Collection.

32. Only decades later did the opening of the Soviet archives document Khrushchev's decision on October 31 to reverse course and resolve to crush the Revolution. See Mark Kramer, "New Evidence on Soviet Decision-Making and the 1956 Polish and Hungarian Crises," *Bulletin of the Cold War International History Project,* issues 8–9 (Winter 1996–97): 358–84.

33. See Gati, *Failed Illusions.*

34. "A review of American-sponsored Radio Free Europe's broadcasts shows that the station cavalierly suggested that Western military assistance might be forthcoming if the rebels held out." *New York Times,* editorial, November 3, 1996. "[RFE] encouraged [the Hungarians] with promises that the U.S. military would rush to their aid." *Süddeutsche Zeitung,* Munich, June 23, 2006. "[After the Poznań riots] CIA could do nothing but feed [Eastern Europeans'] rage." Tim Weiner, *Legacy of Ashes: The History of the CIA* (New York: Random House, 2007), 125ff.

35. "[RFE's] 'informational activities' and broadcasts in the 1950s probably precipitated . . . the Soviet crackdown on Hungary on November 3–4, as well as increased the number of casualties." Johanna Granville, "'Caught with Jam on Our Fingers':

reformer who might have played the positive role in Hungary that Gomułka played in Poland,[36] and that RFE broadcasts were highly emotional, included tactical advice, and otherwise fell far short of normal standards of journalism.[37] Praise for any part of the RFE Hungarian broadcasts during this period is almost totally absent.[38]

Did RFE Hungarian broadcasts urge Hungarians to fight the Soviet Army? The thrust of all commentary was solidarity with the Revolution. On October 24, the Hungarian Service appealed repeatedly to the Hungarian army and police not to " fire on those who fight for freedom" and to regime judges not to impose summary death sentences ("the death penalty is unjust and illegitimate").[39] Many programs relayed with approval domestic Hungarian voices calling for continuing the Revolution and resisting efforts to suppress it—for example, a report on "the unanimous, brave, and heroic strike of the workers."[40] A program on October 28 said that the Nagy government's appeal for a cease-fire had to be respected by the Soviet Army to have any meaning.[41] Three programs aired on October 28–30 (after most

---

Radio Free Europe and the Hungarian Revolution of 1956," *Diplomatic History* 29, no. 5 (November 2005): 811–39; the quotation here is on 811. In fact, RFE figures marginally, if at all, in the ample archival documentation on Soviet decisionmaking in 1956, as surveyed by Kramer, "New Evidence on Soviet Decision-Making."

36. "[RFE broadcast] a massive hate campaign (*Hetze*) against Prime Minister Imre Nagy, the one individual for whom unconditional support in those days might have meant success for the Hungarian struggle for freedom." *SPD-Pressedienst,* organ of the West German Social Democratic Party, May 29, 1957. "[RFE] egged on the most radical insurgent groups to fight on until all of their demands were met." Gati, *Failed Illusions,* 6.

37. "What was absent was an understanding [of the situation in Hungary] . . . and professionalism in daily work." Paul Lendvai, "Die ungarische Revolution 1956: Eine Einleitung," in *Die Ungarnkrise 1956 und Österreich,* ed. Erwin A. Schmidl (Vienna: Boehlau, 2003), 13.

38. Most of this critical literature is uninformed by comprehensive review of the broadcast record. Early negative evaluations were based on personal impressions, secondhand reports, and scattered translated RFE programs and other documents available in U.S. archives. Their validity could have been assessed in part as early as the 1960s by reviewing the program scripts, many with English translations, preserved on microfilm at RFE in Munich. They could be assessed fully only in the last decade, when log tapes (recording transmitter output) of every RFE transmission during the Hungarian Revolution were recovered from the Federal German Archives. Also see the appendix to this chapter, a note on the history of the 1956 RFE Hungarian broadcast archives.

39. Appeals broadcast between commentaries on October 24, NSL transcription; George R. Urban, *Radio Free Europe and the Pursuit of Democracy: My War within the Cold War* (New Haven, Conn.: Yale University Press, 1997), 215–16.

40. Special Workers Commentary, by József Molnar, October 30, 1956.

41. Short Commentary, by Imre Vámos, October 28, 1956.

fighting had temporarily stopped) offered tactical military advice and claimed that the Hungarian fighters were stronger than the Soviet army.[42] A November 1 commentary called on Hungarians to keep their weapons as a guarantee of the freedoms and independence that had been won. "To be clear, we only said . . . do not give up your weapons. We did not say use them when there is no purpose and no sense in it."[43] When the second Soviet intervention began on November 4, RFE Hungarian newscasts repeatedly carried Nagy's words (first broadcast at dawn by Radio Free Kossuth) that "our troops are engaged in a battle" and Hungarian News Agency (MTI) reports that "Soviet troops are waging a general attack against the Hungarian capital."[44] A commentary declared that Hungary was at war.[45] A second emotional commentary that day said that "we, a small people in numbers but a great nation, are fighting against the despotism of the Muscovites. . . . The barricades on which we are shedding our blood will be remembered for centuries to come."[46] A commentary on November 6 said, "the fight of the Hungarian people has not yet ended."[47] A second commentary on that date said that "the fight continues. . . . [It is the workers who] are fighting the terrible, overwhelming Soviet forces the longest, most desperately and unmindful of the lives sacrificed."[48] These programs and others indicated admiration for the insurgents and solidarity with resistance to the Soviet Army. As such they could easily have been interpreted by listeners as encouraging resistance. But no RFE Hungarian broadcast appealed to the Hungarian people to continue armed struggle against the Soviet Army.

Did RFE Hungarian broadcasts promise military assistance from the West? Newscasts had reported accurately John Foster Dulles' speech of October 21 that the United States supported gradual liberalization in Poland.[49]

---

42. "Armed Forces Special" programs by Julian Borsányi and Gyula Litterati-Lootz. It was the latter, a freelance contributor, and not Borsányi (pseudonym Colonel Bell) who, on October 28 at 20:30, famously interviewed former anti-tank artillery officer Gyula Patko on how a "Molotov cocktail" is made (a translation is given by Békés, Byrne, and Rainer, *1956 Hungarian Revolution,* as document 45, 288–89) and interviewed him again on October 30 at 14:51 on the conduct of partisan warfare. I am indebted to Gábor Hanák for clarifying the dates of these broadcasts from NSL transcriptions. The "Colonel Bell" program series began in 1950 and regularly discussed East-West military issues.

43. Special Reflector F-1, by Imre Mikes, November 1, 1956.

44. NSL transcriptions.

45. Special Short Commentary, by László Béry, November 4, 1956.

46. Special Short Reflector I-1, by Imre Mikes, November 4, 1956.

47. Special Short Commentary K-1, by László Béry, November 6, 1956.

48. Special Short Commentary K-2, by Imre Mikes, November 6, 1956

49. "The United States sympathetically observes what is happening in Poland. The United States would welcome the victory of real democracy in Poland and other coun-

Newscasts on October 28 repeatedly carried his remarks in Dallas on October 27 that the United States supported the cause of Hungarian freedom and would assist more independent Eastern European countries economically. "Dulles emphasized the fact that the support of the US is not subject to political conditions. It is not seeking military allies. America's only objective is to see Hungarian and other Eastern European nations once again part of a new, blessed, Europe without partitions."[50] Newscasts reported accurately President Eisenhower's television address on October 31, in which he expressed the hope that Hungary would become a free nation, promised economic assistance to "the new and independent governments" without making it conditional on "adopting of any particular form of society," and repeated that the United States did not seek "potential military allies" in Eastern Europe."[51]

Cold War histories often cite the single case of an RFE broadcast implying that Western military assistance would be forthcoming if the Hungarian revolutionaries held out once the Soviet attacks resumed on November 4.[52] That program was a review of the Italian press and an article in the London *Observer* written before November 4 that anticipated the Soviet intervention and predicted that "if Hungarians can hold out for three or four days [then] pressure on the government of the United States to send military help to the Freedom Fighters will become inevitable. This is what the *Observer* writes today." Hungarian Service editor Zoltán Thury concluded: "The re-

---

tries. But we must not forget that democracy as a form of government can only prevail gradually throughout the world. The American government is making efforts to keep the idea of freedom alive in Eastern-European countries through institutions such as the Voice of America." RFE Hungarian newscast, October 22, 1956, 07:00 hours, repeated throughout the day (NSL transcription); *New York Times,* October 22, 1956. A newscast at 23:00 hours reported: "In Washington, Paris and London the latest Polish events are evaluated with great prudence. In these Western capitals no one wants to encourage developments that might lead to a clash of arms." (NSL transcription).

50. RFE Hungarian newscast, October 28, 1956, 01:00 hours, repeated throughout the day (NSL transcription).

51. RFE Hungarian newscast, November 1, 1956, 06:00 hours, repeated throughout the day (NSL transcription); text in *Department of State Bulletin,* November 12, 1956, 743–45. The "Colonel Bell" program had argued on October 27 the importance of a central insurgent military command for international economic and political—not military—assistance. Julian Borsányi commentary, October 27, 1956, 13:50 hours, NSL transcription.

52. Including the Discovery Channel documentary on the Hungarian Revolution, *Betrayal at Budapest,* which ends with an account of the broadcast of the November 4 *Observer* press item against the visual backdrop of RFE studios.

ports from London, Paris, the U.S. and other Western reports show that the world's reaction to Hungarian events surpasses every imagination. In the Western capitals, a practical manifestation of Western sympathy is expected at any hour."[53] This was the only such program identified in the many internal and external reviews of RFE programming.

The origins of the enduring myth that RFE promised Western military assistance to Hungary may be traceable in part to the broadcasts of other stations. RFE, VOA, and BBC were the dominant Western Hungarian-language broadcasters during this period, but many other foreign radio stations continued or initiated broadcasts to Hungary in Hungarian during the Revolution. Two of these stations explicitly mentioned military assistance from the West. Radio Madrid, staffed by right-wing exiles in the Franco era, quite irresponsibly urged Hungarians to keep fighting because Western volunteers were massing on the Hungarian border (of course they were not). Similarly, the Russian-émigré NTS Radio operating out of Germany claimed that the "Association of Former Hungarian Servicemen" in the West was preparing to aid the insurgent forces.[54] Given the babble of tens of foreign and domestic Hungarian-language broadcasters during this period and the difficulty of reception through jamming for part of the time, listeners could easily but incorrectly have attributed such broadcasts to RFE and assumed that it was RFE that was urging Hungarians to hold out until Western military assistance arrived.[55]

---

53. Special Short World Press 1-2, November 4, 1956, by Zoltán Thury, translation on microfilm reel 189, first broadcast at 18:04. The original Hungarian text was not preserved, but the translation was checked against the original broadcast audio in 1956 and later transcribed by NSL and found to be accurate. Thury's report on international reactions broadcast first at 14:03 on November 4 included a slightly softer conclusion: "It will come to declarations of sympathy and to manifestation of Western public feelings within a very short time." Special Short World Press I-1, November 4, 1956, by Zoltán Thury, original and translation on microfilm reel 189.

54. NTS-sponsored Radio Free Russia in Hungarian at 1005 GMT, October 30, 1956, as monitored by FBIS; Kagan dispatch, *New York Post,* November 26, 1956; RFE New York telex NYC 223, November 26, 1956; Michie, *Voices through the Iron Curtain,* 281; Adolf A. Berle diary entry, December 5, 1956, given by Beatrice Bishop Berle and Travis Beal Jacobs, eds., *Navigating the Rapids 1918–1971: From the Papers of Adolf A. Berle* (New York: Harcourt Brace Jovanovich, 1973), 676. The German government press office notified the Foreign Office on December 12, 1956, that broadcasts to Hungary from a mobile NTS transmitter were being mistaken for RFE broadcasts; FOPA, B 40 Band 112, Fische B 112-3. CIA/IOD attempted, evidently without success, to get Radio Free Russia to admit its responsibility for this broadcast.

55. An example is the recollection of Zoltán Benkő, in *Valóság,* no. 5 (1993): 83,

The November 4 *Observer* item was one program in a critical month of
nearly round-the-clock RFE Hungarian broadcasting of more than 500 programs and was not a significant programming theme. To be sure, many or
even most Hungarians caught up in the Revolution did come to believe that
the West would support them, one way or another, and as discussed below,
Western radio broadcasts evidently encouraged them in that belief. But that
was not because of the content of one RFE program, which arguably had
little if any impact. It was not mentioned by any interviewee in several surveys of Hungarian refugees in late 1956. No program, as noted, advocated
continued military resistance. Hungarian listeners may have drawn encouragement from RFE broadcasts both to keep fighting and to expect Western
aid—but these were actions the programs themselves neither advocated nor
promised.

Did RFE broadcasts undermine Nagy? As outlined above, RFE policy
guidelines for the treatment of Nagy written in New York and Munich em-
bodied skepticism about and generally directed a "wait and see" attitude toward him. RFE Hungarian commentaries, by and large, did not observe these
guidelines (which implied but could have more explicitly cautioned against
undue criticism as well as support of individual Hungarian leaders). There
was a role for sober critical analysis of Nagy's past record, sources of current support, and choices ahead. Instead, many RFE Hungarian commentaries broadcast between October 25 and October 30 were blanket condemnations of Nagy—sometimes in personal, emotional, vituperative tones:

> At the beginning of this tragic week when millions assembled, Imre
> Nagy must have known that they supported him. He should have acted
> the way Gomułka did in Warsaw, banging his fist only once at Party
> headquarters, and [his] criminal past would have been forgotten. . . . But
> Imre Nagy did not bang his fist on the table, he hit the people instead . . .
> [now] an oppressed nation perishes on the barricades facing Imre Nagy's
> Soviet troops and threatened by his order for martial law. . . . [Nagy]
> shouldn't be promising anything, the people have no need for his pro-
> gram, no need for his deceitful popular-front government, no need for
> his rhetoric. They need only his signature . . . to recall the Soviet divi-
> sions . . . this will decide if . . . if he has a drop of loyalty to the nation

cited by Urban, *Radio Free Europe and the Pursuit of Democracy,* 238. A former political prisoner, Benkő escaped from Hungary after the Revolution, worked for RFE as a
freelancer in 1957, and remained highly critical of the 1956 broadcasts.

bleeding from a thousand wounds. . . . He still has a last opportunity to follow the will of the nation. Away with the Soviets! And if not, away with him forever.[56]

Soviet tanks arrive at the behest of Imre Nagy whose hands are steeped in Hungarian blood. . . . Shout "stop!" to the Soviet mercenaries whom you have hideously let loose on the nation! After that "hands up."[57]

The murderer of the people, Imre Nagy and his party leadership with blood on their hands, do not possess the humanity and Hungarian national feeling to resign or to give a documented statement that this killing was not ordered by them.[58]

RFE's New York headquarters first registered concern about the anti-Nagy commentaries and communicated this concern to Munich on November 2, directing that broadcasts "must not at any time—directly or indirectly—take RFE positions for or against individual personalities in the temporary government."[59]

56. Special Reflector IV, by Imre Mikes, October 26, 1956; Gati, *Failed Illusions,* 170.

57. Special Short Commentary, by Miklós Ajtay, October 26, 1956; Gati, *Failed Illusions,* 170.

58. "Agrarius" (Zoltán Nemet) program for farmers, October 30, 11:20 hours, NSL transcription. This was the last such depiction of Nagy; while some commentaries remained critical, by October 29 the emotional condemnations had ceased and criticism was focused on Communists in the Nagy government. Zoltán Károly commentary, November 1, 1956, 11:55 hours; László Béry commentary, November 3, 13:10 hours, NSL transcriptions. Many of the anti-Nagy broadcasts are reprinted by Judit Katona and György Vámos, "Nagy Imre és a Szabad Európa Rádió 1956-ban" [Imre Nagy and Radio Free Europe in 1956], in *Nagy Imre és kora: Tanulmányok és források I* [Imre Nagy and his era: Studies and sources] (Budapest, Imre Nagy Foundation, 2002); and a few are quoted by Urban, *Radio Free Europe and the Pursuit of Democracy,* 221–22; and Paul Lendvai, *1956. One Day That Shook the Communist World: The 1956 Hungarian Uprising and Its Legacy* (Princeton, N.J.: Princeton University Press, 2008), 187–88, drawing on a selection by Benkő; and by Gati, *Failed Illusions,* 170.

59. FEC telex NYC 28, November 2, 1956; FEC memorandum of November 2 telephone call between RFE director Egan (in New York) and RFE European director Condon (in Munich). RFE's New York headquarters evidently focused on the derogatory commentaries only after U.S. government involvement ("Yugoslav intervention vis-à-vis the State Department," RFE letter from Condon to Egan, November 3, 1956) and after review on November 1 of the New York–based Broadcast Review Staff's content report dated October 29, 1956, which summarized some of the anti-Nagy commentaries. A Yugoslav Foreign Ministry official complained to a U.S. Embassy officer on October 31 about RFE broadcasts (admitting he had not listened since October 29) as an "in-

While RFE Hungarian broadcasts are thus properly faulted for emotional derogatory treatment of Nagy, they cannot be faulted for promoting József Cardinal Mindszenty as an alternative political leader,[60] because they did not. Several programs written and aired by the Hungarian Service staff priest called for Cardinal Mindszenty's release from prison "to be permitted to re-turn to Esztergom in order to take over there the governance of the Hungar-ian Catholic Church."[61] Another commentary welcomed emotionally his re-lease from prison on October 31: "Hungary . . . expressed the demand, 'Free Mindszenty and put him back in his lawful position as Primate.' "[62] While RFE commentaries urged and then welcomed Mindszenty's release from prison, advocated his return to clerical authority, and celebrated his moral stature (as did RFE Polish broadcasts with regard to Cardinal Wyszyński), no RFE broadcast treated Mindszenty as a political alternative to Nagy. RFE newscasts on November 2 carried Mindszenty's own emphatic disavowal of that possibility.[63]

---

citement" to "wipe out completely all communism, not even recognize Nagy"; Depart-ment of State telegram, Belgrade no. 584, October 31, 1956, declassified September 12, 1996, NARA 764.00/10-3166. The Yugoslav Foreign Ministry also made a démarche to Deputy Undersecretary of State Robert Murphy in Washington on October 31. Yet a day earlier, another Yugoslav official had criticized Nagy for failing to make a clean break with the Hungarian Stalinists; Department of State telegram, Belgrade no. 570, October 30, 1956, declassified September 12, 1996, NARA 764.00/10-3056. Murphy expressed his concerns to Allen Dulles, and IOD conveyed them to RFE New York (memorandum to the Secretary of State from L. Randolph Higgs, with concurrence of Cord Meyer, No-vember 13, 1956, released to the author in November 2006; memorandum to the DCI from Cord Meyer, November 14, 1956, released to the author in November 2006).

60. See Békés, Byrne, and Rainer, *1956 Hungarian Revolution,* xvi, 245; James Mc-Cargar, "Policy and Personalities," paper presented at conference on "Hungary and the World, 1956: The New Archival Evidence," Budapest, September 26–29, 1996; Urban, *Ra-dio Free Europe and the Pursuit of Democracy,* 308 n. 11, a mischaracterization of Grif-fith's October 31 Daily Analysis cited above, which neither warned against a "Finnish-type solution" nor (while acknowledging Mindszenty's "prestige") advocated promoting him as an alternative to Nagy. Puddington, *Broadcasting Freedom,* 108, quotes Borbándi as telling him a Munich guidance urged favorable coverage of Cardinal Mindszenty as a fu-ture replacement for Nagy. The available record of guidances contains no such instruction.

61. E.g., Special Mindszenty Program, by Károly Fábián, October 26, 1956. This was one of a series of such programs by Father Fábián.

62. Special Commentary, by László Béry, October 31, 1956, 8:14 hours, NSL tran-scription.. For interpretations of this emotional commentary as promoting Mindszenty as an alternative to Nagy, see Granville, " 'Caught with Jam on Our Fingers,' " 832; Lend-vai, *1956,* 187–88.

63. "A [Budapest] reporter asked Mindszenty [at a press conference at his residence]

RFE Hungarian broadcasts also included characterizations of Nagy in unedited rebroadcast of reports and commentaries of the "Freedom Radios" around Hungary. Some of these local radio stations also carried reviews of the many newly established independent newspapers around the country. These independent radio and newspaper accounts included a variety of views on Nagy, both supportive and critical. They generally became more critical of Nagy's leadership in late October (before he clearly distanced himself from the October 24 crackdown on October 28 and included non-communists in his government), shifting to full support for him on November 1 when he promised a return to a multiparty system and international neutrality.[64]

RFE's treatment of Nagy in its Hungarian broadcasts can be explained in part by the fact that (in contrast to the situation in Poland) there was almost no independent information from Hungary during the first days of the Revolution, when international communications were blocked. RFE (as others in the West) labored under the misconception spread by Communist Party chief Gerő that Nagy shared responsibility for the initial decision to "request" Soviet military assistance against the rebels and impose martial law. It was only on October 28 that Nagy acknowledged that the uprising was "a broad democratic mass movement" and not a "counterrevolution." It was only on October 30 that he endorsed a return to a multiparty political system and made clear that the imposition of martial law and initial call for Soviet troops had been taken without his knowledge. These circumstances notwithstanding, the many emotional and negative RFE Hungarian broadcasts about Nagy deviated from U.S. government and RFE policy guidelines. That said, even if Western broadcasts had contributed to more popular support sooner for Nagy, it would arguably have made little or no difference in the outcome of the conflict.

It is in any case difficult to imagine how RFE could or should have taken the same approach to Nagy as it did to Gomułka in Poland or, even more

---

to comment on the reports that say that certain political groups would welcome him as prime minister. Mindszenty's answer was very emphatic, firmly rejecting the proposition, saying, "I am the Primate." And then ending the press conference as he left the room." Newscasts of November 2, 1956, 16:00, 17:00, 18:00 hours, NSL transcription.

64. Excerpts are given in *The Revolt in Hungary: A Documentary Chronology of Events Based Exclusively on Internal Broadcasts by Central and Provincial Radios, October 23, 1956–November 4, 1956,* by Free Europe Committee (New York: Free Europe Committee, 1957). The Communist leaders Losonczy and Donath accepted Nagy's leadership only on October 28–29, but Vasarhelyi only on October 30.

ambitiously, promoted a national reform Communist "Nagyism."[65] Simply
stated, Hungary was not Poland, and Nagy was not Gomułka. In Poland in
October 1956, as discussed above, power resided in Communist Party and
government offices, with the levers of Communist control intact. The danger of future mass protests and armed conflict between Soviet and Polish
military units was the backdrop for the confrontation between the Soviet
and Polish party leaderships that led to Soviet acceptance of Gomułka. In
Hungary, in contrast, an insurgency had begun, the Soviet army and Hungarian Communist forces had already killed hundreds, the institutions of repression and control were crumbling, and power was shifting to the streets.
A national anticommunist and anti-Soviet revolution was under way that no
Hungarian Communist leader could have reversed and that Moscow, after
initial hesitation, was determined to crush.

And Nagy was not Gomułka. Nagy was often indecisive. He issued contradictory statements, initially condemning insurgents and justifying the
Soviet intervention, and then saying the opposite.[66] He was not the Communist Party chief but a prime minister with uncertain powers. He could
not oppose Soviet intervention; it had already occurred. He could not avert
violence; it was increasing daily. He could not win support by endorsing
limited in-system reform; popular demands for decollectivization of agri-
culture, reestablishment of noncommunist parties, free elections, and withdrawal from the Warsaw Pact predated his reemergence on the political

65. See Jan Nowak, "Poles and Hungarians in 1956," paper presented at conference
on "Hungary and the World, 1956: The New Archival Evidence," Budapest, September
26–29, 1996; Nowak-Jeziorański, *Wojna w eterze.* Gati, *Failed Illusions,* contends that
"[RFE] should have enthusiastically, and with great effect, supported Nagy during the
second week of the revolt, but it did not" (p. 6). Let us imagine a counterfactual Hungarian scenario: A peaceful student protest in Miskolc is broken up by the AVH (internal security forces) and tens of students are killed. Responding to ferment outside and
within the party, Nagy replaces Gerő as Communist Party chief and purges the leadership of the worst Stalinists. He gains control of the internal security apparatus while acknowledging legitimate reform demands of students and others, so long as Communist
Party rule is not threatened. He quickly releases Cardinal Mindszenty from prison. He
vows to defend Hungarian national interests, while urging all Hungarians to acknowledge the geopolitical reality of Soviet influence, including continued membership in the
Warsaw Pact. In such a scenario, RFE's Hungarian Service would have done well to
have conditionally supported Nagy in the same way that the Polish Services supported
Gomułka. But that scenario in no way describes Hungarian reality in October and November 1956.

66. Gati, *Failed Illusions,* chap. 5, provides a masterful reconstruction and interpretation of Nagy's political life.

scene and were escalating. Under these circumstances, RFE's proper role was not to condemn or endorse Nagy (or Nagyism), but rather to report the range of domestic and international opinion about him and explain his circumstances, yet refrain from original judgmental commentary.

If RFE broadcasts could not reasonably treat Nagy as a Gomułka, did they unnecessarily undercut him by overplaying radical political (meaning anticommunist) demands by Hungarian insurgents? RFE could hardly ignore these demands, just as it could not ignore the calls of the Poznań demonstrators in June for freedom as well as bread. RFE relayed (with explicit U.S. government authorization, as noted above) reports of the many, now noncommunist domestic radios that conveyed demands for radical political change issued by noncommunist revolutionary councils and other independent organizations and media that mushroomed around Hungary after October 23.[67] One such RFE program of November 1 carried (by then noncommunist) Radio Free Kossuth (Budapest) and Radio Free Győr reports on the newly formed National Council of Transdanubia's decision to support continued labor strikes, a report from Radio Szombathely on the local Roman Catholic bishop's prayers for fallen Freedom Fighters, and additional reports from Radio Free Kossuth (Budapest) on popular demands for withdrawal from the Warsaw Pact, a purge of Communist leaders from the Smallholders' Party, and peasant demands for economic and political freedoms.[68] Judging by review of a sample of several of these rebroadcasts (all of which were revoiced, not a replay of the original sound), RFE limited itself to relaying the substantive information they contained without undue emotion or third-party editorial comment. One example is RFE's report on the eighteen-point demand of Miskolc students issued over Radio Free Miskolc on October 26.[69]

Were RFE Hungarian broadcasts responsible journalism? By all accounts, both contemporaneous reviews and current sampling, the quality of too many—but certainly not the majority—of RFE Hungarian broadcasts during the Revolution was poor. A December 1956 internal RFE policy review found many good programs; 171 of 308 programs were rated excel-

67. By October 30, the Communist media-control system had disintegrated. Radio Kossuth Budapest became Radio Free Kossuth on that date. Debrecen, Dunapentele, Eger, Győr, Kaposvár, Miskolc, Nyíregyháza, Pécs, and Szombathely also operated as Free Radios. RFE established a special unit in Vienna to monitor these Free Radios, most of which had low transmitter power.

68. Special Győr Report F1, by Emil Csonka, November 1, 1956.

69. As cited by Michie, *Voices through the Iron Curtain,* 225–27.

lent or good. But the remainder were rated mediocre or worse, and Griffith concluded that the bad and mediocre programs overshadowed the many outstandingly good ones. The top-of-the-hour ten-minute newscasts (a mainstay of programming not examined in any of the postmortems or by any of the critics) were dispassionate, objective, and professionally competent by any standard (judging by a few that I have sampled and the comprehensive analysis of Gábor Hanák).[70] Hungarian Service correspondent reports from European capitals and the United States were factual. It was the series of Munich political commentaries that all too often failed to meet minimum journalistic standards, because they included far too much emotion, preaching, unsubstantiated opinion, condescension, vituperation, and tactical advice. These failings characterized most of the programs graded as "D" or "F" in the December 1956 review discussed below. Additionally, as noted above, four programs egregiously disregarded policy guidelines, three by offering tactical military advice[71] and the one press review implying Western assistance. Perhaps the worst journalistic aspect of RFE Hungarian programming during this period was periodic anonymous exhortations injected into the broadcasts, such as "Safeguard Revolutionary Unity!" and "With Murderers There Is No Peace. Repeal Martial Law Immediately!" Looking back at 1956 with the hindsight of thirty years, Griffith found the overall tone of the Hungarian broadcasts to have been "insufficiently professional, too emotional, and too didactic. They transgressed against the overriding importance of objectivity and therefore of credibility."[72]

RFE Hungarian programs improved in November. The same broadcasters who had aired overly emotional and prescriptive commentaries during the heady days before November 4 now broadcast professional programs, just as they had before October 23. An example is László Béry's November 20 commentary on deportations of prominent revolutionaries and UN and

70. E.g., the 17:00 (Budapest time) newscast on October 25, CD from original reel 1884, track 11, Hoover Archives. It covered fighting in Budapest, factory strikes, the curfew, closed schools, chaotic transportation, anti-Soviet placards, appointment of Kádár as party secretary, Nagy's speech that day, a fire in the National Museum, and reactions abroad from London, New York, Warsaw, and the Council of Europe. Gábor Hanák of the National Széchényi Library has comprehensively reviewed the newscasts as broadcast and concurs in this judgment (personal communication).

71. László Borhi attributes the idea for such programs to Griffith. I have found no evidence to support this interpretation. László Borhi, "Liberation or Inaction? The United States and Hungary in 1956," in *Die Ungarnkrise 1956 und Österreich,* ed. Erwin A. Schmidl (Vienna: Boehlau Verlag, 2003), 143.

72. Griffith, "Interview."

Red Cross activities to assist Hungary.[73] After the Revolution was crushed, RFE began a daily series of special programs devoted to personal messages from refugees to relatives back in Hungary reporting (with first names or pseudonyms) their safe arrival in the West.[74] Some 200,000 messages of this kind were broadcast, a major public service. To cite one testimonial, László Ivanits later recalled how a priest who sought him out on a train in Germany conveyed to RFE, and thus to his aunt and parents in Hungary, his message that "the blond-haired, blue-eyed boy from Raday Street is on his way to America."[75]

Looking back in 2000, Arch Puddington aptly summarized what the Hungarian Service could and could not have done in 1956:

> Hungary presented RFE with a more formidable challenge than did Poland. RFE did not have the option of encouraging the people to remain in their homes and avoid bloodshed. Hungary was at war; thus the challenge for RFE was to support the goals of the revolution through honest, non-polemical reporting, to provide a realistic evaluation of the international response to Hungary's plight, and to avoid becoming a participant in the upheaval. Unfortunately, RFE fell short on all three goals.[76]

Controversy without End

After the Revolution was crushed, and as criticisms of RFE's role multiplied in the international media, RFE Hungarian broadcast policy was intensively reviewed both inside and outside RFE. The internal reviews were the most comprehensive and the most critical. An RFE Program Department evaluation concluded "that discipline was maintained in the Polish Desk and that it was slack in the Hungarian."[77] A Free Europe Press Division review characterized the Hungarian broadcasts as "inexpert due to poor content, emotional tone, and inadequate programming techniques," in contrast to the Polish broadcasts, which they found to be "consistently excellent,

---

73. Special Commentary A-2, by László Béry, original text and translation on microfilm reel 156.

74. E.g., Special Messages H-3 by Katalin Hunyadi, November 9, 1956, text on microfilm reel no. 165.

75. *Centre Daily Times,* State College, Pa., December 24, 2006.

76. Puddington, *Broadcasting Freedom,* 100.

77. "Program Department Report for the Period 1 October–1 December 1956" (Wright Memorandum), December 3, 1956.

showing restraint, strict adherence to policy, and masterful programming techniques." The reviewers described the Hungarian Service senior editors as "out of touch with the situation in their country, inadequately trained in professional radio techniques, and politically out of tune with the patriots. The chain of command within the [Hungarian Service] broke down, and discipline was not enforced."[78]

The most thorough review, conducted by the Office of the Political Advisor, the so-called Griffith Report,[79] covered 308 programs or 70 percent of all non-news broadcast coverage during the period. It assigned letter grades to the programs as follows: A-78, B-93, C-81, D-37, and F-19. This meant that 171 of the 308 programs were judged to be at the "A" or "B" level, while 56 programs were judged to be at the "D" or "F" level. It also assigned letter grades to the programs of the 26 principal broadcast editors; only 12 of the 26 were at the "A" or "B" level, while 3 senior editors were at the "D" level. The report concluded that in the first two weeks after October 23,

> although there were few genuine violations of policy, . . . the application of policy lines was more often than not crude and unimaginative. Many of the rules of effective broadcasting technique were violated. The tone of the broadcasts was overexcited. There was too much rhetoric, too much emotionalism, and too much generalization. The great majority of programs were lacking in humility and subtlety. [Hungarian Service] output for the first two-week period in particular had a distinct "émigré" tone; too little specific reference was made to the desires and demands of the people in the country. An improvement is discernible toward the end of this first two-week period. By the first days of November con-

78. "Review of RFE and FEP Operations in Hungary and Poland, 1 October–1 December 1956" (hereafter, Walker Memorandum), December 7, 1956.

79. "Policy Review of Voice of Free Hungary Programming, 23 October–23 November 1956" (Griffith Memorandum, drafted by Paul Henze), December 5, 1956, reprinted (without supporting appendices) by Békés, Byrne, and Rainer, *1956 Hungarian Revolution*. Appendix I contains the summary evaluation of each program. Appendix II evaluates the performance of the individual Hungarian Service broadcasters. Appendix III contains excerpts of the written RFE policy guidances for the period. In a separate memorandum, Griffith concluded that "[RFE's] role in respect to creating exaggerated ideas of Western aid was primarily one of reflecting Western statements rather than what it said itself." "Lessons of the Polish and Hungarian Revolutions," RFE memorandum to Galantiere from Griffith, March 11, 1957, Office of the Political Advisor Political Report RFE/M (57) 4.

siderably more frequent reference was made to the "freedom stations" in Hungary and the demands of the local revolutionary councils, and policy guidance on key questions such as the role of Imre Nagy was applied with greater refinement.

It remains puzzling that what the veteran Reuters journalist Michael Nelson termed a "sober and balanced internal report"[80] did not consider the derogatory personal attacks on Nagy as policy violations. They clearly were.

The CIA commissioned its own review from a set of RFE transmitter tapes borrowed from the Portugal transmitter site. Allen Dulles later summarized this review as follows: "I had three Hungarian-speaking employees of ours listen to all the tapes of broadcasts during the period of October 23 to November 4, 1956. They found that Radio Free Europe neither incited the Hungarian people to revolution nor promised outside military intervention."[81] The generally positive internal CIA review indeed made those points, adding that the broadcasts reported on but did not call for strikes, provided straight news accounts of statements of President Eisenhower and senior American officials, covered the reports on the various independent radio stations, and did not promote individual Hungarian leaders (and did not carry the appeal of some independent radio stations that Cardinal Mindszenty should become premier). More negatively, the review concluded, RFE did offer some advice on political demands, carried sustained criticism of Nagy, along with other Hungarian Communist leaders, and was on occasion emotional in tone.[82] Earlier, on November 20, 1956, and before systematic review, Dulles wrote to President Eisenhower that RFE broadcasts had been generally consistent with U.S. policies but that RFE "went somewhat beyond specific guidances in identifying itself with Hungarian patriot aims, and in offering certain tactical advice to the patriots."[83]

The German Foreign Office borrowed a second set of RFE broadcasts during the Revolution recorded from the RFE transmitters in Biblis—the

80. Michael Nelson, *War of the Black Heavens* (Syracuse: Syracuse University Press, 1997), 74.

81. FEC letter to Harlow Curtice, Chairman of the Crusade for Freedom, November 16, 1957; also see Cord Meyer, *Facing Reality: From World Federalism to the CIA* (New York: Harper & Row, 1980), 126.

82. CIA memorandum, "Report on a Review of Radio Free Europe Broadcasts Beamed to Hungary, from 24 October to 4 November 1956," January 14, 1957, released to the author in March 2007.

83. "Memorandum from the Director of Central Intelligence (Dulles) to the President, November 20, 1956," document 199, in *FRUS*, 1955–57, XXV, 473–75.

set later deposited in the Federal German Archives and now available for research—and conducted its own review. Preliminary results were discussed with RFE management in Munich on November 27,[84] and were communicated to the U.S. government via the Bonn Embassy on December 20.[85] The German review cleared RFE of the charge of promising military help to the Revolution but criticized some programs on grounds of offering tactical advice and attacking Nagy. The German Foreign Office accurately concluded that RFE management was sometimes ignorant of the exact nature of the broadcasts. Asked about RFE broadcasts to Hungary by an East Berlin journalist at a press conference on January 25, 1957, Chancellor Konrad Adenauer said that press reports that "Radio Free Europe had promised armed support of the West to the Hungarians is not in conformity with the facts " but added that some of the broadcasts had contained "remarks . . . subject to misinterpretation."[86] The main criticism of RFE's treatment of Nagy at the time came from German Social Democrats, who viewed the German government review as insufficiently critical of RFE, in part by downplaying its attacks on Nagy.[87]

This specific SPD critique caused the CIA/IOD to review separately the relevant broadcast texts in translation. The reviewing IOD officer concluded that "from 23 thru 31 October not only did Nagy get no breaks from RFE, he was very openly and uncompromisingly attacked. . . . It was not until 1 November that any sort of let-up on the attacks against Nagy could be discerned and that was a backhand deal; . . . on November 2 RFE made its first sympathetic reference to Imre Nagy."[88]

Reviews by the Council of Europe, the United Nations, and a congressional committee also generally cleared RFE of wrongdoing.[89] The State De-

84. RFE Munich telex MUN 321, November 27, 1956.

85. "Editorial Note," document 228, in *FRUS, 1955–57,* XXV; Embassy Bonn dispatch, 2416, December 20, 1956, released to the author in November 2006. I could not locate the review itself in the German Foreign Office Political Archive, notwithstanding helpful efforts of the Political Archive staff.

86. *New York Times,* January 26, 1957.

87. *SPD-Pressedienst,* May 29, 1957, quoting excerpts of RFE criticisms of Nagy.

88. CIA/IOD memorandum dated June 5, 1957, released to the author in February 2007.

89. A Council of Europe committee cleared RFE of wrongdoing but used the occasion to call for future European participation in the operation; Council of Europe, Consultative Assembly, Committee on Non-Represented Nations, *Radio Free Europe,* report presented by M. Goedhart. April 27, 1957. The "Kelly Committee" focused on linking foreign information programs to foreign policy; Foreign Relations Committee [Sub-

partment was more critical. A State Department memorandum prepared jointly with Cord Meyer for Secretary of State Dulles on November 13 (replacing a State Department draft that the CIA viewed as unfairly critical) stated that the broadcasts had not caused the uprising nor promised American aid, that RFE policies had State Department approval, and that RFE was specifically authorized to give full coverage to broadcasts of the patriot radios, but that "over-zealous Hungarian employees of RFE" had encouraged the revolutionaries and offered certain tactical advice.[90] While Allen Dulles defended RFE's broadcasts at a meeting of the interagency Operations Coordinating Board on November 21,[91] Deputy Undersecretary of State Robert Murphy, after reviewing selected commentaries, criticized them for attacking Nagy and for overly close identification with the Revolution.[92]

Edward T. Wailes (who had arrived in Budapest to head the American Legation only on November 2) and his deputy, Leonard Meeker, concluded from their reading of broadcast texts that while criticism of the Radios was overdone, "RFE scripts often had a tone which fed the hopes of the people beyond the point of reality." But they told IOD officers in the spring of 1957 that they did not think that cautionary, antiviolence broadcasts would have held back the Revolution.[93] Forwarding Murphy's memorandum to Allen Dulles, Meyer noted that RFE had been authorized to act as a "communications center" for the revolutionaries and thus inevitably became identified with the revolutionary cause.[94] The State Department would have the last word. It would make use of the controversy over RFE Hungarian broadcasting in 1956 and a second controversy that developed in early 1957 over

---

committee headed by New York Democratic Congresswoman Edna Kelly], U.S. House of Representatives, report issued May 16, 1957; United Nations, *Report of the Special Committee on the Problem of Hungary,* June 20, 1957, cleared the Radio of the charge of provoking the uprising but said it perhaps gave an impression that Western aid was forthcoming. Also see Puddington, *Broadcasting Freedom,* 103–4.

90. Department of State memorandum to the secretary of state from L. Randolph Higgs, with the concurrence of Cord Meyer, November 13, 1956, released to the author in November 2006; CIA memorandum to the DCI from Cord Meyer, November 14, 1956, released to the author in November 2006.

91. "Memorandum for the Record by the Counselor of the Department of State (MacArthur), November 21, 1956," document 201, in *FRUS,* 1955–57, XXV.

92. State Department memorandum to CIA, November 26, 1956, released to the author in November 2006.

93. CIA/IOD memorandum, March 18, 1957, released to the author in March 2009.

94. CIA/IOD memorandum to the DCI from Meyer dated November 29, 1956, released to the author in November 2006.

broadcasting to Poland to strengthen its control over "private" RFE and RL broadcasts for which the U.S. government publicly claimed to bear no responsibility.

Breakdown of Control

The record indicates that RFE's written policy guidances conformed to U.S. policy deliberations for international information programs in October and November 1956 but that many Hungarian broadcasts did not. There was a breakdown of control, but it was not between the U.S. government and the FEC/RFE, but rather within the FEC/RFE itself. Internal friction began while the Revolution was under way. RFE director W. J. Conerey Egan (in New York), following up his communications on the treatment of Nagy the previous day cited above, on November 3 conveyed to RFE European director Condon his criticism of the Hungarian broadcasts for "serious if not flagrant violations" of policy and directed a prebroadcast review of programming by the American management and limitation of commentary.[95] Egan's strong language notwithstanding, the four programs previously cited and negative treatment of Nagy were the only real departures from specific policy guidances at this juncture, although the emotionalism of many commentaries were at odds with overall RFE broadcasting policy and standards. In a letter from Condon to Egan dated November 5, the Munich management staunchly defended its approach (thus indicating its insufficient knowledge of what had been on the air), initially granting that only that a few inadvisable programs had been broadcast.

This breakdown of control within the FEC and RFE had many causes. A new FEC president without postwar European experience, retired General Willis D. Crittenberger (a West Point classmate of President Eisenhower) had assumed office on the eve of the Revolution. There was a history of long-standing bureaucratic conflict between the FEC and RFE New York, on the one hand, and RFE Munich on the other.[96] In Munich, management

95. RFE New York telex, NYC 39, November 3, 1956.
96. FEC counselor Galantiere (in New York) wrote to departing FEC president Shepardson in June: "I am very sorry the way matters . . . are going in RFE. There is a deep gulf between Munich and New York. Whereas Munich is in the stream of the wise and tactful tradition built up these past six years, and handles East European problems with a judicious admixture of regard for the American interest and respect for the political realities and for the exile's feelings and point of view, RFE/New York is deserting RFE traditions and turning the organization into a shrill-voiced USIA." FEC memorandum, June 26, 1956.

responsibilities were divided between the policy and program departments (the program department hired the Hungarian and all other broadcasters, while the policy office advised on the content of broadcasts). The American policy staff failed to adequately discuss key programs with the Hungarian broadcasting management before broadcast.[97] Editorial responsibility within the Hungarian Service was poorly defined.

The breakdown of control also involved personnel failures, specifically a Hungarian Service director, Andor Gellért, who performed poorly (a problem exacerbated by illness)[98] and a Hungarian broadcast staff that was on balance more "rightist" than opinion in Hungary, demoralized to some extent by recent history (Hungary was truncated after World War I and was an Axis-allied power in World War II), and lacking the discipline engendered by past military resistance. This was in contrast to the Polish Service staff, no less anticommunist but more in tune with local conditions, veterans of the protracted Warsaw Uprising, and able to maintain discipline in a crisis.[99] Perhaps the fatal flaw was that Gellért's deputies performed abysmally; the worst programs—those that were overly emotional, offering tactical advice, vituperative—were written by the senior editors of the service, whose job should have been to set a model of good programming and require it from others. These senior editors were not primitive propagandists. In normal circumstances, they were capable of airing good programs. For example, László Béry and Imre Mikes, whose programs were rated in the December 1956 Griffith review as the poorest of all (with an average grade of D+), wrote reasonable commentaries both before and after the Revolution. They were evidently overcome by emotion and unrealistic expectations with the unexpected outbreak and violent turn of the Revolution.

To be sure, under the very best of circumstances, the RFE Hungarian Service would have faced an enormous challenge in 1956. The outbreak of the Hungarian Revolution surprised everyone, not least everyone at RFE. Gyula Borbándi (at the time a broadcaster; later deputy director) recalled that the Hungarian Service was unprepared, stunned, excited, lacking in su-

---

97. Editorial responsibility within RFE always rested with the respective Broadcasting Service directors. Broadcasts were only in exceptional cases preapproved by American management.

98. Jan Nowak's impression after talking to Gellért during the height of the crisis was that he was very sick and had lost contact with his staff. Nowak-Jeziorański, *Wojna w eterze,* 284.

99. Paul Smith concluded that "the Hungarian Service of RFE was smaller in staff and neither as experienced or politically astute as the larger Polish Division." Paul A. Smith, *On Political War* (Washington, D.C.: National Defense University Press, 1989), 209.

pervision because of Director Gellért's illness, and overwhelmed by the quantity of information pouring in.[100] The fact remains that "the chain of command within the [Hungarian] Desk broke down, and discipline was not enforced."[101] RFE Munich leadership acknowledged problems with the Hungarian Service later in November, noting that while the Hungarian Revolution was generally "leftist," RFE Hungarian broadcasters were generally "'rightist' in political orientation and they tended over the years to become more and more shrill, emotional and over general in tone, to an extent where we have for some time felt that rather drastic measures are needed to de-emotionalize their scripts."[102] The RFE Munich management had indeed long been aware of poor leadership and staffing of the Hungarian Service and negativism in its programs but had been able to make only limited improvements.[103]

It is clear in retrospect that the American management at RFE Munich devoted insufficient attention to the content of the Hungarian broadcasts in the crisis period, in part because it assumed a common understanding of broadcast policy from and expected discipline within the Hungarian Service (both of which, unlike the case of the Polish Service, did not exist) and because it lacked the monitoring, linguistic, and translation capabilities necessary for critical prebroadcast discussion, real-time broadcast monitoring, and speedy postbroadcast review. RFE management's limited Hungarian-language capabilities were diverted to providing New York and Washington (and the international media) with translations of the extensive broadcasts of the Hungarian Freedom Radios.[104] Some of management's attention was diverted by what seem in retrospect to have been secondary concerns.[105]

100. Gyula Borbándi, *Magyarok az Angol Kertben: A Szabad Europa Rádió Törtenete* [Hungarians in the English Garden: The History of Radio Free Europe] (Budapest: Europa Könyvkiadó, 1996), 205–77.

101. Walker Memorandum.

102. RFE Munich telex to New York, MUN 236, November 20, 1956.

103. Letters to Griffith from Henze, July 27 and August 5, 1953, devoted to problems in the Hungarian Service (Henze Correspondence).

104. Communication from William Rademaekers to the author, 2006. Rademaekers was the only Hungarian speaker in the RFE American management in 1956.

105. Part of October 29 and 30 was devoted to general roundtable discussions with outside experts, including Peter Wiles, Franz Borkenau, and Edmond Taylor; RFE Munich, Office of the Political Advisor, Background Information USSR, October 1956. Griffith was absent for several crucial days, October 31–November 2, having been ordered by the FEC to travel to Paris for consultations with CIA deputy director Frank Wisner not about RFE broadcasts but about how the U.S. government should deal with

There was an alternative model. Radio Liberty's Russian broadcasts during this period (some directed specifically to Soviet forces in Hungary) were much more tightly controlled and restrained. RL president Howland Sargeant, based in New York and advised by Boris Shub, directed early in the crisis that RL broadcasts limit themselves to news reporting and abstain from carrying opinion pieces from international media and especially to avoid original commentary. State Department officials endorsed this approach, maintaining that RL "can fulfill highly important role simply by transmitting to Soviets all available hard facts of rapidly evolving situation."[106] RL broadcasters and American management in Munich understandably resented these limitations as undermining RL's mission of providing views as well as news and indicating a lack of trust in their capability to make sound editorial judgments. They adhered to the restrictions while arguing against them and soon obtained their relaxation.[107]

Personnel changes followed RFE's 1956 Hungarian crisis—for the better in the Hungarian Service, for the worse in the American management. In early 1957 the Hungarian Service was reorganized. István Bede was promoted to replace Gellért (who moved to the New York office) as director, and Károly András was appointed deputy director, replacing Viktor Mátyás, who was dismissed, along with twelve other staff members, including Zoltán Thury (who had prepared the November 4 *Observer* press review). Imre Mikes's commentaries were suspended until mid-1957. Julian Borsányi (whose "Colonel Bell" series had carried the "Molotov Cocktail" program) was protected by his position on the employee works council. Borbándi was threatened with termination on the unrelated grounds that he was too "leftist"; Griffith argued successfully against that step. The new Hungarian Service team would prove to be effective professional broadcasters in the 1960s and beyond.

Most of the FEC and RFE senior management also changed; by the end of 1958, Crittenberger, Egan, Condon, Griffith, Henze, and others had departed for a variety of reasons. Their immediate successors were less knowledgeable about Eastern Europe and less capable managers, an organizational

---

a future coalition government in Hungary; RFE Munich telex MUN 336, October 31, 1956; McCargar, "Policy and Personalities"; Griffith interview with the author, 1992.

106. State cable, November 1, 1956, as reported in CIA cable dated November 2, 1956, released to the author March 2009.

107. "Telegram from the Consulate General at Munich to the Department of State, October 30, 1956," document 142, in *FRUS,* 1955–57, XXV; RL [Munich] Weekly Airgram Report, November 2 and 16, 1956.

deficit overcome only in 1961 with the appointments of John Richardson Jr. as FEC president, G. Rodney Smith as RFE director, and R. V. Burks and then Ralph E. Walter as RFE policy directors.

To recapitulate, some RFE Hungarian broadcasts in October 1956 departed from U.S. government and RFE policy and standards in their emotional commentaries and their negative treatment of Imre Nagy. Three programs offered tactical military advice, and one program implied Western assistance. These failures overshadowed the many high-quality programs that were broadcast, especially professional newscasts in several weeks of nearly round-the-clock programs. The failures were primarily the responsibility of the Hungarian Service director and his senior staff, who enjoyed great autonomy and trust in the decentralized RFE "partnership" structure. They were assumed to be the best judges, within overall RFE policy, of what was and was not responsible and effective broadcasting. Instead, they failed to live up to the injunction the 1952 guidance quoted in chapter 2 to not "allow their hearts to run away with their heads."

Ultimately, of course, these failures were the responsibility of the American FEC and RFE management as a whole who had hired the Hungarian Service directorate and failed to monitor its broadcasts closely enough.[108] Given the staffing and outlook of the Hungarian Service at the time and the fast-moving pace of events, Condon, Griffith, and their subordinates could not realistically have reshaped the broadcasts during the crisis. Nor—given RFE's mission and the satisfactory performance of the Hungarian Service before the outbreak of the Revolution—could they realistically have preemptively banned all commentary. What they could have done after October 23 was to ban all commentaries except for a few approved in full translation in advance. Less would have been much better. But that would have required a better appreciation of the sensitivity of broadcasts in a revolutionary situation and a much better knowledge of program content. These major organizational weaknesses would be corrected in the 1960s.

The Dilemma of Crisis Broadcasting

An RFE-commissioned survey of one thousand Hungarian refugees in Austria published in February 1957 concluded that foreign radio had been their

---

108. RFE management's unfamiliarity with the content of the Hungarian broadcasts at the time is evident in the RFE Munich dispatch to RFE New York of November 5, 1956, cited above, which praised director Gellért, minimized the problems within the Hungarian Service, downplayed the significance of condemnations of Nagy, and ignored the emotional content of broadcasts.

major source of information during the Revolution on both domestic and foreign developments. Ninety percent had listened to foreign radio, and of these, 81 percent listened to RFE frequently and 67 percent listened to both VOA and the BBC frequently. Radio Vienna, RIAS, and Radio Vatican also had significant listenerships.[109] A separate survey of Hungarian refugees by the Austrian Institut für Markt-und Meinungsforschung found that 72 percent of interviewed refugees listened to Western radio daily, with the highest percentage tuning in to RFE.[110] State Department interviews with refugees in Europe and IOD staff interviews with refugees at Camp Kilmer, New Jersey, showed high listenership.[111] Anecdotal evidence of listening to RFE in Hungary abounded.

RFE unquestionably had large audiences in Hungary during the 1956 Revolution. It also had a great impact. But many foreign stations broadcast in Hungarian, and even after radio jamming (temporarily) ended on October 24, listeners sometimes could not determine which station they heard. In the aftermath of the crushed Revolution, feelings of betrayal emerged in Hungary, and collective guilt in the West, along with a search for scapegoats. Western journalists in Hungary focused disproportionately on RFE to the exclusion of other stations; the reports and later book of the journalist Leslie Bain were perhaps most influential in this context.[112] All Western broadcasters shared in some proportion the credit or blame for the impact of the broadcasts in 1956.[113]

109. "Hungary and the 1956 Uprising: Personal Interviews with 1000 Hungarian Refugees in Austria," International Research Associates, Inc., February 1957, summarized in RFE Audience Analysis Section, Special Report 12, March 1957; full text in the RFE/RL Collection.

110. RFE press release, December 23, 1957.

111. "A Myth about Radio Free Europe" [letter to the editor], by William Lloyd Stearman, *Washington Post,* June 27, 2009.

112. Leslie B. Bain, *The Reluctant Satellites: An Eyewitness Report on East Europe and the Hungarian Revolution* (New York: Macmillan, 1960).

113. And in crises key actors are not necessarily listeners. As one Freedom Fighter told me, "We were fighting in the streets; we did not have time to listen to radio stations." There are no detailed examinations of BBC and VOA broadcasting during the Hungarian Revolution; a useful introduction is Rawnsley, *Radio Diplomacy and Propaganda.* Copies of the BBC Hungarian broadcasts were deposited in the National Széchényi Library and Hungarian Radio in Budapest. The BBC Written Archives Centre, Reading, contains texts of 1956 BBC Hungarian broadcasts (as cited by Rawnsley). Comparable VOA archives have not been located. A BBC commentary on October 26 sympathized with the Hungarian Revolution but excluded Western military support. Another BBC commentary on October 27 denounced the Nagy government (Rawnsley, *Radio Diplomacy and Propaganda,* 89, 92), apparently contradicting Urban's claim (*Radio Free Europe and the Pursuit of Democracy,* 231) that BBC Hungarian broadcasts "backed

RFE Hungarian broadcasts evidently contributed to the belief among Hungarians that, one way or another, the West would support them in securing a triumph of the Revolution. The RFE-commissioned survey of refugees in Austria indicated that half the respondents thought that American broadcasts had given the impression that the United States was willing to fight the Soviet Union to save Hungary. That was not because of the explicit content of programs; as noted, only one program during the critical month could be interpreted as directly suggesting Western assistance, and none of the interviewees referred to that program. It was rather because RFE projected to Hungary the sympathy and moral and humanitarian support of the entire Western world for the Hungarian cause, leading Hungarian listeners to misread the messages and overestimate Western support.

After the Revolution was crushed by the Soviet Union, Western journalists, State Department officials, and several émigré interview projects reported a variety of views about RFE held by Hungarian émigrés, including criticism of the RFE Hungarian broadcasts from Hungarians prominent in the Revolution. The Socialist Party leader Béla Kovács, for example, claimed that "US radio misled Hungarians into believing they could count on effective US aid in event of trouble with Soviets."[114] Hungarians were understandably encouraged and emboldened by the broadcast of Western press reviews and correspondent reports that conveyed accurately the widespread sympathy—in Western Europe as much as in the United States—for their cause. The Hungarian Service broadcast the passages of the Republican and Democratic parties' election platforms, a Senate resolution, and the remarks of American politicians across the political spectrum supporting eventual freedom of the captive peoples. These sentiments were by no means confined to the United States. On the eve of the Revolution, RFE reported from Strasbourg on Council of Europe discussions about the "cap-

[Nagy] without hesitation throughout the revolution." BBC programs did not feature political commentaries as did RFE. VOA broadcast only 1 hour and 45 minutes of original Hungarian programs daily during the Revolution, characterized by USIA as "calm, factual, and objective; . . . certain programs even warned the freedom fighters to be cautious"; USIA memorandum to President Eisenhower from Abbott Washburn, November 19, 1956, NARA II, RG 306, A141, Box 1, declassified March 30, 2009. A VOA review is cited in document 185, in *FRUS, 1955–57*, XXV, 437; VOA Hungarian Munich chief Boros' emotional commentaries were evidently not broadcast; Rawnsley, *Radio Diplomacy and Propaganda*, 79.

114. Kovács' resentment of RFE was reported by the American Legation in Budapest on November 19. "Telegram from the Legation in Hungary to the Department of State, November 19, 1956," document 198, in *FRUS, 1955–57*, XXV.

tive nations," concluding with the words of chairman Étienne de la Vallée-Poussin from Belgium: "Today we are only speaking, but tomorrow we will have to act. History is marching along at increased speed. The rigidity of the Soviet system is not the same as before. Let the unity and determined attitude of the West be the answer. Only thus can we solve the essence of the question: the problem of the united, indivisible, and free Europe."[115]

After October 23, RFE reported the outpouring of support for the cause of the Revolution across the political spectrum in Western Europe (including the noncommunist European Left) as well as in the United States. Press reviews ranged from *L'Osservatore Romano* to the *Daily Worker.* Correspondent reports covered demonstrations and relief efforts around the world. An RFE Hungarian broadcast on October 29, for example, included correspondents' reports on solidarity with Hungary at "an enormous New York manifestation in favor of the Hungarian cause [outside the UN]," on a demonstration of five thousand in Cleveland that proclaimed "Long Live Hungary! Help for the Hungarian People," and on a statement of the Social Democratic Party of Sweden proclaiming that "in a country whose people wish to live in freedom, all attempts to perpetuate the rule of oppressors over small nations must remain unsuccessful."[116] Another correspondent's report from Vienna described the relief efforts of the International Red Cross; the collection of food and medicine in Dublin; the arrival in Vienna of food, clothing, and blood from the Finnish Red Cross; and donations of food, clothing, and blood in West Berlin and Munich.[117] Hungarians could be further encouraged by RFE reports (which were dispassionate and noted Soviet objections, although perhaps not often enough) about Western diplomatic efforts on their behalf, such as U.S. ambassador Henry Cabot Lodge's appeals at the United Nations beginning on October 28 first to forestall Soviet suppression of the uprising and then to legitimize the Nagy government.[118]

115. From Our Correspondent No. C-14, "Report from Strasbourg," by Szabolcs Vájay, original and translation on microfilm reel 153.

116. Special Report C-2, by Katalin Hunyadi, original and translation on microfilm reel 185.

117. Special Red Cross Vienna Report, by József Koble, Hungarian text on microfilm reel 187, translation by Margit Grigory, Hoover Institution.

118. Special UNO Program No. C-1, October 29, 1956, by László Mezőfy, original and translation on microfilm reel 187. Internal U.S. government discussions about other nonmilitary measures to assist the Hungarian insurgents, however problematical, were cut short by preoccupation with the Suez Crisis, which began on October 29 with Israel's occupation of the Sinai with French and British support. Gati, *Failed Illusions,* 162ff, provides a critical review of U.S. policy deliberations.

It was this international reporting, all highly professional, that posed the dilemma of RFE broadcasting to Hungary in 1956. As George Urban wrote: "Supposing that Radio Free Europe *had confined* itself to bland observations through the period—the perceptions in the minds of listeners would still not have been very different. Given Radio Free Europe's mandate—and a similar mentality which informed the broadcasts of the Central European Service of the BBC—a 'positional' kind of incitement was inevitable. Surrogate broadcasting from Munich and BBC broadcasting in the languages of Central and Eastern Europe from London were a form of encouragement simply because they, and the sentiments they reflected, existed."[119] The same applied to the Voice of America.

Listening to the emotional personal commentaries of Hungarian broadcasters, the Hungarian audience could think they heard the voice of the West.[120] Listening to objective reports of declarations of moral and economic support in the 1956 U.S. electoral campaign and declarations and demonstrations of support and relief efforts around the world after October 23, the Hungarian audience heard widespread support for their cause. Knowing that RFE broadcast almost around the clock in Hungarian and viewing it—program content totally aside—as an authoritative voice from the United States, the Hungarian audience could easily conclude that, somehow, Hungary would not be abandoned by the West to a Soviet fate.[121]

This, then, was the dilemma—as relevant today as it was in Hungary in 1956—of an external communicator who accurately conveys news and in-

119. Urban, *Radio Free Europe and the Pursuit of Democracy,* 219; emphasis in the original.

120. Katona and Vámos, "Nagy Imre es a Szabad Europa Radio 1956-ban." A Hungarian-American who left Hungary in 1945 and who sampled some of the broadcasts in 2006 commented: "I can see how possible interpretations that help is somehow coming could have been deduced from the totally empathetic, emotional tone and delivery."

121. One embittered Hungarian-American told Frank Wisner that Western radios and especially RFE "had appeared to promise but had failed to deliver . . . the rescue of the Satellite peoples, whom by our deeds and actions we have been inciting to rise against their Soviet and Communist masters." CIA memorandum of conversation in the U.S. Ambassador's Residence, Vienna, November 9, 1956, released to the author in March 2007. Hungarian parliamentarian Ilona Marothy, interviewed at Camp Kilmer in December 1956, reflected: "In the second phase of the revolution the Hungarian people, even if with bitterness, acknowledged the fact that the West will not help, because of higher political consideration[s] cannot help the Hungarian freedom fight with arms. . . . In between the lines [RFE] had sown in the soul of the people the hope of Western armed help. When this proved to be impossible and false, the bitter reaction was inevitable: 'This radio also gives promises only and states lies.'"

formation into a crisis region but risks its misinterpretation by the audience as signifying the promise of outside material or other specific support for a particular cause when that is not the case. Responsible journalism can thus become inadvertent incitement. It was not specific promises or advocacy by RFE Hungarian broadcasters, but rather a combination of the emotional tone of some commentaries, the accurate reporting of Western solidarity with the Hungarian cause, and the very existence of RFE that evidently led many Hungarians to the conclusion that the United States supported the Revolution (which was true) and would not let it fail (which was false). As the two Hungarian-speaking officers in the Budapest Legation observed in the spring of 1956, "RFE, very likely much more than VOA, symbolizes to the Hungarian people the active interest of the United States Government in Hungarians and Hungary. The danger is that the symbol is a static one in that RFE still seems to symbolize to Hungarians future Western liberation of their country."[122] Hungarians' belief in that symbol is testimony to the influence that RFE came to assume in Hungary—exaggerated because it vastly overrated RFE's authority and ability to affect the course of events and encouraged illusions of Western military support of the Hungarian insurgents that was never in prospect.

In the end, the historical record demonstrates, as the American and European governments concluded at the time, that the journalistic lapses of the RFE Hungarian Service, although serious, could not have inspired, provoked, or by themselves prolonged the Hungarian Revolution or caused the Soviet Union to suppress it. Nor, by any reasonable reading, could the U.S. government's policy guidance to RFE after 1953 and especially in 1956 be held to have encouraged or sustained the uprising. Yet almost certainly the combined effect of predominantly professional programming by RFE and other Western stations broadcasting to Hungary in October 1956, and the American and European expressions of sympathy for Hungary's struggle for freedom that all broadcasters conveyed in the course of journalistic reporting, did in fact nurture the hopes of Hungarians for Western military intervention that would never happen.

Western leaders and their broadcasters failed to appreciate that a nation locked in a desperate struggle for freedom would be inclined to understand moral support as tantamount to a pledge of material support. RFE was the dominant broadcaster to Eastern Europe at the time, and it was perhaps in-

---

122. Budapest Legation Dispatch 172, March 28, 1956, drafted by Nyerges and Katona. Released to the author in April 2010.

evitable that RFE would bear the brunt of disappointment, even in the absence of its flawed programming. This searing experience remains a signal lesson for international communication in crisis situations.

The Doldrums at RFE after 1956

With the crushing of the Hungarian Revolution and reassertion of Soviet control over Eastern Europe, RFE fell into an institutional crisis that lasted nearly five years. Soviet reversal of an almost-completed self-liberation ended hope of any foreseeable restoration of freedom and independence to Eastern European countries. Although much of the international criticism directed at RFE's 1956 Hungarian broadcasts was undeserved, and its constructive Polish broadcasts were ignored, the controversy had a corrosive effect on the institution as a whole. FEC and RFE management turned over and its competence declined, staff morale worsened, the State Department's influence over RFE operations increased, and CIA officials themselves began to express doubts about the future of the autonomous influence project they had spawned and nurtured.

By 1958, as noted above, most key officials responsible for successfully launching RFE, developing the theory and practice of surrogate broadcasting, and running the Radio for the first eight years had departed—some of them under pressure from FEC president Crittenberger before he resigned and against the wishes of the CIA/IOD, some of them on their own volition. Their immediate successors—FEC president Archibald Alexander, RFE director Thomas H. Brown Jr., RFE European director Erik Hazelhoff, and RFE policy adviser J. David Penn—lacked their predecessors' regional expertise and sensitivity about émigrés. Uncertainty about mission fueled bureaucratic rivalry between Munich and New York. Demands from the State Department and the CIA for greater control of émigré broadcasters, including preclearance by Americans of broadcasts, called into question the surrogate radio model of American-émigré partnership. As his departure from Munich neared, Griffith commented caustically but accurately on a U.S.-government-encouraged FEC reorganization plan (never implemented) that would have centralized American control over the broadcast services:

> The main problem seems to me that the command positions . . . are occupied by people with little interest and less knowledge of psychological warfare per se, and of the areas and regimes with which we deal. . . .

Unfortunately, this lack of knowledge and ability is most strikingly present among that group—RFE's American staff—which the paper proposes to expand at the expense of exile control. . . . The paper's proposals require that Americans take over the direct conduct (as opposed to control) of psychological warfare operations; this seems to me a sure road to disaster. We have a much higher-level pool of talent from which we are able to draw among the East European emigrations than among those Americans whom we might hope to get. . . . As for "mediocre ability," certainly some of our editors and writers are mediocre, but our Americans are, generally, more so.[123]

In the end, practical realities in Munich trumped policy directives from Washington.[124] The ground truth was that even Americans with the requisite language and country knowledge could preclear only a fraction of the daily programming—and those Americans had departed and not been replaced. As Griffith accurately wrote in August 1957, "Our control on output, due to lack of personnel who have left, is even less than existed before the Hungarian Revolution and [is] the antithesis of commitments which have been made."[125] Revisiting Munich in 1961, he observed that "there is in fact practically no control over RFE broadcasts by Americans, and that enormous efforts will be required to reestablish it."[126] Only in the early 1960s was a practical program-monitoring mechanism introduced; the Broadcast Analysis Department, which reported to the RFE director, was staffed by émigrés, monitored programs after and very selectively as they were broadcast, and produced for RFE management daily and weekly English-language program summaries and same-day spot reports of editorial problems.

Griffith also resisted efforts from the revamped FEC staff in New York to dictate what today would be called broadcast "spin" that would have called into question the credibility of RFE broadcasts. A case in point was FEC New York Weekly Directive No. 34, dated November 28, 1957, issued in the wake of the Soviet launching of *Sputnik* (the first Earth satellite), which cautioned against broadcasting reviews of the Western press reflect-

123. FEC memorandum from William E. Griffith, June 9, 1958. Griffith consistently argued against efforts at prebroadcast control, e.g., FEC memorandum to Hazelhoff from Griffith, "Re: Re-Imposition of Pre-Broadcast Control in RFE," January 16, 1958.
124. This included a directive to the FEC from Allan Dulles himself.
125. RFE memorandum to Egan from Griffith and Delgado, August 8, 1957.
126. William E. Griffith, "Conversations in Munich, June 15–17, 1961, re Radio Free Europe," June 21, 1961, copy in RFE/RL Collection.

ing "temporarily depressed and basically unsound press opinions about facts that allow far more than one interpretation." Griffith and audience research director Robert Sorensen reacted sharply to this suggestion to slant coverage to favor "sound" opinion, arguing that "it is naïve for us to assume that we can spoon-feed our listeners our own special rose-colored view of world affairs, or to assume that they will accept this view."[127] Responding to this criticism, FEC New York replaced Weekly Directive No. 34 with Weekly Directive No. 35, issued on December 12, 1957, which was equally problematic for RFE managers in Munich. The new directive read: "When presenting press opinion we must . . . always clarify what we ourselves feel to be true." In meetings in Munich on January 2 and 3, 1958, American and exile managers alike rejected FEC president Crittenberger's notion (as explained by Hazelhoff) that "credibility and objectivity" could detract from accomplishing the RFE mission. In Sorensen's words: "Credibility is not an abstract consideration. It is a prerequisite of effectiveness. If we are not credible to our listeners, whatever hope we express will seem silly to them. Whatever influence we expect to exercise has to be grounded on credibility. Credibility is the prerequisite for everything else." Polish Service director Jan Nowak added: "It is the Communists who believe in selectivity in press reviews. People consequently do not believe them. Nor will they believe us if they find us doing the same thing." And Romanian Service director Noel Bernard said that "we are broadcasting to convince our audience. We must approach them in such a way so as to seem credible and convincing to them."[128] CIA/IOD officers followed the dispute with dismay —and with sympathy for the Munich point of view.

Inside RFE, adverse international publicity connected with the Hungarian broadcasts, uncertainly about the future of the organization, and management ineptitude led to turmoil within the Hungarian Service, outright revolt in the Czechoslovak and Polish services, and an overall decline in staff morale. RFE became for many of its staff less a calling and more a permanent employer. Nothing symbolized this transformation more than the introduction of a pension plan in 1958. German labor law, discussed in chapter 2, made it increasingly difficult for management to promote, reward, or fire staff based on merit.

The Hungarian Service was recast and improved with new hires, but this occurred only after a number of Hungarian broadcasters were terminated in

---

127. RFE memorandum to Hazelhoff from Griffith and Sorensen, December 2, 1957.
128. RFE memoranda of record, January 3 and January 6, 1958.

early 1957 and sought redress in German Labor Court, resulting in more negative publicity.[129] The Czechoslovak Service staff revolted in November 1960 over the appointment of the unpopular Oswald Kostrba as service chief to replace the highly respected Julius Firt. RFE European director Hazelhoff overreacted by firing eighteen supposed ringleaders of the revolt, whereupon most of the remaining Czechoslovak staff sided with the terminated broadcasters and threatened to stop work. The terminated broadcasters, with trade union backing, filed suit in Munich labor court, and the FEC legal counsel advised that they would prevail. FEC president Alexander then intervened, ousting Hazelhoff, Penn, and another of his deputies and reinstating all the Czechoslovak broadcasters.[130] The controversy resulted in yet another round of unfavorable publicity in the German media.[131] Polish Service staff, underestimating the constraints imposed by German and U.S. government policies, threatened to strike if they could not more directly espouse Polish national interests on the Western frontier (Oder-Neisse) issue. They were mollified by a minor concession, presented by Nowak as a victory in a dispute on the larger policy issue that he in fact did not win.[132] Alexander's vacillation during these controversies, on top of his delay in cutting New York administrative staffs and shifting the RFE management headquarters to Munich, led the FEC Board, urged on (but not dictated to) by the CIA, to obtain Alexander's resignation, effective May 1, 1961.[133]

Disarray within RFE in the late 1950s was accompanied by pressure on the organization from without. The Soviet crackdown in Hungary and RFE's lapses in broadcasting to that country provided the State Department with cause and pretext to argue within the U.S. government for scaling back RFE broadcasts while increasing the State Department's policy influence over both RFE and RL. At issue was not policy oversight, always the prove-

129. E.g., "Nine Hungarians Sue Radio Free Europe" (in German), *Süddeutsche Zeitung,* May 18–19, 1957.

130. RFE memorandum, "Background on Czechoslovak Desk Situation," by J. David Penn, December 1, 1960, copy in DDRS.

131. *Frankfurter Allgemeine Zeitung,* December 21, 1960.

132. RFE memorandum to C. D. Jackson from Jan Nowak, October 14, 1960, copy in DDRS.

133. FEC press release, April 20, 1961. FEC chairman John C. Hughes, C. D. Jackson, Allen Dulles, and Cord Meyer discussed the matter on March 12, 1961. FEC general counsel Richard S. Greenlee provided a damning account of Alexander's management failures in an FEC memorandum addressed to FEC vice president Yarrow and an IOD officer, "Reorganization of Free Europe Committee, Inc."

nance of the department, but an effort to curtail RFE operations and involve State in daily broadcasting.

The State Department's bureaucratic offensive, originating in the Office of East European Affairs, championed by Ambassador Jacob Beam from Warsaw after 1957, and supported by Deputy Undersecretary of State for Political Affairs Robert Murphy, had four objectives: to halt RFE technical modernization and give budgetary priority to VOA; to restructure RL and devote part of its capabilities to Asian-African broadcasts; to begin the phase-down of RFE Polish and Hungarian broadcasts; and to reduce émigré involvement in RFE (ideally replacing émigré service chiefs with bilingual Americans). These proposals reflected misperceptions and were based on exaggerated views of three things: RFE's failings in Hungary, liberalization impulses of the Gomułka regime in Poland, and the influence of émigré organizations on RFE and RL broadcasts.[134]

The first step in this bureaucratic offensive was a Bureau of the Budget (BOB) freeze, requested by Robert Murphy, on RFE's previously approved Portugal transmitter modernization project and RL's pending Spanish transmitter project. The next step was the establishment at State Department initiative of an interagency Committee on Radio Broadcasting Policy (CRBP) outside the Operations Coordinating Board framework, comprising State, USIA, and CIA representatives and chaired by Deputy Assistant Secretary of State for Public Affairs E. Allen Leightner Jr. (who was knowledgeable about all the U.S.-funded radios from his past service as consul general in Munich). Murphy and Director of Central Intelligence Dulles agreed on March 2 that it was the responsibility of the CRBP to ensure that policies governing broadcasts "are consistent with [U.S. government] policies" and to define the respective roles of RFE, RL, VOA, and RIAS so as to eliminate duplication and maximize effectiveness.[135]

---

134. The opening shot in this offensive was a memorandum prepared in the State Department's Office of East European Affairs and forwarded to the CIA on January 10, 1957. The U.S. ambassador in Prague, U. Alexis Johnson, generally supported the office's proposals. Ambassador Bohlen in Moscow was indirectly critical of RL, although RL president Sargeant, having met with Bohlen, drew a more optimistic interpretation of his views. CIA memorandum to Helms from Meyer, May 1, 1957, released to the author in March 2009; AMCOMLIB memorandum of record from Sargeant, March 9, 1957.

135. CIA memorandum to Dulles from Helms, February 11, 1957, released to the author in March 2009; FEC memorandum to Condon from Griffith, March 30, 1957; FEC memorandum from CIA, WN (HL) 9015, August 2, 1957; Puddington, *Broadcasting Freedom,* 118–20.

Beginning in mid-1957, the CRBP issued a series of relatively standardized U.S. government policy guidances for each RFE, RL, and VOA broadcast country.[136] The FEC and AMCOMLIB then issued paraphrases of the documents, redacted to obscure their U.S. government provenance, as binding policy directives for RFE and RL.[137] USIA promulgated corresponding guidances for VOA.[138]

The 1957 CRBP guidances defined RFE's mission as promoting the autonomy of the Eastern European countries from the Soviet Union, including national Communist tendencies as an intermediate stage. RFE was to promote evolutionary internal change by constructively criticizing regime shortcomings and by offering information about alternative, especially European, approaches. It was to enhance its effectiveness through impartial and objective selection of news and comment. It was enjoined from engaging in condescension and excessive polemics (although it was not to dignify the Kádár regime by calling it a "government"), using inflammatory material, insulting national pride, offering tactical advice, and broadcasting dull commentaries. It could cover viewpoints differing from those of the U.S. government. It could also serve as an instrument of "unannounced" U.S. government policy—a notion never explained and never implemented.

All this differed little from FEC policy statements for RFE before the fall of 1956, albeit with more emphasis on the likely limits to liberalization, more broadcast prohibitions, and a certain amount of presumptuous involvement in broadcast technique (no "dull commentaries"). The significance of the country guidances, as Puddington noted, related less to specifics of broadcasting policy "than to the State Department's intention to play a more

---

136. The papers were drafted by the CRBP, shared with FEC and AMCOMLIB in draft, and the final versions incorporated broadcaster suggestions. The CRBP paper for the Soviet Union was "Gray Broadcasting Policy toward the Soviet Union," approved by Committee on Radio Broadcasting Policy, May 1, 1958, released to the author in October 2004. The CRBP country paper for Hungary, "RFE Broadcasting Policy towards Hungary," August 20, 1957, is reproduced by Puddington, *Broadcasting Freedom,* 326–36, which also summarizes the FEC version of the guidance for Czechoslovakia, 118–20.

137. FEC letter from CIA, WN (VS) 9060, August 22, 1957. The derivative FEC guidances were issued as Special Guidances 28–32 in the fall of 1957.

138. USIA memorandum to Larson from Bradford, August 29, 1957, NARA II RG 306, A141, box 1, declassified March 30, 2009; Nicholas J. Cull, *The Cold War and the United States Information Agency: American Propaganda and Public Diplomacy, 1945–1989* (Cambridge: Cambridge University Press, 2008), 144.

intrusive role in shaping the station's political approach."[139] To deemphasize émigré connections, the CRBP ruled that the names of the RFE services should be changed. The Voice of Free Poland (Głos Wolnej Polski), for example, would become the Polish Service of Radio Free Europe (Rozgłośna Polska Radia Wolna Europa).

This new U.S. government review process centered in the CRBP had several consequences. First was the precedent of State Department–drafted country broadcast policy papers (albeit with FEC and ABCOMLIB management input); theretofore the department had limited itself to approving general FEC- and AMCOMLIB-drafted papers. Second was the precedent of formal interagency review of broadcast policy and of selected broadcasts (generally weekly samples, in translation) in a venue where RFE and RL, represented by the CIA, were overshadowed by VOA, represented by USIA and State.

Third was the perhaps surprising conclusion of this official U.S. government review that RFE and RL programs, to be more effective, should be more "European" and less "American." To that end, the CRBP endorsed establishment of an RFE European Advisory Committee—an idea first entertained by the FEC in the early 1950s as the "Umbrella" project and recommended by the Council of Europe after 1956.[140] The CRBP emphasized that

---

139. Puddington, *Broadcasting Freedom,* 120. FEC management sought to emphasize the positive in the guidances, and thus expand its freedom of action, in a letter to the CIA, NW-OT-9100, November 14, 1957.

140. The Council of Europe's review of RFE's 1956 Hungarian broadcasts had led it to suggest more focus on European issues and involvement of Europeans in RFE broadcasting. Planning begin in 1957 for what would become the RFE West European Advisory Committee (WEAC), comprising former high officials and other prominent public figures from Western European countries. The FEC had in 1952 considered organizing such a group—the so-called Umbrella project—but found that prominent Europeans knew too little about the FEC and RFE to want to join (personal communications from Paul B. Henze, 2006; RFE memorandum by William E. Griffith and Richard Condon, April 4, 1953; FEC memorandum to Shepardson from Galantiere, " 'Umbrella' Committee, or Panel," August 6, 1954). Adverse publicity about RFE in the wake of the Hungarian Revolution led the U.S. government and the FEC to revisit the idea of a European committee of advisers. With State Department endorsement, Allen Dulles approved the project in May 1958, candidates were sought and endorsed, and the WEAC held its inaugural meeting in Paris in May 1959. The membership included such prominent Europeans as Robert Schuman, Paul van Zeeland, Sam Watson, and Alastair Buchan; FEC Letter to CIA, "West European Advisory Committee," FC-1258, May 28, 1959. In the 1960s and thereafter, the WEAC assisted RFE with European media relations, maintaining good relations with its host governments (Germany, Portugal, and later Spain), and providing testimonials to the U.S. government on the importance of the operation. See John Richardson Jr., *A New Vision for America: Toward Human Solidarity through Global Democracy—a Memoir* (New York: Ruder Finn Press, 2006), 107–10.

programming about America was the provenance of VOA, which was to concentrate its broadcasts on American policy and life and avoid commentary on domestic Eastern European issues.[141] Indeed, CRBP country papers for VOA emphasized more than had pre-1956 policy documents VOA's role as the official voice of the U.S. government. Fourth was the recommendation that broadcasts should have a stronger elite-focused component—leading to the inauguration in June 1958 of a "University of the Air" series of democracy programs concentrating on European experiences prepared at the College of Europe in Bruges for all five RFE broadcasting services.

The fifth consequence of the CRBP process was a series of detailed cautions, in the wake of Soviet suppression of the Hungarian Revolution, on avoiding broadcast tone or content that could give listeners unrealistic hopes about Western actions to free them from Communist rule. Sixth was a list of topics judged to be sensitive in bilateral relations, (for example, defections from Poland or the future of Cardinal Mindszenty, who remained in the U.S. Legation in Budapest) that were prohibited from broadcast without prior State Department approval. Seventh and most important was a marked inconsistency and ambiguity about the Radios' "surrogate function." The Polish country paper, for example, declared that RFE should support "temperate resistance to Soviet domination" and "evolutionary change" and "take advantage of the latitude that it enjoys as compared with [Western] government stations," and "concern itself with the internal affairs of Poland." Yet, the guidance cautioned, RFE "will avoid involvement in affairs which Poles in general would regard as peculiarly their own concern" and avoid "dwelling on aspects of internal conditions and shortcomings of which the Poles themselves are aware."[142] Such self-contradictory language led the IOD staff member then responsible for RFE to the (perhaps exaggerated) conclusion that, as defined by the CRBP, the area of overlap between RFE and VOA programming was almost 90 percent, raising the question of RFE's continued existence. The FEC's reaction was to emphasize the positive and to underline both RFE's latitude as a nonofficial station and the continued importance of commentary on domestic matters, strong language to refer to outright regime crimes and clear injustices, programs targeted at Communist elites, and programs on national heritage.[143]

141. Cull, *Cold War and the United States Information Agency,* 144.

142. FEC "Special Guidance on RFE Broadcasts to Poland," September 30, 1957. Nowak objected to the constraints of the guidance in memoranda to Hazelhoff dated November 4 and 6, 1957.

143. FEC memorandum to CIA/IOD, NW-OT–9100, November 14, 1957.

Beginning in 1958, the CRBP periodically reviewed a selected week of country broadcasts by RFE, RL, and VOA services. State Department reviewers generally took the lead and had little criticism of VOA broadcasts. Their evaluation of RFE was mixed. Bulgarian programming was judged positively; Romanian programming, critically ("avoidance of adequate discussion of Romanian internal issues"); Czechoslovak programming, generally positively, although some programs were characterized as "nonconstructive diatribe"; Hungarian programming, bland ("quite a number of programs were devoid of any interest to the Hungarian people"); and Polish programming, negatively. (The critique of Polish broadcasting is discussed in chapter 4.)[144]

RFE, RL, VOA, and RIAS broadcasting was also reviewed at the fourth annual "Schramm conference" of U.S. government-supported broadcasters held in Paris in September 1957. By then the State Department's anti-RFE campaign had weakened, and there was general agreement (except from the representative from the Prague Embassy) on the continued need for both VOA and RFE and RL. Reflecting the post-1956 atmosphere, the Schramm conference report emphasized that "evolution, not revolution, is the only programming policy now justified by political realities and audience temper. . . . The Satellite audience does not want us to broadcast *hope* to them. Our very presence is sufficient to suggest hope. The audience rather wants *realism*."[145]

Beset by internal demoralization and U.S. government pressure, the Radios also had their public detractors. Chastized by the State Department for broadcasts seen as too "hard," the Radios were simultaneously subjected to criticism from the American Right for being too "soft." Prominent radio commentator and columnist Fulton Lewis Jr. launched a multiple-month campaign in October 1957 against RFE in his syndicated Knight Features columns and his weekly Mutual Network radio broadcasts, accusing it of financial mismanagement, being soft on Communism, and receiving secret funding from the CIA. William F. Buckley Jr.'s *National Review* seemed to accept some of Lewis's accusations, calling editorially for an independent

---

144. FEC memoranda from CIA, February 27, 1959; WN 9822, June 27, 1958, WN-9823, June 27, 1958; WN 9929, September 9, 1958. The RFE Political Advisor's Office in Munich was more critical of Bulgarian programs. FEC memorandum to Griffith from Henze, "Shortcomings of our Bulgarians," June 29, 1957.

145. Cull, *Cold War and the United States Information Agency,* 146 n. 49, citing the Dwight D. Eisenhower Presidential Library's copy of the Report of the Chairman [Schramm]; emphasis in the original.

committee of anticommunists to survey FEC operations.[146] FEC and CIA officials, working with the White House staff, influential members of Congress, and finally Vice President Richard Nixon, were able to defuse the charges, and Lewis moved on to other causes.[147] His anti-RFE campaign, however unfair, did have one positive consequence. It hastened a series of internal reviews (including a Booz, Allen & Hamilton management study and a CIA inspector general study) that led to long-needed administrative reorganization of the FEC and RFE in 1960 and 1961.[148]

During this period, as before and since, some of the most dubious suggestions for the Radios came from their strongest supporters. C. D. Jackson, the inveterate political warrior, suggested to Allen Dulles in February 1959 that the U.S. government should react to renewed repression in Eastern Europe by reviving the concept of liberation to light "a powerful and effective counter-brush fire." Two years later, during the 1961 Berlin crisis, he would describe the Radios as "an instrument in being, which can be used to make the enemy say 'ouch' . . .—a program designed to create Soviet concern in Eastern Europe and to make Khrushchev think twice before pressing the Berlin issue."

All these developments led to questioning within the U.S. government about the very concept of unattributed or "gray" broadcasting and the utility of RFE and RL in particular, and to some soul-searching on these matters within the CIA itself. In the spring of 1960, Allen Dulles floated internally (how seriously is unclear) the notion of "Freedom Radios" that would merge RFE and RL, expand freedom broadcasts to other parts of the world, and become truly private enterprises free of CIA involvement. In 1959 the U.S. Advisory Committee on Information, chaired by Mark May and with cognizance over USIA, asked a series of pointed questions about RFE and RL that implied their declining value. The President's Committee on Information Activities Abroad chaired by Mansfield Sprague (the "Sprague Committee"), which was established in 1960 to update the "Jackson Committee" recommendations and included Allen Dulles and C. D. Jackson as members, concluded that RFE and RL had been "slow or unsuccessful in adjusting their message to changing conditions and prospects in the satel-

---

146. "Mr. Lewis and Radio Free Europe," editorial, *National Review*, March 29, 1958.

147. Nixon endorsed RFE at a Crusade for Freedom fund-raising luncheon in New York on March 16, 1960. RFE News Room release, March 18, 1960.

148. FEC copy, "Organizational Survey, Free Europe Committee, Inc.," Booz, Allen & Hamilton, July 30, 1958.

lite countries, and to changes in the United States broadcast policy line."[149] Assistant Secretary of State Foy Kohler, in discussion with the committee staff, saw no difference between the proper roles of VOA and RFE and RL.[150] A Kennedy administration national security directive gave USIA the authority to preempt RFE and RL broadcasts and use their facilities in case of national emergency.[151] Richard M. Bissell Jr., Frank Wisner's successor as CIA deputy director for operations from 1959 to 1961, sided with what seemed to be the perennial view of the Bureau of the Budget that "much of what is being done [by RFE] is of marginal value to the U.S. government" and later suggested that RFE facilities might be made available to private U.S. and European organizations.[152]

At the CIA working level, the IOD tried to involve itself more in FEC operations, generating a stream of recommendations on reorganizations, personnel changes, and broadcasting content. The IOD staff officer responsible for RFE noted, not inaccurately, that "FEC/RFE has hardening of the arteries; . . . the drive and imagination which characterized it in the early 1950s are no longer there." State Department and CIA policy guidances on the need for restraint and caution notwithstanding, Cord Meyer criticized the RFE editorial line in mid-1961 as "about as tough as limp spaghetti and more cautious than VOA." A member of his staff viewed the FEC New York Daily Guidance Summaries so negatively that he thought it a plus that they seemed to be ignored in programming. Searching for fresh ideas, IOD staff consulted some of the founding RFE managers, including program manager William Raphael and RFE director Robert Lang, both by then in commercial American radio, for suggestions on improvements. An IOD officer pointed to RFE and RL duplicative administrative and technical facilities (also flagged in the Booz, Allen & Hamilton management study) and seconded a suggestion from the Bureau of the Budget that the two organizations be merged. The IOD's lack of confidence in FEC management at the turn of 1961 was indicated by the tone of its reaction to the FEC monthly

149. "Conclusions and Recommendations of the President's Committee on Information Activities Abroad," December 1960, Helms Collection; redacted preliminary version in President's Committee on Information Activities Abroad; VOA/RFE/RL and RIAS, April 22, 1960, DDRS.

150. "Sprague Committee" memorandum of conversation, March 30, 1960, DDRS.

151. National Security Action Memorandum No. 63, July 24, 1961, released in full to the author in March 2009, redacted version at the John F. Kennedy Presidential Library.

152. CIA/IOD, memorandum of conversation [with BOB, State, USIA, and CIA officials], November 27, 1961, released to the author in March 2009.

policy directive for January 1961, which it found to be "incredibly naïve; . . . the draft appears to us beyond repair and should be discarded. . . . A major reorganization and personnel changes in the RFE policy structure are urgently needed."[153]

This general malaise was reflected in an FEC memorandum (unsigned, but evidently written by C. D. Jackson) as the Kennedy administration took office in early 1961:

> [The FEC] has suffered from a creeping demoralization because it felt that the Executive Committee South [that is, the CIA] was not fighting to preserve the spirit and purpose of the organization, but had actually allowed the purpose to be whittled away by the State Department, USIA, and NSC, that this excellent instrument of political warfare had become little more than the Poor Man's Information Agency. . . . Radio Free Europe . . . is in dreadful condition. It is torn asunder by the conflict between New York and Munich; it is permeated by a sense of impotence brought about by the constant emasculation of what it considers its rightful and needed function; it is irritated, if not enraged, by the systematic sniping at "exile domination" when it knows that the American personnel is intellectually incapable of exercising the right kind of control; it is depressed and frightened by constant budgetary pressure by business-office characters incapable of any qualitative appraisal.[154]

This was an apt description of the state of affairs in the FEC and RFE at the turn of 1961. The patient was indeed sick. But it would recover.

Appendix: A Note on the History of the 1956 RFE Hungarian Broadcast Archives

All RFE and RL programs were recorded at the transmitter sites as broadcast but retained for only a few months in accordance with German, Portuguese, and Spanish transmitter licensing requirements. Copies of these "log" tapes (programs recorded as broadcast over the transmitters at Biblis, Germany) of RFE Hungarian (and also Polish and Czech/Slovak) broadcasts for the period October 19–November 13, 1956, are available at the

---

153. FEC memorandum from the CIA, EC-1436, January 5, 1961.
154. Aide-memoire on the Free Europe Committee, March 6, 1961, DDRS.

Hoover Archives, the National Széchényi Library and Hungarian Radio in Budapest, and the Federal German Archives in Koblenz. These RFE tapes were used by the German Foreign Office for its own review and then deposited in the Federal German Archives. It is that accident of history that preserved them. Copies were retrieved from archaic media through cooperation between the Federal German Archives, Hungarian Radio, and RFE/RL. They have been transcribed in full by the National Széchényi Library. Only a few audio (studio) recordings of RFE Hungarian broadcasts for the years before and after these dates (until the 1960s) have been preserved. Copies of many program texts (scripts) for the period, organized by subject and not chronologically, are available on preservation microfilm at the Hoover Archives and the National Széchényi Library, through cooperation between those two institutions and RFE/RL. Some of the program texts are accompanied by English translations. The Hoover Archives contains a set of (often inaccurate) English summaries of major programs. The inaccuracy of these summaries is one explanation for why the RFE management was less knowledgeable than it should have been at the time about program content. Useful in interpreting the 1956 Hungarian broadcasts are the following RFE documents, all in the Hoover Archives: Office of the Political Advisor [Munich] Daily Analysis of Developments in Hungary, October 24–November 2, 1956, November 3–9, 1956, and November 10–16, 1956; Outline of Events and RFE Guidances up to and during the Hungarian Revolution of October–November 1956; Broadcast Review Staff [New York], political content report for weeks of October 20–26, October 27–November 2, and November 3–9, 1956.

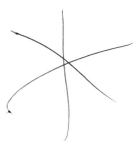

Chapter 4

Bridge Building in the 1960s

RFE emerged from its post-Hungary doldrums only in 1961, when it was revitalized under the leadership of a new FEC president, John Richardson Jr. A young lawyer who had passionately supported the cause of the Hungarian Revolution and then organized a flow of medicines to Poland after October 1956, Richardson implemented long-overdue management and administrative reforms. He immediately cut the worldwide staff of nearly 1,800 by more than 130 (some 50 in the New York headquarters). He transferred management of RFE from New York to Munich and confirmed as RFE director retired general G. Rodney Smith, who had been hired by FEC president Archibald Alexander as general vice president. Although Smith's background was in military logistics (and his lack of regional expertise initially concerned the CIA/IOD and Richardson), he quickly won the respect of the broadcast chiefs and American staff in Munich. R. V. Burks, an academic expert on Eastern Europe, became policy director, followed in the fall of 1965 by Ralph E. Walter (who had been an assistant to William Griffith, and who subsequently worked on émigré issues for the FEC and then headed the RFE office in New York). Walter reconstituted the system of country policy assistants that had collapsed after 1956, hiring for each RFE broadcast country young Americans with language and country knowledge.[1]

Richardson proved to be an effective bureaucratic infighter in Washington. He organized to good effect a dinner to bring together Munich broadcasting service chiefs with top officials of the Bureau of the Budget, State Department, and White House and demonstrate RFE's expertise. He pleaded

---

1. I served as policy assistant for Poland between September 1966 and September 1969.

continuously with the CIA for ample budgets.[2] He argued for an increase in the worldwide nonradio operations of the FEC and oversaw an expansion of the FEC's mission to the developing world, creating the International Development Fund to supply anticommunist émigré speakers and publications to developing countries facing Communist threats.[3] While maintaining regular contact with the CIA/IOD, including monthly visits to CIA Headquarters,[4] he actively pursued direct contacts with policymakers and occasionally made end runs around the CIA to the State Department, the White House, Attorney General Robert Kennedy, and members of Congress in his efforts to promote the FEC (and ensure its funding). He was able to obtain U.S. government approval for new RFE capital expansion projects.

Richardson was indeed a talented manager and skilled advocate within the U.S. government bureaucracies for the FEC. Cord Meyer considered him the most effective FEC president.[5] Richardson also had a crusading streak and, harking back to the role played by FEC directors in the early 1950s, sought not just to promote the FEC but also to influence overall U.S. foreign policy. Some of his efforts logically followed from his position as FEC president—for example, his suggestions to the State Department and the national security adviser in 1963 arguing against any kind of nonaggression agreement with the Soviet regime and seeking to counter the perceived demoralizing impact of détente on the Eastern European peoples.[6] Other policy initiatives, such as those advanced in contingency planning during the 1961 Berlin crisis, amounted to disinformation schemes (for example, a plan to plant false rumors about Soviet designs on Polish territory to exacerbate Soviet/Polish friction, or a plan to spread rumors of a UN peacekeeping presence on the Polish–East German border) that were impossible to reconcile with credible broadcasting and fortunately were never approved.[7] He

2. FEC personal letter to Richard Helms, June 28, 1962; FEC memorandum to CIA, FC 1194/63, October 10, 1963; FEC memorandum from CIA, EC 2870, October 23, 1963; FEC memorandum to CIA, FC 4192, April 20, 1966, FC 4280, May 13, 1966 (in which Richardson argued that it was absolutely essential to increase the FY1967 FEC budget allocation of $19 million by $200,000, i.e., 1 percent).

3. FEC memorandum by John Richardson, "The Free Europe Committee; A Description and a Proposal," October 27, 1961. Copy in DDRS.

4. John Richardson Jr., *A New Vision for America: Toward Human Solidarity through Global Democracy—a Memoir* (New York: Ruder Finn Press, 2006), 110.

5. Cord Meyer, *Facing Reality: From World Federalism to the CIA* (New York: Harper & Row, 1980), 115.

6. FEC letter to Bundy from Richardson, July 16, 1963.

7. Kennedy Administration National Security Action Memorandum No. 58, June 30, 1961, directed the secretary of state and the director of central intelligence to recom-

issued a broadcast guidance calling for an information campaign on the consequences of war in Europe based on the assumption that enhanced antiwar sentiment among Eastern Europeans could serve as a constraint on Soviet behavior. But he quickly revoked it in the face of opposition from both émigré and American managers in Munich, who argued that such a campaign linked to the Berlin crisis (as opposed to normal reporting) would be counterproductive and damaging to RFE's credibility.[8]

Richardson also succeeded in improving relations with the State Department. As RFE expanded its research and analysis capability, drawing on an increased flow of information from Eastern Europe, American (and other Western) embassies became dependent on RFE for information about the region (and even "their" countries). The chargé d'affaires in Budapest told RFE in 1962 that "we would simply be lost without your research papers."[9] On occasion embassies requested specific research studies that they lacked the capability to conduct, for example, analyses of the 1962 Czechoslovak Party Congress and of Sino-Czechoslovak relations requested by the Prague Embassy. Informal consultations between RFE and RL officials and analysts and U.S. Embassy officials visiting Western Europe became standard practice.[10] Deputy Undersecretary of State U. Alexis Johnson came to hold a more positive view of RFE than when he served as ambassador to Czechoslovakia from 1953 to 1958.[11] Embassy evaluations of RFE broadcasts, which had often been highly critical in the late 1950s, became generally pos-

---

mend contingency measures "for inciting progressively increasing instability in East Germany and Eastern Europe" to deter Soviet aggression in Berlin, document 53, in *Foreign Relations of the United States,* ed. U.S. Department of State (hereafter, *FRUS*) (Washington, D.C.: U.S. Government Printing Office, various years), 1961–63, vol. XIV. The CIA/IOD solicited ideas from the FEC but reacted negatively to the disinformation scheme; FEC memorandum from CIA/IOD, EC-1765, June 13, 1961. Richardson and FEC chairman Ernst Gross met with Secretary of State Dean Rusk on June 17 and presented their ideas in a paper titled "The Free Europe Committee and the Berlin Crisis." FEC directors C. D. Jackson and Whitney Debevoise followed up with Deputy Undersecretary of State U. Alexis Johnson on July 20; Jackson described the FEC and RFE as an instrument that "can be used to make the enemy say 'ouch'." An editorial in *Life* magazine on July 14, 1961, written by Jackson, claimed that "RFE has the power to stir up almost any degree of unrest that may suit our purposes." FEC memorandum to CIA from Richardson, FRC-5777, August 10, 1961. As in the 1950s, RFE Munich American and émigré chiefs were appalled by such rhetoric.

8. "FEC Guidance for RFE on the Berlin Situation," NYC telex 124, August 22, 1961; MUN telex 147, August 25, 1961.

9. FEC memorandum to CIA, FC 8057, July 30, 1962.

10. I participated in such consultations in Munich and Vienna.

11. Remarks to an RFE Fund luncheon, March 7, 1962.

itive. The Budapest Legation now viewed RFE as "still fill[ing] a special need in Western and U.S. media to Hungary." The Warsaw Embassy registered "the important place which RFE fills in the Polish society." The Bucharest Embassy viewed RFE broadcasts as "both technically and substantively effective." The Munich Consulate-General concluded that "RFE's chief value . . . lies in its ability, a unique one among Western radio stations, to broadcast accurate and timely comments on the internal developments in the target countries."[12] Senior State Department, USIA, Bureau of the Budget, and CIA officials agreed in the fall of 1962 on the continued importance of the FEC's operations and its requirement for sufficient funds. (The Bureau of the Budget remained generally skeptical, but assistant director Robert Amory, a former CIA official, was supportive). They also agreed that, as had been the practice before 1957, the FEC would henceforth take the initiative in drafting revised country broadcast policies and submit them to the CIA and the State Department for approval. Though financial budgets never met the FEC's expectations, operating budgets remained relatively constant in real terms, and additional capital funds for new transmitters in Portugal were approved in 1963.[13]

By 1962, RFE and RL had emerged from the doldrums, but without the personal support at the top of the U.S. government they had enjoyed in the past. With Allen Dulles' retirement from the CIA in the fall of 1961, the FEC could no longer look to the director of central intelligence himself as their advocate and "case officer." From 1962 to 1965, the highest CIA official regularly involved with the Radios was Richard Helms, the deputy director for operations. Helms had no involvement with the Radios in their early years, but he now became a steadfast supporter (and after 1965, as director of central intelligence, was instrumental in ensuring their survival at the turn of the 1970s). The Johnson White House, with other priorities, ended its promotion of the RFE Fund, as the Crusade for Freedom had been renamed in 1960. An internal administrative CIA task force recommended in 1965 that the CIA's control over the FEC (which was of more concern than the RLC) be increased.[14] Discussions within the U.S. government in 1965 on

12. Department of State airgrams: Budapest A-5, July 11, 1964; Warsaw A-107, July 30, 1964; Bucharest A-44, August 7, 1964; Munich A-8, July 7, 1964. All released by NARA, January 29, 2008.

13. CIA Letter to Richardson from Deputy Director of Central Intelligence Carter, January 4, 1963, released to the author in September 2007; FEC correspondence with CIA, FC 1194/63 and EC 2870, both October 1963.

14. The review concluded: "The Free Europe Committee, under officers and direc-

reviving a Radio Free Asia led National Security Advisor McGeorge Bundy to commission a "Panel on U.S. Government Radio Broadcasting to the Communist Bloc," charged with reviewing the continued relevance of RFE, RL, and VOA broadcasting and the advisability of a Radio Free China. The panel's four members (three of whom had been connected with or otherwise supportive of RFE in the past) recommended in April 1966 that "the present general missions of VOA, RFE, and RL be continued" and (with one abstention) endorsed the Radio Free China proposal.[15] The NSC accepted the panel recommendations, but the Radio Free China initiative became moot with the revelation in 1967 of CIA funding of the Radios.

Broadcasts and Controversies

The history of RFE (more so than RL) in the 1960s was shaped by interplay between what had become two distinct tracks of U.S. policy toward the Soviet bloc. The first track continued to focus on efforts via RFE and other information channels such as USIA libraries to influence Eastern European society—to keep hope of a better future alive, to give a voice to dissidents and political opposition, to promote civil society—in current terminology, to promote gradual system change using soft power. The new, second track of U.S. policy sought to influence the behavior of the Communist regimes themselves in a more liberal and national direction, and this required dealing directly with them.[16] It is the long shadow of the controversy over RFE's 1956 Hungarian broadcasts and the tension thereafter between the two tracks

---

tors convinced of their own independence and sometimes hostile to CIA, has taken the bit in its teeth to such an extent that its relationship with CIA is not that of a true proprietary. This independence has permitted waste, mismanagement, and costly excursions into [non-broadcasting] fields. . . . The Radio Liberty Committee . . . has remained responsive to the Agency's wishes."

15. "Report of the Panel on U.S. Government Radio Broadcasting to the Communist Bloc," April 28, 1966, released with minor redactions by NARA October 30, 1997, DDRS. The panel was comprised of Zbigniew Brzezinski, William E. Griffith, John S. Hayes, and Richard S. Salant. In contrast to the CRBP, which was dominated by the State Department, the CIA took the lead in organizing the panel and provided its staff director.

16. This was advocated by Brzezinski and Griffith in their 1961 article and by Brzezinski in his 1965 book. See Zbigniew Brzezinski and William Griffith, "Peaceful Engagement in Eastern Europe," *Foreign Affairs* 39, no. 4 (Spring 1961); and Zbigniew Brzezinski, *Alternative to Partition: For a Broader Conception of America's Role in Europe* (New York: McGraw-Hill, 1965).

of U.S. policy that explain the evolution of RFE and RL broadcasting in the 1960s.

RFE continued to provide a full broadcast menu of news, features, and entertainment, in line with its mission as a substitute home service. However, it now added programming for the elites. There were more programs on Western and especially Western European democratic institutions and on the ferment in the Communist world. In 1962 policy director R. V. Burks inaugurated a special series featuring translated documentation of the Sino-Soviet dispute, which was broadcast after midnight without commentary not for the general audience but for the express purpose of making these programs available to regime monitors who would transcribe them for top party leaders.[17]

The tension between the two tracks of U.S. policy toward Eastern Europe especially shaped the controversies about RFE's Polish and Romanian services in the 1960s.

Poland

As previewed in chapter 3, in-system reforms in Poland in the fall of 1956 led State Department officials to question the continued utility of RFE's Polish broadcasts.[18] The Warsaw Embassy (headed by Ambassador Jacob Beam after mid-1957) took a relatively optimistic view of Poland's liberalizing reforms (as did CIA analysts in the Directorate of Intelligence) and viewed RFE's Polish broadcasts as hampering their efforts to improve ties with and influence Polish Communist elites. The issue was joined early; State Department officials were critical of RFE's Polish broadcasts in the run-up to the Polish parliamentary election of January 20, 1957. They reacted in part to Western press articles uncritically reflecting Polish regime accusations.[19] RFE had given Gomułka the benefit of the doubt in October 1956, but the Gomułka regime (unlike the Romanian regime in the 1960s) never reciprocated and never viewed RFE as even a limited and conditional partner. RFE's Polish broadcasts in early 1957 in fact accepted the in-

17. FEC memorandum to Richardson from Burks, June 27, 1962.
18. Arch Puddington summarizes the controversy; see Arch Puddington, *Broadcasting Freedom: The Cold War Triumph of Radio Free Europe and Radio Liberty* (Lexington: University Press of Kentucky, 2000), 120–27.
19. *New York Times,* January 17, 1957, quoting *Trybuna Ludu*'s accusation that "RFE swindlers" were using preelection broadcasts to promote "anarchy instead of order" and "push Poland into the arms of the reactionaries."

evitability of Gomułka's single-slate ballot (the perceived alternatives being Polish Stalinists or Soviet invasion), yet pointed out that the elections were hardly free and reminded voters both of Gomułka's backsliding on promises to exclude candidates with unsavory pasts and their right to cross particular candidates off their ballots. Only one commentary went beyond providing information and offered tactical advice: "One should procure a pencil, and delete the names of all who are abhorrent to the community. Delete those who are the worst."[20]

RFE's detractors in both Washington and the Warsaw Embassy believed that blanket criticism of the Gomułka regime could cause it to backtrack on reforms that included improving ties with the West, allowing Poles to travel, and ending radio jamming within Poland. Hence the language of the FEC 1957 Polish country guidance that "RFE should address [issues in] its discussion of internal affairs . . . only to the extent that they serve to promote policy objectives with regard to Poland. It is of the utmost importance that the content and matter of such discussion [of Polish internal affairs] be carefully calculated to aid in the gradual attainment of objectives without stimulating or encouraging developments which might force a regime reversion to Stalinist methods or risk Soviet intervention."[21] The underlying assumptions were spelled out more clearly in the Committee on Radio Broadcasting Policy's original Polish guidance, which viewed Poland as the test case for evolutionary change, foresaw enhanced U.S. economic and cultural ties with Poland to promote that course, and defined broadcasting's primary task as providing straight news and information about the Western world.

The 1957 Polish country guidance was supplemented by a stream of ad hoc policy directives. A fall 1957 CIA/IOD guidance cleared with the State Department on broadcast coverage of the closing of the independent journal *Po prostu* emphasized that broadcasts should encourage restraint and nonviolence: "It is therefore essential to prevent a Hungary-type situation from developing, even though it may mean temporary (we hope) setbacks in some of the freedoms which the Polish people have forced from the So-

20. Polish Service commentaries by Tadeusz Zawadzki and W. Trościanko, January 9, 1957, and by S. Zadrozny, January 11, 1957. In response to State Department concerns, the "blacklist" program was discontinued by January 18; FEC NYC and MUN telex no. 148, January 18, 1957. Nowak instructed his staff on January 18 that "no program . . . can express any instructions, directives, advice, or appeals to the listeners"; RFE Munich telex MUN 145, January 18, 1957. RFE Polish broadcasts on the election were reviewed in FEC memorandum to Crittenberger from Egan, January 31, 1957.
21. "Special Guidance No. 29 on RFE Broadcasts to Poland," September 30, 1957, 4.

viets and the Polish regime."[22] This was an unnecessary admonition; restraint and nonviolence were precisely what the Polish Service had encouraged in June and October 1956 and thereafter. That Washington thought it needed to command restraint indicated how poorly it understood the role of the RFE Polish Service in 1956 and the outlook of its staff, and how much Soviet suppression of the Hungarian Revolution had overshadowed and distorted critical thought within the U.S. government about Eastern Europe.

The CRBP charter called for regular review of RFE, RL, and VOA broadcasts, creating a forum where State Department officials could object to specific RFE Polish programs. Reviewing a week of January 1958 broadcasts, for example, State Department representatives objected to only one VOA program but to fifteen RFE programs that, in their view, variously erred in wrongly disparaging the West German Social Democratic Party, raising the Polish Western border issue, overemphasizing Western military strength, suggesting proper voting behavior, fanning worker discontent, suggesting that the Rapacki Plan for European disarmament was of Soviet origin, publicizing a gloomy poem by Adam Ważyk, overreporting the Polish émigré press, oversimplifying the causes of Polish inflation, adopting a preaching tone, satirizing Marshal Rokosovsky, and misreporting Khrushchev's drinking habits.[23]

Such criticisms reflected less exaggerated concern about specific violations of agreed-on policy than fundamental reservations about the continued utility of RFE as even a restrained critic of the Gomułka regime. In that view, if RFE had to exist, the less it said about Polish internal affairs, the better. That view led the State Department to generally disapprove interviews with defectors, which according to the 1957 country guidance required advance Department approval. One such disapproved case was an interview with Andrzej Krajewski, who escaped with his family from Poland in October 1959 by flying a sports plane to Denmark.[24] Another escapee, Irena Świat-Ihnatowicz, provided material for a "New Class" series of broadcasts in late 1958 based on her experiences working in the household of the minister of industrial construction. A third escapee, Andrzej Zukowski, was interviewed on the situation of Polish Stalinists in prison. Interviews with the latter two were approved in advance by Erik Hazelhoff and William Grif-

22. FEC memorandum from CIA, WN(VS) 9213, October 8, 1957.
23. FEC memorandum from CIA, WN-9708, May 1, 1958.
24. The interview was recorded on March 20, 1960, submitted to the State Department, disapproved, and never broadcast. It is preserved in the RFE/RL Collection.

fith in Munich but broadcast without referral to the State Department, much to its consternation.[25]

It was the job of the State Department to deal with and attempt to influence the Gomułka regime, so it was inevitably sensitive to complaints about RFE from the Polish government. Such complaints were incessant and served to demonstrate RFE's impact. Polish foreign minister Adam Rapacki complained about RFE's focus on Polish internal affairs to Secretary of State Dulles in October 1957.[26] Gomułka repeatedly denounced RFE in a private meeting with Vice President Nixon in Warsaw on August 3, 1959 (with Milton Eisenhower, Ambassador Beam, and Deputy Assistant Secretary of State Foy Kohler present), claiming "the U.S. Government–financed RFE [pours] out hours of abuse daily into Poland."[27] Deputy Premier Piotr Jaroszewicz complained about RFE to Secretary of State Christian Herter in April 1960. In February 1959, Ambassador Beam, criticizing a number of specific RFE programs, suggested that the United States might be better served by dispensing with RFE and expanding VOA's Polish broadcasts. Beam's critique was seconded by Milton Eisenhower and by USIA director George Allen, following their visit to Poland with Nixon.[28]

A more pessimistic view of Polish political developments after 1956 was taken by the RFE Polish Service, by Griffith (who remained in Munich through 1958), and by the CIA/IOD, which generally defended RFE programming.[29] RFE could cite support for its approach from the Polish Catholic

25. FEC memorandum from CIA/IOD, EC-89, January 23, 1959; FEC memorandum to CIA/IOD, FC-469, February 13, 1959.

26. FEC memorandum from CIA, WN (VS) 9397, December 17, 1957.

27. Department of State, memorandum of conversation, August 3, 1959, released to the author in November 2006; document 74, in *FRUS, 1958–60,* X, part II.

28. USIA memorandum to the president from director George V. Allen, August 19, 1959, DDRS; Puddington, *Broadcasting Freedom,* 124.

29. Nowak outlined his views in an FEC memorandum to European Director Erik Hazelhoff dated August 27, 1959, copy in DDRS. "Any policy [the one Nowak attributed to the Warsaw Embassy] which puts excessive emphasis on the liberal tendencies of the Polish Communist leadership and underestimates the importance and role played by popular resistance must be self-defeating from the point of view of American objectives in Poland." The CIA/IOD provided its assessment in a January 1959 memorandum to Allen Dulles: "Our assessment of RFE's current broadcasts is that they are based on excellent information, that they are geared to straightening out the distortions in regime propaganda and preventing further slippage from the 'October freedoms,' that their policy is realistic, that it conforms with currently agreed-on policy papers, that while there is an occasional mistake, on the whole they are remarkably good and effective." It also conveyed its positive assessment directly to the Department of State; CIA/IOD memo-

Church. Hazelhoff, together with Jan Nowak and Father Tadeusz Kirschke (the Polish Service staff priest), were reassured about the Church's favorable view of RFE's Polish broadcasts by high Church officials who accompanied Cardinal Wyszyński to Rome in October 1958. Wyszyński himself always avoided direct contact with RFE, given the delicacy of his position, but during his Rome visit he denied (through Church intermediaries) press accounts (originating with the AP correspondent in Warsaw) that he had criticized RFE, adding that he viewed RFE as having a restraining influence on regime policy against the Church.[30] One of the intermediaries, Archbishop Józef Gawlina (head of the Polish Catholic Church outside Poland) repeated this endorsement the following year to both FEC president Alexander and Deputy Undersecretary of State Robert Murphy.[31]

The differences between the State Department and RFE about the Polish broadcasts were aired at length in a December 1958 meeting in Munich between Warsaw Embassy first secretary Thomas A. Donovan and Griffith. As recounted by Griffith, "As far as retrogression in Poland is concerned, Mr. Donovan stated that one could not see very many traces of it. . . . We . . . do not regard Mr. Donovan's comments re analysis or programming as valid. . . . Our basic guidances require us to combat [regression]"[32] Ambassador Beam and Kohler maintained that the Polish Service should be closed or limited in scope, and following a contentious meeting of State Department, CIA, and RFE officials on April 23, 1959, the FEC at the CIA/IOD's urging, and doubtless also in self-defense, directed further restraint in RFE's Polish broadcasts, including "striking more constructive, positive notes" about the Polish internal situation, and more control by the American management.[33] The CIA/IOD itself now became more critical, agreeing with the State Department after reviewing another week of programs that the

randum to Joseph W. Scott from Cord Meyer, March 18, 1959, dissenting from the negative evaluation of RFE programs in Warsaw Embassy dispatch 301, February 19, 1959, released to the author in March 2009.

30. FEC memorandum to Hazelhoff from Nowak, October 31 1958; FEC memorandum by Hazelhoff on conversations in Rome, November 3, 1958.

31. FEC memorandum to CIA/IOD from Alexander, August 31, 1959; FEC memorandum to Brown from Nowak, October 5, 1959, reporting on Gawlina's recent meeting with Murphy.

32. FEC memorandum by Griffith, December 29, 1958; Puddington, *Broadcasting Freedom,* 131.

33. CIA memorandum to Dulles from Meyer, April 28, 1959, released to the author in March 2009; FEC memorandum from CIA, EC-324, May 1, 1959; FEC memorandum to Hazelhoff from Brown, May 13, 1959.

broadcasts "do not carry out the spirit of Special Guidance No. 29. . . . The total impact of the broadcasts for this week is negative and pessimistic."[34]

The dispute became heated and spilled over into the Western media and into RFE's Polish broadcasts (through RFE interviews with Polish travelers).[35] Reacting to George Allen's blanket critique of the Radios to President Dwight D. Eisenhower, C. D. Jackson used the occasion of a dinner with the president and other top officials on September 10 to argue the utility of political broadcasting alongside diplomacy. "For ambassadors to be getting high blood pressure because an instrument of political warfare is 'making trouble' for them is ridiculous."[36] Jackson was supported by Vice President Nixon, who during his visit to Poland the previous month had been impressed by RFE's role in reporting his itinerary (not publicized by official Polish media) resulting in large welcoming crowds—a positive view only strengthened by Gomułka's private diatribes.[37] The controversy was only moderated in meetings in September and October 1959 between Allen Dulles, Ambassador Beam, Foy Kohler (now assistant secretary of state for Europe), and FEC president Alexander.[38] Kohler continued to believe that RFE was far too critical of the Gomułka regime and "was on the verge of being counterproductive."[39] Ambassador Beam continued to view some RFE Polish programming as excessively negative and polemical. USIA director George Allen regularly questioned a continuing need for RFE and RL. And lower-level State Department officials continued to object to the scope of RFE's Polish broadcasts on events such as the April 1961 Polish elections.

This controversy about the effectiveness of U.S.-sponsored surrogate broadcasting to Poland after 1956 developed from different assumptions

34. FEC memoranda from CIA, EC-417, June 12, 1959; EC-651, September 3, 1959.

35. *New York Times,* July 10 and 11, 1959; Philippe Ben dispatch, *Le Monde,* July 16, 1959; *Neue Zürcher Zeitung,* July 27, 1959; Information Item 3202/59, "Polish Intellectual Comments on Ambassador Beam's Criticism of RFE," July 30, 1959; FEC memorandum to CIA, FC-1591, July 14, 1959.

36. Undated memorandum by C. D. Jackson, as cited by Puddington, *Broadcasting Freedom,* 125.

37. See ibid., 125–26.

38. *New York Times,* July 7 and 11, 1959; FEC letter to Board of Directors from Alexander, August 13, 1959; CIA memorandum of conversation [with Undersecretary of State Douglas Dillon and Ambassador Beam] by Dulles, September 15, 1959, released to the author in March 2009; FEC memorandum from Alexander, September 15, 1959, a sanitized version of Dulles' memorandum.

39. Comments to the "Sprague Committee" staff, memorandum of conversation, March 30, 1960, DDRS.

about the political dynamics in Poland. Was the glass half full and filling? Or was it half empty, and emptying? The State Department and especially the Warsaw Embassy and Ambassador Beam—who had to deal with regime officials daily in implementing the U.S. policy of promoting cultural, educational, economic, and personal ties between Poland and the West—took a relatively optimistic view of Poland's internal relaxation and autonomy from the USSR.

RFE, conversely, was focused on promoting evolutionary system change and drew more pessimistic conclusions. By the mid-1960s, it became apparent to all observers that RFE's interpretation had been proven correct and was by then generally accepted throughout the U.S. government. So it was appropriate for RFE commentaries to take a critical approach to internal Polish developments after 1956. But the Polish Service would have strengthened its position within the FEC and in Washington if its programs had been more responsive to the spirit of the August 1957 policy guidance and included more coverage of Western European developments, more elite-focused programs, and less negativism and personal invective.[40] Reviewing RFE's Polish broadcasts in the fall of 1959 from his new position at the Massachusetts Institute of Technology, William Griffith called for more objectivity in RFE's Polish programming, which he judged "close to an all-out attack on the regime. . . . Anti-regime polemics are often extreme in tone and are frequently concentrated on Gomułka personally."[41]

It was personal invective, a matter of style and tone more than content, that provided the most ammunition to the critics of the Polish Service. As one example, Vice Minister of Education Eugenia Krassowska had been helpful to the United States in starting up Ford Foundation exchange programs in Poland. So one can understand the unhappiness of the Ford Foundation, the State Department, and Ambassador Beam when an RFE commentary described her as a "venomous ant."[42] Such ad hominem attacks violated the prohibitions of the 1957 and revised 1960 country broadcast policy guidances on avoiding vituperation and sarcasm. Though not a daily occurrence, they happened often enough to concern the U.S. government

40. The CIA/IOD, which generally supported RFE against State Department criticisms, criticized RFE on these grounds in mid-1959; FEC memorandum from CIA/IOD, EC-417, June 12, 1959, with appendix, "Critical Comments on RFE Polish Scripts for 14–20 March 1959."

41. William E. Griffith, "RFE and the Polish Situation," November 4, 1959, RFE/RL Collection.

42. Wiktor Trościanko, "The Other Side of the Coin," October 25, 1960.

and distorted its overall assessments of the content of RFE broadcasts. And though perhaps music to the ears of some listeners, such personal criticisms were not essential to effective programming and were harmful to the FEC and RFE in Washington. Both Polish Service director Jan Nowak and the RFE American management can be faulted for allowing them to continue.

As the Gomułka regime in the 1960s continued to retreat from many liberalization measures of 1956–57, the U.S. Embassy in Warsaw and State Department officials in Washington responsible for Eastern European affairs came to share RFE's analysis of post-1956 political regression and endorse RFE's usefulness in Poland. A revised FEC 1960 guidance on broadcasting to Poland, while retaining all the restraints of the 1957 guidance, reemphasized the importance of RFE's mission to "provide the Polish nation by radio with a truly 'free press' which will inform and support them in defending, and if possible, expanding their 'margin of freedom,' while throwing an *accurate, balanced* spotlight on moves which clearly work against freedom."[43]

Personnel changes on both sides also helped defuse the controversy, as First Secretary Donovan left Warsaw and the new American management under Rodney Smith took over in Munich. By August 1961, when he met Smith in Munich, Ambassador Beam had become more positive about RFE, describing it as a "decided plus in furthering U.S. objectives in Poland."[44] Thereafter, in contrast to its earlier evaluations, the Warsaw Embassy regularly offered positive evaluations of RFE's Polish broadcasting,[45] and praised its publicity of cases of internal repression, such as the trial in 1964 of Melchior Wańkowicz (a writer sentenced but then released for allegedly

43. FEC memorandum, "RFE Broadcasting Policy toward Poland," January 13, 1960; emphasis in the original. This guidance was based on a revised CRBP guidance issued on October 21, 1959, and finalized at a meeting on that day between Dulles, Kohler, Beam, and Alexander.

44. In the 1970s, Ambassador Beam became chairman of the FEC Board and one of RFE's strongest advocates, defending it against criticism from Richard T. Davies, then ambassador in Warsaw, which he dismissed as "localitis." See FEC memorandum, "Report on a Trip to Europe, January 23–February 1, 1975, by Jacob D. Beam; Walter interviews with the author.

45. In mid-1962, the embassy granted that its analysis had changed and it now viewed RFE as doing "an effective job in an important and complex undertaking." It added in mid-1964: "There is no question about its value as a bridge of truth to the Polish people. . . . The reporting officer . . . has been particularly impressed during the last year or two with the important place which RFE fills in the Polish society. It appears to be growing more important." Warsaw Embassy A-107, July 30, 1964.

providing a dissident text to RFE). A further revision of the Polish country guidance in 1964 reiterated that it was RFE's task to provide Poland with a radio "free press" that would support the Polish people's "margin of freedom" while highlighting regressive developments.[46] A subsequent directive by RFE policy director Burks stated that "a major task of the Polish [Service] will be to help prevent further retrogression in Poland."[47] But RFE remained conscious of the need for restraint. Noting in mid-1964 increased economic difficulties, intellectual protest, and assertiveness by the Catholic Church, FEC president Richardson emphasized the need for RFE's Polish broadcasts to exercise restraint by "continued scrupulous observance of the cautionary clauses written into the [country guidances]" while making every effort "to channel popular pressures along paths which are at the same time non-violent and effective for the attainment of limited constructive goals."[48]

The convergence of State Department and RFE views after 1961 on the general contours of Polish political developments did not end the controversy between them on specific issues. In the early 1960s, the two organizations came to disagree on the nature and significance of the so-called Partisan faction within the Polish Communist Party made up of secret police veterans led by Interior Minister Mieczysław Moczar.[49] Drawing on "inside information" from Polish informants and Western journalists based in Warsaw, RFE on June 30, 1962, inaugurated a six-part series on Moczar's effort to take over the party leadership from Gomułka. State Department and CIA analysts were dubious. It was neither surprising nor illegitimate for analysts in different organizations to make differing judgments about developments within Communist regimes. In this case, however, the differing analyses resulted in a successful effort by the State Department to control RFE broadcast policy on the issue. Much bureaucratic paper was devoted on all sides to assessing whether the "Partisans" were indeed an organized

46. "Radio Free Europe Broadcasting Policy toward Poland," enclosure to FEC memorandum from CIA, EC-2958, May 7, 1964.

47. RFE memorandum, "Special Guidance for Broadcasts to Poland," June 1, 1964.

48. FEC memorandum by John Richardson, "Special Memorandum on the Situation in Poland," May 14, 1964.

49. See A. Ross Johnson, "Poland: The End of the Post-October Era," *Survey,* July 1968; David Floyd dispatch, *Daily Telegraph,* July 2, 1962; RFE memorandum to Burks from Nowak, July 11, 1962; RFE background report, "The 'Partisan' Group in Poland's Communist Party," July 30, 1962; FEC memorandum, "Genesis, Outcome, and Consequences of the 'Partisans' Coup d'État in June of 1963," April 1, 1964.

"faction" or only an inchoate intraparty "grouping," whether they aimed to oust Gomułka or only to influence him, and how they should be treated in RFE's Polish broadcasts. State Department policy guidance, relayed through the CIA, in fact banned programs (including Western press surveys) focused on the issue and even forbade use of the term "faction" in broadcasts between 1962 and 1966.[50]

The entire controversy about the "Partisans" was less harmful than unnecessary. It demonstrated RFE's potential to influence developments within the upper levels of the Polish Communist Party (while raising the questions about whether RFE overestimated the strength and cohesion of the "Partisan" grouping and whether in any case the anti-"Partisan" campaign was a legitimate activity for a surrogate broadcaster). It also illustrated the temptation for U.S. government policy officials in the 1960s, having accepted the continued utility of RFE and RL, to attempt to micromanage covertly the ostensibly nongovernmental overt broadcasters, RFE and RL, on domestic Soviet Bloc political issues.

If bureaucratic controversy about the "Partisans" and the resulting restrictions on RFE's Polish broadcasts on the subject were a case of State Department policy overreach, the same cannot be said about State's policy guidance on the broadcast treatment of Poland's western frontier on the Oder-Neisse rivers. World War II had moved Poland some 200 miles westward; it had been forced to surrender eastern Poland to the USSR while gaining control of former German lands in the West. Polish sovereignty over the latter was a sine qua non for all Poles, noncommunists no less than Communists. But the Potsdam Agreement had defined the Oder-Neisse border as provisional, pending a German peace treaty, and American presidents and the German chancellor regularly restated this policy position. The FEC

---

50. FEC president Richardson first directed a halt to the broadcasts on July 19, citing sensitive intra-U.S. government discussions on RFE transmitter modernization. FEC memorandum, July 25, 1962; FEC telex NYC 92, July 19, 1966. An FEC "Special Guidance on the Polish Partisans," September 29, 1962, formalized the ban. The FEC (lacking CIA / Covert Action Staff support) tried and failed to ease the restrictions in 1965. FEC memorandum to CIA, FC-3018, February 2, 1965; FEC memorandum from CIA, EC-2348, February 9, 1965; FEC memorandum to CIA, FC-3074, February 17, 1965. The restrictions were lifted only in July 1966 (FEC memorandum to CIA, FC-4398, June 30, 1966; FEC memorandum from CIA, EC-2463, July 25, 1966) after the Panel on U.S. Government Radio Broadcasting to the Soviet Bloc raised the issue with higher State Department officials and after RFE had prepared a series of broadcasts with Polish military defector Władysław Tykociński, who discussed the Partisan faction (and long after the subject had been widely discussed in the Western press).

made clear before the inauguration of Polish broadcasting from Munich the constraints this policy imposed: "What is certain is that the Western powers . . . have no present intention of offending the Germans by agreeing to demands that they here and now guarantee the present Western frontiers of Poland. . . . The Oder-Neisse line is not a frontier problem; it is a European problem. . . . RFE prefers that this topic be discussed as little as possible by the Voice of Free Poland."[51] Preparing in 1952 the future broadcasting license for RFE (discussed in chapter 2), the German Foreign Office made clear to the FEC its expectation that "the subject of the Oder-Neisse line should not be treated in RFE broadcasts." In providing the German government with its assurance—a condition of the license—that RFE "will abstain from supporting or promoting political endeavors which in the opinion of the Federal Government are in conflict with basic objectives of its policy," the FEC explicitly included the Oder-Neisse and other German border questions.[52] German officials nonetheless immediately faulted some of the broadcasts for violating this pledge.[53]

An unconstrained "surrogate" Polish service would have espoused without reservation the permanence of Poland's post–World War II Western border. In principle, RFE's broadcast services had some latitude to carry material that did not reflect U.S. policy. The 1960 RFE Polish country guidance stated that RFE "may give fair coverage to significant viewpoints which are not necessarily in accordance with the views of the U.S. Government." But the guidance also stated that RFE broadcasts "must not prejudice American interests," and on the Oder-Neisse issue this was the operative phrase. RFE was constrained by U.S. policy and especially by its German location. American interests in a stable, pro-Western Federal Republic of Germany took precedence over immediate Polish interests. It was the State Department's proper responsibility in the 1950s and 1960s to insist that RFE commentary and features on the issue (as distinct from news reports) not get ahead of U.S. and West German policy (and German domestic politics). That would have threatened U.S.–West German relations. More specifi-

51. FEC memorandum, "Guidance No. 13 for Broadcasts to Poland," March 6, 1952.

52. FO letter to Condon from Kaumann, 454-08 II/9764/52, August 6, 1952, FOPA, B10, band 1908, A5488; FEC letter to Hallstein.

53. Letter to U.S. consul-general Charles J. Thayer from Bavarian minister-president Hans Ehard, October 8, 1952, objecting to a Polish Service broadcast on September 19, 1952 (Trościanko, "Other Side of the Coin"), which referred to territories "recovered . . . after years of German and Soviet occupation," copy in FOPA, B10, band 1908, A5489.

cally, it would have given German officials grounds to question continuation of RFE's broadcasting license, which as noted in chapter 2 reserved the Bonn government's right to review all broadcasts and order immediate cessation of transmissions it judged to harm German interests. In the years 1970–71, the Foreign Office would formally review RFE's Polish broadcasts—the second of only two such cases of German review of broadcasts in RFE's entire history. As much as the RFE Polish Service chafed at these restrictions, it and RFE would not have survived had they been blatantly violated.

As noted in chapter 3, broadcast policy on the Oder-Neisse issue was the immediate cause of the Polish Service's threatened strike in October 1960. Though most requests referred to the State Department in 1960 for clearance of Oder-Neisse programs had been granted, the process was cumbersome, some proposed programs were killed preemptively within the FEC, and the Gomułka regime stepped up its press attacks on the Polish Service for failing to distance itself from statements by Chancellor Adenauer and other influential West Germans that the Oder-Neisse boundary remained provisional. When approval was withheld for a Polish broadcast on an upcoming Polish-American Congress meeting in the United States that would have discussed the border issue, the entire Polish Service staff threatened to strike, protesting that "instead of countering Communist propaganda we are, in fact, helping the Communists to create the impression among our listeners that only they are defending Polish interests in this vital issue."[54]

After meeting with the FEC and RFE management on October 18, Allen Dulles brokered compromise program language with Foy Kohler that Nowak accepted, over the objections of some of his staff, and the strike was averted. Though the Polish Service thus won a minor concession in October 1960, basic policy restrictions on broadcast treatment of the Oder-Neisse issue remained.[55] The controversy was reported in the German press, and RFE

54. RFE Polish Service staff statement, October 13, 1960.

55. FEC memorandum by Archibald Alexander, "Post-Mortem on Oder-Neisse and Polish American Congress Scripts and Threatened Polish Desk Sit-Down," November 1, 1960. Nowak chronicled restrictions on the Oder-Neisse material in an FEC memorandum to Hazelhoff on April 13, 1960, and in an FEC memorandum to C. D. Jackson, October 14, 1960, copy in DDRS. A compromise was made more difficult when in September two of Nowak's commentaries endorsed by RFE management were disapproved, while a Trościanko commentary of September 29 with a minor endorsement of the Oder-Neisse was broadcast without clearance. Hazelhoff was entirely sympathetic to the arguments of the Polish Service, but was prepared to fire everyone if they stopped work; RFE Munich telex, MUN 19, October 18, 1960. At the time, Nowak saw the out-

management sought to reassure the Foreign Office that "the case demon-strates careful American oversight of the content of broadcasts to be sure that nothing is said that could in any way contradict German interests."[56] When the Polish Service (with RFE management approval and notification to the CIA) covered statements in support of the Oder-Neisse border made at the 1961 Polish Constitution Day celebrations in the United States, the State Department objected to the CIA's failure to obtain advance clearance. State rejected efforts by the FEC in 1961 and 1962 to ease the restrictions on Oder-Neisse coverage.[57] Nowak attempted to force the issue again in July 1964 after the revised June 1964 policy paper for Poland was issued, declaring that "we [the Polish Service] feel unable to accept the policy pa-per in its present form." RFE director Smith, never one to countenance in-subordination, met privately with Nowak; "the upshot is of course that the guidance is operative and Nowak is preparing a new memo of agreement for presentation to the [RFE management] policy board."[58]

The best efforts of FEC president Richardson notwithstanding, restric-tions on broadcasts about the Oder-Neisse border were significantly eased only in 1966 as Germans gradually reconciled themselves to the loss of what was still commonly called "Eastern Germany."[59] The restrictions were

---

come as a "victory," but he complained in spring 1964 that "RFE policy [on the West-ern border issue] has become recently more rigid and prohibitive than at any time be-fore"; see Jan Nowak-Jeziorański, *Wojna w eterze* (Kraków: Znak, 2000), 396–97. Also see FEC memorandum to RFE director Chester Ott from Nowak, April 17, 1964.

56. *Süddeutsche Zeitung,* December 7, 1960; RFE letter to the Foreign Office from Ernst Langendorf, December 16, 1960, FOPA, B12, band 387.

57. FEC memorandum from CIA, EC-1906, August 11, 1961; FEC memorandum from CIA, EC-2096, December 12, 1961, responding to FEC memorandum to CIA, FC-6188, October 19, 1961 with enclosure, "The Oder-Neisse Issue and Radio Free Eu-rope," September 2, 1961; FEC memorandum from CIA, EC-2958, May 7, 1964, which stated that "it would be feared that active discussion of the German-Polish boundary is-sue in RFE broadcasts would be stimulated rather than 'de-activated,' which the [CRBP] considered prejudicial to stated U.S. policy and long-term interests."

58. RFE memorandum to Burks from Nowak, July 27, 1964; RFE memorandum to Burks and Collins from Smith, July 30, 1964; RFE informal memorandum to Burks from Collins, August 8, 1964; revised RFE memorandum to Burks from Nowak, August 8, 1964.

59. Ostdeutschland, as distinct from Mitteldeutschland or "Middle Germany," the appellation for the German Democratic Republic. An FEC memorandum from CIA, EC-2447, dated March 29, 1966, recorded U.S. government approval to permit limited fea-tures and commentaries on the issue with the advance approval of the director of RFE. These changes were proposed by the FEC in a memorandum to the CIA, FC-3987, Feb-ruary 1, 1966.

eliminated entirely only in 1972, when a treaty between West Germany and Poland legitimized the postwar border.

More important in the mid-1960s than these policy controversies was the role the RFE Polish Service began to play in reinforcing domestic political dissent. By then, the Polish variety of Communism had degenerated into a peculiar hard/soft system—prosecutions and harsh prison sentences for political transgressions, on the one hand, and continuing liberalization of foreign travel and contacts with the West, on the other. This mixture of repression and relaxation spawned the first significant indigenous opposition currents—the "Open Letter to the Party" of then-Marxist dissidents Jacek Kuroń and Karol Modzelewski, the 1964 "Letter of 34" dissident intellectuals, and the student revolt of March 1968. RFE became the megaphone for these first stirrings of indigenous opposition, regardless of political cast, Marxist and non-Marxist.

RFE's ability to cover Polish internal developments was facilitated by the relative opening up of communication from Poland, which permitted broadcasters and officials to maintain personal contacts with important Polish individuals traveling in the West.[60] There were frequent contacts with the Polish Church hierarchy and, most important, regular meetings in Rome between the Polish Service staff priest, Father Tadeusz Kirschke, and Archbishop Bolesław Kominek of Wrocław and Archbishop Gawlina, representing the Polish Catholic Church outside Poland. Lay Catholic leaders of the Znak parliamentary group, including Stanisław Stomma, Jerzy Turowicz, Jacek Woźniakowski, and Stefan Kisielewski, regularly met Polish Service broadcasters in the West. A Polish Service broadcaster had met in 1956 in Rome with reform economist Oskar Lange (then briefly a member of the reformist Polish government, who urged RFE to be a "positive opposition"). Nowak later met with other regime figures traveling in the West, including by his own account (to the present author) Mieczysław Rakowski (then chief editor of the weekly *Polityka,* later the Communist Party first secretary). Polish Service broadcasters also met with regime journalists (including Ignacy Krasicki), parliamentary deputies (including Konstanty Łubieński), and others. The motives for and utility of these conversations varied. Some interlocutors simply wanted to provide RFE with information to improve its broadcasts. Other interlocutors, such as Krasicki, sought to

60. E.g., an RFE Polish Service memorandum dated December 17, 1962, reporting writer Jan Kott's views on developments in Polish cultural and political cycles, as expressed in conversation with Polish Service staff in Italy earlier that month.

embroil RFE in intraparty factional conflict. Still other interlocutors were simply Interior Ministry messengers charged with the task of acquiring information about RFE or encouraging redefections. In varying degrees, all served RFE as a source of information about developments inside Poland.

These personal contacts supplemented information that RFE gathered by monitoring regime media and by interviewing travelers, including some officials, in its news bureaus around Western Europe. The Polish Service also benefited from a number of informal "correspondents" in Poland. Two such contributors became well known after 1989. One, Józef Szaniawski, a journalist working for the official Polish News Agency, for twelve years provided RFE with information about Poland that he gathered in the course of his official duties but that could not be published in Poland (or could only be published in internal Communist Party bulletins). He was jailed in 1985 for his cooperation with RFE, and was released only in 1990. The other, Władysław Bartoszewski, the foreign minister after 1989, supplied "inside information" to RFE for three decades via the Austrian Culture Center in Warsaw.[61]

RFE's mission, in Poland as elsewhere, was never to foment revolution, but to "keep hope alive" and maintain a tie with the West (in which it succeeded), and in the years before 1956 to encourage the formation of a passive opposition movement (at least in Czechoslovakia and Hungary, in which it failed). Now its role—which would become its most important one—was to report, comment on, and in the process help expand authentic, existing opposition voices. Its role was to be a megaphone. Its coverage of intellectual ferment in Poland in the 1960s was followed by coverage of the December 1970 protests on the Baltic Coast characterized by the same prudence evidenced in its reporting on the 1956 events in Poland.[62] Reacting to criticism of some 1970 broadcasts by the Polish government and the State Department, a CIA assessment of early 1971 concluded:

> In [our] judgment totality of coverage was entirely responsible and [the Polish Service] performed with exceptional competence and professional

61. Szaniawski's and Bartoszewski's remarks at a conference on Radio Free Europe in Polish and Western politics, Warsaw, November 30–December 1, 2007, in *Radio Wolna Europa w polityce polskiej i zachodniej,* ed. Andrzej Borzym and Jeremy Sadowski (Warsaw: Stowarzyszenie Wolnego Słowa, 2009), 137–68.

62. FEC memorandum, "Insight into a Relationship: A Study of the Polish Crisis of 1970–1971 and Radio Free Europe Broadcasts," May 15, 1971.

brilliance during the crisis and subsequently. Charges that it deviated from established policy guidelines or was guilty of irresponsible broadcasting are without foundation.

The laudatory record of the Polish Service in the second half of the 1960s and early 1970s notwithstanding, there were occasional missteps. In May 1965, the Polish Service broadcast a "manifesto" or "composite" that reflected genuine opposition voices in Poland but was created as a document in Munich, not Poland—an error criticized by FEC management and not repeated.[63] Its special programming on the regime-controlled 1965 elections correctly pointed out voters' legal right to cross off names from the single list of candidates but violated the prohibition on tactical advice in again (as had happened in January 1957) seeming to single out specific names for deletion. The broadcasting of a scurrilous protest song on February 8, 1970, the use of unconfirmed "inside information" obtained through personal contacts, and instances of ad hominem criticisms of Communist leaders led RFE director Walter to insist on prior discussion of all broadcasts using "inside information."[64] Nowak dutifully complied and discussed sensitive political commentaries with Walter in advance, and though there was agreement on most of them, some program language was modified at Walter's request, and occasionally a Polish Service script (including some written by Nowak) was rejected.[65] But problems continued. A January 1971 commentary, broadcast contrary to redaction by Nowak's deputy, mocked Communist Party leader Stanisław Kociołek. Chapter 8 will discuss how such personal invective would once again become both cause and pretext for more

63. RFE Special Polish Program No. 3019, May 29, 1965; RFE Daily Guidance Summary, May 29, 1965; FEC memorandum to Richardson from Ott, June 5, 1965, with Richardson's annotation of June 8, "The action violated my basic policy as well as basic guidance."

64. RFE memorandum to Broadcasting Department directors from Walter, "Use of Criticism in Broadcasting; Need for Reliable Information and Facts," June 9, 1970. Nowak, in a memorandum to his deputies dated June 10, insisted on strict adherence to these guidelines.

65. An example of a modified text was Nowak's commentary of January 27, 1971, "In Search of a Third Way," which initially described "Moczar's methods" as "corpses, beating, etc."; FEC memorandum to Durkee from Walter, February 1, 1971. An example of a rejected text was Nowak's proposed program of December 21, 1970, using alleged eyewitness accounts of regime atrocities in the crackdown on the Polish coast; FEC memorandum to Durkee from Walter, December 21, 1970, enclosing the text of the proposed program.

generalized criticisms of RFE's Polish broadcasts in Polish regime circles, in Washington, and in Bonn.

Romania

In the mid-1960s, many Western observers of the Soviet Bloc, disappointed by Gomułka's backtracking on foreign policy autonomy and domestic reform, turned their attention to Nikolae Ceauçescu's Romania as a promising example of "national Communism." They focused on the autonomous role in international affairs to which Romania seemed to aspire as it distanced itself from Soviet policies on a number of issues of importance to the United States. Romania took a neutral position on the Sino-Soviet dispute, established diplomatic relations with West Germany, refused to follow the Soviet lead and sever relations with Israel after the June 1967 war, opposed Soviet intervention in Czechoslovakia in 1968, delayed tighter Soviet control over the Eastern European military establishments, and in 1972 ended cooperation with the KGB and Eastern European intelligence agencies.

It was a straightforward matter for RFE and RL to "cross-report" the emerging Romanian foreign policy deviation to the rest of its broadcast region. This was in line with the policy of informing audiences about developments elsewhere in the Soviet orbit pointing in the direction of foreign policy autonomy. The revised RFE Romanian broadcasting guidance approved by the CRBP in 1965 emphasized RFE's role in promoting "the strengthening and consolidation of Romanian independence from Soviet control, the expansion of Romanian relations with the West."[66]

As for domestic conditions in Romania, while the Romanian Service continued to point out shortcomings, RFE, like most Western observers, initially viewed the Ceauçescu regime as an improvement over that of its predecessor. RFE's Romanian broadcasts generally complied with the language of the 1965 guidance that "comment on internal affairs should be essentially constructive, calm and reasoned, avoiding a belligerent tone [as well as] denunciation and personal attacks or ridicule."[67] Ceauçescu, for his part, seemed initially to find RFE more useful internationally in publicizing and reinforcing Romanian autonomy within the Soviet Bloc than threatening to

66. "Radio Free Europe Broadcasting Policy toward Romania," EC-2375, April 12, 1965.
67. Ibid.

his regime at home. Attempting to put the best face possible on Romanian policies in order to improve relations with the West, Ceauçescu continued the practices introduced by his predecessor, Gheorghe Gheorghiu-Dej, of ending both jamming of RFE broadcasts (on July 29, 1963) and regime media attacks on RFE. The Ceauçescu regime actively sought an implicit understanding with RFE, suggesting in 1965 that RFE send correspondents to Romania, drawing the attention of RFE correspondents to Ceauçescu's speeches in 1966 criticizing the USSR, and even hinting that that Romanian Service chief Noel Bernard would be welcome in Bucharest. Sharp criticism of RFE in *Romania Libera* on November 4, 1969, signaled the end of this "armistice" and the resumption of regime media condemnations. By then, domestic repression had increased, and RFE Romanian broadcasts had become much more critical.

Romanian foreign policy "exceptionalism" within the Soviet Bloc was a reality, and undoubtedly useful to the West at the time. But as it distanced itself from the USSR, the Ceauçescu regime became increasingly repressive at home. It was RFE's proper role to publicize and criticize that repression. This almost inevitably led to conflict with the State Department and especially with Ambassador Leonard Meeker in Bucharest—a replay of the tension between the State Department and RFE in the late 1950s and early 1960s over Poland—who was on the front lines in working to tie Romania more closely to the West.

Much State Department criticism of RFE's Romanian broadcasts at the time focused on the commentaries of the service director, Bernard Noel. After having been director of the service in the 1950s, Bernard had been ousted in 1958 following negative evaluations of Romanian broadcasts at that time by the FEC and the CRBP and as a victim of bureaucratic conflict between FEC New York and RFE Munich. After he was rehired in 1963, he ably led the Romanian Service in the late 1960s and effectively focused much of its programming on internal repression in Romania. The Romanian Service attracted the largest audience of any RFE service, and Bernard himself became a legend in Romania.

But as had happened earlier with the Polish Service, Bernard weakened the position of the service within RFE and in Washington by allowing it (and himself) to engage in personal invective against Ceauçescu and others in his regime. An example was Bernard's *Listeners' Mail* program of January 24, 1971, which detailed the perquisites of and abuse of power by the head of a sports association. Though the condemnation was doubtless music to the ears of the Romanian audience, and Bernard said he had other confirmation of the facts, the ad hominem criticism was in violation of agreed policy.[68] This put RFE director Walter in the difficult position of defending RFE's Romanian broadcasts critical of Ceauçescu's domestic repression while having to admonish Bernard for his use of personal invective and to insist on reviewing his sensitive political commentaries prior to broadcast. In Walter's words, in response to the Bucharest Embassy's criticism of Bernard's commentaries in November 1969,

There is no real question about our policy on personal attacks, and the slippage which has taken place in a few instances is certainly unfortunate. While it is intended that these errors will not be repeated, I hope it is clear to all concerned that we have no intention of ceasing criticism of Romanian regime policies and practices where it is appropriate. Our criticism should be responsible and to the point. Every effort will be made to assure that such is the case.[69]

Controversy over RFE's Romanian broadcasting continued into the early 1970s. Walter and Ambassador Meeker met in Munich in May 1970 but did not resolve their differences. The Bucharest Embassy continued to view RFE's Romanian Service broadcasting on Romanian domestic issues as "too harsh and querulous, particularly in that it does not offer sufficient or adequate 'constructive criticism' and positive suggestions to balance the condemnations." The CIA's Covert Action Staff served primarily as an intermediary between the State Department and RFE in this controversy, but it evaluated the Romanian broadcasts on balance favorably, finding that "the Romanian [Service] fulfills its function of offering informed, construc-

68. RFE notes exchanged between Walter and Bernard, January 30 and February 1, 1971.

69. RFE memorandum by Walter, December 11, 1969, in response to embassy criticism of Bernard commentaries on November 8, 11, and 26. Bernard's November 8 commentary focused on Ceauşescu's use of a "transparent mask of primitive and doubtful nationalist demagogy" to impose a "personal dictatorship" and a "revolting personality cult." The embassy viewed such language as "totally detrimental to what [the U.S.] is trying to achieve in Romania." Walter had earlier admonished Bernard for a "crude attack" on Romanian minister of education Constantinescu on October 2, in Press Review and Political Program No. 318; RFE memorandum for the record, October 10, 1969. The program included the rhetorical question: "What respect can this man at the head of the Education Ministry inspire when he suffered such a tragic failure in his own family, when his own daughter killed her mother?"

tive commentary on Romanian problems, in line with long-established policy directives."[70]

The controversy was partly defused in 1971, when Walter required his prior approval for sensitive political broadcasts of the Romanian Service.[71] Protraction of the unresolved issues was perhaps in part due to changes in the RFE organizational structure. With Walter's promotion to RFE director in 1968, he continued to perform the function of policy director, a position that had been abolished. A CIA official pointed out at the time, not unreasonably, that a full-time policy director, of the caliber of Griffith, Burks, or Walter himself, might have been able to devote more attention to and deal more quickly with ongoing policy issues.

Czechoslovakia

RFE's broadcasts to Czechoslovakia in the 1960s were the subject of policy differences within the U.S. government similar to, although not as heated as, those involving Polish and Romanian broadcasts. The Czechoslovak Service staff's "revolt" in 1960 and its mishandling by the RFE American management resulted in adverse publicity in Czechoslovakia and Germany and weakened the standing of the service within the FEC and in Washington.[72] Earlier, RFE's Czechoslovak broadcasts had upset the State Department for inadvertently taking a policy position on ongoing negotiations involving the sale of a steel rolling mill to Czechoslovakia.[73] In late 1960 and early 1961, the U.S. Embassy in Prague suggested the possibility of a deal whereby the Czechoslovak authorities would cease jamming if RFE ended its commentaries on domestic Czechoslovak affairs. Indeed, Ambassador Christian M. Ravndal questioned whether RFE was needed at all, because "liberation" was dead, and closing RFE might lead the Czechoslovak regime to end "jamming of VOA." But such criticism soon faded. Comprehensive Prague Embassy reviews of RFE's Czechoslovak broadcasts in 1962 and 1964 were generally positive (while pointing out some continuing usage of aggressive and vituperative tone and vocabulary). By 1964, the embassy had come to view RFE as the only American endeavor having any influence

70. FEC memorandum from CIA / Covert Action Staff, EC-2724, June 15, 1970.

71. RFE memorandum by Walter, "Approval of Romanian BD Commentaries on Present Situation in Romania," August 26, 1971.

72. *Frankfurter Allgemeine Zeitung,* December 21, 1961.

73. Night Commentary B-388, September 2, 1958.

on internal Czechoslovak developments, and that in a positive direction promoting liberalization.

The CIA/IOD generally defended RFE against State Department pressure throughout the early 1960s to curtail or end coverage of domestic Czechoslovak affairs. But in one case in 1961—the so-called Barak affair—IOD (under pressure from other CIA units) sought to influence RFE's programming for operational purposes. At issue was broadcast treatment of the dismissal on June 24, 1961, of Rudolf Barak as minister of the interior. The IOD encouraged RFE to play this up, and speculate on the ramifications and possible ouster of other ministry officials, evidently hoping to encourage unrest and possible defections within the Czechoslovak Intelligence Service. The IOD criticized the June 26, 1961, FEC Daily Guidance Summary for not taking "a more imaginative and aggressive approach to capitalizing on—or attempting to create—difficulties in the Communist Czech hierarchy."[74] As one of Cord Meyer's officers wrote to the FEC, "While we are all concerned about credibility, we are equally concerned about probing areas where the enemy is vulnerable."[75] Asked in a telephone call by another IOD officer to relay this message to RFE Munich, along with a request to broadcast an unsubstantiated report that Barak's foreign intelligence chief, Jaroslav Mueler, and two subordinates had been arrested, Ralph Walter (then serving with RFE in New York) replied that he would do so but recommend that it be disregarded—as it was.[76] Walter drafted the formal FEC response to the CIA, which argued that "we have deliberately adopted the policy of avoiding presentation of premature conclusions on the basis of what is clearly incomplete information. . . . There is a basic difference between reporting manufactured stories and encouraging speculation about the fate of an individual the regime is unlikely to put before the public eye."[77]

The Barak case is instructive on two counts. It is the only known case after the early 1950s of the IOD, and later the Covert Action Staff—normally the staunch protectors of RFE from efforts of other CIA operational units to

74. FEC memorandum from CIA, EC-1824, June 30, 1961.
75. FEC letter to Yarrow from CIA, July 1, 1961.
76. Walter interviews with the author.
77. FEC memorandum to CIA, FC-5608, July 7, 1961. Barak was in fact arrested in January 1962 and sentenced to imprisonment for fifteen years, ostensibly for corruption. Mueler was ousted in November 1961, and subsequently several of his subordinates were dismissed. Personal communication from Prokop Tomek of the Czech Military History Institute, 2009.

utilize it for their own missions—attempting to slant RFE broadcasts for operational purposes. That IOD's efforts failed demonstrated the extent of the FEC's autonomy that allowed it to disregard such pressure.

Coda

As these controversies about RFE broadcasts in the 1960s unfolded, in 1967 the "cover" of the many covert influence projects established at the outset of the Cold War by the OPC and the CIA at the direction of the White House began to unravel. RFE and RL were the largest of these projects and, as will be discussed in chapter 8, they were nearly disbanded in the early 1970s before being transformed into ongoing public broadcast and research organizations outside the CIA's orbit. As this process got under way, the Radio's performance and utility would be again tested in crisis. The high marks given RFE's broadcasting during the Soviet military suppression of Czechoslovakia's attempted self-liberation in 1968 would help make this transformation possible.

Chapter 5

Czechoslovakia, 1968

The Soviet military occupation of Czechoslovakia on August 20–21, 1968, had consequences extending far beyond that country. It demonstrated the determination of the Soviet leadership to resist even evolutionary change of a communist system. It filled a major gap in Soviet military planning that required stationing Soviet forces adjacent to Western Europe as a first strategic echelon for offensive operations in a European military conflict.[1] A combination of circumstances precipitated the Soviet action—unrest in Poland, foreign policy autonomy in Romania, domestic reform currents challenging communist orthodoxy in Czechoslovakia, spillover in the Soviet western borderlands, and a more flexible West German approach to the East that began to undercut East Germany. The Soviet occupation temporarily froze some of these developments but reinforced others. It led a growing number of formally loyal intellectuals and regime officials to become disillusioned with, dissent from, and then oppose the communist system. Two prominent examples were Andrei Sakharov, who had called the Prague Spring "so valuable for the future of socialism and mankind,"[2] and Colonel Ryszard Kukliński, who concluded that Poland's national existence was threatened and resolved to share Warsaw Pact military plans with the West.[3]

1. A. Ross Johnson, *East European Armed Forces and Soviet Military Planning: Factors of Change* (Santa Monica, Calif.: RAND Corporation, 1989), 9–10.
2. Andrei Sakharov, *Thoughts on Progress, Coexistence, and Intellectual Freedom* (New York: W. W. Norton, 1968).
3. Benjamin Weiser, *A Secret Life: The Polish Officer, His Covert Mission, and the Price He Paid to Save His Country* (New York: PublicAffairs, 2004), 47ff.

The unfolding developments in Czechoslovakia in 1968 were not a high priority for Western countries, which then were focused on Vietnam, détente, and internal social unrest. There was probably more attention in the spring of 1968 to the mounting Czechoslovak crisis at RFE and RL than in any other Western organizations. Western radio was more than an observer, however, because it had impact, providing news and information about the West and other Communist countries and disseminating to large audiences the ferment in Czech and Slovak intellectual circles after 1966. Clear evidence of the Soviet leadership's perception of that impact is the fact that it quickly resumed or intensified its jamming of all Western radio broadcasts. On August 21, Moscow resumed jamming VOA and BBC Russian broadcasts after an interval of five years and intensified jamming RL. Jamming was reinstated in Czechoslovakia (and also briefly in Hungary, which had terminated jamming on February 1, 1964) and intensified in Poland and Bulgaria.

Support for Reform Communism

RFE's purpose in broadcasting to Czechoslovakia in the 1960s was defined in a March 1965 policy memorandum as promoting "peaceful evolution toward internal freedom and national independence, the reduction of Czechoslovak contributions to Soviet strength, and the further weakening of the external cohesiveness of the Soviet Bloc." Broadcasting was to help Czechs and Slovaks obtain a "margin of freedom." Short-term priorities included enhanced programming for elites focused on promoting decentralization and reformist currents within the Czechoslovak Communist Party.[4]

In line with this guidance, RFE broadcasts gave full coverage to the reformist currents of the "Prague Spring" following the removal of Antonín Novotný as Communist Party chief in January and his replacement by Alexander Dubček. RFE saw as its task "to help maximize the existing and incipient social pressures which demand progress, . . . from piecemeal re-

4. FEC memorandum, "FEC Policy for RFE Broadcasting toward Czechoslovakia," May 10, 1965, a minor redaction of "Radio Free Europe Broadcasting Policy toward Czechoslovakia," March 1965, as approved by the Committee on Radio Broadcasting Policy (FEC memorandum from CIA, April 12, 1965). See also Arch Puddington, *Broadcasting Freedom: The Cold War Triumph of Radio Free Europe and Radio Liberty* (Lexington: University Press of Kentucky, 2000), chap. 9, 142–52.

form to a fundamental overhaul of the political system." To this end, RFE would seek to "extend the internal communication system available to the forces of reform, . . . place the Czechoslovak reform thinking into a broader context, . . . [and] emphasize specific, institutional approaches and solutions." Its task was "sustaining the momentum of change and accelerating the pace of evolution toward a more genuinely pluralistic political system."[5] But RFE avoided amplifying indigenous Czechoslovak voices calling for a multiparty system and an independent foreign or security policy, or otherwise blatantly confronting the USSR. This gradualist approach conformed to the very limited guidance the State Department and the CIA were providing at the time.[6]

As the Warsaw Pact conducted military exercises around and in Czechoslovakia throughout the spring and summer of 1968, RFE officials were concerned about the danger of Soviet intervention, as indicated by a policy guidance of July 11 and an internal memorandum of July 19 on contingency planning for an invasion that was viewed as probable. This was a prominent topic in daily policy meetings.[7] The July 11 guidance underlined RFE's responsibility not to increase the "severe and contradictory pressures" faced by the Czechoslovak reform leaders. A guidance of August 16 similarly counseled caution.

Such caution put RFE in the position of urging restraint on Czechs and Slovaks who understandably wished to expand their "margin of freedom" as quickly and widely as possible. Many democratic reforms were in fact introduced in the spring of 1968, including the unshackling of the domestic media. Radio Prague, freed of most Communist Party controls, "said things which Radio Free Europe didn't dare broadcast," recalled Karel Jezdinský, a Radio Prague reporter who later worked for RFE.[8] RFE's uncomfortable role as the voice of caution about the pace of reform was illustrated by a remarkable, unprecedented visit of the editors of the Czechoslovak newspapers *Student* and *Obrana Lidu* to the RFE building in Munich in July. An internal RFE transcript of the far-ranging discussions during this visit be-

5. RFE memorandum, "Special Guidance on the Winds of Change in Czechoslovakia, February 29, 1968."
6. State Department and CIA guidance, as indicated in an FEC memorandum dated March 19, 1968, was bland, reminding RFE of such basics as stick to "established facts," don't "get in advance of story," "keep presentation low-keyed and unexcited," and "avoid comparisons with 1956."
7. The author was a participant in these policy meetings throughout 1968.
8. Jezdinský interview with Puddington, *Broadcasting Freedom*, 147.

tween the RFE broadcasters and their sympathetic but critical elite listeners provides an illuminating interpretation of RFE's origins, organization, post-1956 policies, and American-émigré partnership.[9] The RFE managers urged the visitors from Prague not to publish a story on their visit. As RFE director Ralph Walter reported to the FEC in New York: "I urged [Czechoslovak Service chief Jaroslav] Pechacek to do everything in his power to forestall publication of anything on RFE in view of Czechoslovak situation. . . . We can only hope that political judgment will restrain journalistic enthusiasm at *Student* at least until—hopefully—things cool down."[10] *Student* nonetheless published a positive account of the visit that same month, promptly drawing fire from Soviet and orthodox Czechoslovak Communist media.

There were two reasons for RFE's restraint. First, RFE management (like the U.S. State Department and most Soviet watchers of the day) believed (reasonably, but in the event wrongly) that small steps away from Communist dogma were less likely than bold reformist actions to provoke a Soviet crackdown. A policy guidance of August 18 reflected this assumption, stating that RFE broadcasts should "acknowledge that to maintain flexibility for internal reform, the Party leadership must seek to give the least offense to its orthodox allies." Second, RFE was determined not to repeat the errors it made broadcasting to Hungary in 1956. Walter cautioned his staff on July 18 that broadcasts would be monitored internally "as part of an effort to keep down excitability in any form."[11] In the spring, he had circulated the internal review of 1956 Hungarian broadcasts, the so-called Griffith Report, to his policy staff (including the present author) and told them to study its lessons. He made the importance of the 1956 experience clear in a later interview:

> We heeded the lessons of the Hungarian Revolution. We were cautious, because we were conscious of the possibility of an invasion. . . . We felt that we had to be more responsible than the people who were enjoying this period of liberalization.[12]

9. FEC document, "The Discussion [with editors of *Student*] as Tape Recorded in RFE on Sunday, July 7, 1968."

10. FEC memorandum to Yarrow from Walter, July 15, 1968. A CIA/CA official noted on a copy of this memorandum "*Very* responsible attitude"; emphasis in the original.

11. FEC memorandum from Walter, July 18, 1968, as cited by Puddington, *Broadcasting Freedom*, 148.

12. Walter interview with Puddington.

RL followed the same gradualist approach. An RL policy guidance of June 20 called (somewhat disingenuously) for RL programs to "portray Czechoslovak citizens as undertaking liberalizing and progressive reforms 'within' the socialist framework and to suggest that these represent a creative development of Marxism within the Czech national context" and "to impress on Soviet listeners that Czechoslovakia should be permitted to conduct its affairs without interference from the outside since the Czechoslovakian reforms are no threat to the USSR itself." RL broadcasts were not to suggest that "Czechoslovakia may leave the Communist camp" or that domestic reforms "may go beyond the socialist framework."[13]

Post-invasion Restraint

As Soviet and Warsaw Pact armed forces occupied Czechoslovakia in the early hours of August 21, 1968, RFE and RL implemented contingency plans prepared in the summer for round-the-clock broadcasting with increased transmitter power. RFE dedicated its medium-wave transmitter near Munich (normally shared by Czech/Slovak and Polish programs) solely to broadcasts to Czechoslovakia. RL increased transmitter power directed at Soviet troops in Czechoslovakia. RFE had multiple sources of information in the immediate postinvasion period—reports from Western journalists in Czechoslovakia, monitoring of the free Czech and Slovak radios that operated for some time, and the Czechoslovak news agency CTK and other free media telex services that were the last external channel to the outside world.

Both Radios sought to keep their audiences informed while bending over backward to avoid even the appearance of encouraging active resistance to the Soviet invasion, fearing that it might end in violence. The line between providing information and restraint was not always clear. Reporting to Washington from Prague, Ambassador Jacob Beam (who had headed the interagency working group on Hungary in 1956, before serving as ambassador to Poland) called for "extreme caution" in RFE and VOA broadcasts, noting the pitfalls of either encouraging or discouraging restive youth. RFE reported most of the information broadcast by underground radios that began operating within Czechoslovakia after the occupation, except for ap-

13. RL Broadcast Guidance, "The Current Situation in Czechoslovakia, June 20, 1968."

peals for active resistance to the occupiers. This policy was established bottom-up; Ralph Walter set the policy in Munich, and it was then endorsed by the Department of State in conversations between Deputy Under-secretary Charles Bohlen and Cord Meyer.[14]

RFE banned any discussion in its programs of Czechoslovak neutrality —even reports from within Czechoslovakia or from the Western press in newscasts. More restrictively, an RL guidance of August 27 suggested "straight news on [Czechoslovak] reaction as reported by such as Reuters and UPI, deleting their references to the reports and reaction of clandestine [Czechoslovak opposition] transmitters." RL beamed its regular Russian program to Soviet forces in Czechoslovakia, but without any special messages or appeals to Soviet soldiers.

At RFE, Walter insisted that he or his American policy staff approve in advance all commentaries on the invasion. He directed at 02:50 Munich time on August 21 that no press commentary on the invasion be aired until evaluated by the policy office. A second directive at 12:28 banned all commentary on the movement of Warsaw Pact forces. Another directive at 12:54 reminded broadcast chiefs to "make certain that the tone of your broadcasts is as even and normal as possible. This is not the time to allow emotions to influence even voicing of programs." Policy Advisor Robert Tuck took a similar approach at RL, directing at 12:00 on August 21 that "all news features and commentaries will be checked by the policy office as soon as written and before broadcast." Not all the details of this prebroadcast review can be documented because, as Walter noted at the time, "we are handling guidance problems orally because of pace of events."[15] This approach represented an unprecedented degree of prebroadcast control by the American RFE management in crisis conditions. As such, it represented a modification of the American-émigré "partnership" model, a revision made necessary by the failure of the original model in the 1956 Hungarian broadcasts. RFE commentaries approved all emphasized calm and discipline. The first Czech commentary broadcast on August 21, for example, condemned the invasion, noted that Czechs and Slovaks had no way to expel the aggressors, and concluded that "nothing would be worse in this historical moment than despair and lack of prudence."[16]

14. CIA memorandum for the record from Meyer, August 22, 1968, released to the author March 2009.
15. FEC telex MUN 70, August 22, 1968.
16. RFE Czechoslovak Daily Broadcast Analysis Report 181, August 22, 1968.

On August 28, 1968, the Soviet Union announced the signing of the Moscow Protocol between the Soviet leadership and the Czechoslovak leadership it had abducted to Moscow, allowing Dubček to remain in office while severely constraining his powers. The State Department and CIA initially sought to ban RFE or RL commentary on the agreement. RFE objected, and in fact was able to cover (while downplaying) questioning within Czechoslovakia of the wisdom of the Moscow Protocol. (Václav Havel was one who privately questioned the wisdom or necessity of the Moscow Protocol at the time).[17] RFE continued to ignore, even in newscasts, appeals from within Czechoslovakia for nonviolent resistance reported in the Western press. Unlike its coverage of the Hungarian Freedom Radios in 1956, RFE did not report such messages from clandestine radios inside Czechoslovakia. Reports on other subjects (some of them later confirmed as accurate) were excluded from broadcasts in the immediate postinvasion period on the grounds that they might prove inflammatory as well. Hence reports of KGB arrests of Czech intellectuals, reports of a U.S.-Soviet "spheres of influence" agreement, and Western reports of Soviet demands for the permanent stationing of Soviet troops in Czechoslovakia were not aired at the time.[18] The assumption underlining this approach was that Dubček would still be able to salvage something of the Prague Spring after the intervention, that postinvasion Dubček was the lesser evil to Alois Indra or other pro-Soviet Czechoslovak leaders. Most of this turned out to be wishful thinking, neglecting the possibility that Dubček would become neither conquering hero, defiant prisoner, nor triumphant martyr—the only possibilities envisaged in an RL guidance of August 22—but rather the compromised agent of "normalization." It had happened before in Czechoslovakia. President Edvard Beneš, summoned to Moscow in 1946, had signed a coerced "Moscow Agreement" that kept him in office but in retrospect only prepared the way for the Communist coup of February 1948.

A year later, the "Prague Spring" of 1968 was history. Apart from more powers for the Slovak Communist regime vis-à-vis the central Communist Party organization in Prague, Czechoslovakia reverted not to Stalinism but to the status quo ante of January 1968. Czech and Slovak historians will

---

17. Private letter to an unnamed correspondent in the United States, late September 1968, copy in RFE/RL Collection.
18. RFE memorandum by Walter, "Subjects Played Down by RFE during Czechoslovak Crisis," September 11, 1968.

continue to debate whether it was better or worse for Czechoslovakia that Dubček presided over what the Soviets and orthodox Czechoslovak Communists called "normalization." Did Dubček mitigate or ease the Soviet-imposed crackdown? Was this better or worse for Czechs and Slovaks in the ensuing two decades? If arguably the latter, then RFE broadcasts after August 1968 gave Dubček too much credit, in contrast to Hungary in 1956, when RFE broadcasts gave Imre Nagy too little.

Whatever the judgments, the issue became moot in April 1969, when Gustáv Husák replaced Dubček as party first secretary (and Dubček himself was banished to Ankara as Czechoslovak ambassador, a prisoner in his own embassy, and later exiled to the forestry service in Slovakia). RFE broadcasts characterized Husák, (in the words of one Czech commentary) as "a politician who will strictly observe the line demanded by Moscow, without showing the slightest respect for the people's opinion and will."[19] Few would question that assessment, but once again, and almost predictably, some State Department officers now criticized RFE for an excessively harsh approach to domestic Czechoslovak affairs. After 1968, RFE's Czechoslovak Service reverted to its traditional role of a saturation home service, providing news, information, and features about Czechoslovakia and the world banned from controlled domestic media. One indicator of its success was the size of its audience, which had declined dramatically in the spring of 1968 and now again increased.[20]

Lesson Overlearned?

Organizations routinely review past crises to understand their successes and failures. They draw up "lessons learned."[21] But lessons can be overlearned, and organizations, like armies, can prepare themselves to fight past battles. Was that the case with RFE and RL broadcasting to postinvasion Czechoslovakia in 1968? RFE's painful experience with Hungarian broadcasting in 1956 properly focused it in 1968 on an external communicator's cardinal responsibility to avoid even implicit encouragement of violence. That

19. RFE Czechoslovak Service commentary by Sláva Volný, August 4, 1969. Volný was one of several Czech journalists prominent in the Prague Spring who left Czechoslovakia after August 1968 and joined the RFE Czechoslovak Service.
20. FEC memorandum, September 30, 1968.
21. FEC memorandum, "Czechoslovakia 1968: A Chronology of Events and the Role of Communications" (two parts), October 1968.

responsibility led it to ignore calls from within Czechoslovakia for nonviolent resistance to the post–August 21 "normalization," a qualification of its mission of providing full and objective news and information. Both Radios were widely praised, at the time and later, by listeners and U.S. government officials, for their restraint in 1968.[22]

It was arguably not RFE's proper role to omit or downplay coverage of appeals by legitimate domestic Czechoslovak voices for postcommunist democratic institutions or for international neutrality in the period before August 21. Nor, arguably, was it RFE's proper role to give Dubček as much of the benefit of the doubt as he received in RFE commentaries after the Soviet occupation. In both cases, RFE and RL were conforming to U.S. policy. That RFE and RL could not at least soften that approach was testimony to the continuing burden of RFE's 1956 Hungarian experience and the extent of the policy consensus that gradual in-system reforms could both prove viable within an Eastern European country and acceptable to the Soviet Union.

Spillover: The Impact on the Soviet Bloc after 1968

One consequence of the 1968 "Prague Spring" was spillover of the liberalizing Czechoslovak media to the western USSR, much to the consternation of the Soviet leadership. "All this propaganda affects us as much as it affects you," Brezhnev told the Czechoslovak leadership in early 1968.[23] As Amir Weiner concluded in his study of this issue, "Thanks to the Czechoslovak media, western Ukrainians, the most rebellious Soviet nationality, could now watch, read, and draw their own conclusion on issues that were still strictly taboo in their country."[24] The Soviet reaction was first to ignore

22. The prominent writer Milan Kundera said at the time that he was "very impressed by [RFE's] programs because of their restraint, accuracy and objectivity, and because of the wise and 'statesmanlike' tone and standpoint expressed in the some of its commentaries. . . . This appreciation is shared by other writers, as well as by television and radio workers." A listener, injured by Soviet artillery in Prague on August 21, wrote at the time that "I realized that you were aware of the responsibility for the words you put on the air, which have a multiplied effect"; RFE memorandum, "Roundup of Reports from Czechoslovak Listeners," September 26, 1968.

23. Cited by Mark Kramer, "The Czechoslovak Crisis and the Brezhnev Doctrine," in *1968: The World Transformed,* ed. Carole Fink, Philipp Gassert, and Detlef Junker (New York: Cambridge: Cambridge University Press, 1998), 143.

24. Amir Weiner, "Foreign Media, the Soviet Western Frontier, and the Hungarian

the Prague Spring in Soviet media and then, when it was evident that information was spilling over anyway, to organize a massive counterpropaganda campaign.

RFE and RL and other Western broadcasters countered this counterpropaganda and took over the function of "spillover"—which they had reinforced all along—after August 21, 1968, providing extensive coverage of the Soviet occupation to the USSR and the other Eastern European countries. In identifying so clearly with the reformist currents of the Prague Spring, and then in covering the invasion and its aftermath, all Western radio stations helped debunk the Soviet propaganda line that "creeping counterrevolution" had been nipped in the bud in Czechoslovakia; that "the Soviet armed forces came in time." An RL guidance of August 21 called for broadcasts to "review the facts of the Czechoslovak developments since January showing their peaceful nature and loyalty to 'socialist' commitments and alliances. Commentaries will be calm in tone and content." Messages like this helped many in the Soviet orbit conclude that Brezhnev-style communism was bankrupt and that reform communism was an illusion. That realization was the first step toward the dissent and opposition movements that were to develop in the 1970s and 1980s. Soviet suppression of the Prague Spring was the watershed—and the broadcasts of RL and RFE helped make it so.

---

and Czechoslovak Crises," in *Cold War Broadcasting: Impact on the Soviet Union and Eastern Europe—A Collection of Studies and Documents,* ed. A. Ross Johnson and R. Eugene Parta (Budapest: Central European University Press, 2010), chap. 15.

Chapter 6

Radio Liberty in the 1960s

In comparison with the tumultuous history of the FEC and RFE in 1956 and thereafter, AMCOMLIB (renamed the Radio Liberty Committee, RLC, in January 1964) and RL (Radio Liberation was renamed Radio Liberty in 1959) enjoyed a quieter life during these years. Less was at stake for the U.S. government foreign policy establishment. RL broadcasts in 1956 were not controversial. AMCOMLIB lacked the public face of the FEC—it had no counterpart to the Crusade for Freedom, and its directors (formally, trustees), all prominent Americans, eschewed the publicity and the policy role sought by C. D. Jackson and other FEC directors. RL's impact during these years was uncertain at best—and would remain so until the 1970s, when internal pressures for change and active dissent began to emerge in the USSR. Indeed, during deliberations of the interagency Committee on Radio Broadcasting Policy in 1957, the State Department argued unsuccessfully for abolishing RL on the grounds that the broadcasts had no discernible impact and yet were unnecessarily condescending and provocative.

Such criticism notwithstanding, CRBP program reviews gave higher marks to RL than to VOA Russian broadcasts, and in March 1957 the CRBP approved the continuation of broadcasts by Radio Liberty under revised policy guidelines.[1] Following the conclusion of an agreement in principle facilitated by the U.S. Embassy in Madrid between the Spanish government

---

1. "Gray Broadcasting Policy toward the Soviet Union," approved by Committee on Radio Broadcasting Policy, May 1, 1958, released to the author in October 2004. In May 1959, the Russian Service and nine other RL language services changed their names in the vernacular from "Liberation" to "Liberty." The remaining eight services had always called themselves in the vernacular "Liberty."

and AMCOMLIB on July 15, 1957,[2] the NSC authorized proceeding with the Spanish transmitter project at Playa de Pals on the Costa Brava—a clear indication that the U.S. government intended for RL not to disappear but to expand. An additional capital expansion program to increase the power of transmitters and antennas in West Germany, Spain, and Taiwan was approved in 1963. By the mid-1960s, RL programs were broadcast from these three locations on thirty shortwave frequencies over transmitters with a combined power of nearly 2 million watts.

The CRBP's rationale for endorsing the continuation of RL was that it had a mission different from that of VOA. VOA was directed in May 1958 to "place even greater emphasis than heretofore on straight news and factual information about important U.S. and world developments, on exposition of U.S. policies, and on a valid delineation of the values, institutions, and procedures which characterize American life. . . . Materials dealing with internal Soviet affairs . . . shall constitute no more than a minor portion both of programming as a whole and of any single program." In the spirit of that policy guidance and analogous guidance for Eastern Europe, VOA closed its Munich programming center, which had employed some two hundred émigrés who naturally had focused their attention on the USSR and Eastern Europe, duplicating the work of RL and RFE broadcasters. VOA also strengthened its centralized news operation, inter alia reducing the editorial authority of émigré broadcasters.

RL was directed by the CRBP to "assume an émigré face" (but not to represent any émigré organization) and focus on the USSR. Its mission was "encourag[ing] whatever evolutionary development is manifested in the Soviet system, along lines consistent with U.S. security objectives and the legitimate aspirations of the peoples of the Soviet Union." The station "assumes the role of a catalyst, disseminating information and views on domestic Soviet and foreign developments, suppressed or distorted by the regime, which will stimulate independent thought, feed existing and latent currents of dissatisfaction with official policies and skepticism about the prevailing Soviet system, and make Soviet citizens more conscious of desirable alternatives to various aspects of that system." RL's primary target audience was the elite, the "politically alert" in the Soviet system, who could best be reached with responsible and accurate news and calm and thoughtful com-

2. AMCOMLIB memorandum from Sargeant, "Assistance Given to Amcomlib by Ambassador John Davis Lodge and Minister-Counselor Homer Byngton, Jr.," July 23, 1957.

mentary. On the Soviet nationalities question, RL was to adhere to the policy of "non-predeterminism," meaning that "it is the right of the people themselves to determine the over-all state structure of the USSR when they are free to do so." RL was to comment on international affairs from "an enlightened Soviet-émigré point of view . . . [and] avoid creating the impression that it represents the primary interests of the United States or the West in general, . . . [and giving] fair coverage of legitimate points of view not necessarily in accord with the public position of the U.S. Government."[3]

These principles were incorporated in a revised RL Policy Manual dated November 15, 1958, that was drafted by AMCOMLIB and approved by the CIA and the State Department.[4] This 1958 Policy Manual was a revision and not a repudiation of the June 29, 1956, Policy Manual—another indication that October 1956 was not the watershed in U.S. policy or broadcasting strategy from "liberation" to "liberalization" that is often assumed. The revised Policy Manual was a document intended for RL staff and was thus silent on the issues of U.S. foreign policy goals and U.S. government funding for RL spelled out in the CRBP document. It defined RL's purpose as assisting the Soviet people to achieve "some form of representative government" of a nature and at a pace of their own choosing. Thus it was RL's task to focus broadcasts primarily on Soviet domestic affairs,

> to break down the isolation separating them from the outside world; to strengthen their faith in the eternal values of liberty as indispensable to genuine human progress; to fortify the convictions of those consciously opposed to the present regime and encourage them with information about their friends and allies abroad; to bring into sharp focus existing subconscious opposition; to foster doubt and dissatisfaction with existing inequities as steps on the road to opposition.

These principles shaped an updated RL surrogate radio mission statement drafted in 1959 by Gene Sosin, then RL's policy coordinator in New York, following an unusual tour of the USSR:[5]

3. "Gray Broadcasting Policy toward the Soviet Union."
4. RL Policy Manual, November 15, 1958.
5. RL and RFE personnel were normally banned from travel to the Soviet Bloc. The circumstances of this unusual trip are described by Gene Sosin, *Sparks of Liberty: An Insider's Memoir of Radio Liberty* (University Park: Pennsylvania State University Press, 1999), 81–86.

Radio Liberty speaks not as an official voice of a foreign government, but as a voice of opposition to the one-party dictatorship in a land where such opposition is forbidden. It speaks not only about what is going on outside the USSR but also about internal events, in the way that an opposition radio or newspaper would if it were tolerated within the USSR. ... Its image is psychologically internal, identified with the listener who is striving toward the common goal of full personal and political liberty for every individual Soviet citizen. ... It is a reliable, constructive critic of Soviet reality, giving listeners a perspective on Soviet life and stimulating them to think independently and to draw their own conclusions. By establishing rapport with its audience as a voice of opposition broadcasting from the outside, but speaking from inside the Soviet mind and heart, Radio Liberty can attract Soviet listeners because of its special message and mission, regardless of the increasing competition from Soviet TV and other radios abroad which speak for foreigners, not for the Soviet man.[6]

RL undertook comparative studies of Western broadcasting content in an effort to demonstrate its special role. One such review noted that RL devoted much more broadcast time to Soviet affairs than did VOA and that even where there was overlap, the perspectives differed. VOA's coverage of domestic Soviet affairs generally involved an international aspect, whereas RL provided an inside picture of Soviet developments "directly related to the listener in terms of his own history, life situation, interests, aspirations, and experiences."[7] One such inside picture was Boris Pasternak's banned novel *Doctor Zhivago,* which RL covered in 1958 (following its publication in Italian in the West) and serialized verbatim at dictation speed in 1959 (after it had been published in Russian in the West).[8]

Having survived the post-1956 reappraisal of U.S. international broadcasting, RL expanded its operations in the 1960s. Yet it lacked the support within the U.S. government that RFE had by then come to enjoy. Soviet ex-

6. AMCOMLIB memorandum, "Radio Liberty's Current Programming Policy" [by Gene Sosin], October 19, 1959.

7. AMCOMLIB memorandum, "RL's Mission and Output in Relationship to That of VOA," September 6, 1962.

8. Although AMCOMLIB obtained an original Russian text in early 1958, concerns about compromising Pasternak and the Italian publisher's copyright delayed verbatim broadcasts until 1959.

perts at the State Department and other U.S. government agencies viewed RL broadcasts less as a positive instrument of political and social change in the USSR than as a project that did no harm, should not be terminated under Soviet pressure, and might someday prove useful as a bargaining chip to obtain concessions from the USSR (for example, to end jamming of VOA). In the 1960s, Ambassador Llewellyn E. Thompson Jr.'s views from Moscow ranged from uncertain to negative and always envisaged the possibility—occasionally floated by Soviet officials—of such a trade-off.

Doubts about RL's utility were eased only in part by its ability to "surge" during crises. RL had beamed its regular Russian program to Soviet forces in Hungary after 1956 and continued this practice throughout the 1960s. During the 1961 Berlin crisis, it beamed its regular Russian program to Soviet forces in East Germany thirteen hours daily. Later, in the wake of the Cuban missile crisis, with NSC approval and the cooperation of U.S. commercial broadcasters, it also broadcast its regular Russian program to Soviet forces in Cuba over medium-wave U.S. commercial transmitters.[9]

Organization Transformed

To support broadcasts focused on Soviet affairs, RL had by the early 1960s built up a capability to gather and analyze information about the USSR comparable to that created by RFE in the early 1950s. RL bureaus were established in London, Paris, and Taipei, supplemented by correspondents in many countries. RL's media monitoring service tracked some hundred Soviet radio stations and press agencies and some two hundred Soviet publications. RL established its own research unit, RL Research, led first by Viktor Zorza and then John Nicholson and Albert Boiter, to support broadcasting (and serve CIA analysts and the larger Western community interested in Soviet affairs). RL Research developed what became a comprehensive "Red Archive" of information obtained from its various sources. It established the first large samizdat archive, directed by Peter Dornan. Under the direction of Max Ralis, it launched a program of interviewing Soviet travelers for information both about reactions to RL broadcasts and about Soviet life.[10]

9. The 1963 AM broadcasts to Cuba were approved by the NSC "Special Group" on April 9, 1963; NSC memorandum for members of the Special Group, April 9, 1963, declassified September 29, 1998, reprinted by Sosin, *Sparks of Liberty,* 98.
10. Sosin, *Sparks of Liberty,* 73ff.; James Critchlow, *Radio Hole-in-the-Head: Ra-*

AMCOMLIB continued to support Soviet émigré activities unrelated to broadcasting. It funded the Institute for the Study of the USSR. And its Special Projects Division, headed by Isaac Patch, published a biweekly newspaper, *Nashe Obshchee Delo,* and a quarterly journal for the Soviet émigré community, *Problems of the Peoples of the USSR.* It also published Russian translations of Western literature and organized a counterpart to the FEC book program (see chapter 2) that made Western and émigré literature available to Soviet travelers and others.

Howland Sargeant had assumed the presidency of AMCOMLIB in 1954, at a time when it was more closely controlled by the CIA than the FEC. But by the early 1960s, he had acquired much of the same autonomy enjoyed by John Richardson as FEC president. Because he was always sensitive to the line between gathering information for broadcasting and collecting intelligence for government purposes, he insisted that no personal information identifying RL interviewees in the West be released to the U.S. government unless it had his personal approval. He rejected a CIA suggestion to hire a KGB defector, Peter Deryabin, on the grounds that it would be resented by RL staff and hurt morale. He and Richardson ended the practice of allowing a few RL and RFE employees to act as double agents, pretending to work for the other side in gathering information about the Radios in order to counter the Soviet Bloc intelligence operations directed against them.

Sargeant sought to develop a public profile for AMCOMLIB and thus help ensure its continued existence. He proposed establishing a separate nonprofit corporation on the model of the FEC's Crusade for Freedom / RFE Fund to raise private funds. The CIA rejected that project, citing the increased practical difficulties of maintaining "cover" in the foundation and nonprofit worlds by the early 1960s but doubtless also wary of another freewheeling organization led by powerful individuals outside the U.S. government. Sargeant did raise some private funds for the Institute for the Study of the USSR, including a Ford Foundation grant to finance a summer seminar in Munich in 1958 for young American and European scholars in the Soviet field.

RL's low public profile had its advantages. RL was spared public criticism in the United States, such as Fulton Lewis Jr.'s verbal broadsides against

dio Liberty—An Insider's Story of Cold War Broadcasting (Washington, D.C.: American University Press, 1995), 99–112; Leo Bogart, "In Memoriam: Max Ralis 1916–1999," *Public Opinion Quarterly* 63, no. 2 (Summer 1999): 261–62; R. Eugene Parta, *Discovering the Hidden Listener: An Assessment of Radio Liberty and Western Broadcasting to the USSR during the Cold War* (Stanford, Calif.: Hoover Institution Press, 2007), 1–4.

RFE. Its low profile eased its relations with the West German government (aided by the efforts of a very effective emissary, the Vienna-born lawyer Paul Moeller). In 1963 the Bonn government favorably cited this low profile in lengthening the term of RL's broadcasting license renewal from four to eight years (subsequently extending the same treatment to RFE). RL was rarely mentioned after 1967 in public references to the CIA's support for RFE.

Internally, AMCOMLIB was plagued with the same bifurcation between a small New York headquarters and a large Munich broadcasting center that burdened RFE. Munich program directors Richard Bertrandias and Francis S. Ronalds shaped RL broadcasts, but AMCOMLIB was even slower than the FEC to shift all executive responsibility for RL operations to Munich. In theory, RL senior management relocated to Munich in 1964, and Lewis W. Shollenberger (a journalist at the American Broadcasting Company) was appointed executive director, reporting to President Sargeant in New York. In practice, Shollenberger's authority was undercut by constant interference from RLC staff in New York. Only when Walter K. (Ken) Scott assumed the position of executive director in 1966 did RL management responsibilities shift fully to Munich, as they had for RFE under Rodney Smith in 1962.[11]

RL broadcasts, like those of RFE, faced competition from VOA, the BBC, and other mainstream Western broadcasters. It also faced competition from a number of émigré broadcasters that carried extremist, chauvinist, irredentist, and sometimes incendiary programs. The most important of these extremist broadcasters were "Radio Free Russia," operated out of Germany by the NTS (and sometimes confused even in the Bonn government with RL), and broadcasts on Radio Madrid that an AMCOMLIB policy official, Catherine Dupuy, accurately described as "bad policy, bad journalism; . . . the tone is on the whole inflammatory; the content represents reaction at its most extreme,"[12] and that seemed to serve only to demonstrate the Franco regime's hatred of communism. These extremist broadcasters evidently had little impact in the USSR. RL's main "competition" were in fact the Soviet jamming stations, which limited the reception of RL broadcasts for much of the Soviet audience. This explained at least in part the more extensive audience reach of the unjammed VOA and BBC during those years.[13]

11. Many positive changes in the RL organization by 1963 were chronicled in an AMCOMLIB memorandum to Sargeant from Richard Bertrandias, RL's departing Munich program director, May 31, 1963.

12. AMCOMLIB memorandum to Sargeant from Dupuy, "Programs Broadcast from Radio Madrid in Languages of Eastern Europe and the USSR," December 18, 1961.

13. RLC memorandum, "Soviet Jamming of Radio Liberty," n.d. [1965]

Message Refined

With RL's relevance as a medium in the late 1950s and early 1960s widely questioned within the U.S. government, its message remained a subject of criticism. Initial CRBP reviews had given RL higher marks than VOA's Russian broadcasts. But when reviewing broadcasts during the last quarter of 1957, a CIA/IOD officer found RL programs on internal Soviet affairs to be "frequently ironic, contemptuous, didactic, hortatory, denunciatory, and, on occasion, little short of provocative." Reviewing the broadcasts in the fall of 1959, an IOD officer with Soviet expertise found no violations of the 1958 Policy Manual but reflections of a lack of sophistication on current political developments and a sometimes strident tone, especially in the Ukrainian service.

The strongest critique of the RL message came not from outside but from within. Critically reviewing Russian Service programming in mid-1957, Boris Shub concluded that news reports and press reviews dwelt on the minutiae of East-West diplomatic and military relations to the exclusion of domestic Soviet and broader Western matters: "Total effect: an enemy station masquerading as a friend." More fundamentally, Shub wrote, there was too much emotion and instant analysis and too little of the richness of Western and émigré writings: "We do not give the audience an uncensored, undiluted flow of vital ideas." Shub outlined seven essentials of effective programming—principles that RL would attempt to implement in the 1960s: "scrupulous respect for the facts"; respect for the intelligence of the listener; elimination of verbal bombast; balanced domestic and international news; a full spectrum of Western and Soviet thought and opinion; modern radio reporting technique; and a recognition of Soviet listeners' patriotism, sense of progress, and optimism for the future.[14]

Simultaneously, RL broadcasts were denounced as politically suspect by two AMCOMLIB trustees, its founders Isaac Don Levine and Eugene Lyons, who was also its first president. Levine and Lyons complained to AMCOMLIB president Sargeant and independently to Allen Dulles and Deputy Undersecretary of State Loy Henderson that RL broadcasts had become "appeasement of Red imperialism," "leftish, Marxist, anti-Western and even pro-Soviet," the result of "infiltration by elements set upon subverting from within the purposes and policies of Radio Liberation."

However implausible these accusations, the authority of the messengers made it impossible for Sargeant and the CIA to ignore them. Sargeant in-

14. AMCOMLIB memoranda to Bertandrias from Shub, May 3 and June 28, 1957.

vited them to prepare a critique of several months of broadcasts, while the CIA/IOD itself undertook several internal reviews. AMCOMLIB also commissioned external reviews; an examination of February 1959 Russian programming by George Kline of Bryn Mawr College found the broadcasts to be of "high quality—solid, informative and interesting. They meet the standards set by the RL Policy Manual, with certain exceptions."[15] The outcome was a basic defense by both Sargeant and the CIA of the broadcast record, along with an admission by RL's Munich managers (some of whom were replaced) that there had been a few violations of policy and some ineffective programming. All agreed that there was a need to improve the evaluation and control of programming along the lines recommended by Shub.[16] The Levine-Lyons critique was partly deflected from RL to the U.S. government by the issuance in the midst of the controversy of the May 1958 CRBP policy document for RL referenced above. Lyons and his fellow AMCOMLIB trustee Reginald Townsend criticized this U.S. government policy document for reflecting the "illusion" of coexistence with the USSR and imposing unwanted restraints on RL. But they and Levine agreed that matters could be worse ("considering the political climate in Washington today we have a firmer paper than could have been expected"—Levine) and concluded that the policy document gave RL considerable programming latitude.[17] Renaming Radio Liberation as Radio Liberty was the last straw for Lyons, and he resigned from AMCOMLIB.[18]

However unwelcome the Levine-Lyon controversy was for AMCOMLIB and the CIA, the ensuing program reviews and Shub's earlier critique had the

15. AMCOMLIB memorandum, "Evaluation of Radio Liberation Scripts (Month of February 1959)," by George L. Kline, April 24, 1959.

16. AMCOMLIB letter to Lyons and Levine from Sargeant, December 2, 1957; AMCOMLIB letter to Sargeant from Levine, March 15, 1958; AMCOMLIB memoranda, "Actions Taken to Strengthen the Programming of Radio Liberation," and "Evaluations of Programming by Radio Liberation," from Sargeant, April 9,1958; AMCOMLIB letter to Sargeant from Lyons, April 17, 1958; AMCOMLIB memorandum, "Some Highlights of Recent Events," by Sargeant, May 1, 1958; AMCOMLIB letter to Sargeant from Richard Bertrandias [RL Munich program director] with detailed response to Levine's criticisms, May 5, 1958; AMCOMLIB letter to Bertrandias from Sargeant, May 12, 1958; AMCOMLIB memorandum for the record, "Review of Steps Taken to Strengthen Radio Liberation Programming," by Sargeant, May 27, 1958; AMCOMLIB memorandum to Sargeant from Bertrandias, May 28, 1958; AMCOMLIB memorandum to Sargeant from Robert F. Kelley, May 30, 1958.

17. AMCOMLIB memorandum, "Review of Country Paper with Key Members of the Board of Trustees, by Assistant to the President [Yedigaroff]," May 28, 1958.

18. Lyons interview with John Scott, September 1, 1976, RFE/RL memorandum to Mickelson from Scott, September 10, 1976.

positive result of helping to anchor five principles in Munich, New York, and Washington that would thereafter guide RL programming. The first principle was that effective broadcasting had to focus on the mindset and interests of the audience, not on those of émigrés or U.S. officials. The second principle was that newscasts, to be credible, had to report the bad along with the good involving the United States and the West generally and to avoid confusing news with commentary. The third principle was that broadcasts could, on occasion, be critical of U.S. government policy. The fourth principle was that commentary from a "leftist" or socialist perspective was sometimes the most effective counter to the injustices of the Soviet system. And the fifth, overarching principle was that liberation was not an event but a process—that "evolution is necessary to prepare the way for a democratic revolution."

In 1960, Robert Tuck (who had earlier overseen RL in the CIA/IOD)[19] became RL's Munich policy adviser, and he dedicated himself to implementing these five principles. Reviewing RL's output in mid-1962, he still found many problematic broadcasts—"unproductive criticism of the regime from a generally negative point of view; . . . many completely unnecessary digs and crudely propagandistic tone which keep recurring in too many scripts from all desks . . . [and] scripts . . . preoccupied with showing our hatred of the Soviet system and Communism instead of our interest and regard for the Soviet citizen."[20] This critique led him to draft a policy memorandum, "Radio Liberty's Task and Tone," a sophisticated analysis of the various categories of RL listeners and the best approach to reach them. He concluded that "an overall friendly tone is all-important from the point of view of sharpening Radio Liberty's criticism of Soviet policy and the impact of that criticism on the listener." RL's task, he suggested, was to "offer [Soviet listeners] constructive encouragement and relevant, meaningful alternatives which they can use in their own way to weaken the regime and better their condition."[21]

These themes were emphasized in a December 1963 CRBP update of the 1958 RL policy guidance. RL was now specifically told to promote pluralism and "encourage the free exchange of peoples and ideas between the So-

19. Sosin, *Sparks of Liberty*, 86; Tuck interview with the author.

20. Quoted in AMCOMLIB memorandum from CIA, "Radio Liberty Programming," July 13, 1962.

21. AMCOMLIB draft PPS, "Radio Liberty's Task and Tone," August 16, 1962. A CIA officer nonetheless found the draft to be too hard-line and called for a revision to spell out a "soft sell" with "much greater emphasis on positive versus negative programming; . . . our task is to stimulate and exploit evolutionary changes within the USSR which will make the regime less onerous to its subjects and less of a threat to world peace"; AMCOMLIB memorandum from CIA, August 30, 1962.

viet Union and non-Communist countries." The station's proper image was now defined as "the voice of free erstwhile Soviet citizens speaking to fellow countrymen who are still under Communist domination." RL was to "represent everything in the émigré community which illustrates the advantages and superiority of a free society." To maximize its impact, RL should emphasize news and explanatory comment and "have a reasoned, friendly tone and ensure that its programs are consistent with the contemporary language and psychology of the Soviet peoples." This updated document emphasized the importance of programs on divisions within the Communist world, especially the Sino-Soviet split, and on the isolation of the top Communist Party leadership from Soviet society. While observing the policy of non-predeterminism on the nationality question, RL programs to the Soviet nationalities "should foster pride in language, history, culture, and individuality."[22]

Promulgation of the 1963 CRBP policy update occasioned a revision of RL's internal Policy Manual.[23] More significant than the textual changes was the process itself, which consumed twenty-eight months from the first draft of the CRBP document to the final Policy Manual text. The case serves as a reminder that policy documents emerging from such a process often have little immediate relevance for operations and that the institutional and bureaucratic differences they engender are usually papered over, not resolved. Although USIA representatives on the CRBP had approved the December 1963 policy document, USIA later questioned RL's émigré image— a key factor distinguishing it from VOA. Tuck's draft of the revised Policy Manual was another negotiated paper that was eventually approved with minor changes by RLC management, the RL Council of [Émigré] Editors, the CIA, and the State Department. During the review process, the nationality service chiefs in Munich were able to include the significant point (absent from the original drafts) that non-predeterminism did not presume "that we think the present structure of the USSR should remain intact."[24]

22. "Gray Broadcasting Policy toward the Soviet Union."
    23. RLC document, Radio Liberty Policy Manual, May 12, 1965. Tuck elaborated some of these themes in a paper, "Influencing Political Change by Broadcasting to the Soviet Union," prepared for the September 1966 meeting of the American Political Science Association; RLC memorandum, "Evolution of Radio Liberty Policy 1952–1967," July 21, 1967.
    24. RLC memorandum to Sargeant from Tuck, May 10, 1965; RLC memorandum to Tuck from Joan B. Malukoff, April 9, 1965; AMCOMLIB memorandum to Advisory Board [CIA] from Sargeant, "Updating of Radlib Country Paper," February 19, 1963.

The 1965 RL Policy Manual that eventually emerged from this process was more specific than its predecessor on RL's role "to stimulate independent individual thinking rather than to incite group action." It incorporated Tuck's emphasis on "a tone of friendliness" and dignity in the broadcasts, which should appear to the listeners as "a guest in the living room." RL's task was to provide factual information and alternative views on Soviet, international Communist, and Western affairs. But it was to "avoid generalized, vituperative, or undocumented attacks against Soviet leaders and wholesale condemnation of Soviet domestic and foreign policies" and "avoid adopting a condescending tone, or presenting material in such a way as to imply an assumption of the political naïveté of the listener." It was to avoid negativism, emotionalism, and pejorative terms. This long list of "don'ts" was an indication that the kinds of programming they sought to ban were a continuing problem for RL's managers well into the 1960s.

RL's editorial policy on topical issues in the late 1950s and 1960s was based on these assumptions and was elaborated in a series of policy position statements (PPSs), forty-one of which were issued between May 1957 and June 1962. These PPSs were generally not written in Washington but rather drafted by RL and then submitted to the CIA/IOD and, through it, to the State Department for approval or revision. The "buy-in" of broadcasters was facilitated by the inclusion of the RL Council of Editors—the émigré chiefs of all the broadcast services—in the process.

Most PPSs contained situational analyses that (the title notwithstanding) only implied an editorial policy and were routinely endorsed by the CIA and the State Department. Examples were the PPSs "Free Exchange of Information and Ideas" (November 3, 1960), "The 22nd Party Congress" (September 26, 1961), "The USSR and China" (1967), and "The Soviet Union and International Communism" (July 1, 1969).

A second category of PPSs conveyed "enlightened émigré" editorial perspectives on international affairs that sometimes departed from U.S. government policies and—RL's U.S. government-approved charter notwithstanding—invariably led to State Department criticism and occasional revision of the document in question. Examples were the PPSs "Military Technological Achievements" (May 5, 1961), which was criticized for not sufficiently dramatizing the Soviet military threat; "Poland" (February 18, 1960), which was criticized for overstating Gomułka's retreat from the high tide of 1956 reforms; and "Latin America" (revised June 1, 1960), which was criticized for covering developments contrary to as well as supportive of U.S. policy.

Just as was true for RFE, some of the issues addressed by these PPSs gave rise to extensive bureaucratic debate on matters of minor and some- times only stylistic importance. The case of an early PPS on disarmament and nuclear testing, dated April 4, 1957, was illustrative. Although the State Department had minor reservations, it finally endorsed the PPS in July after only stylistic changes. And though the PPS was a joint product of AMCOMLIB New York and RL Munich American policy officials and émi- gré service chiefs, New York AMCOMLIB officials were initially inclined to accept State's reservations, but took a harder stance after objections from Munich. Underlying such controversies were different conceptions of the Radios' role and specifically their connection to current U.S. government policy positions. Notwithstanding the CRBP's endorsement of separate missions for VOA and RL in 1957 and the State Department's approval of the May 1958 broadcast policy statement, State's officials would remain op- posed to broadcasts that deviated from official U.S. government policy, while the CIA defended the RL principle that "it is inherent in the concept of an émigré voice that it will not parrot the official U.S. line at every point."[25]

Most contentious was the Soviet nationalities issue. "Non-predeterminism" on Soviet nationality matters often involved the AMCOMLIB and RL in controversy with émigré organizations calling for national independence for their homelands. Captive Nations Week in the United States always oc- casioned such controversy. Preparing for this week in 1960, RL planned to play down the Western discussion and avoid mentioning specific "nations" such as Ukraine, notwithstanding a joint resolution of Congress of July 1959 that did precisely this.[26] Such restraint notwithstanding, the State De- partment's criticism increased in the mid-1960s, with the CIA Covert Ac- tion Staff countering by defending RL in 1967 against accusations that RL Ukrainian programming "intended to encourage narrowly nationalistic, separatist, and anti-Russian attitudes on the part of Ukrainian listeners."

This line of criticism led RL to draft a series of nationality annexes to its Policy Manual, beginning with Ukraine in 1968. The annex specified that RL Ukrainian broadcasts should "preserve and stimulate the growth of Ukrainian cultural values and national identity, reflecting in its broadcasts a continuity in the history and life of the Ukrainian nation which antedates the Soviet era and will persist and flourish in the future." Broadcasts should

25. AMCOMLIB memorandum by Richard Bertrandias, April 3, 1957; AMCOMLIB New York Airgram 306, June 11, 1957.
26. AMCOMLIB PPS, "Captive Nations," April 1960.

"emphasize not only the aim of truly representative government, but also stress the importance of achieving political, economic, and social reforms in the present system." RL would not prejudge "the ultimate outcome of exercise of the right to self-determination, whether it be independence, federation, or alliance."[27]

The State Department's approval of this annex, and similar annexes to the Policy Manual for the other RL nationality services, did not end the matter. State's officers remained critical of the balance of RL broadcasts based on these policy documents. Reviewing the PPS "The Nationality Question" (April 17, 1970), the State Department asked that it be revised to include a statement that "specifically, in its output Radio Liberty takes care not to be identified with a program of separatism and dismemberment of the USSR, which can only alienate and unite all Russians, who still constitute the dominant and ruling element in the USSR and the primary target of RL broadcasts." RL officials viewed such language as accusatory and excessively Russo-centric, and it was evidently never incorporated into a revised PPS.

To be sure, AMCOMLIB and RL had no monopoly on wisdom, and occasionally intervention by the U.S. government in fact did improve RL broadcasts. One such example involved programming on the resumption of nuclear weapons testing by the United States in 1962. In that case, the CIA/IOD's intervention led RL to broadcast not two individual commentaries, as originally planned, but a discussion among five scientists, three of them Nobel Prize winners—most prominently Linus Pauling, who criticized the U.S. testing, and Edward Teller, who defended it.[28]

Intra-Radio and interagency controversies about RL and RFE policy statements—and later analyses of them by scholars—sometimes lost sight of the fact that these policy documents were only a framework for discussions within RL and RFE about broadcasts, not the broadcasts themselves. They often recorded ("memorialized," in bureaucratese) a consensus reached through prior discussion among émigré broadcasters and American managers. Few if any RL PPSs or RFE policy guidances were unilateral directives from American managers to émigré broadcasters. No RL PPS and no RFE policy guidance was ever translated verbatim and broadcast. That would have amounted to central scripting—which was common at the time at VOA

27. Radio Liberty Policy Manual Annex, "Ukrainian Broadcasts," November 1968.
28. RL Russian Service, "Special Features," no. 271, April 16, 1962; English translation in Hoover Archives. The text of the final program, quite exceptionally, was reviewed by the CIA/IOD before broadcast. See also Sosin, *Sparks of Liberty*, 93–96.

and the BBC but anathema to the concept of surrogate broadcasting, "a joint endeavor of Americans and émigrés," which purposefully devolved editorial responsibility, within broad guidelines, to émigré broadcast service chiefs. As an RL Munich policy official, Edward Van Der Rhoer, observed at the time:

> I am still at a loss to understand why the slight change in emphasis [in revisions of the PPSs] was considered so important. . . . The formulations contained in a given PPS are seldom if ever broadcast in the form stated. We provide in our statement of background, assumptions, and objectives certain rather general guidelines which in turn provide a skeleton rather than the flesh and bones of our programming.[29]

In the RL case, the few exceptions to the "bottom-up" flow of policy statements from Munich to New York to Washington and back involved sensitivities of foreign governments whose goodwill was the prerequisite for continued RL operations. This was the case with a 1962 PPS on broadcast coverage of Spanish topics, which reemphasized the provision of the RL Policy Manual banning broadcasting from local transmitters of "any material harmful to the interests of the host governments which might embarrass the radio in the conduct of its relations with the host governments." Thus the 1962 PPS directed that any material critical of Spain could be broadcast only from RL's German transmitters.[30] This was a problematic solution to a hypothetical problem; there is no known case of an RL broadcast critical of one of the host countries (Spain, Germany, Taiwan) being broadcast only from the others.

By the late 1960s, the quality of RL broadcasts had improved considerably relative to the early 1950s. RL had recruited new staff members from among recent political émigrés. It had become a more effective communicator focused on Soviet affairs from an "enlightened émigré perspective," "as a native entity, but one free of the restrictions imposed on domestic institutions,"[31] albeit identified as a "U.S. station" by many listeners.[32] RL's impact depended on conditions in the USSR, which began to change dra-

29. AMCOMLIB memorandum by Edward Van Der Rhoer, June 14, 1961.

30. AMCOMLIB memorandum from the CIA, "Interim Guidance for Radio Liberty Broadcasts from Spain" (draft), July 11, 1962.

31. RLC brochure, "The Relevance of Radio Liberty in 1969."

32. RLC memorandum from policy advisor [Tuck], "The Americanization of Radio Liberty," October 25, 1965.

matically in the late 1960s. As dissident voices emerged in the USSR, RL was now ready and able to amplify them. It broadcast, often at dictation speed, the growing literature of dissent that could not be published in the USSR: the writings of Andrei Sinyvaski and Yuri Daniel; Andrei Sakharov's book *Thoughts on Progress, Peaceful Coexistence, and Intellectual Freedom;* Andrei Amalrik's essay "Will the Soviet Union Survive until 1984?"; Aleksandr Solzhenitsyn's novel *Cancer Ward;* Svetlana Alliluyeva's memoir *Twenty Letters to a Friend;* and much more. It was just at this juncture, as RL began to demonstrate its real potential after fifteen years of investment and as the Soviet Union increased its efforts to counter it, that RL was marked for termination by the Nixon White House.

Chapter 7

Impact and Countermeasures

The Iron Curtain was not just concrete and barbed wire. It was also an "information curtain" intended to isolate Soviet Bloc populations from outside information that might challenge communist truths. Control of information was a key element of the communist system, and Western efforts to penetrate that information curtain with RFE, RL, and other broadcasters constituted a major challenge to the regimes.

In the 1950s, the Radios could marshal only limited evidence of their impact, primarily letters from listeners,[1] limited surveys among refugees, and counterattacks in regime-controlled media. However, beginning in the 1960s, audience surveys among more than 150,000 travelers to the West, now-accessible internal regime surveys that had once been secret, and retrospective internal surveys commissioned after 1989 all indicated remarkably large regular audiences for Western broadcasts—about one-third of the urban adult Soviet population and close to half the Eastern European adult populations after the 1950s.[2] These large audiences were further increased by extensive word-of-mouth amplification.

Reinforcing the evidence of the impact of the Radios from survey data, both Communist and postcommunist elites later testified to the importance

---

1. E.g., the Polish Service received 2,184 letters in the course of 1957. RFE Assessments Memorandum, Audience Analysis Section, "Poland: Audience Response to Western Broadcasts, July–December 1957," no. 67, June 1958. Though some letters were doubtless a product of deception operations—see Ladislav Bittman, *The Deception Game* (Syracuse: Syracuse University Research Corporation, 1972), 148ff—most were genuine and made their way through the censors.

2. R. Eugene Parta, *Discovering the Hidden Listener: An Assessment of Radio Liberty and Western Broadcasting to the USSR during the Cold War* (Stanford, Calif.: Hoover

of Western broadcasts. Václav Havel said that RFE/RL's "influence and significance have been great and profound." Former Hungarian propaganda chief János Berecz said: "I became convinced that Western broadcasts were among the accepted sources of information among the youth." East German spymaster Markus Wolf said in his memoirs that, "of all the various means used to influence people against the East during the Cold War, I would count [Radio Free Europe and RIAS] as the most effective." And the great Russian novelist Aleksandr Solzhenitsyn wrote of "the mighty non-military force which resides in the airwaves and whose kindling power in the midst of communist darkness cannot even be grasped by the Western imagination."[3]

Another measure of the Radios' impact was the magnitude of the resources the Communist regimes devoted to countering Western broadcasts. Their efforts included technical interference with the broadcasts (jamming), reprisals against listeners and other efforts to discourage listening, blocking the flow of information to the Radios, penetration of the Radios with agents, intimidation of Radio staffs, and public and private propaganda and disinformation intended to turn European public opinion against the Radios. This chapter examines these countermeasures, and carries the story of the Radios forward beyond the CIA period to the end of the Cold War.

At Stalin's personal directive, the USSR and its allies organized radio jamming on a massive scale,[4] arguably spending more on jamming than the West did on broadcasting—$150 million yearly, according to U.S. government estimates of the late 1960s. Romania ended jamming in 1963 and Hungary in 1964, but jamming of all RL and RFE broadcasts to Bulgaria, Czechoslovakia, and (less effectively) Poland continued until November

Institution Press, 2007); A. Ross Johnson and R. Eugene Parta, eds., *Cold War Broadcasting: Impact on the Soviet Union and Eastern Europe—A Collection of Studies and Documents* (Budapest: Central European University Press, 2010); Helmut Aigner, oral history interview with R. Eugene Parta, Vienna, August 2005, Hoover Archives. A review by Oliver Quayle and Company validated RFE's methodology of surrogate survey research; FEC copy, "An Informal Survey of Opinion Research at Radio Free Europe," prepared by Oliver Quayle and Company, October 1970.

3. These quotations are from Johnson and Parta, *Cold War Broadcasting;* Markus Wolf, *Man Without a Face: The Autobiography of Communism's Greatest Spymaster* (New York: PublicAffairs, 1997), 261; and Alan L. Heil Jr., "The Voice of America: A Brief Cold War History," in *Cold War Broadcasting,* ed. Johnson and Parta, chap. 3.

4. "USSR Council of Ministers Decree No. 4028-1849ss of October 24, 1951," translation in *Cold War Broadcasting,* document 43; RLC memorandum, "Soviet Jamming of Radio Liberty," n.d. [1965].

1988.[5] Soviet Bloc regimes organized counterpropaganda in their domestic media, while at the same time secretly circulating transcriptions of monitored Western broadcasts among top officials to provide them with information not available from their own controlled media or intelligence services. Even counterpropaganda had to acknowledge and thus amplify in the local media some information provided by Western Radios. Soviet Communist Party ideological secretary Piotr Demichev lamented, "It is not unusual that works polemicizing with bourgeois ideology turn out to be in effect reproductions of bourgeois books and articles."[6] The same held true for polemics with Western broadcasts.

Soviet Bloc security services also took reprisals against listeners and attempted through propaganda and police measures to interrupt the flow of information to the Radios about domestic developments. For example, 4,400 people were sentenced to labor camps in Poland between 1950 and 1954 for spreading "hostile propaganda," in part from Western radio broadcasts.[7] The Polish security service attempted to neutralize "Operation Spotlight" by collecting copies of the brochures with Józef Światło's revelations that had reached Poland by balloons and the mails.[8] Hungarian "New Course" leader Imre Nagy condemned the "base slander . . . from balloons and dirty leaflets" sent by émigré "vermin, . . . pitiable tools of foreign hostile aims."[9] The official news agency CTK denounced the mailing of leaflets to Czechoslovakia.[10] In mid-1955, Budapest relatives of RFE Hungarian staff members were forced to resettle to a town near the Soviet border.[11] The security

5. See the overview of Soviet Bloc jamming given by George Woodard, "Cold War Jamming," in *Cold War Broadcasting,* ed. Johnson and Parta, chap. 4. Jamming of RFE Polish broadcasts within Poland ended in 1956 but continued from the USSR.

6. *Einheit* (East Berlin), no. 9, 1968, as cited in RFE Research paper, "The New Character of Communist Reaction to RFE Broadcasts," n.d. [1970].

7. Paweł Machcewicz, *"Monachijska menażeria": Walka z Radiem Wolna Europa* (Warsaw: Instytut Pamięci Narodowej, ISP, 2007), 86.

8. Protocol of Session of the Committee for Public Security, February 14, 1955, AIPN, IPN KdsBP, 1, k. 43–44, Instytut Pamięci Narodowej, Warsaw. I am indebted to Andrzej Paczkowski for a copy of this document.

9. RFE monitoring of Kossuth radio transmission of speech by Imre Nagy to the People's Front Congress, October 24, 1954. A Hungarian escapee told RFE that on October 10 "Sopron was snowed under with leaflets." RFE information report from Vienna, October 22, 1954.

10. CTK, September 5, 1956.

11. RFE report, "Retaliatory Measures by AVH against RFE Relatives in Hungary," July 22, 1955; article in *Truth* (London), August 10, 1956; Allan A. Michie, *Voices through the Iron Curtain: The Radio Free Europe Story* (New York, Dodd, Mead, 1963), 284.

services also attempted to track and arrest individuals who were secretly providing RFE and RL with information. For example, László Geresby and his wife were arrested in Hungary in 1967 for cooperating with RFE, and a Polish Press Agency journalist, Józef Szaniawski, was arrested in 1985 after supplying "inside" information to RFE for twelve years.[12]

The Communist regimes also directed their intelligence services to penetrate the Radios, to wage political warfare against them in Western Europe, and to attempt to woo away or take reprisals against their staffs. An October 1954 Polish intelligence service directive tasked the service to penetrate RFE, uncover its contacts and sources, and plant false material that could compromise it.[13] These efforts were concentrated against RFE and RL (among all Western broadcasters) because both were more focused on domestic developments in the Soviet Bloc than other Western broadcasters and because both were located in Munich (and thus were more accessible to penetration than VOA in Washington or the BBC in London).

Penetration for Information Collection

The efforts of the Soviet Bloc's intelligence services to penetrate the Radios began in the 1950s but increased in the 1960s. They enlisted collaborators already in the West through blackmail, appeals to patriotism, or monetary payment. Less frequently, they dispatched career agents with elaborate cover stories who sought employment with RFE or RL. The Polish intelligence service was the most active in this regard. It recruited a Polish broadcaster ("Fonda") in 1963 and thereafter utilized a series of collaborators. Best known was Andrzej Czechowicz, who (contrary to Polish regime claims that he was prepared for his assignment in Poland), was evidently recruited while already in the West. Czechowicz collected information from his desk in the Polish research section for several years before returning to Poland to denounce RFE in a staged press conference on March 8, 1971, and in numerous publications. Other (self-admitted) collaborators who surfaced later in Poland were Andrzej Smoliński (who also worked in Polish research) and Mieczysław Lach (who worked in the audience research department). The Polish intelligence service actively sought the cooperation of other Poles at

12. In 1963, Polish party leader Gomułka denounced Poles who passed information to RFE. See Machcewicz, *"Monachijska menażeria."*
13. FEC memorandum from CIA, W (JS) 5604, January 25, 1955.

RFE. It established a reporting relationship with Wiktor Trościanko, a highly respected senior broadcaster, who may have thought he was somehow promoting the cause of his National Democratic Party but over time provided the Polish regime with considerable information about the internal workings of the RFE Polish Service.[14]

The Czechoslovak intelligence service utilized Pavel Minařík between 1968 and 1976, when he was surfaced in Prague.[15] Communist-era Interior Ministry files contain reports from Bulgarian and Hungarian informers as well. One alleged Romanian agent within RFE was arrested by the German authorities in July 1981.[16]

The most important Soviet Bloc spy in the Munich Radios was Oleg Tumanov, the KGB's principal source within RL. Tumanov joined RL in 1966 and initially presented himself when he surfaced in Moscow in 1986 as a patriot who had come to his senses and returned home. In fact, as he himself later admitted (and Oleg Kalugin confirmed), Tumanov was a KGB agent placed within RL who reported extensively on the organization for twenty years.[17]

The East German intelligence service (the Ministry for State Security's Main Directorate for Intelligence, the HVA, headed by Markus Wolf) had no direct interest in RFE or RL (which did not broadcast in German, although RFE did produce research reports on East Germany, which the HVA obtained and translated into German). Although RFE and RL employed hundreds of German citizens in Munich and at its German transmitter stations, HVA records at the Office of the Federal Commissioner (BStU) suggest that it had only a few of its own collaborators within RFE and RL, some of these as a direct service to the KGB. One such informant was "Krüger," who provided reports on RL's organizational and personnel issues from 1976 to the mid-1980s. Earlier reports were evidently provided by another

14. Machcewicz, *"Monachijska menażeria,"* 174–218, provides details and documentation from Interior Ministry archives now deposited at the Instytut Pamięci Narodowej; also see Andrzej Czechowicz, *Siedem trudnych lat* (Warsaw, 1st ed., 1973; 2nd ed., 1974).

15. Minařík's "revelations" were published as *Navrat Rozvĕdčíka* (Prague, 1976) and *Vozvrashchenie razvedchika* (Moscow: Progress, 1977).

16. Jack Anderson, "The Ante Rises Over Radio Free Europe," *Washington Post,* July 25, 1981.

17. Oleg Tumanov, *Confessions of a KGB Agent* (Chicago: Edition Q, 1993); Oleg Kalugin, *The First Directorate: My 32 Years in Intelligence and Espionage against the West* (New York: St. Martin's Press, 1994), 194–97.

informant.[18] More important were HVA intelligence reports on attitudes about RFE and RL in the West German government, including reports on views hostile to the Radios held by some in the Brandt government, who (the reports claimed) even welcomed Soviet Bloc pressure against the Radios.[19] The archives also document East German assistance to the Czechoslovak and Polish intelligence services in intercepting in West Berlin letters sent to RFE and to the Bulgarian service with information on RFE traveler surveys carried out in Vienna.

The purpose of these Soviet Bloc penetration efforts was uniformly to collect information, not to influence RFE/RL operations. Soviet Bloc agents gathered everything they could get their hands on: internal memoranda, the internal telephone book, research reports, traveler survey questionnaires and reports, lists of home addresses of staff, broadcast guidances, and virtually all other printed materials. A key target was the identity of Soviet Bloc travelers who were interviewed in various Western European cities by RFE or RL bureau staff. One set of these interviews solicited reactions to the broadcasts. A separate set of interviews conducted by RFE until 1971 (and described in chapter 2) sought information—political, economic, social, and biographic data—about developments in the target countries; this information was circulated internally as "information items" and was utilized in research and broadcasting. Some of this was micro-level information, such as work conditions in a particular factory. Other information concerned the activities of top regime officials, often provided by regime elites who "leaked" the information to the West so that it would be broadcast and thus weaken rivals within the ruling establishment.[20] This source information was closely held within RFE, and no reports containing this information have been lo-

18. "Rosenholz" "Krüger" file case XV 2740/76, BStU, released to the author; Richard H. Cummings, *Cold War Radio: The Dangerous History of American Broadcasting in Europe, 1950–1989* (Jefferson, N.C.: McFarland & Co., 2009), 194–95; MfS report on RL personnel changes, March 6, 1974, HA22-5555/41, BStU.

19. MfS Information No. 993/70, "Information über die Einschätzung der Haltung der Bundesregierung zur Tätigkeit der Sender 'Freies Europe' und 'Radio Liberty,'" September 23, 1970, MfS HA X, 541, BStU, translation in *Cold War Broadcasting,* ed. Johnson and Parta, document 4.

20. A Polish intelligence service document referred to material reaching RFE "provided by a person holding a high Party position in Poland. Texts or reports from sessions of the Politburo are also delivered in this way via London or New York to Munich." "Notatka informacyjna dotycząca ujawnionych kontaktów z Rozgłośnią Polską RWE" [Note concerning uncovered contacts with the RFE Polish Service], July 21, 1962, AIPN, IPN 01299/358, k. 9–10, as cited by Machcewicz, *"Monachijska menażeria,"* 143.

cated in Soviet Bloc security service archives. Nonetheless, some of it was probably obtained.[21]

Soviet Bloc collaborators and agents within the Radios provided, in addition to documentary material, analyses of personnel and policy issues—some of which, in retrospect, were quite perceptive. For example, Minařík (who was sometimes viewed as a bungler) provided dispassionate and accurate analyses of program and policy changes in the RFE Czechoslovak Service following the Soviet occupation in August 1968.[22] And a still-unidentified Polish collaborator provided a sophisticated analysis of personal relationships within the RFE Polish Service before 1988.[23]

Although Soviet Bloc agents or collaborators within RFE and RL thus collected much information about the Radios, there is no evidence that they attempted to influence the content of the radio broadcasts and little evidence that they were specifically tasked to sow dissension among the ranks. They operated as collectors of information, not agents of influence. The most important Soviet penetration agent, as noted above, was Oleg Tumanov, who worked for the KGB in RL for twenty years, until 1986. By his own later account, his assignment was to collect information on RL, especially its contacts with Soviet travelers, and also to use his RL job as cover to collect information on the anti-Soviet émigré organization Narodno-Trudovoy Soyuz (National Alliance of Russian Solidarists) and other anti-Soviet activities in West Germany. His KGB superiors repeatedly discouraged him from any initiatives in his work as a broadcaster that might raise suspicions. As he later boasted, "Fortunately there were never any mistakes in my work. I was always very careful to see that my cover was not exposed; that is to say that the official cover for my work as an agent was always faultless. I am proud to have created a whole series of new programs for Radio Liberty."[24]

---

21. The preserved Eastern European security service files are generally open to researchers. Czechowicz claims that he obtained and transmitted to Warsaw the identities of hundreds of Polish informants; Czechowicz interview with the author, Warsaw, July 2004. Polish Interior Ministry archives at the Institute of National Remembrance contain copies of 429 information "Items" obtained by Czechowicz but no information on the sources of these reports. RFE's procedures for protecting source information (detailed in a memorandum "Information Reporting", n.d.), if followed, would have precluded Czechowicz's access to source information.

22. Czechoslovak intelligence report in German translation dated November 10, 1968, ZAIG 22324, BStU, and subsequent reports.

23. Polish Interior Ministry report on the RFE Polish Service, January 15, 1988, Instytut Pamięci Narodowej.

24. Tumanov, *Confessions of a KGB Agent,* 178.

The Soviet Bloc's intelligence services, under the tutelage of the KGB, regularly exchanged intelligence reports obtained from collaborators within RFE and RL. The Bulgarian Interior Ministry's archives document these exchanges between the Bulgarian KDB and the KGB. The East German Ministry of State Security files at the BStU contain numerous Bulgarian, Czechoslovak, Hungarian, and Polish intelligence reports in German translation. They contain no Romanian Securitate reports, even from the period before 1972 when the Securitate was responsive to the KGB and participated in Soviet Bloc multilateral intelligence activities.[25]

Public and Private Campaigns against "Ideological Subversion Centers"

Soviet Bloc media and officials had denounced RFE and RL broadcasts from the outset. Supplementing these ideologically based denunciations, information collected from and about RFE and RL by Soviet Bloc intelligence services was put to operational use, informing propaganda and disinformation actions in Western Europe intended to turn public opinion against the Radios and thus close them down or at least drive them out of Germany. These covert efforts supported a major Soviet Bloc effort, described in chapter 8, to reinforce reservations of the Brandt government about the Radios and concerns of the International Olympic Committee about holding the 1972 Summer Olympic Games in Munich. After Czechowicz was surfaced in Warsaw in March 1971, some of his accusations against RFE were used in Poland's diplomatic protests about RFE to the West German and U.S. governments in May 1971.

This anti-Radio campaign intensified after 1975, as the Helsinki Final Act emboldened dissidents in the Soviet Bloc and as the Radios took on a new role as amplifier of internal dissent. But as early as the Geneva Conference of 1955, the Soviet Union had sought to make an issue of RFE and RL in diplomatic discussions. At the October 1955 foreign ministers' meeting in Geneva, Soviet foreign minister Vyacheslav Molotov denounced the exile voices on RFE as "the scum of society thrown out of the people's democracies." In 1959, Polish Communist leader Gomułka complained to U.S. vice president Richard Nixon that RFE broadcast "hours of abuse daily

25. Several of the documents published in *Cold War Broadcasting,* ed. Johnson and Parta, provide details of this information exchange.

into Poland." And in 1972, Soviet leader Leonid Brezhnev complained to President Nixon about the harm to good bilateral relations caused by "constant blather by some American publications and various radio stations, such as Radio Free Europe, etc."[26]

The public campaign against RFE, RL, and other "subversive" Western information programs was the focus of a series of multilateral Soviet Bloc intelligence service meetings involving the Soviet, East German, Polish, Hungarian, and Bulgarian services. (The Romanian Securitate did not participate; Soviet-Romanian intelligence cooperation ended in 1972, and the Securitate then became a target, rather than a junior partner, of the KGB.) An initial multilateral meeting was held in Havana in 1974 devoted to coordinating the fight against "ideological subversion." The key meeting was held in Prague in 1976 and chaired by Oleg Kalugin. Follow-up coordination meetings were held in Budapest in 1977, Warsaw in 1979, Moscow in 1980, Sofia in 1983, and Prague in 1986.

The key 1976 Prague conference was opened by Czechoslovak interior minister Jaromir Obzina, who claimed that the Helsinki Final Act and prior revelations in the United States of CIA funding for RFE and RL had created favorable circumstances for a public media campaign that would discredit the Radios in the eyes of Western Europeans. The conference adopted a "Work Plan for the Joint Measures of the Intelligence Organs of the [Six Countries] against the Centers of Ideological Subversion—The Radio Stations 'Free Europe' and 'Liberty,'" with the minimum objective of removing RFE and RL from Europe and with the maximum objective of closing them down entirely. This work plan envisaged (1) overt propaganda from Soviet Bloc countries utilizing information from Czechowicz, Minarik, and other informants to expose the Radios "as ideological subversive centers of the USA working at the direction of the CIA"; (2) covert efforts to influence international public opinion, including "Operation Spider" (the details of which are unknown) to demonstrate that the Radios were in violation of international law, along with statements by "progressive groups" and letters to parliamentarians; (3) holding a "public tribunal against RFE and RL on the territory of a socialist country"; (4) efforts to isolate the Radios in international organizations such as the International Olympic Committee; (5)

---

26. U.S. Department of State, *Foreign Relations of the United States* (hereafter, *FRUS*) (Washington, D.C.: U.S. Government Printing Office, various years), *Soviet-American Relations. The Détente Years 1969–1972*, 997.

measures to exert psychological pressure on the Radios' employees, including exploitation of nationalist conflicts and anti-Semitism; (6) continued information collection, including information on "the role and position of the U.S. intelligence agencies in the subversive activity of RFE and RL"; and (7) interrupting the flow of information from the "socialist countries" to the Radios.[27]

The archives of the Communist intelligence services document the implementation of parts of this work plan. Efforts at penetration continued. Official media in all the Soviet Bloc countries launched a new anti-Radio campaign utilizing material from the intelligence services. As one example, an article prepared by the MfS was published in *Volksstimme* in Vienna and then reprinted in *Izvestia* on May 17, 1975. A treatise was published in Vienna by Emil Hoffmann on the "illegal" status of RFE and RL; the work was a product of the MfS, and copies of successive drafts are preserved in the archives.[28] The Czechoslovak Interior Ministry covertly published a brochure on Radio officials in English, German, Slovak, French, and Spanish intended to expose them as Western intelligence officers. Conversely, the notion of a public tribunal was evidently quickly dropped, and there is little evidence of enhanced efforts to exacerbate tensions at the Radios from within.

The public anti-Radio campaigns in domestic and international media included targeted disinformation. For instance, the Polish Interior Ministry established Group D in Department III in the early 1970s for the purpose of "programming of inspiration and disinformation activities toward anticommunist centers." One product of this effort was the accusation in the second edition of Czechowicz's book that RFE Polish Service director Jan Nowak had collaborated with the Nazi occupiers in Warsaw at the outset of World War II.[29]

These public disinformation efforts had a private counterpart. The most serious case involved allegations (subsequently disproven) that RFE Polish

---

27. "Arbeitsplan für gemeinsame Aktionen der Aufklärungsorgane der VRB, UVR, DDR, VRP, UdSSR, und ČSSR gegen die Zentren der ideologischen Diversion—die Runkfunkstationen 'Freies Europa' und 'Liberty' Übersetzung aus dem Russischen. Entwurf, 13 February 1976, Prag," MfS HA XX; ZMA 914, BStU. English translation in *Cold War Broadcasting,* ed. Johnson and Parta, document 21.
28. MfS HA IX, 1231 Bd. 2; HA IX 16133, BStU.
29. Czechowicz, *Siedem trudnych lat;* Machcewicz, *"Monachijska menażeria,"* 289ff.

Service deputy director Alexander Żenczykowski (Zawadzki), a hero of the Home Army, was a Polish intelligence service collaborator. The allegation, evidently made by a high-level Polish defector, was taken at face value for some time, until a polygraph interview and other evidence indicated it was witting or unwitting disinformation.[30]

Persuasion, Intimidation, Reprisals

In the early 1950s, a number of violent actions were taken against RFE and RL employees, freelancers, and physical facilities that were almost certainly organized by the KGB. German and American occupation authorities thwarted evident preparations to bomb an RFE balloon-launching facility and the Holzkirchen transmitter site. RL Azerbaijani service chief Abdul Fatalibey and Belorussian service broadcaster Leonid Karas were murdered in Munich in 1954. Other broadcasters were harassed. (Some of these actions may have targeted individuals for émigré activities separate from their role at the Radios).[31] In 1959, in the now-famous "Saltshaker" episode, a Czechoslovak intelligence service officer planed to place the poison atropine in saltshakers in the RFE cafeteria (a plot thwarted by a double agent).[32] Subsequently, as the Cold War fronts hardened and implicit "rules of the game" developed, there is little evidence of violent actions undertaken by Soviet Bloc intelligence and security services against Radio staff. Agents and collaborators (including "Fonda" and Minařík) regularly suggested to their superiors bombings or other physical actions

30. John Richardson Jr., *A New Vision for America: Toward Human Solidarity through Global Democracy—a Memoir* (New York: Ruder Finn Press, 2006), 113. Richardson identified the deputy director as Zawadzki in an interview with the author, 2008. The RFE/RL security files document the same allegation made by individuals close to the Polish regime to RFE Polish Service staff members (during RFE-approved contacts). They also document (perhaps part of the same disinformation effort) at least one Polish regime approach to Zawadzki to persuade him to return to Poland.

31. See James Critchlow, *Radio Hole-in-the-Head: Radio Liberty—An Insider's Story of Cold War Broadcasting* (Washington, D.C.: American University Press, 1995), 55–67; Cummings, *Cold War Radio,* 34–39.

32. Arch Puddington, *Broadcasting Freedom: The Cold War Triumph of Radio Free Europe and Radio Liberty* (Lexington: University Press of Kentucky, 2000), 227; Cummings, *Cold War Radio,* 51–52; Bittman, *Deception Game,* 11–12; *The Guardian,* December 17, 1959.

against Radio facilities, but these proposals never reached the stage of operational planning.

If violence subsided, efforts by the Communist regimes to pressure individual RFE and RL journalists to return to the homeland (or to remain in place and spy) did not. In the 1950s, regime efforts to influence RFE and RL staff involved reprisals against relatives at home—dismissal from jobs, forced relocation, arrests, and other harassment. In many cases, the "redefection" campaigns of 1954–56 involved such pressure on relatives.[33] Subsequently a softer approach was generally used, in the form of approaches by acquaintances or relatives allowed to travel to the West under the condition that they attempt to persuade the broadcaster to return home (or cooperate in place) and that they report on their activities. As an indication of the scale of this effort at times, RL reported sixteen Soviet approaches to its broadcasters over a three-month period in 1962 aimed at persuading them to redefect.

Polish Interior Ministry files at the Instytut Pamięci Narodowej (Institute of National Remembrance) reviewed by Paweł Machcewicz and RFE/RL corporate security files reviewed by the author indicate many other regime approaches to RFE staff. Most were pro forma—the price of a relative being able to travel—and quickly rebuffed. A few led to one or two rounds of RFE-approved conversations, with each side trying to learn more about the other (and—the house of mirrors of intelligence operations—each side knowing that the other side knew this, and so on), evidently to little avail.

Although Soviet Bloc regimes generally avoided physical violence against RFE and RL personnel after the 1950s, there are two notable exceptions. The first was the assassination in London in September 1978 of Georgi Markov, a Bulgarian exile writer who had been an "insider" with knowledge of the Bulgarian Communist leadership secrets and who subsequently became a contributor to BBC, RFE, and Deutsche Welle Bulgarian-language broadcasts. Markov was killed by ricin poisoning, following prior unsuccessful assassination attempts on both Markov and Bulgarian Service broadcaster Vladimir Kostov, a defector from the Bulgarian intelligence service, and repeated efforts at intimidation. Bulgarian Interior Ministry archives, informed Bulgarian analyses, a Scotland Yard investigation, and

33. Michie, *Voices through the Iron Curtain,* 275ff. As one example, *Rude Pravo,* July 13, 1956 (RFE translation, July 17, 1956) carried an interview with Helena Bušová-Kasalová, who redefected in 1956 along with her husband Karel Kasal; both had worked at RFE.

the testimonies of Oleg Kalugin and Vasili Mitrokhin indicate that his murder was carried out by Bulgarian agents with KGB "technical" assistance.[34]

The Bulgarian Communist Party's leadership had a clear motive for silencing Markov, an "unwelcome priest" with firsthand knowledge of the party leadership who was personally hated by Bulgarian party chief Todor Zhivkov. A Bulgarian Interior Ministry analysis of 1977 singled out Markov's broadcasts (along with those of three other recent defectors) as especially threatening because "they criticize and slander everything and everybody related to the Bulgarian-Soviet friendship and the building of our socialist Motherland."[35] Less clear is the KGB's motivation for violating the unwritten "rules of the game"—avoiding violence against enemies on the territory (in this case the United Kingdom) of the strategic adversary—on an issue of secondary importance to the Kremlin. According to Mitrokhin, "Andropov eventually accepted Kryuchkov's argument that to refuse would be an unacceptable slight to Zhivkov."[36]

The second and major exception was the series of violent physical assaults on the RFE Romanian staff and the RFE building in Munich undertaken by the Romanian Securitate after the mid-1970s. This violence may be explained by the growing siege mentality of the Ceauşescu regime, the impact on the Romanian population of the RFE Romanian Service, and, ironically, Romania's autonomous course on the international scene, which included the independence of the Securitate from the KGB and thus the absence of a certain restraining influence. As Nestor Ratesh has written, "As Ceauşescu was crisscrossing the West, collecting honors and playing the respected statesman, within his inner circle he plotted feverishly against Radio Free Europe."[37]

Ceauşescu's plotting resulted in the bombing of the RFE/RL building in Munich in February 1981. It is now well documented that the Securitate

34. Jordan Baev, "Bulgarian Regime Countermeasures against Radio Free Europe," in *Cold War Broadcasting,* ed. Johnson and Parta, chap. 13; Kalugin, *First Directorate,* 178–83; Christopher Andrew and Vasili Mitrokhin, *The Sword and the Shield: The Mitrokhin Archive and the Secret History of the KGB* (New York: Basic Books, 1999), 388–89. See the full account given by Cummings, *Cold War Radio,* 58–91.

35. "Analysis of Foreign Propaganda against the People's Republic of Bulgaria in 1977," May 11, 1978, Bulgarian Interior Ministry Archive, fond 22, record 1, document 65, translated in *Cold War Broadcasting,* ed. Johnson and Parta, document 1.

36. Andrews and Mitrokhin, *Sword and the Shield,* 388–89. Yuri Andropov was then head of the KGB and Vladimir Kryuchkov was chief of its foreign intelligence directorate.

37. Nestor Ratesh, "Radio Free Europe's Impact in Romania during the Cold War," in *Cold War Broadcasting,* ed. Johnson and Parta, chap. 10; Ion Mihai Pacepa, *Red Horizons: Chronicles of a Communist Spy Chief* (Washington, D.C.: Regnery Gateway, 1987).

commissioned Ilich Ramirez Sanchez (the international terrorist leader commonly known as Carlos the Jackal) to organize the bombing, although many details remain unclear.[38] First, if the target was the RFE Romanian Service, the bomb exploded far from its offices, causing physical damage and seriously injuring three Czechoslovak service staff. Second, before the bombing, the Carlos group, like other anti-Western terrorist groupings, found refuge in Eastern Europe, living at various times in East Berlin and Budapest, with the knowledge and some support from local security services (and therefore the knowledge and approval of the KGB). Soviet Bloc security services monitored the Carlos group and Securitate officials traveling in Eastern Europe closely enough to have been aware of the preparations for the bombing of the RFE building.[39] If so, perhaps they found it useful to let the operation go forward as an unattributable act of intimidation. Or perhaps the monitoring reports were buried in the bureaucracies. An authoritative MfS Main Division 22 ("antiterrorism" division) memorandum prepared for the minister of state security, Erich Mielke, several weeks after the bombing indicated that the MfS did not know who was responsible, adding, "Unofficial information indicates that responsibility for the attack cannot be attributed to groups known to us operating in the framework of the PLO, nor to the RAF [respectively, Palestinian and West German terrorist organizations]."[40] If the Soviet Bloc intelligence services had for-

38. Carlos was reportedly paid $1 million for the operation, and the four-person operational group led by Johannes Weinrich that carried it out utilized Romanian-supplied explosives and equipment. An intelligence report (not a liaison report) in the MfS files noted that the Securitate established ties with the Carlos group in Prague in 1979. For a detailed discussion and documentation, see Cummings, *Cold War Radio*, 92–121. A different account of the 1981 bombing offered by Kalugin, *First Directorate*, who describes it as a KGB plan executed by the East Germans, is not supported by the documentary evidence. Kalugin may have thought of a bombing in 1979 but lacked firsthand knowledge of KGB foreign operations in 1981, because by then he had left the foreign intelligence directorate and was sidetracked to Leningrad.

39. The Hungarian security service secretly monitored and transcribed the preparations for the bombing of the Carlos group in Budapest; minutes of a meeting with between Czechoslovak and Hungarian interior ministry officials on the Carlos terrorist group and RFE attack, April 24, 1981, translation in *Cold War Broadcasting*, ed. Johnson and Parta, document 26. An East German document dated April 28 on East Germany's MfS talks with the same Hungarian Interior Ministry delegation is translated as appendix A in *Radio Free Europe and the Pursuit of Democracy: My War within the Cold War* by George R. Urban (New Haven, Conn.: Yale University Press, 1997).

40. "Sprengstoffanschlag auf den Sender 'Radio Freies Europe' in München am 21.2.1981," March 13, 1981, MfS HA 22-5555/41, BStU.

merly viewed the Carlos group as a useful instrument in support of "national liberation movements" in the developing world,[41] after the bombing the Carlos group was in effect expelled from Eastern Europe, declined to settle in Havana, and ended up in Damascus. (Carlos and most of his associates were later apprehended, tried in Western countries, convicted of murder during other terrorist attacks, and imprisoned for life.)

Ceaușescu also ordered that several Romanian Service directors and broadcasters be harmed or killed. The Securitate did its best to comply. The Securitate resident in Bonn sent Bucharest a cable on October 22, 1980, titled "Concerning the Compromising and Liquidation of [Romanian service director] Noel Bernard."[42] In some cases the Securitate acted. RFE Romanian broadcaster Monica Lovinescu was brutally attacked in Paris; Pacepa claimed that Ceaușescu had specifically ordered this action against her.[43] RFE Romanian staff received threatening letters. In early February 1981, just before the Munich bombing, three prominent exiled Romanians living in Paris and Cologne, all contributors to RFE, received book bombs disguised as Khrushchev's memoirs in the mail. Lead broadcaster Emil Georgescu was brutally beaten in Munich on January 26, 1981, and then stabbed repeatedly in a second attack on July 28 by two French citizens, who were subsequently apprehended. The Securitate archives contain the operational report of agent "Helmut" on the attempted "annihilation of Iago [Emil Georgescu]."[44] But the Securitate was not omnipotent. In the cases of the three successive RFE Romanian Service directors who died of cancer, although Ceaușescu ordered or wished them silenced, and many Romanians believe to this day that he had them killed, there is no evidence linking their deaths to the hand of the Securitate.[45]

41. MfS Department XXII/8 document of February 10, 1981, translation given by Cummings, *Cold War Radio,* appendix A.

42. As cited by Ratesh, "Radio Free Europe's Impact." For the details and documentation, see Cummings, *Cold War Radio,* 122–70.

43. Pacepa, *Red Horizons,* 35.

44. Ratesh, "Radio Free Europe's Impact."

45. In *Red Horizons,* Pacepa recounts Ceaușescu's orders in 1978 to silence several RFE broadcasters. These orders included using "Radu" (described as a cancer-inducing device employing radioactive thallium isotopes obtained from the KGB in 1970) against RFE Romanian Service director Noel Bernard. By Pacepa's account, the device had been used against political prisoners in Romanian jails. When Pacepa pointed out to Ceaușescu that "we have never had a portable 'Radu,' comrade," Ceaușescu responded, "Let's make one." There is no plausible account of how cancer could be caused by low-level radioactivity in a noncontrolled environment. Bernard died of lung cancer, for

Wrong Target

In summary, Soviet Bloc regimes regarded uncensored Western radio broadcasts (and printed matter distributed in the East) as a major threat. They initiated an elaborate and costly series of countermeasures. These included targeting their intelligence services against Western broadcasters, especially RFE and RL. They accessed much of the Radios' internal information flow and used some of that information in overt and covert media campaigns intended to discredit the Radios in the eyes of their own populations and the West—without evident impact.

Yet it is difficult to document any use made by Soviet Bloc regimes of much of the information they collected. Even when the identity of sources providing information to the Radios was discovered, and sanctions against them could have decreased the outflow of information to the West, evidently little use was made of this knowledge. When asked why not, Czechowicz offered this explanation about Poland: "Most of them were little fish, not worth the effort. Some of them were big fish [Communist Party officials], who could not be touched."[46] Indeed, some of the most important information reaching the Radios about top-level Communist Party controversies came from mid- or even high-level officials within the system who in effect cooperated with RFE and RL. RFE and RL thus also came to play a role in intraregime communications and infighting.

The extensive resources devoted to this information collection effort can be explained in part by the natural impulse of intelligence organizations to learn as much about their adversaries as possible. But the totality of this effort can perhaps best be explained by a belief on the part of the Soviet Bloc intelligence organizations and Communist Party leaderships that the Radios were CIA operations even the 1970s and 1980s and that penetration of the Radios could lead to information about other, hidden, and presumably even more important CIA operations against the Soviet Bloc.

This belief resulted from misplaced "mirror imaging" by the Communist regimes. Even during the two decades of CIA sponsorship, the Radios enjoyed substantial autonomy, remained focused on their broadcasting and research mission, and—impossible as it was for the Soviet Bloc intelligence

---

which radioactivity is an unlikely cause. Vlad Georgescu died of a malignant brain tumor; he could have been exposed to radioactivity while in prison for dissident activity in Romania, but that preceded his affiliation with RFE.

46. Czechowicz interview, 2004.

services to believe—were not utilized for espionage or covert operations.[47] All CIA involvement with RFE and RL ended in early 1972—but the Communist regimes and their intelligence services drew a different conclusion. The Soviet Bloc's countermeasures against the Radios increased, rather than declined. In part this was a reaction to the greater impact of the Radio broadcasts after the 1960s, as dissent and opposition increased in the Soviet Bloc. In part it was a reflection of how the KGB and its junior intelligence partners viewed the world. Extrapolating from their own experience, they assumed that the CIA had closely controlled Radio operations all along, had used the Radios for a variety of purposes unrelated to broadcasting, and— regardless of what was said to the contrary in the U.S. Congress and the American media—continued to control the Radios after 1971. As one example of this mindset, in May 1983 the then-director of the RFE Polish Service, Zdzisław Najder, was sentenced to death in absentia in Poland for treason under martial law. In issuing the sentence, the Military Court stated that the prosecution was initiated "based on the generally known fact that RFE is an organ subordinated to the special services of the United States (overseen and controlled by the CIA) and the fact that all previous directors of the Polish Service were career American intelligence officers."[48]

Post-1989 publications by former Soviet Bloc intelligence officers also illuminate this mindset. Klaus Eichner and Andreas Dobbert, both former officers of MfS HVA Department IX (foreign counterintelligence)—in a book devoted to justifying their past activities and exposing purported CIA activities in Germany that is based on a 1985 internal HVA analysis available at the BStU—contend that after 1971 "the CIA did not cease its activities with RFE/RL. Our analyses confirmed the continued presence of the CIA in these Radios. All key positions in both Radios were occupied by experienced CIA officers."[49] When interviewed in Prague in 1990 by an

47. Cord Meyer, *Facing Reality: From World Federalism to the CIA* (New York: Harper & Row, 1980), 115. See also Sig Mickelson, *America's Other Voice: The Story of Radio Free Europe and Radio Liberty* (New York: Praeger, 1983); Gene Sosin, *Sparks of Liberty: An Insider's Memoir of Radio Liberty* (University Park: Pennsylvania State University Press, 1999); Puddington, *Broadcasting Freedom;* Richardson, *New Vision for America.*

48. See Johnson and Parta, *Cold War Broadcasting,* document 40. In the early 1970s, Najder provided information, largely innocuous, to the Polish intelligence service in order to travel abroad; subsequently he became a major target of the service; Machcewicz, *"Monachijska menażeria,"* 351–62.

49. See Klaus Eichner and Andreas Dobbert, *Headquarters Germany: Die USA-Geheimdienste in Deutschland* (Berlin: Edition Ost, 1997), which reprints material con-

RFE/RL executive, Minařík said that his priority task had been to identify CIA agents on the staff and uncover evidence of a CIA-RFE connection. This was all nonsense. But it was not just propaganda. It was evidently the genuine belief of the MfS, the StB (State Security Service), and their Soviet Bloc partners—for the simple reason that this is how *they* would have done it. Such views in the security services doubtless influenced the perceptions of top Communist Party leaders. When interviewed in 2002, former Polish defense minister, Communist Party first secretary, and president Wojciech Jaruzelski said that he had viewed RFE throughout the entire Cold War as an organ of the CIA.[50]

Preoccupation with the CIA and other Western intelligence organizations thought to be embedded within RFE and RL diverted the Soviet Bloc's intelligence services from what logically should have been their primary task—undermining the Radios' broadcasts from within. In the end, they devoted vast resources to collecting huge quantities of information that served little purpose while searching for hidden Western intelligence operations that did not exist. Meanwhile, they neglected whatever possibilities they might have had to exacerbate the Radios' staff tensions from within and to influence with disinformation or other measures the content of the broadcasts that were the real threat to the political order they were attempting to defend.

---

tained in a 1985 HVA Department IX document alleging that RFE/RL had been and remained a base for CIA operations: "Die Diversionssender 'Radio Free Europe / Radio Liberty,' als Basen für geheimdienstliche Operationen und eine aktive Kontakttätigkeit gegen die socialistischen Länder," June 1985, MfS HAXX, ZMA 914, BStU. Also Günther Bohnsack, interview with the author, Berlin, December 2003. Bohnsack was a former HVA disinformation officer.

50. Wojciech Jaruzelski, oral history interview with Jane Leftwich Curry, Hoover Archives.

Chapter 8

Emergence from the Shadows

Try as they might, the Soviet Bloc regimes had little success in disrupting RFE and RL. Both Radios came to face a threat to their continued existence in the early 1970s and were nearly closed down in June 1971, but that existential threat came not from the East but from within the West. A perfect storm almost sank both Radios—public disclosure of CIA funding, reappraisal by a new German government of its national interests, diplomatic protests from the East, personal hostility of the powerful chairman of the Senate Foreign Relations Committee, and congressional insistence on ending all funding for the Radios from the intelligence budget before making alternative arrangements for open support. Looking back, it is a wonder they survived. That they did was testimony to the reputation for effective broadcasting and high-quality research that they had established among those both inside and outside the U.S. government who were knowledgeable about the Soviet Bloc. That reputation was the basis for support on the part of the majority of Congress, the American media, and the foreign affairs establishment for continuing the Radios in the 1970s and 1980s and beyond.

That reputation and broad support would not have saved the Radios at the end of the 1960s had it not been for the dedicated efforts at critical junctures of a few key individuals in the Johnson administration and Congress. Leadership does matter. Among that small group, most important was the director of central intelligence, Richard Helms, who understood the importance of the Radios, concluded that CIA involvement was not essential to their effective operation, and lobbied for their continuation outside the CIA's orbit. Helms' efforts were supported by USIA director Frank Shakespeare, who might have used the crisis to try to merge RFE and RL with

VOA. But Shakespeare ignored the bureaucratic imperative that "where you stand is where you sit" and strongly supported continuation of both Radios based on the proposition that they had missions different from that of VOA and were important for the United States.[1]

The story of public disclosure in the late 1960s of the CIA's Cold War covert influence projects and the response by the administration and Congress has been told many times.[2] To summarize, the article in the March 1967 issue of the leftist journal *Ramparts* on the CIA's ties with the National Student Association (first reported in the *New York Times* on February 14) led to publicity about the CIA's covert support for a variety of American organizations active abroad. Thomas W. Braden (Cord Meyer's predecessor as head of the IOD, who left the CIA in the mid-1950s) fueled the ensuing controversy with an article, "I'm Glad the CIA Is 'Immoral,'" in the *Saturday Evening Post* on May 8, 1967. A deluge of articles, interviews and congressional hearings followed, ending only in 1976 with the Church Committee hearings.

Reacting to the initial revelations, President Johnson directed comprehensive review within the administration of all such covert influence projects, establishing for this purpose the "Katzenbach Committee," headed by Undersecretary of State Nicholas Katzenbach and including both the secretary of health, education, and welfare, John Gardner, and Helms. In its final report of March 28, 1967, the Katzenbach Committee recommended that all covert funding and support of U.S. educational and private voluntary organizations cease and that (drawing on the experience of the British Council, the Smithsonian Institution, and similar organizations) an alternative public-private mechanism be established "to provide public funds openly for overseas activities of organizations which are adjudged deserving, in the national interest, of public support."[3]

1. See, e.g., "Memorandum from the Director of the United States Information Agency (Shakespeare) to the President's Advisor for National Security Affairs (Kissinger); Subject: Radio Free Europe. June 5, 1970," document 38, in *Foreign Relations of the United States,* ed. U.S. Department of State (hereafter, *FRUS*) (Washington, D.C.: U.S. Government Printing Office, various years), 1969–76, XXIX.

2. See Arch Puddington, *Broadcasting Freedom: The Cold War Triumph of Radio Free Europe and Radio Liberty* (Lexington: University Press of Kentucky, 2000), chap. 12; Sig Mickelson, *America's Other Voice: The Story of Radio Free Europe and Radio Liberty* (New York: Praeger, 1983), chap. 13; Gene Sosin, *Sparks of Liberty: An Insider's Memoir of Radio Liberty* (University Park: Pennsylvania State University Press, 1999), chap. 9; Cord Meyer, *Facing Reality: From World Federalism to the CIA* (New York: Harper & Row, 1980), chap. 5.

3. *American Foreign Policy: Current Documents* (Washington, D.C.: U.S. Govern-

Endorsing the conclusions of the Katzenbach Committee,[4] President Johnson then appointed an eighteen-member committee chaired by Secretary of State Dean Rusk and drawn from the executive branch, Congress, and the private sector to recommend such a public mechanism. It proved far easier to dismantle old programs than establish new ones. The "Rusk Committee" was unable to agree on specific recommendations, resulting in what Cord Meyer aptly termed "unilateral political disarmament in the face of a continuing Soviet challenge."[5] This unpardonable national deficit in foreign influence programs would last for seventeen years, until the establishment of the National Endowment for Democracy under Ronald Reagan's administration in 1984.

The FEC and RLC were minor actors in this drama, which was focused on covert CIA support of such U.S.-based organizations as the National Student Association. U.S. government and specifically CIA support for RFE and RL had been alleged publicly from time to time throughout their history, but the claims had generally been ignored by the American media and public. Even repeated allegations of CIA funding by a popular radio commentator, Fulton Lewis Jr., in the late 1950s were largely ignored.[6] *The Invisible Government,* published in June 1964, devoted part of a chapter on "Black Radio" to RFE and RL, implying that they were financed by the CIA (but quoting RFE and RL spokesmen to the contrary) and including a citation from a December 15, 1956, *Chicago Daily News* article that "the United States Government probably supports RFE with 'unvouchered funds,' but this has never been officially established."[7]

In the wake of the *Ramparts* article, new questions arose about the Radios' sources of funds and their purpose. Max Frankel described RFE in the *New York Times* as "an intelligence agency operation represented as a nonprofit enterprise."[8] Mike Wallace broadcast a report, "In the Pay of the CIA: An American Dilemma," on the CBS-TV Network on March 13, 1967, which argued the duplicity of the Crusade for Freedom's solicitation of citizen

---

ment Printing Office, 1967), 1214–17; Richard Helms, *A Look Over My Shoulder: My Life in the Central Intelligence Agency* (New York: Random House, 2003), 368–70.

4. *Public Papers of the Presidents of the United States: Lyndon B. Johnson, 1967, Book I* (Washington, D.C.: U.S. Government Printing Office, 1968), 403–4.

5. Meyer, *Facing Reality,* 106.

6. E.g., Fulton Lewis Jr., in the *New York Mirror,* November 18, 1957.

7. David Wise and Thomas B. Ross, *The Invisible Government* (New York: Random House, 1964), 318–27.

8. *New York Times,* February 18, 1967.

contributions for an ostensibly private undertaking. The *New York Times* television reviewer of the Wallace report labeled the broadcasts "extracurricular espionage."

Even these and other post-*Ramparts* news reports about RFE's CIA funding had little resonance at the time, and media attention faded. Much to the surprise of the "insiders" involved, the "story" of RFE's CIA connection (RL was rarely mentioned) died out for nearly four years. As Sig Mickelson wrote, Americans were at the time preoccupied with more immediate and serious problems—the Vietnam War, campus protests, street demonstrations.[9] The administration prepared itself "to reply noncommittally or evasively to the questions [about the funding of RFE and RL] which are almost certain to be raised," but in fact rarely were.[10] In late 1968, the syndicated newspaper columnists Rowland Evans and Robert Novak wrote of "continued financing of Radio Free Europe and Radio Liberty from CIA funds."[11] Two years later, *Washington Post* reporter John Goshko filed a long story from Munich that mentioned RFE's CIA connection while praising the objectivity of RFE broadcasts.[12] There was little media follow-up to such stories. CIA funding of the Radios would become a political issue only in 1971, when Senator Clifford Case (R-N.J.), in a speech to the Senate on January 21, became the first American official to acknowledge publicly that the FEC and RLC, and the Radios they operated, had been supported by the CIA.

When the Rusk Committee convened in mid-1967 to consider open public funding of foreign activities of worthy private American organizations, Secretary Rusk excluded the FEC and RLC from consideration, recommending that their fate, given their national security importance and foreign focus, be considered by the "303 Committee" (later the "40 Committee," successors to the Psychological Strategy Board and the Operations Coordinating Board—that is, the NSC interagency committee responsible for all U.S. government covert operations). The "303 Committee" in turn set up a subcommittee, the Radio Study Group (RSG), headed by State Department official William Trueheart and including the Department of Defense, USIA, the Bureau of the Budget, and CIA representatives, to recommend what

9. Mickelson, *America's Other Voice*, 127.

10. "Public Stance on Funding of RFE and RL, Paper Prepared for the President's Press Secretary (Ziegler)," n.d. [February 1969], document 31, in *FRUS*, 1969–76, XXIX. The author attended RFE meetings in 1969 where the RFE Munich press officer dissembled in response to questions from visiting journalists about CIA funding.

11. *Washington Post*, December 5, 1968.

12. *Washington Post*, November 22, 1970.

should be done with the Radios. Drawing on the 1966 study by the Panel on U.S. Government Radio Broadcasting to the Communist Bloc and fresh inputs from U.S. embassies in the broadcast region and from the Radios themselves,[13] the RSG considered a number of options. Rejecting termination or merger with VOA, the RSG recommended in September 1967 that the Radios should continue under CIA auspices but acknowledge U.S. government (but not specifically CIA) support, thus obviating the need for an announced exception to the Katzenbach Committee constraints. There were two dissents: Helms quite realistically viewed this public relations approach as unworkable and suggested instead an announced exception to the Katzenbach guidelines. The BOB dissented entirely, suggesting that RFE be merged with VOA and that RL be liquidated.[14]

   The RSG recommendation to continue covert funding required congressional support. President Johnson, declining to be involved personally, authorized Helms to sound out influential members of Congress on their views, which unanimously supported continuation of the Radios.[15] FEC president Richardson met separately with various members of Congress seeking their endorsement. On the basis of this strong congressional sentiment, BOB director Charles Schultze recommended accelerated or "surge" funding for fiscal years (FYs) 1968 and 1969 (that is, disbursement in December 1967 of funds sufficient for operations through June 1969). The 303 Committee endorsed Schultze's recommendation on December 15, and Pres-

13. E.g., Embassy Moscow Dispatch No. 330, July 24, 1967, DDRS. Ambassador Llewellyn E. Thompson Jr. recommended "that at least for the time being Radio Liberty (RL) continue in operation . . . and . . . keep problem as quiescent as possible at this time." RLC memorandum, "Package for Radio Study Group Chairman, August 21, 1967.

14. This history is summarized in "Memorandum for the 303 Committee," prepared by the Department of State, January 27, 1969, document 28, in *FRUS, 1969–76, XXIX;* CIA memorandum for the 303 Committee from Helms, September 12, 1967, released November 2, 1998, available at www.foia.cia.gov.

15. Helms consulted representatives George Mahon of Texas, Frank Bow of Ohio, and Glenard Lipscomb of California, and senators Richard Russell of Georgia and Milton Young of North Dakota. All these individuals expressed a willingness to support the Radios financially in the round amount of $30 million a year for at least the next fiscal year and possibly longer. Helms, *A Look Over My Shoulder,* 272–73; "CIA Memorandum for the President from Helms, November 14, 1967," DDRS. Morton H. Halperin, the Department of Defense representative who did not dissent from this interagency consensus, would later coauthor a book suggesting the CIA on its own continued covert funding of RFE and RL, which was not the case; Morton H. Halperin et al., *The Lawless State: The Crimes of the U.S. Intelligence Agencies* (New York: Penguin Books, 1975), 54.

ident Johnson approved surge funding of $49 million on December 16.[16] This interim solution avoided both the need for an announced exception to the Katzenbach Committee's guidelines on ending covert aid to private voluntary organizations by December 31 and any requirement for public disclosure of U.S. government support. It funded the FEC and RLC through June 1969 and left to a new administration the decision on what should happen thereafter.[17] The Nixon administration would later rule that RFE and RL were not "educational or private voluntary organizations" and thus were not governed by the Katzenbach policy.[18]

The 1967 interagency review process thus ensured continued covert funding for the Radios until mid-1969, but none of the participants in the process was entirely happy with the outcome nor expected it to last. FEC and RLC managements began to advocate a shift to open congressional funding while retaining the private character of the Radios. In the course of 1967, both committees suggested such a legislative solution to a number of U.S. government officials, including National Security Advisor Walt Rostow.[19] Howland Sargeant sketched in April 1967 a National Council for Freedom of Information, modeled on the abortive International Broadcasting Foundation proposal of 1946, and urged proactive discussions with Congress.[20] In May 1968, the FEC forwarded to Rostow a first draft of suggested legislation establishing an American Council for Private International Communications, Inc., that would be funded openly by Congress and in turn make grants to the FEC and the RLC.[21] Meanwhile, Helms continued to seek assurances of congressional support for the Radios, writing to key members of Congress about the issue in July 1968.[22] The CIA Covert

16. Document 31, original n. 3, in *FRUS, 1969–76,* XXIX.

17. "Radio Liberty and Radio Free Europe" (Schultze Memorandum) [November 20, 1967], released June 1999, available at www.foia.cia.gov and in DDRS; "Action Memorandum from the President's Special Assistant (Rostow) to President Johnson and Attached Memorandum for the Record; Subject: Minutes of the Meeting of the 303 Committee, 15 December 1967," document 197, in *FRUS, 1964–68,* X, and DDRS, from the LBJ Library [with different redactions]; "Memorandum for the 303 Committee," January 27, 1969.

18. State Department Press Officer, January 1971.

19. RLC memorandum from Sargeant, "Conference with Walt Rostow [and John Richardson] on May 12, 1967."

20. RLC draft, "National Council for Freedom of Information," April 25, 1967; RLC memorandum, "Basic Briefing on Three Key Programs of the Radio Liberty Committee," April 17, 1967.

21. FEC letter to Walt Rostow, June 20, 1967.

22. Helms wrote to George Mahon, chairman of the House Committee on Appropri-

Action Staff (CA) strongly supported continuation of the Radios but viewed continued covert funding as the only realistic alternative to liquidation.[23] The BOB for its part continued to view the Radios as an asset of diminishing value that could be allowed to disappear.

Upon assuming office in January 1969, the Nixon administration decided to maintain the status quo for FY 1970—continued covert funding by the CIA of the FEC and RLC with no acknowledgment of U.S. government funding and no declared exception to the Katzenbach Committee funding guidelines.[24] Later that year, as it prepared the FY 1971 budget, the new administration adopted a more negative approach. At President Nixon's direction, the Office of Management and Budget (OMB, as the BOB was now renamed) included operating funds for RFE but initially deleted all funding for RL on the grounds that it "no longer stresses the need to liberate the Soviet Union from Communism." That language indicated a fundamental misunderstanding of RL's purpose and operations and was all too typical of the amateurish involvement of the BOB and OMB in international broadcasting policy issues throughout the Cold War. Quick intervention by Helms and National Security Advisor Henry Kissinger, supported unanimously by the 303 Committee, persuaded Nixon to reverse himself and approve on December 29, 1969, FY 1971 operating funds for RL as well as RFE.[25] It took

---

ations, Representative Glenard P. Lipscomb, Representative Frank T. Bow, Senator Richard B. Russell, chair, Committee on Armed Services, and Senator Milton R. Young. Helms letter to Mahon dated July 8, 1968, released June 1999, available at www.foia.cia.gov.

23. CIA memorandum to DCI, November 13, 1968, released June 1999, available at www.foia.cia.gov.

24. The columnists Rowland Evans and Robert Novak had accurately reported the choices the incoming administration would face; see Rowland Evans and Robert Novak, "Financing of Radio Free Europe Leaves Nixon Sensitive Problem," *Washington Post,* December 5, 1968. General Clay, then chairman of the Board of the FEC, wrote to Nixon on January 24, 1969, asking for "the assurance of long-term financial support." The 303 Committee recommended a continuation of covert funding on February 5, 1969, and President Nixon approved $32.3 million for RFE and RL on February 22. "Memorandum for the Record: Minutes of the Meeting of the 303 Committee, 5 February 1969," document 30, in *FRUS, 1969–76,* XXIX.

25. "Memorandum from Laurence E. Lynn Jr. of the National Security Staff to the President's Assistant for National Security Affairs (Kissinger); Subject: Termination of Radio Liberty, December 18, 1969," document 32, in *FRUS, 1969–76,* XXIX; "Memorandum from the Acting Director of Central Intelligence (Cushman) to the President's Assistant for National Security Affairs (Kissinger); Subject: Termination of Radio Liberty, December 19, 1969," document 33, in *FRUS, 1969–76,* XXIX; "Memorandum from the President's Assistant for National Security Affairs (Kissinger) to President

another round of recommendations by the "40 Committee" (the renamed 303 Committee, with the State Department, Defense Department, and USIA representatives all concurring) in May 1970 to restore modernization funds for the Radios. This marked a return to the status quo ante of full covert funding. But it flew in the face of a national American reappraisal of the role of covert activities in foreign and security policy and would not last a year.

While these developments were unfolding in the United States, a new West German Social Democratic Party (Sozialdemokratische Partei Deutschlands, SPD) government led by Willy Brandt assumed office. Resolved to pursue a new détentist policy—Ostpolitik—to improve relations with Eastern Europe, some of Brandt's associates—especially SPD head Herbert Wehner, Eastern Europe expert Egon Bahr, and security expert Horst Ehmke—viewed RFE (RL less so) as a problem. Their concerns, conveyed privately to American officials and to RFE management,[26] were reinforced by German media attacks on RFE. Illustrative was an article in *Der Stern* on June 6, 1970, titled "Propaganda—Ami Go Home." Reacting to such German views, President Nixon took the position that "the Radio Free Europe broadcasts are not negotiable" and that a "tough line" on RFE was "part of our policy on Germany."[27] Rejecting both a conciliatory State Department

Nixon," n.d., document 34, in *FRUS,* 1969–76, XXIX; photocopies of the memorandum show Nixon's approval date as December 29 [not December 23]. Nixon wavered on his support for RFE and RL, questioning their need for modernization funds at the end of December, but by March indicated "that he had had a change of mind and thought that Radio Free Europe should be continued." "Memorandum for the Record. Talk with President Nixon [from Richard Helms], March 25, 1970," document 147, in *FRUS,* 1969–76, XII.

26. Thomas Raffert, a German SPD member of the West European Advisory Committee, under instructions from Bahr conveyed the Brandt government's concerns to RFE officials in the course of the November 1969 West European Advisory Committee meeting. RFE memorandum for the record from Ralph Walter, November 21, 1969; RFE memorandum to Durkee from Walter, November 24, 1969; "Telegram from the Embassy in Germany to the Department of State; Subject: German reaction to RFE [Foreign Office official] Pommerening's discussion [on May 20] with RFE Director Walter, June 3, 1970," document 36, in *FRUS,* 1969–76, XXIX; Foreign Office memorandum on the meeting, II A3-86, 70/1, FOPA, B40, band 209, fiche B209-1. Bahr had visited RL in November 1967 and seemed impressed with its operation, but opined that he thought RIAS had lost touch with East German conditions and outlived its former usefulness.

27. Charles Bartlett in the *Washington Star,* June 21, 1970, evidently based on a June 9 meeting Nixon held with Frank Shakespeare and William F. Buckley Jr.; Editorial Note, document 39, in *FRUS,* 1969–77, XXIX; "Transcript of Telephone Conversation between the President's Assistant for National Security Affairs (Kissinger) and the Assistant Secretary of State for European Affairs (Hillenbrand), June 9, 1970," document 40, in *FRUS,* 1969–76, XXIX.

draft responsive to German government concerns and a tough formal position paper, the White House decided to use an informal channel and approved soundings in Bonn by CIA/CA official Fred Valtin, who had a long history of personal ties with Brandt and other SPD officials.[28] Valtin's conversations in Bonn in summer 1970 indicated that the German Foreign Office was mostly concerned that the RFE issue, and specifically RFE's Polish broadcasts, would needlessly complicate negotiations with Warsaw on a Polish-German treaty. Bahr and Ehmke, conversely, were focused on more fundamental issues of German foreign policy and sovereignty and told Valtin that RFE and RL would have to leave Germany.[29] Acting under instructions as a White House (that is, not CIA) emissary, Valtin met Chancellor Brandt (with Ehmke present) for nearly two hours on October 14, 1970. Valtin's message that "the President is seriously concerned about the situation"[30] was sufficient for Brandt to respond that he would accept the continuation of the Radios in Germany. He did ask that the U.S. government consider shifting RFE and RL transmitters out of Germany, so as to lessen the political burden on his country, the Federal Republic of Germany (FRG; that is, West Germany), but said if that were not possible, the status quo could continue.[31]

28. Jane C. Valtin, quoted on her late husband's CIA career, in the *New York Times,* August 13, 2004: "Fred helped the Germans establish a postwar government. . . . He hung around with Willy Brandt and helped build the Social Democratic Party."

29. Reports on Valtin's meetings with Foreign Office official Pommerening, State Secretary Ahlers, and Bahr and Ehmke are published in *FRUS,* 1969–76, XXIX, documents 41,42, 46, 48. Document 46 refers to Valtin's meeting with Bahr and Ehmke on June 25 when they said the Radios must leave Germany; a full account of that meeting could not be located.

30. "Memorandum from the Deputy Director of the Bureau of Intelligence and Research (Coerr) to the Assistant Secretary of State for European Affairs (Hillenbrand); Subject: Minutes of the Meeting of the 40 Committee, August 7 and 13, 1970," document 47, in *FRUS,* 1969–76, XXIX.

31. "Memorandum from the Deputy Director for Plans, Central Intelligence Agency (Karamessines) to the President's Assistant for National Security Affairs (Kissinger) and the Under Secretary of State for Political Affairs (Johnson); Subject: Discussion [by Fred Valtin] with Chancellor Brandt on RFE and RL, October 23, 1970," document 49, in *FRUS,* 1969–76. That same day Brandt told an American journalist, off the record and referring to his visit earlier that day from "an American from Washington," that the FRG would not abrogate any agreements with RFE but that he would like to see other European countries cohosting the activities of the station. The Foreign Office subsequently distributed a position paper to government offices and embassies noting the American government's interest in RFE and denying media speculation that Bonn would make concessions to the East on the issue. FEC memorandum to Walter from Langendorf; sub-

The U.S. government committed itself to a study of transmitter relocation and in due course reported to Bonn that it was impractical. Ehmke told Valtin in February 1971 that the FRG did not want the Radios to become a matter of controversy between itself and the United States, and Foreign Minister Walter Scheel did not raise the issue when he met Secretary of State William Rogers in Washington that same month. Henry Kissinger reiterated the White House's interest in the Radios to Bahr in Washington in June 1971, leading him to say that RFE and RL were primarily a matter between the United States and the Soviet Union and suggesting the possibility of a future U.S. approach to the Soviets on some kind of quid pro quo.[32] Brandt closed this chapter in July 1971 with a comment that the Radios were a matter to be resolved exclusively between the United States and the Soviet Union.[33]

The domestic American political controversy about the Radios and the new German Ostpolitik provided the Eastern European regimes, especially the Polish and Romanian governments, with what they viewed as a new opportunity to attempt to curtail or eliminate RFE's broadcasts to their countries. Polish foreign minister Stefan Jedrychowski and Communist Party official Ryszard Frelek signaled in the fall of 1969 Poland's intention to use negotiations on normalizing relations with Bonn to curtail RFE's broadcasts to Poland.[34] The Polish side raised the issue of RFE in the second round of FRG-Polish talks on March 10, 1970, and it gave the German Foreign Office thirteen items related to RFE broadcasts it found objectionable, which were in turn forwarded to RFE.[35] Horst Pommerening of the Foreign Of-

---

ject: "Visit to Bonn, November 6–10, 1970." On October 4, at an event in Munich, Brandt had privately reassured RFE official Ernst Langendorf that the German government would take no action against RFE; "Keine Sorgen, wir tuen nichts in Eurer Sache" (RFE memorandum from Langendorf, October 5, 1970).

32. "Memorandum of Conversation, June 17, 1971," document 56, in *FRUS, 1969–76, XXIX.*

33. Remarks to the Berlin Press Club, RFE memorandum to Durkee from Walter, July 21, 1971.

34. Jedrychowski interview on German Television ARD, October 24, 1969; Frelek, in *Sprawy Międzynarodowe,* September 1969.

35. "Notatka w sprawie radio 'Wolna Europa' w Monarchium," March 5, 1970, FOPA, B40, band 209, fiche B209-1. Of the thirteen items, only ten could be identified as RFE programs. RFE judged five of them as either bordering on or violating policy guidelines prohibiting personal attacks or tactical advice; RFE memorandum to Durkee from Walter, July 16, 1970. A CIA/CA review came to essentially the same conclusion and noted that these were only five cases from 7,000 hours of Polish broadcasts in 1969. FEC copy of CIA memorandum, "Analysis of Polish Documentary Charges against RFE," 1970.

fice conveyed Polish (and some German) concerns to Ralph Walter and Ernst Langendorf during the May 20, 1970, meeting and suggested that the broadcasts not give unnecessary ammunition to the Polish side. Reviewing a month of Polish scripts in mid-1970, the Foreign Office found them generally appropriate, although it noted that all programs had a negative tone.[36]

The German government sought to defuse the issue, informing the Polish government that while it could not interfere in RFE programming, it had urged the RFE management "to avoid non-factual polemics, aggressiveness, and personal disparagement of Polish personalities."[37] The Polish side repeatedly returned to the subject in late 1970 and 1971. Polish foreign minister Jedrychowski raised the matter with German foreign minister Scheel in June 1971.[38] Continuing Polish regime complaints led German officials in September 1971 to exercise their prerogative (for the second and last time in forty-four years of RFE operations in Germany) to review transmitter tapes of certain RFE Polish broadcasts and as a result to criticize some of the programs.[39]

The Polish government also conveyed its objections to RFE broadcasts directly to Washington. Poland gave the U.S. government an aide-memoire dated May 26, 1971, which criticized RFE Polish broadcasts as seriously burdening Polish-American relations.[40] Warsaw also contacted the governments of Britain, Austria, and Denmark and objected to the RFE field offices in those countries. The U.S. Embassy in Warsaw registered its own concerns with some RFE Polish Service coverage of the December 1970

36. Foreign Office Memorandum IIA 3-86.70/1, FOPA, B40, band 209, fiche B209-1.

37. "An Polen Übergebene deutsche Stellungnahme von 23 Juli 1970," FAPO, B40, band 209, fiche B209-1.

38. "Memorandum from Helmut Sonnenfeldt of the National Security Council Staff to the President's Assistant for National Security Affairs (Kissinger); Subject: Polish Complaints to Germans about Radio Free Europe," document 55, in *FRUS, 1969–76,* XXIX.

39. Representative of the views of some Foreign Office officials was a memorandum from von Groll dated January 13, 1971 (FAPO, B40, band 209, fiche B209-1) depicting RFE Polish broadcasts as insufficiently factual, too focused on attacking the Communist regime, and raising a danger that "our detente policy vis-à-vis the East could be undermined by tendentious RFE reporting." Von Groll repeated this criticism, and personal hostility toward Jan Nowak, to Ken Scott of RL in December; RL memorandum to Sargeant from Scott, December 2, 1971.

40. "Telegram from the Embassy in Poland to the Department of State, Subject: Polish Aide-Memoire on RFE, May 26, 1971," document 54, in *FRUS, 1969–76,* XXIX; Polish Foreign Ministry account given by Paweł Machcewicz, *"Monachijska menażeria" Walka z Radiem Wolna Europa* (Warsaw: Instytut Pamięci Narodowej, ISP, 2007), 282.

riots on the Baltic Coast. Reviewing the record again, the CIA/CA reached a different view, concluding that in December 1970 and January 1971 "the Polish Broadcasting Department performed with professional competence and exceptional brilliance."[41] It was clear to all those involved at the time that the issue for the Polish government was not specific RFE broadcasts but, as one Polish official told a German Foreign Office interlocutor, "the existence of Radio Free Europe."[42] As Fred Valtin told German officials in a February 1971 meeting devoted to Polish government complaints: "RFE, to be effective and in fact worthwhile, must engage in commentary, that commentary, to be meaningful, sometimes must be critical, and there [is] thus no way of overcoming the basic Polish charge that RFE broadcasts intervene in Polish domestic affairs."

In the end, with more important issues at stake, and realizing the futility of conditionality, the Polish government set the RFE issue aside and in 1972 concluded a treaty with West Germany formalizing the German recognition of Poland's post–World War II Western border on the Oder-Neisse rivers as permanent, establishing diplomatic relations between the two countries, and facilitating family repatriation of ethnic Germans from Poland.

Although the Polish regime's problem with RFE was not about specific broadcasts but about RFE's very existence as a surrogate radio, the harsh vocabulary and personal attacks on individual leaders in some RFE Polish broadcasts once again—just as in the period after 1956—unnecessarily gave the Polish regime, and RFE's detractors in Bonn and Washington, ammunition for their cause. As Walter said at the time about two questionable programs, "both scripts could have fulfilled the goals of the Polish BD (Broadcasting Department) without resort to use of language which is either so harsh or emotional. This is a continuing problem and a firm editorial hand is always required to cope with it."[43] The RFE Polish Service, and RFE and the FEC as a whole, should have learned that lesson long before and been wise and disciplined enough to exclude such language from broadcasts, whatever the preferences of individual broadcasters or the delight of some of the listeners.

The Romanian regime, having decided after 1967 that RFE was an implacable enemy, also began to complain to the Bonn government about RFE broadcasts and RFE contacts with visitors from Romania. The Romanian

41. CIA memorandum, "Recent Radio Free Europe Broadcasts to Poland [1971], unclassified.
42. RFE memorandum of conversation [in German Foreign Office], May 12, 1971.
43. FEC memorandum to Durkee from Walter, July 16, 1970.

regime's emissaries failed to offer specifics, however, and that allowed the German government basically to ignore the complaints.[44] The other Eastern European countries lodged only minor complaints with Bonn. There is no indication in the German archives that the Soviet Union ever officially complained to Bonn about Radio Liberty.

Preparations for the 1972 Summer Olympic Games in Munich gave Soviet Bloc regimes another opportunity to pressure Bonn on RFE and RL directly, through the International Olympic Committee, and by public suggestions of a boycott. The German Foreign Office, under this pressure, initially suggested to the Radios that they curtail their political broadcasts, concentrate on sports and features, and avoid all contact with Eastern European and Soviet visitors during the Olympics. Foreign Minister Scheel talked about the need for an RFE "armistice" [*Burgfrieden*] during the Olympics. Avery Brundage, head of the International Olympic Committee, wrote to the FEC and RLC on April 20, 1971, suggesting that "it would be appreciated . . . if during the period of the Games when all the foreign visitors are there all political and controversial subjects would be eliminated from your programs." The Radios' managements had made it clear in meetings with German Olympic Committee and Foreign Office officials in February that while they would not initiate contacts with Olympic participants and visitors from the East, they would continue normal programming. FEC chairman Lucius Clay and RLC president Howland Sargeant replied to Brundage that the Radios, while avoiding incidents with visitors, would continue to uphold the principle of freedom of information and would maintain full-service programming during the Olympics. In fact neither Radio altered its operations in any way. Regular RFE and RL programs continued throughout the Olympics, and many visitors to Munich from the East sought out RFE and RL correspondents.[45]

In 1971, the German government's complaints about specific RFE broadcasts would continue, but both Radios could reasonably anticipate continued operations in Germany under the arrangements established in the

44. RFE memorandum to Durkee from Langendorf, October 28, 1968, listing various complaints conveyed to the German Foreign Office; RFE memorandum to Richard Cook from Langendorf, October 24, 1969.

45. RFE memorandum to Durkee from Walter on meeting with Willi Daume and others, February 19, 1971; RFE memorandum of conversation (between Lothar Lahn of the Foreign Office and RFE officials), May 12, 1971; German Foreign Office documentation of the Olympic Games controversy, including copies of the Clay and Sargeant letters, are in FOPA, B40, band 210, fische 210-1 and 210-3.

mid-1950s. The same could not be said for Washington. Senator Clifford Case's Senate speech of January 21, delivered in spite of efforts by the administration to forestall it,[46] effectively foreclosed any possibility of continued covert funding. Case himself was convinced of the importance of the Radios and introduced legislation providing for their continuation with public appropriations (using State Department funds in FY 1972); he was supported by Representative Ogden Reid, who introduced a similar bill in the House. Others in Congress welcomed Case's disclosure as an opportunity to bury the Radios, and they nearly succeeded in doing precisely that.

Bowing to the inevitable after additional internal review,[47] the Nixon administration resolved on public support of the Radios through U.S. Treasury funding of an American Council for Private International Communications, Inc.—basically the FEC proposal of 1968. On May 24, Assistant Secretary of State Martin J. Hillenbrand presented to the Senate Foreign Relations Committee draft legislation to establish such a council, which would "grant support to the activities of private American organizations engaged in the field of communication with foreign peoples." In his testimony, Hillenbrand stressed the importance of retaining the private character of the Radios, arguing that "in contrast to international Radios which are identified as government agencies [for example, VOA], Radio Liberty and Radio Free Europe are able to report and comment on the domestic affairs of other nations much as would any commercial medium operating in a democracy."[48]

The administration's bill was adamantly opposed by the committee chairman, Senator J. William Fulbright. Though he had been an architect of the invaluable international educational exchange programs that still carry his name (and an early member of the Crusade for Freedom's National Council), Fulbright had come to share revisionist historians' critique of American foreign policy as bearing primary responsibility for the Cold War, to

46. "Memorandum from Director of Central Intelligence Helms to the President's Assistant for National Security Affairs (Kissinger); Subject: Senator Case's Proposed Legislation re Radio Free Europe and Radio Liberty," n.d., document 50, in *FRUS, 1969–76,* XXIX.

47. "Memorandum from the Under Secretary of State for Political Affairs (Johnson) to the 40 Committee, Radio Free Europe (RFE) and Radio Liberty (RL), May 12, 1971," document 53, in *FRUS, 1969–76,* XXIX.

48. The bill (S 1936, HR 9330) was modified in discussion with Senator Case to drop the word "Private" from the name and to provide for an eleven-member Board of Directors, with four appointed by Congress and seven by the president (with no mention of Senate confirmation required).

view Soviet control of Eastern Europe as permanent, and to oppose the Radios, which he dismissed as "survivors of the old cold-war mentality" fostering "futile discontent, not for any discernible purpose of policy, but for
purposes of ideological mischief."[49] Fulbright's determination to close
down the Radios, buttressed by Senators Mike Mansfield, Stuart Syming-
ton, and Frank Church, led to deadlock. The Radios faced the very real
prospect of losing all funding at the end of June.[50] Helms alerted President
Nixon to the problem on May 11,[51] and—with no interim funding arranged,
and with the chairmen of both House and Senate appropriations committees
having again ruled out any use of intelligence funds beyond June—he asked
OMB director George Shultz on June 16 for guidance on "what the Administration desires that the Central Intelligence Agency do about the funding and the management of Radio Liberty and Radio Free Europe, effective
1 July 1971."[52] Helms formally advised the FEC and RLC presidents in letters dated June 24 to prepare termination letters for all employees.[53] At the
eleventh hour, with major media strongly supporting continuation of the Radios (for example, "The Essential Business of Radio Free Europe" was the
lead editorial in the *Washington Post* on June 26, 1971), the White House
brokered a compromise whereby the Senate Appropriations Committee on
June 25 included RFE and RL in the USIA joint continuing budget resolution for FY 1972. Congress approved the continuing resolution on July 1.
FEC and RLC direct payments to fifty-five prominent exiles—all that remained by then of the once-extensive émigré support and other special projects—ended and were replaced by State Department–purchased annuities
as authorized by Presidential Directive 72-6.[54]

49. J. William Fulbright, *The Crippled Giant: American Foreign Policy and Its Domestic Consequences* (New York: Random House, 1972), 36–38.
50. "Memorandum from the Under Secretary of State for Political Affairs (Johnson)
to the 40 Committee; Subject: Radio Free Europe (RFE) and Radio Liberty (RL) May
12, 1971," document 53, in *FRUS, 1969–76*, XXIX.
51. "Memorandum from Director of Central Intelligence Helms to President Nixon,
May 11, 1971," document 52, in *FRUS, 1969–76*, XXIX.
52. CIA memorandum for the record, OLC-71-0277, April 23, 1971, released September 2006, CREST CIA-RDP73B000296R0001000400039-5. The daily Journal of
the Office of [CIA] Legislative Council for these months, declassified in CREST, provides details; "Letter from Director of Central Intelligence Helms to the Director of the
Office of Management and Budget (Shultz), June 16, 1971," document 55, in *FRUS,
1969–76*, XXIX.
53. CIA letter to Sargeant from ADCI Cushman, June 24,1971, released to the author in September 2007. The same letter was sent to FEC president Durkee.
54. "Memorandum for the Record, Minutes of the Meeting of the 40 Committee, 22

The White House–brokered compromise of June 1971 providing continued interim funding for RFE and RL involved assurances to key members of Congress with ethnic Baltic constituencies that the Radios would begin to broadcast to the Baltic states. Those broadcasts (as recounted in chapter 1) had originally been planned by RFE but never started because of State Department opposition. Lithuanian, Estonian, and Latvian broadcasts finally began in 1975, initially under RL auspices and after 1984 as part of RFE.

From its inception in May 1949 through June 1971, the FEC and the Crusade for Freedom / RFE Fund received a total of $323.3 million of U.S. government funds through the CIA (and $46 million from private contributions). AMCOMLIB/RLC, from its inception in January 1951 through June 1971, received $158.8 million in U.S. government funds through the CIA.[55] All CIA funding of the Radios ended in June 1971. The CIA exercised residual nonbudgetary oversight until April 15, 1972, when all CIA involvement with the Radios ended after twenty-three years.[56] Evidently the last CIA policy suggestion to the Radios—the approval of a revised RL guidance on arms control—was on February 29, 1972. By March, FEC president William P. Durkee (who succeeded John Richardson in March 1968 and had overseen RFE in CIA/IOD in the early 1950s)[57] responded sharply to a CIA message: "While your information is appreciated, we do not feel such communications appropriate."[58]

The sequel is beyond the scope of this book and is well covered elsewhere.[59] Having lost a battle, Senator Fulbright did not intend to lose the war. He commissioned reports on RFE and RL from the Congressional Research Service, which he assumed would be critical. When they turned out to be positive,[60] he attempted to limit their circulation and discredit them.

June 1971," document 57, editorial fn. 5, in *FRUS,* 1969–76, XXIX. For the legislative history, see "Radio Free Europe and Radio Liberty," 92nd Congress, First Session, Senate, Calendar No. 313, Report 92-319, July 30, 1971.

55. Report to the Committee on Foreign Relations, U.S. Senate, by the Comptroller General of the United States, "U.S. Government Monies Provided to Radio Free Europe and Radio Liberty," May 25, 1972, 14–15, 45.

56. CIA memorandum, "FY 72 Chronology of Key Events," September 19, 1972, released to the author in March 2009.

57. Mickelson, *America's Other Voice,* 42.

58. FEC memorandum to the Executive Committee [CIA] from the President, FC-2119/1972, March 15, 1972.

59. Puddington, *Broadcasting Freedom,* 187–213.

60. James R. Price, *Radio Free Europe: A Survey and Analysis* (Washington, D.C.: Congressional Research Service, 1972); Joseph G. Whelan, *Radio Liberty: A Study of*

Interested parties lobbied Congress on behalf of the Radios, especially an ad hoc Citizens' Committee for Radio Free Europe / Radio Liberty organized by retired Ambassador George Ball. The editorial pages of American media were universally supportive; typical was an editorial, "Saving Free Voices," in the *New York Times* on February 21, 1972, which argued that "for a generation now, Radio Free Europe and Radio Liberty have contributed enormously to enlarging the market place of ideas in Eastern Europe and the Soviet Union." Senator Charles Percy told the Senate on February 22 that "it would be unwise to discard assets which are of great value and cannot be easily reconstructed if abandoned at this time." President Nixon made a strong public endorsement on March 11.[61] On March 24, 1972, Congress approved final FY 1972 funding for the Radios of $36 million through the State Department, an interim solution also adopted for FY 1973. With the favorable report in May 1973 of yet another study group, the Commission on International Radio Broadcasting chaired by Milton S. Eisenhower, and passage in October of the International Broadcasting Act of 1973 (PL 93-129), Congress provided for open appropriations for RFE and RL broadcasting and research in FY 1974 and thereafter through a new federal oversight body, the Board for International Broadcasting.

The Dilemma of Covert Funding

Public disclosure in the late 1960s of CIA support for RFE and RL, however unwelcome to all concerned at the time, could hardly have come as a surprise. Even in the 1950s, CIA, FEC, and AMCOMLIB officials were aware that the "cover" of exclusively private funding was thin and fraying. Too many people—government officials, current and former employees, journalists, foundation officials, corporate executives, and others—knew or suspected the true story. In the words of one FEC official: "The exiles assumed without exception that government funds were involved, and were glad of this evidence of United States interest in their cause. As one elderly Romanian ex-ambassador put it, the FEC's funding was "un secret

---

Its Origins, Structure, Policy, Programming, and Effectiveness (Washington, D.C.: Congressional Research Service, 1972).

61. Percy, as quoted by Sosin, *Sparks of Liberty,* 140; White House Press Release, Department of State Bulletin, April 10, 1972.

de Polichinelle" (an open secret).[62] Things were no different at RL. As James Critchlow wrote, "It was arguably the worst kept secret in the history of statecraft. Without being told officially, I had heard about the CIA involvement well before I joined Radio Liberty, from a friend who worked in Washington, D.C. Most of my colleagues, and not only the American ones, had heard similar revelations."[63] As early as 1952, the FEC prepared an "ice box" statement admitting some U.S. government funding, to be used should the need arise.[64] Crusade for Freedom chairman Arthur Page told the CIA/IOD in 1952 that he anticipated exposure of government funding, "which should alarm no one and . . . a clean breast should be made of the whole activity at the right time." *Washington Post* executive editor J. Russell Wiggins wrote to Page in 1956 that private persons could certainly "assist the government in such an endeavor, . . . [but] there should be no deceit about the matter, and I am a little afraid there has been some deceit."[65]

The Kennedy White House, mindful of the embarrassment created by the U-2 spy plane story (and on the eve of the Bay of Pigs invasion of Cuba), ordered the BOB to consider alternative approaches for various covert projects, including RFE, whose "value may be increasingly jeopardized as their cover grows thinner."[66] It was indeed the case that over time the mechanisms of covert funding became harder to conceal, as state regulatory bodies began to look more closely at the registration and funding sources of nonprofit organizations. In the early 1960s, Representative Wright Patman (D-Tex.) took up this cause. In the course of investigating the tax status of various foundations, he publicly labeled the Kaplan Fund as a CIA funding conduit.[67] By the 1960s, CIA, FEC, and RLC officials were well aware of the increasing likelihood of public disclosure and sought a path toward open congressional appropriations. The chairman of the RFE Fund (successor to the Crusade for Freedom), C. H. Greenewalt, wrote presciently in May 1965: "I think it is only a matter of time until our 'cover' disappears and this could

62. John Foster Leich, "Great Expectations: The National Councils in Exile, 1950–1960," *Polish Review* 35, no. 3 (1990): 183–96.

63. James Critchlow, *Radio Hole-in-the-Head: Radio Liberty—An Insider's Story of Cold War Broadcasting* (Washington, D.C.: American University Press, 1995), 15.

64. FEC memorandum, December 31, 1952.

65. Quoted from the Arthur Page archives by Noel L. Griese, *Arthur W. Page: Publisher, Public Relations Pioneer, Patriot* (Atlanta: Anvil, 2001), 377.

66. National Security Action Memorandum No. 38, April 15, 1961, released by NARA, April 1, 1998, John F. Kennedy Presidential Library (online version).

67. *Washington Post*, September 3, 1964.

happen under circumstances which would be unpleasant for all concerned."[68] As accounts of CIA covert support began to appear in the media in 1967, the FEC and Radio Free Europe Fund boards of directors urged that "the fact of Government financial support be disclosed at an early date; . . . such disclosure, even if it confirmed CIA as the source . . . would relieve present uncertainties and reduce the likelihood of criticism here or in Europe."[69]

Why were the risks of continued covert funding not confronted until the media and Congress forced the issue? Internal discussions at the time within the U.S. government and the Radios included a number of arguments against going public, some bogus and some real. Bogus were the concerns (for example, those expressed by the CIA/CA in the spring of 1967) that acknowledgment of government funding would constrain the Radios' editorial policies, leading them to "pull their punches" so as not to embarrass the United States or complicate diplomatic relations. This argument was a residue of a view dating back to the founding of the Radios that RFE and RL could be harder-hitting (and by implication less responsible) than officially acknowledged communications organs. Such views had always rested on wrong assumptions. They failed to appreciate that the value of the Radios was their domestic or surrogate focus, not their exuberance, that public funding could be combined with distance from government, and that (as Richard Helms said to the Senate Foreign Relations Committee on May 24, 1971) a responsible and effective surrogate broadcaster focused on target country affairs could operate just as effectively with overt funding as with covert funding, continuing to comment on domestic issues of its target countries, provided it was a private organization and not part of the federal bureaucracy. The argument also ignored the U.S. government policy constraints and a decade of increased State Department involvement in editorial issues that applied to the Radios as covertly funded just as they did to the "official" VOA.

If the concern that public funding would necessarily lead to editorial censorship or self-censorship was bogus, two other concerns about going public were very real. First was the well-founded concern that the Radios might not survive an extended congressional debate on alternative funding. This was the view of the CIA Covert Action Staff, perhaps part institutional bias but also realistic analysis, for in fact the Radios came close to not surviv-

68. FEC letter to John Page from Greenewalt, May 3, 1965.
69. FEC letter to Walt B. Rostow, special assistant to the president, n.d. [June 1967].

ing the transition.[70] Second were sensitivities of the foreign host countries
—West Germany, Portugal, and Spain. Germany hosted the program centers of both RFE and RL as private organizations, and all three countries had
granted transmitter licenses to the Radios as private broadcasters. German
Foreign Office archives reviewed by the author make clear that the German
government had no doubt about U.S. government and specifically CIA support for RFE and RL,[71] and the Portuguese and Spanish governments surely
had the same view. "Don't ask, don't tell" was a useful approach for all parties. The European governments assumed but did not seek confirmation of
U.S. government support, because having granted broadcasting licenses and
other concessions to formally private organizations, they could disavow responsibility for their operations when convenient. U.S. government soundings to the three host governments in the late 1960s about their views of open
U.S. government sponsorship of the Radios were uniformly negative, and
this was an important and legitimate policy consideration in the decision to
maintain the status quo from 1967 to 1971. As it turned out, these fears were
exaggerated, for all three countries renewed broadcasting licenses for the
still private RFE and RL after 1971 under interim State Department and then
regular funding from the Board for International Broadcasting. When the
RFE/RL transmitter sites were federalized in the mid-1990s, Germany authorized a continuation of transmissions from Biblis and Lampertheim. But
hindsight is not foresight, and none of this was at all certain in the 1960s.

Life after the CIA

In the early 1970s, after two decades of CIA funding and oversight, RFE
and RL emerged from the shadows as experienced full-service surrogate

70. CIA records reviewed by the author contradict the contention of Victor Marchetti
and John D. Marks that CIA elements had become disenchanted with the Radios and that
CIA internal studies "in each case" supported this viewpoint. Nor does the record support
the other claims related to RFE/RL in the book—that CIA analysts doubted the utility of
the Radios "for years," that CIA officers at the Radios "made all the important decisions
regarding the programming and operations," and that the Radios provided the CIA with
"covert assets which could be used against" the Soviet Bloc. Victor Marchetti and John D.
Marks, *The CIA and the Cult of Intelligence* (New York: Alfred A. Knopf, 1974), 167–70.

71. E.g., a Bavarian Interior Ministry review of RFE dated August 13, 1957 (FOPA,
B12, band 386) suggested that RFE and RL were guided by the State Department and
overseen by the American intelligence service.

broadcasters. They operated for the final two decades of the Cold War and beyond with open public funding. It was only then that the initial investment made during the CIA years was fully returned, as the Radios demonstrated their value as providers of information to and amplification of dissent from within the USSR and Eastern Europe. The FEC and the RLC, freed of earlier émigré-related activities, now focused solely on broadcasting and research. They merged in 1976 as RFE/RL, Inc., with RL and RFE as the major operating divisions until the early 1990s (when all research was consolidated in the RFE/RL Research Institute and a single broadcasting division was created). RFE/RL moved its broadcast center to Prague in 1995. Today it continues to provide domestically focused news and information to all parts of the former Soviet Union except the Baltic states, to the Western Balkans, and to Afghanistan, Iran, Iraq, and the Tribal Areas of Pakistan.

During the 1970s and 1980s, RFE broadcasts to Poland and Romania had the largest audiences and the most impact.[72] RFE's role was quite different in the two countries. In Poland, individual dissent began to coalesce into organized opposition with the founding of the Committee for the Defense of Workers, KOR, in 1976 and the emergence of Solidarity, encompassing 10 million people, in 1980–81. Romania under an increasingly repressive Ceaușescu regime, conversely, remained an atomized society. Writing in 1977, RFE director J. F. Brown described RFE's differing tasks in the two countries:

> Poland, with its powerful Church, powerful private peasantry, powerful workers, and assertive intellectuals, is a state where the ruling apparatus can have few illusions about its totalitarian power. In fact, there is real political interplay in Poland and the Polish [Service] joins fully in this interplay. In Romania there is no political interplay; despite the flurry of dissent this spring it is still a case of the individual against the state. RFE's impact, therefore, must necessarily be on an individual basis.[73]

That legacy continues. In Poland and Romania today, documentaries, television and radio programs, exhibits, and research projects regularly feature RFE.

---

72. For a discussion of the impact of the various RFE and RL services in the 1970s and 1980s, see the country chapters in *Cold War Broadcasting: Impact on the Soviet Union and Eastern Europe—A Collection of Studies and Documents,* ed. A. Ross Johnson and R. Eugene Parta (Budapest: Central European University Press, 2010).

73. RFE memorandum to William A. Buell from Brown, September 1, 1977.

Elsewhere in Eastern Europe, RFE helped spread the message of Charter 77 in Czechoslovakia. But the Czechoslovak Service, notwithstanding an influx of talented journalists after 1968, was generally less effective until the late 1980s (in part because of jamming) than VOA, which took over part of its surrogate radio function. The Hungarian Service extensively covered "goulash communism" reforms in Hungary. Promotion of piecemeal liberalization did not spare it from controversy; denounced as hostile by the Kádár regime, it was criticized by some inside and outside Hungary as overly accommodationist. The Bulgarian Service achieved real political impact only when indigenous dissent developed in the late 1980s.

Radio Liberty audiences surpassed those of other Western broadcasters only after 1988, when jamming still directed only at RL broadcasts finally ceased. RL's impact was demonstrated earlier, as audiences soared to obtain information about the shooting down of a Korean Airlines plane in 1983, the Chernobyl nuclear reactor disaster in 1986, and the war in Afghanistan. Equally important was RL's role among elite audiences in spreading dissident literature—samizdat. Uncensored information provided to Soviet audiences by RL and other Western broadcasters contributed to the limited freeing of Soviet media—glasnost—under Mikhail Gorbachev. Broadcasts to the then-Soviet republics (especially to the Baltic states from the Estonian, Latvian, and Lithuanian services, which were by then part of RFE) contributed significantly to the end of Communist rule and the breakup of the USSR.

During the 1970s, the Jimmy Carter administration's support enabled the Radios to fend off another round of German government criticism during the chancellorship of Helmut Schmidt. RFE/RL was able to renew its transmitter leases in Spain and Portugal after the end of the Franco and Salazar eras. In Portugal, leftist forces hostile to RFE were strong in the area of the Gloria transmitters. What helped save them was the local RFE-run industrial school, originally established to train skilled workers for the transmitter facilities, and an associated health clinic, both open to the local community as well.

Given this record and the reasonable projection after the early 1970s of indefinite public funding, it may seem surprising that RFE/RL's English Garden headquarters in Munich was not a happier workplace during these years and that governance of the publicly funded yet private Radio was so troubled. Arch Puddington has provided an overview of both developments in the final chapters of his book *Broadcasting Freedom.* The merger of RL and RFE created competition for resources and frictions between staffs of what had been two quite distinct organizations. RL's managers, for example, understandably resented the fact that the RL Ukrainian Service was half the size of the RFE Bulgarian Service. New waves of émigrés brought talent and recent experience but were often at odds with older generations, and this exacerbated tensions within individual broadcast services. The "Solidarity" wave of Polish broadcasters had a different outlook and temperament than earlier émigrés. Broadcasters from the new Soviet emigration, many of Jewish origin, were at odds with earlier generations. Munich was sometimes referred to as a golden cage; disgruntled broadcasters had limited alternative career options, few if any as well paid. And of course no one could know the end of the story and foresee the day when Munich's broadcasters would be recognized and honored by strangers in Eastern Europe and the USSR by the sound of their voices alone.

In the new atmosphere of open funding and oversight after 1971, infighting was often taken outside RFE/RL to the media, the executive branch, and Congress. In this sense, RFE/RL became a regular part of the American system of government. In one famous case fueled by internal dissension, a congressional hearing considered the propriety of a single broadcast, a 1977 Orthodox Easter interview with Archbishop Valerian Trifa, head of the Romanian Orthodox Church in the United States, then facing denaturalization hearings for war crimes.

Internal controversies were also taken directly to the oversight body, the Board for International Broadcasting (BIB). The peculiar BIB structure— a federal agency established with the sole purpose of overseeing one private corporation, each with its own board—was a formula that guaranteed continuous conflict over authority, policy, and operations. That conflict was exacerbated by a full-time BIB staff, which in the 1970s profiled itself in opposition to the Radios' management (unlike the CIA/IOD and CA staffs, which were generally supportive). Congress reduced that built-in conflict by further blurring the line between oversight and management with enactment in 1982 of the so-called Pell Amendment to the International Broadcasting Act. This amendment made the federal BIB, whose members were appointed by the president and confirmed by the Senate, the Board of Directors of the private nonprofit corporation. A BIB inspector general's office was established to conduct normal audits but was located in Munich and quickly became a magnet for employee grievances that should have been handled inside the private corporation.

None of this problematic governance, it may be noted in passing, was inevitable. Two years after passage of the Pell Amendment, Congress char-

tered the National Endowment for Democracy to promote democratic transformation in Communist and other countries. Like the Radios, the endowment was funded by Congress and operated in a larger U.S. foreign policy
context. But Congress entrusted responsibility for fiscal oversight and governance to the endowment's private board of directors.

The Reagan administration enhanced the importance and financing of the
Radios. Frank Shakespeare, who had been very supportive of RFE and RL
as director of USIA during the Nixon administration, was appointed BIB
chairman. The administration increased funding for all international information programs, including international broadcasting. It launched major
transmitter modernization and augmentation projects, including a facility in
Israel for broadcasts to Soviet Central Asia (never completed) and a second
transmitter complex for Eastern Europe in Portugal (completed just at the
end of the Cold War).

In the 1970s, RFE and RL programs were criticized by a number of individuals both inside and outside the U.S. government as insufficiently anticommunist,[74] and the BIB under Shakespeare resolved to sharpen the
broadcast message, looking beyond what it saw as excessive Radio concern
with reforming Communist systems to democratic transformation (or what
was once called self-liberation). Shakespeare replaced most top RFE/RL
managers, and in the process, as had happened at RFE after 1956, some of
the most capable veterans departed.[75] Personnel changes did not, however,
lead to the radical revamping of the message that the Radio critics advocated and defenders feared. In fact, changes in program content were min-
imal. This was in small part due to standard organizational inertia and bureaucratic resistance. In larger part, it was due to continued acceptance by
all those involved of RFE/RL's decentralized structure and attention to audience feedback. That structure empowered émigré broadcast service chiefs
and counted on them to use their talents and understanding of their countries to reach their audiences. They and higher management benefited from
a constant stream of audience reaction to the broadcasts, based on the extensive polling of travelers described in chapter 7.

Malcolm S. (Steve) Forbes Jr. took over chairmanship of the BIB in 1984.
He put an end to BIB staff "freelancing" and entrusted his new president
(veteran broadcaster E. Eugene Pell) and that president's senior managers

74. E.g., James L. Tyson, *U.S. International Broadcasting and National Security*
(New York: Ramapo Press, 1983).
75. These changes are discussed by Puddington, *Broadcasting Freedom,* 262ff.

to run the Radios.[76] To be sure, controversy about program content continued. The Polish Service verged in the mid-1980s on becoming an uncritical Voice of Solidarity. Some Azeri Service broadcasts during the 1989 Baku rioting were potentially inflammatory. But the broadcasts that led to these and other controversies resulted from exuberance or inattention of broadcast service chiefs, not "anticommunist" dictates from on high.

BIB oversight had the decided advantage of ending direct State Department involvement in broadcast policy. American ambassadors continued on occasion to object to RFE and RL programs, as was their right and responsibility, but editorial policy was now set in Munich, within the framework of broad guidelines promulgated by the BIB, and was never vetted with State Department or other U.S. government offices. Radio top management was empowered to make judgments about what was responsible and effective broadcasting, in partnership with the émigré broadcast service directors. Most broadcast review by American management, relying on the Broadcast Analysis Department, remained post facto, but key political programs and commentaries were discussed and agreed on in advance.

Three examples from my time as RFE director (1988–91) may be instructive. During the years 1988–89, as RFE covered the semi-free elections, Round Table deliberations, power sharing between Premier Tadeusz Mazowiecki and President Wojciech Jaruzelski, and the rebirth of democratic Poland, Ambassador John Davis often communicated, quite reasonably, his general concern that RFE's Polish broadcasts remain prudent and cautious (my response was that we were always cautious). But he did not attempt to tell us what to broadcast or not broadcast; the Polish Service knew its business and did its job. In December 1989, as violence in Timişoara paved the way for Ceauşescu's downfall, RFE's Romanian broadcasts reported those developments to the rest of the country while avoiding the exaggerated accounts of fatalities carried by much of the Western press and reminding the Romanian military of its obligations to Romanian society. All this was decided in Munich, without any outside "policy guidance." And in 1991–92, as Czechs and Slovaks discussed whether the Czechoslovak state should continue, Czechoslovak Service director Pavel Pechacek and I agreed that RFE's job was to report the range of views in Czechoslovakia while avoiding even an implicit editorial position on the desirability of two states ver-

76. I served as director of RFE from the fall of 1988 until mid-1991, as director of the RFE/RL Research Institute from 1991 to 1994, as acting president in 1994, and as counselor until 2002.

sus one. That was an issue to resolve in Prague and Bratislava, not in Munich. There was some dissent on this approach from within RFE, but there was no "guidance" of any kind from outside.

Coda

In the 1980s, buffeted by the various developments and controversies just recounted, RFE and RL veterans sometimes looked back to an earlier Golden Era, when—as they saw it—the CIA provided the money, protected them from outside inquisitors, and basically left them alone. That was, as this book has hopefully demonstrated, a much oversimplified view of an arrangement that could not last. RFE and RL existed only because they metamorphosed from émigré projects that were logically conducted by a CIA entrusted by American policymakers with tasks of influence, as well as traditional tasks of espionage. By the 1960s, the Radios were an anomaly for the CIA, assuming a large part of its budget for influence activities but operating outside the usual framework of administrative control. Both Radios could have operated openly in the 1960s, but the Kennedy administration considered and rejected that option. It was to the credit of the CIA in those years that it oversaw and defended within the U.S. government bureaucracy that influence project and then, when the hand was forced, oversaw the emergence of RFE and RL from the shadows.

Chapter 9

Public-Private Partnership

[The Free Europe Committee] is directed by individuals not only of some public stature but possessing specific experience in the field of diplomacy and psychological warfare. If an ostensibly private instrumentality is desired which will do no more than carry out automatically directions from Washington, a different type of personnel will have to be found. . . . The individuals now directing the [FEC] are intensely loyal citizens. . . . They can be counted upon to go to the utmost in giving effect to Governmental policies when these are clearly and authoritatively established. A long step forward would be accomplished by recognizing the [FEC] to be a partner on an equal footing, subject only to the final authority of the Government on points of public policy.

—DeWitt C. Poole, president of the Free Europe Committee, 1950[1]

Imperative Autonomy

The literature about RFE and RL falls into two distinct categories. Books about the CIA usually treat RFE and RL (and their parent committees, FEC and AMCOMLIB/RLC) as success stories; yet they often depict the Radios in their first two decades pejoratively as CIA tools.[2] Books about RFE and

1. FEC memorandum by De Witt Poole, October 2, 1950, also available at www .foia.cia.gov.

2. Stacey Cone labeled RFE and RL "CIA conduits" and "CIA-run Radios" and criticized the American media for failing to expose them; Stacey Cone, "Presuming a Right to Deceive. Radio Free Europe, Radio Liberty, the CIA, and the News Media," *Journalism History* 24, no. 4: 148–56. Tim Weiner, *Legacy of Ashes: The History of the CIA* (New York: Random House, 2007), 36, labeled the FEC as a "front" organization comprised of American VIPs "recruited by Dulles and Wisner as cover for the true manage-

RL (cited in the bibliography) written before the 1970s are silent on any CIA role, while books written after the 1970s acknowledge CIA funding but generally downplay the role of the CIA and other U.S. government agencies in their operations.

It is the thesis of this book, based on extensive research in the archives of the CIA, RFE/RL, and other archival collections, that the relationship between the CIA and the Radios was far more nuanced. In the terminology that defined inside debate on the issue in the early 1950s, the Radios were not CIA "instrumentalities" but rather "chosen instruments." As discussed in chapter 1, the émigré projects that would become RFE and RL were conceived within the U.S. government, not outside it. George Kennan properly credited himself as father of the concept, one element of the larger program of political warfare that he developed as head of the State Department's Policy Planning Staff (and in the 1970s disavowed). The birth was midwifed by Frank Wisner, as head of the Office of Policy Coordination (and later the CIA's deputy director for operations), and by Allen Dulles, as a prominent New York lawyer with close Washington ties and as a consultant to the National Security Council. A group of prominent Americans in private life, many of them veterans of the Office of Strategic Services or other government agencies, were responsible for shaping RFE, engaging the émigrés, and ensuring the autonomy from government that was essential to the success of the projects as substitute free domestic media—as surrogate radio. RL was launched as an "instrumentality" but evolved into a "chosen instrument" as well.

Three factors explain this autonomy—this essential distance from government. First and foremost, autonomy was dictated by operational requirements. Round-the-clock radio produced in Europe and focused on internal developments in distant lands required current information and immediate editorial decisions. Neither could be supplied by Washington, although none of the parties involved were clear about these constraints at the outset. Some Office of Policy Coordination and CIA officers quickly came to view the FEC and RFE as spinning out of their hands and sought to avoid a repetition with AMCOMLIB and RL by imposing tighter controls. The FEC's directors, conversely, initially complained about the lack of policy

---

ment." (Dulles in fact recruited himself well before he joined the CIA). Hugh Wilford, *The Mighty Wurlitzer: How the CIA Played America* (Cambridge, Mass.: Harvard University Press, 2008), acknowledged the independent existence of other CIA-supported organizations but in the case of the FEC downplayed its importance and stressed OPC control of an émigré-heavy "proprietary."

guidance and absence of current intelligence from Washington, which they thought were needed for successful broadcasting.

The operational requirement for autonomy was reinforced by the personalities on the FEC. Most were prominent members of the foreign affairs establishment who had extensive World War II experience in political and psychological warfare. They fashioned an organization out of the original Office of Policy Coordination concept and had no intention (as indicated in DeWitt C. Poole's statement quoted at the outset of this chapter) of "fronting" a government operation where all important decisions were made elsewhere. Several FEC directors touted exuberance over what they viewed as the bureaucratic timidity of the U.S. government. As C. D. Jackson told Cord Meyer on one occasion, "I don't believe that in all history any men marched to successful battle chanting 'Don't Rock the Boat.'"[3] Although AMCOMLIB lacked an analogous activist board, by the late 1950s its president, former assistant secretary of state for public affairs Howland Sargeant, was able to establish a similar degree of autonomy as an operational necessity.

Finally, the CIA—and specifically its International Organizations Division and later its Covert Action Staff, the units with responsibility for the Radios—was wise enough to exercise restraint, generally to avoid efforts at micromanagement, and to allow the managers of the Radios to do their jobs. Overseeing the FEC from the outset and the AMCOMLIB (initially the responsibility of the Soviet Russia Division of the CIA Operations Directorate) after 1953, the IOD under Tom Braden and Cord Meyer and the Covert Action Staff under their successors advocated the cause of the Radios within the CIA and the U.S. government, defended their yearly financial budgets, and protected them from other CIA departments that were tempted to use them for espionage or disinformation or simply impose standard CIA administrative norms and procedures. That the IOD could do this was in no small measure because of the special role of Allen Dulles. As a private citizen helping to organize the FEC, he emphasized its need for autonomy, and he stuck to this view after he became director of central intelligence. Retaining a strong personal interest in the FEC and RFE especially, he often acted as their "case officer," made himself personally available to FEC and RFE executives, and almost always backed the IOD in intra-CIA controversies about the Radios.

3. FEC letter to Cord Meyer from C. D. Jackson, January 12, 1960.

This large sphere of autonomy allowed the FEC and AMCOMLIB to develop and refine not just broadcast tactics but also strategy. It was RFE director Robert Lang and RFE political adviser William E. Griffith who formulated the concept of "surrogate broadcasting." It was Samuel Walker, head of the FEC's press division, who was the strategist of the printed word influence programs—first leaflets, then books. It was RFE audience research director Henry Hart and RL audience research director Max Ralis who conceived of doing "surrogate" audience research among travelers and provided the results to VOA and the BBC as well. The initiative on influence strategy flowed from the FEC and AMCOMLIB to the U.S. government, not the other way around.

Autonomy is not independence. The FEC and AMCOMLIB/RLC and the Radios they supported had far more freedom of action than would pertain in a special assistance government contract, but they had more constraints than would pertain with an unrestricted grant. The CIA reserved certain powers. It drew up "administrative plans" to regularize oversight and finances, but in general language (and in the case of the FEC unilaterally, because the FEC was never forced to sign the agreements). It controlled financial budgets. It generally advocated the Radios' cause with the Bureau of the Budget and later the Office of Management and Budget (which were never strong supporters) and with key congressional committee chairmen. But it sometimes imposed fiscal constraints—some reasonable, some less evidently so. While the State Department set overall policy, the CIA was an active interface between State and the Radios, usually advocating the Radios' cause but sometimes itself taking a stand on a policy issue contrary to that advocated by the FEC or AMCOMLIB/RLC.

The CIA had veto power over the hiring of personnel (as did the German government over personnel based in Germany), but it almost never exercised that power, even in the early days at RFE (albeit more so at RL in those years). The CIA's approval was required for salary increases of FEC and AMCOMLIB/RLC executives to keep them in line with U.S. government pay scales, but while a few increases were delayed, none was permanently denied. Also, the CIA's approval was needed for major human resources programs such as pension plans, but such approval was often pro forma because, as internal CIA reviewers noted, these were provided by the committees as complete draft packages that were difficult to modify. The CIA placed a few of its own officers within both organizations, but it respected the conditions demanded by successive presidents of both the FEC and AMCOMLIB/RLC that those officers report in fact and not just on paper solely to the presidents. RFE/RL and CIA records and memoirs by and interviews with participants are conclusive on this point.[4] Reviewing the history as documented in both FEC/RLC and CIA archives, it is remarkable how little the CIA interfered in FEC and AMCOMLIB/RLC operations —even when its oversight responsibilities might have argued for more intervention[5]—and how uninformed was the contention of two disaffected former CIA insiders that "CIA officers in the key management positions at the [Radio] stations made all the important decisions regarding the programming and operation of the stations."[6] It is equally remarkable that most differences between the CIA and FEC and AMCOMLIB/RLC were resolved not by fiat but by negotiation.

Once the FEC and AMCOMLIB and their Radios were up and running, the CIA acted on their behalf as an "invisible hand" within the U.S. government at critical junctures in the 1950s and 1960s. Also, the CIA was the interface with the State Department on policy issues. In the 1950s, it provided the technical monitoring of the RFE and RL signals, along with those of VOA, and coordinated assessments of jamming in the Technical Panel

4. James Critchlow, *Radio Hole-in-the-Head: Radio Liberty—An Insider's Story of Cold War Broadcasting* (Washington, D.C.: American University Press, 1995), 17; Gene Sosin, *Sparks of Liberty: An Insider's Memoir of Radio Liberty* (University Park: Pennsylvania State University Press, 1999), 29; CIA memorandum to DCI from CA, December 14, 1967, released June 1999, available at www.voia.cia.gov. There were never more than a handful of CIA officers within either the FEC or the RLC. While they doubtless provided CIA with internal information on the Radios, the available record contains only one case of their operating outside the FEC or RLC chain of command. That case involved an occasional suggestion in the early 1960s from one of the CIA officers to RFE news director Gene Mater to run a specific story. Mater judged the suggested stories to be irrelevant for the Eastern European audiences and declined to run them (Gene Mater, interview with the author, Washington, December 15, 2009). Yet the same CIA officer objected to an IOD suggestion to encourage RFE to run as news an unsourced story on a Soviet issue. CIA/CA officers were greatly overstating the case when they argued (in the December 1967 memorandum): "If . . . it were necessary to remove these Agency employees [from the Radios], the effect would be to reduce drastically our control over the operation. It might also cripple the Radios as such."

5. Sargeant observed in 1957: "I cannot find evidence that . . . the backstoppers [i.e., the CIA] were able to reflect adequate and timely substantive advice to the project by means of any carefully thought-through evaluation of the significance of the basic principles of the [policy] paper *translated into operational terms*." RLC memorandum, "The IG Report," by Howland Sargeant, n.d. [March 1957]; emphasis in the original.

6. Victor Marchetti and John D. Marks, *The CIA and the Cult of Intelligence* (New York: Alfred A. Knopf, 1974), 135.

for International Broadcasting on which all U.S.-funded Radios were represented. It helped the Radios gain access to major defectors such as Józef Światło and Władysław Tykociński.

Equally important, the CIA protected the Radios from irresponsible outside interference, especially domestic American anticommunist hysteria of the early 1950s. It helped spare them the negative impact that McCarthyism had on VOA. The CIA inspector general conducted a defensive security review of FEC and AMCOMLIB staffs in response to public and private accusations that the committees housed "leftists" and were penetrated by Communist agents, but few·if any FEC or AMCOMLIB employees were forced to leave. Allen Dulles persuaded a congressional committee chairman to fire one particularly hostile staff member spreading such accusations. The CIA worked with the White House and key senators to defuse Fulton Lewis Jr.'s anti-RFE campaign. It obtained the help of the AFL-CIO in thwarting efforts of U.S. trade unions to organize RFE employees in Germany in violation of German law. It helped ensure the passage of the "Rodino Bill" sponsored by Representative Peter J. Rodino (D-N.J.), which credited employment with the FEC and AMCOMLIB/RLC outside the United States toward the waiting period for U.S. citizenship and thus allowed ninety-eight employees and their immediate family members to become U.S. citizens in 1967 (and many others after that). It worked with the Immigration and Naturalization Service to secure immigration visas for certain Radio employees working abroad.[7] It provided RFE and RL research analyses to policymakers. Most important, under the leadership of Richard Helms, it managed the transition to overt funding of the Radios—which was by no means assured.

Inside the CIA, Allen Dulles insisted from the outset that the Radios, as "gray" influence projects (that is, overt, except for the source of funds and oversight), should not be involved in other covert action projects and should not be involved in espionage. In 1952, he directed that "we should *never* [emphasis in the original] use NCFE [FEC] or RFE cover for our people who are engaged in a mission of an SI [espionage] or SO [covert action] type. This is to be distinguished from the situation where we place one of our people into the RFE organization for the purpose of assisting that activity as such—and for liaison with us." It was the job of the IOD and later the Covert Action Staff to patrol this border between open communications in-

7. FEC president Richardson acknowledged the importance of CIA support for the Rodino Bill in an FEC memorandum, December 21, 1967.

struments and related information gathering, on the one hand, and espionage and disinformation, on the other. As Cord Meyer recalled:

> Pressure to distort the purpose of the radios also came occasionally from within the Agency. Ingenious schemes to use the radios in disinforma- tion campaigns against particular Communist leaders were raised with us from time to time, and my answer to all such proposals was negative. Compromise of the reputation for reliable accuracy that the broadcasts had come to enjoy was not worth the ephemeral and dubious advantage that might be gained by the use of false information. Similarly, we did not attempt to mix apples and oranges by allowing the American and ex- ile staffs to be used for secret agent operations.[8]

It was the merit of Tom Braden and Cord Meyer, as heads of the IOD, and their successors as heads of the Covert Action Staff, that they enforced these boundaries with very few exceptions, rejecting the occasional argument of others in the CIA that operational interests should take precedence over the accuracy of political reporting. In the early 1950s, RFE evidently carried at the CIA's behest some coded messages to individuals in Eastern Europe, but these ended in 1956. After that year, there is only one known case (in 1982) of RFE/RL broadcasts being used for anything other than providing infor- mation to their regular audiences.[9] And after 1956, the only known instance of a CIA attempt to utilize RFE for disinformation was the effort in 1961 to encourage RFE to "spin" its coverage of the dismissal of Czechoslovak interior minister Rudolf Barak so as to encourage defections within the Czechoslovak Intelligence Service—something RFE refused to do.

There were, to be sure, occasional attempts to "spin" RFE programs. But the enemy of credible broadcasting was not at the CIA but within the FEC itself. In one notorious case in 1956, FEC New York issued a guidance, "On Objective Truth," arguing that there is no such thing and that representative Western press reviews on Soviet-American détente broadcast on RFE might undermine anticommunists' morale. As discussed in chapter 3, policy ad- viser William E. Griffith and the Munich broadcast chiefs strongly objected, and the guidance was ignored. Virtue was not the provenance of one side.

---

8. Cord Meyer, *Facing Reality: From World Federalism to the CIA* (New York: Harper & Row, 1980), 118.

9. See Michael Nelson, *War of the Black Heavens* (Syracuse: Syracuse University Press, 1997), 177.

In 1956, RFE would have benefited from adhering to the CIA's more restrained views on broadcasting to Hungary, even if this had meant canceling most commentary. And in the 1960s, FEC and AMCOMLIB/RLC would arguably have been able to expand and improve RFE and RL broadcasts if they had focused on this core mission and not resisted the CIA's efforts to reduce their subsidiary émigré activities.

Information and Intelligence

RFE and RL were overt organizations with overt broadcasts and overt publications, and as such they had a responsibility to avoid actions that might appear as espionage and threaten to undermine their credibility as providers of objective information. Conversely, their effectiveness as surrogate broadcasters depended on their ability to obtain up-to-date information from within the closed countries to which they broadcast. To this end, as described in chapter 2, they monitored regime media; talked with Western journalists, academics, and other travelers to the region; gathered information from Eastern European and Soviet travelers to the West; and polled these travelers for their use of RFE and RL broadcasts. For most citizens of free countries, such information gathering is considered normal journalism. The Communist regimes that sought to prevent it regularly denounced it as espionage.

There is no clear division between gathering information and collecting intelligence. As one student of intelligence agencies has noted, "All intelligence is information, but not all information is intelligence."[10] RFE/RL and CIA records indicate that the Radios did a commendable job of avoiding initiatives that in Western if not Eastern eyes might have been perceived as intelligence collection. RFE sidestepped occasional CIA efforts to obtain military information from travelers that was not relevant to broadcasting. It rejected occasional offers from well-meaning Eastern Europeans to organize networks of informants in the East.[11] But the Radios themselves crossed the line on a few occasions. In 1955, an RFE broadcaster sought assistance

10. Mark M. Lowenthal, *Intelligence; From Secrets to Policy* (Washington, D.C.: CQ Press, 2006), 2.

11. Jan Nowak-Jeziorański, *Wojna w eterze* (Kraków: Znak, 2000), 74, recounts early offers to establish a network in Poland, which he rejected. Much later, shortly after I became director of RFE in November 1988, I learned that one of my service chiefs was tasking a recently organized network of paid collaborators in Eastern Europe to obtain "inside information." That clearly crossed the line, and I ended it.

from a French Embassy employee in Prague in obtaining Czechoslovak government documents—leading an IOD officer to write: "I propose that we remind [FEC president] Whitney [Shepardson] that one of the best ways of labeling RFE as an espionage apparatus is for it to engage in espionage." Most problematic cases involved volunteers. One was Edmund Ekesiobi, a Nigerian (Biafran) student accredited as a journalist in Prague, who on a visit to West Germany in 1967 contacted RFE "cold" and in the following months provided RFE with internal Czechoslovak Communist Party documents.[12] The most renowned case involved Władysław Bartoszewski, who would become Polish foreign minister after 1989 and who proudly describes himself as RFE's "oldest secret collaborator" in Poland. For almost thirty years, he used the Austrian diplomatic pouch to pass to RFE information about internal developments in Poland that was banned from the censored Polish media.[13] In both cases, RFE would have found itself hard put to decline the offers of information. But given the international controversy after 1967 about the Radios' CIA connection, RFE became especially sensitive about such activities and attempted (unsuccessfully for some time, in the case of Bartoszewski) to call a halt to both efforts. This sensitivity, along with the availability of other sources of information about Eastern Europe after the 1960s and a lack of qualified interviewers, led RFE to abandon its regular program of soliciting information from travelers and after 1971, less understandably, to purge the "information items" from its files.[14] RFE service chiefs and staff (especially in the Polish Service) continued to obtain important information about domestic developments in meetings with opposition and regime figures visiting Western Europe, recording their discussions in ad hoc memoranda.[15]

12. RFE memorandum to Walter from William Robinson, "Nigerian Student at Charles University," November 21, 1967.

13. Paweł Machcewicz, *"Monachijska menażeria": Walka z Radiem Wolna Europa* (Warsaw: Instytut Pamięci Narodowej, ISP, 2007), 225—59; Władysław Bartoszewski, remarks at a panel on secret RFE collaborators at a conference on Radio Free Europe in Polish and Western politics, Warsaw, November 30—December 1, 2007, in *Radio Wolna Europa w polityce polskiej i zachodniej,* ed. Andrzej Borzym and Jeremy Sadowski (Warsaw: Stowarzyszenie Wolnego Słowa, 2009), 137—68.

14. Early "information items" series are preserved on microfilm in the RFE/RL research collection at the Open Society Archives, and occasional "items" are to be found in RFE/RL corporate archive subject files at the Hoover Archives. But a valuable Cold War archive was lost.

15. RFE memorandum to Walter from Robert J. Knauf, "Survey of BD [Broadcast Department] Sensitive Reporting Procedures," March 30, 1971. Many reports of discussions with visitors from Poland in the 1970s and 1980s are preserved in the RFE/RL research collection at the Open Society Archives.

Dilemmas of Mission and Oversight

Since the end of the Cold War, and the subsequent two decades of open congressional appropriations to support RFE and RL (which in 1976 were merged into one organization, RFE/RL, Inc.), many dedicated listeners to the Radios in Eastern Europe and the former USSR have asked why U.S. government support was ever concealed, and why the CIA was involved at all. This book has explored the rationale for this history. The FEC and AMCOMLIB were established in the late 1940s and early 1950s as covert instruments of "political warfare"—a term that grates for many today, but meant opposing with nonmilitary means what was then judged to be an implacable opponent. Thus, this was a use of soft power. NSC Directive 10/2 of June 1948 entrusted the Office of Policy Coordination, later the CIA, with this responsibility. Although the Radios engaged solely in open communication (radio broadcasts, printed matter), concealment of U.S. government support was initially justified on the grounds that the Radios would convey hard-hitting antiregime messages to countries with which the United States maintained diplomatic relations and for which it could not assume responsibility. In Frank Altschul's words of 1950, RFE would be "supplementing the Voice of America in a field in which the Voice must be restrained because it is an agency of Government." Assistant Secretary of State Edward Barrett made the same argument: "Many things could be said by Radio Free Europe which we could not say [on VOA] since they do not openly reflect government policy."[16]

This particular justification quickly disappeared, as most of those involved with the enterprise came to realize that the key to making an impact in the broadcast region was not aggressive content pleasing to Americans but rather domestically focused messages that would be credible to audiences. Yet belief in the value of deniability persisted, as indicated by Henry Kissinger's 1971 question to the 40 Committee: "If there is an item [for the Radios] in the [federal] budget, how do we avoid getting stuck with responsibilities for the broadcasts?"[17] The fact that Communist regimes viewed

16. Letter to Cecily Goodhart, March 31, 1950, as cited by Priscilla Roberts, "Frank Altschul, Lazard Freres, and the Council on Foreign Relations: The Evolution of a Transatlantic Thinker," *Journal of Transatlantic Studies* 1, no. 2 (2003): 175–213, n. 123; "Record of the Undersecretary's Meeting, February 2, 1951," document 611, in *Foreign Relations of the United States,* ed. U.S. Department of State (hereafter, *FRUS*) (Washington, D.C.: U.S. Government Printing Office, various years), 1951, IV, part 2, 1217–18.

17. "Minutes of the 40 Committee Meeting, March 31, 1971," document 51, in *FRUS,* 1969–76, XXIX.

the Radios' domestic focus as hostile interference in internal affairs did not mean that U.S. government sponsorship had to be hidden. RIAS concentrated on internal East German issues with open U.S. government (and West German) support, while RFE's unacknowledged U.S. government support did not obviate the perceived need within the U.S. government to set overall policy and attempt to forestall complaints from U.S. embassies that RFE and RL were complicating their dealings with their host governments.

If aggressive programming was quickly abandoned and if the perceived advantages of "deniability" were mostly illusory, the question remains— Why the CIA? The answer is simply that the reality of U.S. foreign policy and domestic politics in the early Cold War period was such that RFE and RL could only have been founded with covert CIA sponsorship. RIAS evolved from an operating radio station that was the voice of the American military occupation in Berlin, whereas RFE and RL were set up from scratch. With VOA expanding, and fighting for larger budgets, it would have been impossible to justify to Congress and the public a second U.S.-government-funded international radio broadcaster. Even if the need could have been justified in terms of separate missions, there was no U.S. government agency other than the CIA that could oversee it, and no part of the federal budget other than that for intelligence activities from which to fund it.

Secret activities are a perpetual dilemma for open societies, even in wars, both hot and cold. RFE and RL could only have come into being with unacknowledged U.S. government support. As this book has documented, they were in no sense rogue CIA operations; overall policy was set by the State Department, and federal budget officials and the chairmen of key congressional committees controlled financial allocations. U.S. government and/or CIA involvement was widely assumed by foreign governments, allies and opponents, and by the American "political class." Covert CIA sponsorship did not taint these efforts; on the contrary, it made them possible in their first two decades.[18]

The degree of openness of FEC and AMCOMLIB/RLC printed word programs was a function of the media employed. Balloon-delivered leaflets

18. Frances Stoner Saunders, author of the critical study *The Cultural Cold War: The CIA and the World of Arts and Letters* (New York: New Press, 1999), was later willing to entertain the proposition "that in those early years that it was important to do it and that, if the only way to do it was covertly, then it had to be done covertly, because otherwise nothing would be done at all"; she said this in an interview with W. Scott Lucas, "Revealing the Parameters of Opinion: An Interview with Frances Stoner Saunders," *Intelligence and National Security* 18, no. 2 (Summer 2003), 27.

were a highly visible activity that generated demand for the leaflets in Eastern Europe and favorable publicity for the FEC at home. The follow-on FEC and AMCOMLIB/RLC "book programs" throughout the 1960s were the opposite, for good reasons that had little to do with the CIA as the source of funds. The book programs relied on networks of organizations and people outside the United States and the support or tolerance of foreign governments that suspected or knew what was going on, found them a worthy endeavor, and were ready to contribute and cooperate passively or even actively on one condition—that there be no publicity, that they remain covert programs. CIA funding was not the problem; the same issue would have arisen if the funding had been from the Defense Department, USIA, or the Ford Foundation.

More problematic was the Crusade for Freedom (after 1960, the RFE Fund). The crusade's efforts to mobilize Americans in the anticommunist cause was a perfectly legitimate activity in the American tradition of private organizations devoted to causes of all kinds, both foreign and domestic. The crusade's public mobilization efforts—the local committees, the Freedom Bell, the collection of millions of signatures, trips of local organizers to see the Iron Curtain close up, enormous pro bono media publicity provided by the Advertising Council—were driven by the eminent private citizens who headed the FEC and the crusade, not the CIA. What was problematic for American democracy was use of the crusade and later the fund as a cover to raise funds for RFE from American citizens who as taxpayers were already its unknowing majority stockholders.

A crusade contributor complained early that the Eisenhower administration had violated its pledge to restore honesty to government. The crusade, he wrote, "must be either a citizen operation or a government operation or at least a surcease of this business of collecting money from the public under false pretenses and using the American people merely as a smokescreen."[19] John Richardson later reflected:

> I now regard as wrong the concealed use of taxpayer money for exile activities and to "cover" those of the Radio Free Europe Fund, both intended to influence American public opinion. They were . . . a covert infringement by the federal government on the free market of ideas on which the health of our democratic system depends. This is an entirely

---

19. Crusade letter to Samuel F. Pryer from Joseph Pew, January 11, 1954.

distinct issue from concealment of CIA sponsorship of broadcasts to a denied area in a situation like that of the Cold War.[20]

Many contributed to this duplicity—the CIA and FEC to be sure, but equally culpable were corporate and media executives who responded to Allen Dulles' appeals to support the Crusade for Freedom and who could have had little doubt about his role, journalists who knew or suspected that the U.S. government was involved, and presidents Eisenhower, Kennedy, and Johnson, who hosted crusade luncheons at the White House for major corporate contributors who were the principal source of crusade revenue.

20. John Richardson Jr., *A New Vision for America: Toward Human Solidarity through Global Democracy—a Memoir* (New York: Ruder Finn Press, 2006), 93. See Arch Puddington, *Broadcasting Freedom: The Cold War Triumph of Radio Free Europe and Radio Liberty* (Lexington: University Press of Kentucky, 2000), 188—89. A 1950 OPC memorandum acknowledged the ethical issue but concluded that it was proper to seek private contributions for an unacknowledged government-supported activity.

Chapter 10

Influencing Others: Lessons Learned, Overlearned, and Unlearned

Radio Free Europe and Radio Liberty are today generally acknowledged to have played an important role in bringing the Cold War to a peaceful end. As the United States has sought to influence foreign populations since the 1990s, and especially since the September 11, 2001, terrorist attacks, RFE and RL have often been cited as models. The terms in which they are praised —they "told the truth" "we [dissidents and opposition] wanted to make sure that somebody was listening [to us]"[1]—are accurate. But the history of the first two decades of the Radios under CIA auspices provides more specific lessons about what works and what does not in efforts to influence others using international communications, lessons confirmed by RFE and RL practice in the 1970s and 1980s. The Cold War experience cannot directly be transferred to current efforts, in a quite different political, media, and technological world, to communicate with purpose to peoples abroad. Yet the RFE and RL Cold War experience does suggest seven key lessons for policymakers and communicators.

The first lesson is that information provided from outside can only reinforce indigenous opposition to repressive regimes, never create that opposition. It was the often unappreciated merit of the Radios in their earliest years that they promoted indigenous self-liberation, never "liberation" by others. Any ambiguity on that score ended not in 1956, with the failure of the Hungarian Revolution, but in 1953, with the suppression of the East German uprising. But it was an error of FEC strategists in the years between

---

1. Secretary of State Condoleezza Rice's remarks at Georgetown University, January 18, 2006.

242 Influencing Others: Lessons Learned, Overlearned, and Unlearned

1953 and 1956 to think that RFE could serve as catalyst for a passive resistance movement to Communist rule that did not yet exist. RFE and RL, along with VOA, the BBC, and other Western broadcasters, served as a lifeline to the West and kept hope alive for individuals during the entire Cold War. In the words of a young Hungarian refugee interviewed in January 1957, "Hearing about freedom wakes similar desires and keeps hope for freedom alive." But the Radios could reinforce political challenges to repression only after indigenous dissent and opposition had developed in the late 1960s in the Soviet Bloc.

The second lesson is that external media can serve as a "free press" for unfree countries, as substitute free national media, provided that they are properly organized and able to marshal the resources needed for the task. It was the merit of the FEC and RLC that they understood this from the outset, the wisdom of the CIA and the U.S. government that it provided those resources, and the merit of RFE's and RL's managers that they developed the editorial, information gathering, analytic, audience analysis, and quality control capabilities necessary for the task. They also understood that successful substitute media—surrogate broadcasting, as the substitute home services came to be known—required more than simply a focus on target country developments. They required views as well as news, and opinion or commentary or analysis in addition to objective newscasts and features. They also came to understand after 1953 that it was this mix of domestic-focused news, comment, and features that was important, not "hard-hitting broadcasts." They came to understand that verbal bombast, however satisfying to some in the West, was counterproductive with the audience in the East.

The third lesson is that a successful surrogate broadcaster cannot be an overt or covert voice of the United States or any other foreign country—a Voice of America (as VOA was conceived) in disguise. Surrogate media must reflect universal values of freedom and tolerance symbolized by the United States at its best. Their purpose is to promote the freedom of others in the American interest. But they cannot usefully parrot topical U.S. government policy positions to skeptical audiences. Words on this point come easily; the 1957 Committee on Radio Broadcasting Policy country papers affirmed that RFE would "give fair coverage to legitimate points of view which are not necessary in accord with the public position of the U.S. Government," and the International Broadcasting Act of 1973 provided that RFE and RL broadcasts "should not be inconsistent with the broad principles of American foreign policy." Actions come harder; this book has cited examples of U.S. government efforts (fortunately often unsuccessful) to shape broadcasts more in line with official American policies of the day.

The fourth lesson is that if surrogate broadcasting is to be successful, it must be credible to its audience. Its news must be as balanced and objective, and as well sourced, as possible. It must, in the words of the first VOA broadcast (which are equally applicable to surrogate broadcasting), provide "the bad news as well as the good." But its newscasters and commentators must also be credible to the audience—meaning that they must speak the same language, culturally and ethnically as well as linguistically. This involves giving editorial authority to individuals from "there," talented émigrés enjoying editorial autonomy in partnership with Americans (of whatever ethnic background), who ultimately are responsible for broadcasts and publications.

The fifth lesson is the special responsibility of an external communicator in crises. It is the job of any surrogate broadcaster to reinforce and amplify incipient independent media in repressive societies, whether in Hungary during the 1956 Revolution, Poland under Solidarity, or the Soviet Union under Gorbachev. There is always a danger of unintended consequences; during crises, responsible journalism can be inadvertently inflammatory, because audiences can mistake reporting for exhortation.

That said, a surrogate broadcaster (like any external communicator) has a special responsibility to avoid encouraging violence. Revolution and violent opposition to tyranny hold an honorable place in the history of free peoples, but they cannot be the business of external communicators. It was the merit of RFE that its Polish Service discouraged violent opposition to Communist rule in Poland in 1956 and amplified Solidarity's peaceful challenge to Communist rule in 1980. It was the merit of RFE that its Czechoslovak Service promoted calm and discouraged active opposition to Soviet repression in 1968. It was the failure of RFE that its Hungarian Service contributed to rather than restrained unrealistic expectations about the triumph of the violent Hungarian Revolution.

In crisis situations, the external communicator must sometimes suspend normal standards of journalism and limit reporting; it must censor itself. To cite a later example (from my time as RFE director), it was appropriate for the *New York Times* to cover details of the violence between ethnic Hungarians and ethnic Romanians in Transylvania in 1990. It would have been inflammatory for RFE/RL to broadcast those reports back into Hungary and Romania, and it did not. Every crisis requires editorial judgment; sometimes the choices are clear-cut and sometimes they are not. To cite a more recent example, in October 2000 RFE/RL's South Slavic Service gave saturation coverage to preparations around Serbia for the march on Belgrade that brought down Milošević. Broadcasters offered no advice, but they had little doubt that coverage of the preparations (ignored in the Milošević-controlled state media) would increase the number of marchers. It was the right call, but if October 20 had ended in violence, RFE/RL would have been criticized for inflaming the situation.

The sixth lesson is to resist any temptation to "play God," for broadcasters to forget that outside is not inside, and to pretend to know the interests of the audiences better than the audiences themselves. RFE and RL generally resisted that temptation. After 1953 there were only isolated cases of the Radios offering tactical advice.

Judgments about RFE's editorial policy at key Eastern European historical junctures will doubtless continue to vary. RFE arguably erred in failing to give Imre Nagy any benefit of the doubt throughout most of the Hungarian Revolution. RFE arguably tilted in favor of Dubček in the fall of 1968 to the neglect of other views (including those of Václav Havel at the time) that were less charitable about his role after the Soviet invasion. RFE arguably involved itself more than it should have in conflict within the Polish Communist Party in the late 1960s.

The Radio arguably found the right balance in 1980–81 (just as it had in its broadcasts to Poland in 1956), when the Polish Service provided full coverage of (and thus contributed to) Solidarity's rise but then, as tensions mounted, stressed the "possibilities and limits imposed by geo-politics . . . both the Party and the nation must take into account the stand of the Soviet Union."[2] RFE director J. F. Brown, who consulted daily with Polish Service director Zygmunt Michałowski on Polish Service programs, reflected later: "The great difficulty was avoiding specific advice. . . . Both Michałowski and I felt strongly that well-fed, well-paid, well-housed exiles enjoying the safety and security of living in the West were never in any position to proffer advice to listeners living in the hardships and the dangers of Eastern Europe."[3] Following the imposition of martial law, the Polish Service reported but downplayed the incident at the Wujek mines, where nine miners were killed by police, fearing that highlighting the violence could have been incendiary. It did not carry unconfirmed reports of regime atrocities that appeared in

2. Commentary by Michałowski before the imposition of martial law, as quoted by Arch Puddington, *Broadcasting Freedom: The Cold War Triumph of Radio Free Europe and Radio Liberty* (Lexington: University Press of Kentucky, 2000), 270.
3. J. F. Brown, unpublished manuscript on Radio Free Europe, 2005, 135–38.

some Western media after December 1981. But it then provided full coverage of the suppression of Solidarity under martial law.

The seventh and final lesson, and perhaps the most important one, is that successful surrogate broadcasting (indeed, any successful foreign influence program) is a long-term proposition. It requires sustainable support that is difficult to reconcile with the natural inclination of all governments—and especially the U.S. government—to seek short-term indicators of success, to appraise the utility of specific country broadcasts on a yearly basis, to demonstrate from one budget cycle to the next that a particular project is (as current U.S. government jargon terms it) "moving the needle." In the case of broadcasting, and indeed all foreign influence programs, this is an unrealistic, indeed pernicious expectation.

In the 1950s and 1960s, CIA and Radio officials of necessity made use of whatever evidence they could muster, such as listener letters and verbal regime attacks, to demonstrate the Radios' impact within the U.S. government bureaucracy. But they planned for the long term. It was only in the 1960s that RFE could plausibly demonstrate, through massive traveler polling, that it had large audiences. It was only in the 1970s, as dissent developed within the USSR, that RL could plausibly demonstrate an echo-chamber effect. If RL's utility as of 1970 is judged solely by the evidence of impact by that date, then the Nixon administration's initial decision to terminate it was reasonable. Why waste the money? When RL's utility is judged by the evidence of its impact by 1991, then termination in 1970 would have been a huge mistake. Why did we squander the opportunity? If RFE's utility in the 1970s in Czechoslovakia is judged only by its relatively limited impact at the time, then a decision to close the Czechoslovak Service might seem reasonable. Its utility is better judged by its role in amplifying the dissent of Václav Havel and other Charter 77 figures and its impact during the Velvet Revolution.

The Radios had their failures, to be sure, as well as their successes over the years. They made their share of mistakes. But it is to their credit that they remained focused on long-term payoff. The United States rightly touts transparency of political decisionmaking as a core democratic value. Yet it was arguably only the covert oversight and funding of Radio Free Europe and Radio Liberty by the Central Intelligence Agency during their first two decades that made possible the investment in their capabilities that allowed them later to contribute much to the collapse of the Soviet Union and the emergence of a Europe "whole and free."

Bibliography

Memoirs and Interviews

Aigner, Helmut. Oral history interview with R. Eugene Parta, Vienna, August 2005, Hoover Archives.

Bohnsack, Günther. Interview with the author, Berlin, December 2003.

Borbándi, Gyula. *Magyarok az Angol Kertben: A Szabad Europa Rádió Törtenete* [Hungarians in the English Garden: The History of Radio Free Europe]. Budapest: Europa Könyvkiadó, 1996. I am indebted to Margit Grigory for a summary of parts of this book.

Brew, Arthur. Interview with the author, Stanford, Calif., 2004.

Brown, J. F. Unpublished manuscript on Radio Free Europe, 2005.

Buckley, James L. *Gleanings from an Unplanned Life: An Annotated Oral History.* Wilmington, Del.: ISI Books, 2006.

Conference, "Hungary and the World, 1956: The New Archival Evidence," Budapest, September 26–29, 1996. Papers by former RFE officials William E. Griffith, "RFE and the Hungarian Revolution and the Polish October"; Jan Nowak, "Poles and Hungarians in 1956"; Paul B. Henze, "Recollections of Radio Free Europe: Its Evolution in the 1950s and the Hungarian Revolution"; and James McCargar, "Policy and Personalities."

Critchlow, James. *Radio Hole-in-the-Head: Radio Liberty—An Insider's Story of Cold War Broadcasting.* Washington, D.C.: American University Press, 1995.

Czechowicz, Andrzej. Interview with the author, Warsaw, 2004.

Drygas, Maciej J. "Fale w eterze." *Karta,* no. 38, 2003. (Interviews with former Polish jammers and Polish listeners to RFE.)

Ethridge, Mark F. Oral History Interview, Truman Presidential Museum and Library, 1974, www.trumanlibrary.org/oralhist/ethridge.htm.

Grew, Joseph C. "National Committee for Free Europe." *American Foreign Service Journal* 26, no. 9 (September 1949).

Griffith, William E. Interview with László Ribansky of RFE/RL, Bonn, May 13, 1986, RFE/RL Collection.

Henze, Paul B. Interviews with the author, Washington, Va., 2005–8.

———. Personal correspondence, 1952–57.

———. "Radio Free Europe's Early Years: Reflections on Broadcasting to Poland." Conference paper, Warsaw, April 26, 2002.

Hollyer, David L. "Winds Aloft: When Radio Free Europe Flew Balloons." *QST,* April 2001, 49–52.

 Johnson, A. Ross. "A Half-Century of RFE/RL Broadcasting to Hungary: The Endgame." In *Országos Széchényi Könvtár.* Budapest: National Széchenyi Library, 2001.

Leich, John Foster. "Freeing Europe." Unpublished autobiographical paper, n.d.

———. "Great Expectations: The National Councils in Exile, 1950–1960." *Polish Review* 35, nos. 3–4 (1990).

———. Interview with the author, December 2007.

Leinwoll, Stanley. "Freedoms Radio." *Electronics Now,* September 1997.

Lodeesen, Jon. "Radio Liberty (Munich); Foundations for a History." *Historical Review of Film, Radio, and Television* 6, no. 2 (1986).

Mater, Gene. Interview with the author, Washington, D.C., December 15, 2009.

 Matthews, John. P. "The West's Secret Marshall Plan for the Mind." *Journal of Intelligence and Counterintelligence* 16, no. 3 (2003): 409–27.

Michie, Allan A. *Voices through the Iron Curtain: The Radio Free Europe Story.* New York: Dodd, Mead & Company, 1963.

Mickelson, Sig. Oral history interviews with 87 RFE, RL, and former CIA officials in 1981–82, Sig Mickelson Collection, Hoover Archives.

Miller, Stephen. "Inside Radio Free Europe." *Partisan Review,* no. 1, 2003.

Nowak, Jan. "War on the Airwaves: A Frontline Report." Unpublished manuscript. This manuscript is based on *Wojna w eterze* but contains additional material.

Nowak-Jeziorański, Jan. "RWE a CIA." *Karta,* no. 38, 2003.

———. *Wojna w eterze.* Kraków: Znak, 2000.

Patch, Isaac. *Closing the Circle: A Buckalino Journey Around Our Time.* Privately printed, Wellesley College Printing Services, Wellesley, Mass., 1996.

———. *They Made a Difference: Friends Remembered.* 2002. Privately printed.

Rademaekers, William. Correspondence with the author, 2006.

Richardson, John, Jr. Interviews with the author, Washington, 2003 and 2008.

———. *A New Vision for America: Toward Human Solidarity through Global Democracy—a Memoir.* New York: Ruder Finn Press, 2006.

———. Oral History Interview, February 9, 1999, Foreign Affairs Oral History Collection of the Association for Diplomatic Studies and Training, Library of Congress. Available at http://memory.loc.gov.

Rowson, Richard C. "The American Commitment to Private International Political Communications: A View of 'Free Europe'." *Law and Contemporary Problems* (Duke University School of Law), Summer 1966.

Ruckstuhl, Charles E. "The Beginnings of Electronic Warfare." *World & I* 18, no. 10 (October 2003).

Sosin, Gene. *Sparks of Liberty: An Insider's Memoir of Radio Liberty.* University Park: Pennsylvania State University Press, 1999.

Staar, Richard R. *Born under a Lucky Star; Reminiscences.* New York: Oxford University Press, 2002.

"Tajni i świadomi współpracownicy RWE" [Secret RFE Collaborators], panel for a conference on RFE history, Warsaw University, December 1, 2007 (reminiscences by Władysław Bartoszewski, Józef Szaniawski, Piotr Jeglinski, and Włodzimierz Odojewski). In *Radio Wolna Europa w polityce polskiej i zachodniej,* ed. Andrzej Borzym and Jeremy Sadowski. Warsaw: Stowarzyszenie Wolnego Słowa, 2009.

Tuck, Robert. Interview with the author, Chapel Hill, N.C., April 2004.

———. "Radio Liberty." Unpublished speech to the Kiwanis Club, Charlotte, March 6, 1997.

———. "Radio Liberty; Broadcast Policy Operations." Undated.

 Urban, George R. *Radio Free Europe and the Pursuit of Democracy: My War within the Cold War.* New Haven, Conn.: Yale University Press, 1997.

Van Der Rhoer, Edward. Interview with the author, Washington, August 2004.

Walter, Ralph E. Interviews and correspondence with the author, 2003–8.

Wolf, Markus. Interview with the author, Berlin, September 2005.

Archival Collections

Archive of Contemporary Documents, Polish State Archives, Warsaw.

Bavarian State Archive, Munich.

Institute of National Remembrance, Warsaw.

Office of the Federal Commissioner for the Preservation of the Records of the Ministry of State Security, Berlin.

 Oral History Collection and RFE Hungarian Broadcast Transcriptions Collection, National Széchényi Library, Budapest.

Political Archive of the Foreign Office, Berlin.

 Records of the Central Intelligence Agency on Radio Free Europe and Radio Liberty.

RFE/RL Corporate and Broadcast Collections, Hoover Archives, Hoover Institution on War, Revolution, and Peace, Stanford University, Stanford, Calif.

RFE/RL Research Collection, Open Society Archives, Budapest.

Robert F. Kelley Papers, Georgetown University Library Special Collections Division, Washington.

 U.S. National Archives and Records Administration, College Park, Md.

Documentary Collections

Békés, Csaba, Malcolm Byrne, and János M. Rainer. *The 1956 Hungarian Revolution: A History in Documents.* Budapest: Central European University Press, 2002.

The Department of State Policy Planning Papers 1948. New York: Garland, 1983.

Free Europe Committee. *The Revolt in Hungary: A Documentary Chronology of Events Based Exclusively on Internal Broadcasts by Central and Provincial Radios, October 23, 1956–November 4, 1956.* New York: Free Europe Committee, 1957.

U.S. Department of State, ed. *Foreign Relations of the United States,* volumes for 1946–72; also *Soviet-American Relations. The Détente Years 1969–1972.* Washington, D.C.: U.S. Government Printing Office, various years. Also available at http://history.state.gov/historicaldocuments/.

Warner, Michael, ed. *CIA Cold War Records: The CIA under Harry Truman.* Washington, D.C.: Center for the Study of Intelligence, 1994.

Books and Articles

Abshire, David M. *International Broadcasting: A New Dimension of Western Diplomacy—The Washington Papers,* vol. 4. Beverly Hills, Calif.: Sage, 1976.
———. *Saving the Reagan Presidency: Trust Is the Coin of the Realm.* College Station: Texas A&M University Press, 2005.
Andrew, Christopher, and Vasili Mitrokhin. *The Sword and the Shield: The Mitrokhin Archive and the Secret History of the KGB.* New York: Basic Books, 1999.
Bain, Leslie B. *The Reluctant Satellites: An Eyewitness Report on East Europe and the Hungarian Revolution.* New York: Macmillan, 1960.
Barnouw, Erik. *The Image Empire: A History of Broadcasting in the United States, Volume III—from 1953.* New York: Oxford University Press, 1970.
Barrett, Edward W. *Truth Is Our Weapon.* New York: Funk & Wagnalls, 1953.
Berle, Beatrice Bishop, and Travis Beal Jacobs, eds. *Navigating the Rapids 1918–1971: From the Papers of Adolf A. Berle.* New York: Harcourt Brace Jovanovich, 1973.
Bittman, Ladislav. *The Deception Game.* Syracuse: Syracuse University Research Corporation, 1972.
Bogart, Leo. "In Memoriam: Max Ralis 1916–1999." *Public Opinion Quarterly* 63, no. 2 (Summer 1999): 261–62.
Borhi, László. "Liberation or Inaction? The United States and Hungary in 1956." In *Die Ungarnkrise 1956 und Österreich,* ed. Erwin A. Schmidl. Vienna: Boehlau Verlag, 2003.
Borzym, Andrzej, and Jeremy Sadowski, eds., *Radio Wolna Europa w polityce polskiej i zachodniej.* Warsaw: Stowarzyszenie Wolnego Słowa, 2009.
Braden, Thomas W. "I'm Glad the CIA Is 'Immoral'." *Saturday Evening Post,* May 20, 1967.
Browne, Donald R. *International Radio Broadcasting: The Limits of the Limitless Medium.* New York: Praeger, 1982.
———. "Radio in the American Sector, RIAS Berlin." In *Western Broadcasting Over the Iron Curtain,* ed. K. R. M. Short. New York: St. Martin's Press, 1986.
———. "RIAS Berlin: A Case Study of a Cold War Broadcast Operations." *Journal of Broadcasting,* Spring 1966, 119–35.
Brzezinski, Zbigniew. *Alternative to Partition: For a Broader Conception of America's Role in Europe.* New York: McGraw-Hill, 1965.
Brzezinski, Zbigniew, and William Griffith. "Peaceful Engagement in Eastern Europe." *Foreign Affairs* 39, no. 4 (Spring 1961).
Chamberlin, William Henry. "Émigré Anti-Soviet Enterprises and Splits." *Russian Review* 11, no. 1 (January 1952): 16–23.
———. "Russians Against Stalin." *Russian Review* 13, no. 2 (April 1954): 91–98.
Cline, Ray S. *The CIA under Reagan, Bush & Casey: The Evolution of the Agency from Roosevelt to Reagan.* Washington, D.C.: Acropolis Books, 1981.
Cold War Broadcasting Impact: Report on a Conference Organized by the Hoover Institution and the Cold War International History Project of the Woodrow Wilson International Center for Scholars, Stanford University, October 13–16, 2004. Stanford, Calif.: Hoover Archives, 2005. Available at http://hoorferl.stanford.edu/cooperation.php and at www.cwiph.org.
Cone, Stacey. "Presuming a Right to Deceive. Radio Free Europe, Radio Liberty, the CIA, and the News Media." *Journalism History* 24, no. 4: 148–56.

Corke, Sarah-Jane. *US Covert Operations and Cold War Strategy.* New York: Routledge, 2008.

Coste, Brutus. "Propaganda to Eastern Europe." *Public Opinion Quarterly* 14, no. 4 (Winter 1950–51): 639–66.

Critchlow, James. "Public Diplomacy during the Cold War: The Record and Its Implications." *Journal of Cold War Studies* 6, no. 1 (Winter 2004): 75–89.

Cull, Nicholas J. *The Cold War and the United States Information Agency: American Propaganda and Public Diplomacy, 1945–1989.* Cambridge: Cambridge University Press, 2008.

Cummings, Richard H. *Cold War Radio: The Dangerous History of American Broadcasting in Europe, 1950–1989.* Jefferson, N.C.: McFarland & Co., 2009.

———. "The Ether War: Hostile Intelligence Activities Directed against Radio Free Europe, Radio Liberty, and the Émigré Community in Munich during the Cold War." *Journal of Transatlantic Studies* 6, no. 2 (August 2008): 171–88.

———. *Radio Free Europe's "Crusade for Freedom": Rallying Americans Behind Cold War Broadcasting, 1950–1960.* Jefferson, N.C.: McFarland & Co., 2010.

Czechowicz, Andrzej. *Siedem trudnych lat.* Warsaw, 1st ed., 1973; 2nd ed., 1974.

Eichner, Klaus, and Andreas Dobbert. *Headquarters Germany: Die USA-Geheimdienste in Deutschland.* Berlin: Edition Ost, 1997.

Fulbright, J. William. *The Crippled Giant: American Foreign Policy and Its Domestic Consequences.* New York: Random House, 1972.

Garczynski, Joyce. "The Effects of Radio Free Europe and Radio Liberty on Communist Governments and Audiences." Unpublished paper, Annenberg Trust at Sunnylands, 2005.

Gati, Charles. *Failed Illusions: Moscow, Washington, Budapest, and the 1956 Hungarian Revolt.* Washington, D.C., and Stanford, Calif.: Woodrow Wilson Center Press and Stanford University Press, 2006.

Granville, Johanna. " 'Caught with Jam on Our Fingers': Radio Free Europe and the Hungarian Revolution of 1956." *Diplomatic History* 29, no. 5 (November 2005): 811–39.

———. *The First Domino: International Decision Making during the Hungarian Crisis of 1956.* College Station: Texas A&M University Press, 2004.

Griese, Noel L. *Arthur W. Page: Publisher, Public Relations Pioneer, Patriot.* Atlanta: Anvil, 2001.

Grose, Peter. *Gentleman Spy: The Life of Allen Dulles.* Boston: Houghton Mifflin, 1994.

———. *Operation Rollback: America's Secret War behind the Iron Curtain.* Boston: Houghton Mifflin, 2000.

Haight, David. "The Papers of C.D. Jackson: A Glimpse at President Eisenhower's Psychological Warfare Expert." *Manuscripts,* Winter 1976, 27–37.

Hajdasz, Jolanta. *Szczekaczka czylii Rozgłośnia Polska Radia Wolna Europa.* Poznań: Media Rodzina, 2006.

Halperin, Morton H., et al. *The Lawless State: The Crimes of the U.S. Intelligence Agencies.* New York: Penguin Books, 1975.

Heil, Alan L., Jr. *Voice of America: A History.* New York: Columbia University Press, 2003.

Helms, Richard. *A Look Over My Shoulder: My Life in the Central Intelligence Agency.* New York: Random House, 2003.

Hill, Cissie Dore. "Voices of Hope: The Story of Radio Free Europe and Radio Liberty." *Hoover Digest,* no. 4 (2001): 187–204.

Holt, Robert T. *Radio Free Europe.* Minneapolis: University of Minnesota Press, 1958.

Holt, Robert T., and Robert W. van de Velde. *Strategic Psychological Operations and American Foreign Policy.* Chicago: University of Chicago Press, 1960.

Hoopes, Townsend. *The Devil and John Foster Dulles.* Boston: Little, Brown, 1973.

Johnson, A. Ross. *East European Armed Forces and Soviet Military Planning: Factors of Change.* Santa Monica, Calif.: RAND Corporation, 2006 (orig. internal report N-2856-AF, 1989).

———. "To the Barricades: Did Radio Free Europe Inflame the Hungarian Revolutionaries of 1956? Exploring One of the Cold War's Most Stubborn Myths." *Hoover Digest,* no. 4 (2007): 167–78. A longer version of this article appeared in Hungarian in *Aetas,* no. 2 (2007): 147–73.

Johnson, A. Ross, and R. Eugene Parta, eds. *Cold War Broadcasting: Impact on the Soviet Union and Eastern Europe—A Collection of Studies and Documents.* Budapest: Central European University Press, 2010.

Johnston, Gordon. "Listening to the Voices: The BBC's Central-European Service in the Early Days of the Cold War." Paper presented at a conference on Central and Eastern Europe in the Cold War, 1945–89, Warsaw, October 16–18, 2008.

Kalugin, Oleg. *The First Directorate: My 32 Years in Intelligence and Espionage against the West.* New York: St. Martin's Press, 1994.

Kasprzak, Michał. "Radio Free Europe and the Catholic Church during the 1950s and 1960s." *Canadian Slavonic Papers,* September–December 2004.

Katona, Judit, and György Vámos. "Nagy Imre és a Szabad Európa Rádió 1956-ban" [Imre Nagy and Radio Free Europe in 1956]. In *Nagy Imre és kora: Tanulmányok és források I* [Imre Nagy and his era: Studies and sources]. Budapest, Imre Nagy Foundation, 2002. I am indebted to Margit Grigory for summarizing and translating parts of this chapter.

Kennan, George F. *Memoirs. 1925–1950.* Boston: Little, Brown, 1969.

———. "What Is Policy? Lecture to the National War College, December 18, 1947." In *Measures Short of War: The George F. Kennan Lectures at the National War College, 1946–1947.* Washington, D.C.: National Defense University Press, 1991.

Kohler, Foy D., and Mose L. Harvey. *The Soviet Union: Yesterday, Today, Tomorrow— A Colloquy of American Long Timers in Moscow.* Miami: University of Miami Center for Advanced International Studies, 1985.

Kovrig, Bennett. *The Myth of Liberation: East Central Europe in U.S. Diplomacy and Politics since 1941.* Baltimore: Johns Hopkins University Press, 1973.

Kramer, Mark. "The Czechoslovak Crisis and the Brezhnev Doctrine." In *1968: The World Transformed,* ed. Carole Fink, Philipp Gassert, and Detlef Junker. New York: Cambridge: Cambridge University Press, 1998.

———. "New Evidence on Soviet Decision-Making and the 1956 Polish and Hungarian Crises." *Bulletin of the Cold War International History Project,* issues 8–9 (Winter 1996–97): 358–84.

Lendvai, Paul. *1956. One Day That Shook the Communist World: The 1956 Hungarian Uprising and Its Legacy.* Princeton, N.J.: Princeton University Press, 2008.

———. "Die ungarische Revolution 1956: Eine Einleitung." In *Die Ungarnkrise 1956 und Österreich,* ed. Erwin A. Schmidl. Vienna: Boehlau, 2003.

L'Hommedieu, Jonathan H. "Broadcasting to the Baltic, 1950–1975: U.S.-Baltic Émigré Relations Concerning the Role of Radio Free Europe and Radio Liberty Broadcasts and U.S. Foreign Policy." MA thesis, University of Turku, Finland, 2006.

Lisann, Maury. *Broadcasting to the Soviet Union.* New York: Praeger, 1975.

Lowenthal, Mark M. *Intelligence; From Secrets to Policy.* Washington, D.C.: CQ Press, 2006.

Lucas, W. Scott. "Beyond Freedom, Beyond Control: Approaches to Culture and the State-Private Network in the Cold War." *Intelligence and National Security* 18, no. 2 (Summer 2003).

———. "Revealing the Parameters of Opinion: An Interview with Frances Stoner Saunders." *Intelligence and National Security* 18, no. 2 (Summer 2003).

Machcewicz, Paweł. *"Monachijska menażeria": Walka z Radiem Wolna Europa.* Warsaw: Instytut Pamięci Narodowej, ISP, 2007.

———. *Rebellious Satellite: Poland 1956.* Washington, D.C., and Stanford, Calif.: Woodrow Wilson Center Press and Stanford University Press, 2009.

Marchetti, Victor, and John D. Marks. *The CIA and the Cult of Intelligence.* New York: Alfred A. Knopf, 1974.

Marchio, Jim. "Resistance Potential and Rollback: US Intelligence and the Eisenhower Administration's Policies toward Eastern Europe, 1953–1956." *Intelligence and National Security* 10, no. 2 (April 1995): 219–41.

Mastny, Vojtech. *The Cold War and Soviet Insecurity.* New York: Oxford University Press, 1996.

Matthews, John P. C. *Explosion: The Hungarian Revolution of 1956.* New York: Hippocrene Books, 2007.

———. *Tinderbox: East-Central Europe in the Spring, Summer, and Early Fall of 1956.* Tucson: Fenestra Books, 2003.

Meyer, Cord. *Facing Reality: From World Federalism to the CIA.* New York: Harper & Row, 1980.

Mickelson, Sig. *America's Other Voice: The Story of Radio Free Europe and Radio Liberty.* New York: Praeger, 1983.

Miscamble, Wilson D. *George F. Kennan and the Making of American Foreign Policy.* Princeton, N.J.: Princeton University Press, 1992.

Mitrovich, Gregory. *Undermining the Kremlin: America's Strategy to Subvert the Soviet Bloc, 1947–1956.* Ithaca, N.Y.: Cornell University Press, 2000.

Nałęcz, Daria, ed. *50 lat rozgłośni polskiej radia wolna europa.* Warsaw: Polish State Archives, 2003.

Nelson, Michael. *War of the Black Heavens.* Syracuse: Syracuse University Press, 1997.

Ostermann, Christian F., ed. *Uprising in East Germany, 1953.* Budapest, Central European University Press, 2001.

Pacepa, Ion Mihai. *Red Horizons: Chronicles of a Communist Spy Chief.* Washington, D.C.: Regnery Gateway, 1987.

Paczkowski, Andrzej. *Trzy twarze Józefa Światły.* Warsaw: Prószyński Media, 2009.

Parta, R. Eugene. *Discovering the Hidden Listener: An Assessment of Radio Liberty and Western Broadcasting to the USSR during the Cold War.* Stanford, Calif.: Hoover Institution Press, 2007.

Pleikis, Rimantas. *Jamming.* Vilnius, 1998.

Pool, Ithiel de Sola. "Opportunities for Change: Communications with the U.S.S.R." Paper delivered at a Radio Liberty workshop, New York University, November 20, 1965.

Presidential Study Commission on International Radio Broadcasting. *The Right to Know: Report of the Presidential Study Commission on International Radio Broadcasting.* Washington, D.C.: U.S. Government Printing Office, 1973.

Price, James R. *Radio Free Europe: A Survey and Analysis*. Washington, D.C.: Congressional Research Service, 1972.

Propas, Frederic L. "Creating a Hard Line toward Russia: The Training of State Department Soviet Experts, 1927–1939." *Diplomatic History* 8, no. 3 (July 1984): 209–26.

Puddington, Arch. *Broadcasting Freedom: The Cold War Triumph of Radio Free Europe and Radio Liberty*. Lexington: University Press of Kentucky, 2000.

Rawnsley, Gary D. *Radio Diplomacy and Propaganda: The BBC and VOA in International Politics*. New York: St. Martin's Press, 1996.

Reisch, Alfred. *Hot Books in the Cold War: The West's Secret Book Distribution Program behind the Iron Curtain*. Forthcoming.

———. " 'Ideological Warfare' during the Cold War: The West's Secret Book Distribution Program behind the Iron Curtain." *Foreign Policy Review* (Budapest) 6 (2009): 160–76.

Rexin, Manfred, ed. *Radio: Reminiszenzen. Erinnerungen an RIAS Berlin*. Berlin: Vistas Verlag, 2002.

Richmond, Yale. *Cultural Exchange and the Cold War: Raising the Iron Curtain*. University Park: Pennsylvania State University Press, 2003.

Roberts, Priscilla. "Frank Altschul, Lazard Freres, and the Council on Foreign Relations: The Evolution of a Transatlantic Thinker." *Journal of Transatlantic Studies* 1, no. 2 (2003): 175–213.

Russell, Richard L. *George F. Kennan's Strategic Thought: The Making of an American Political Realist*. Westport, Conn.: Praeger, 1979.

Sakharov, Andrei. *Thoughts on Progress, Coexistence, and Intellectual Freedom*. New York: W. W. Norton, 1968.

Saunders, Frances Stoner. *The Cultural Cold War: The CIA and the World of Arts and Letters*. New York: New Press, 1999.

Schwartz, Lowell H. *Political Warfare against the Kremlin: US and British Propaganda at the Beginning of the Cold War*. New York: Palgrave Macmillan, 2009.

Shackley, Theodore. *Spymaster: My Life in the CIA*. Dulles, Va.: Potomac Books, 2006.

Smith, Jean D. *Lucius D. Clay: An American Life*. New York: Henry Holt, 1990.

Smith, Paul A. *On Political War*. Washington, D.C.: National Defense University Press, 1989.

Stępniak, Władysław, ed. *Wokół rozgłośni polskiej radia wolna europa*. Warsaw: Polish State Archives, 2002.

Stockton, Bayard. *Flawed Patriot: The Rise and Fall of CIA Legend Bill Harvey*. Dulles, Va.: Potomac Books, 2006.

Thomas, Evan. *The Very Best Men*. New York: Simon & Schuster, 1995.

Thompson, Nicholas. *The Hawk and the Dove: Paul Nitze, George Kennan, and the History of the Cold War*. New York: Henry Holt, 2009.

Tumanov, Oleg. *Confessions of a KGB Agent*. Chicago: Edition Q, 1993. Also in German: *Geständnisse eines KGB-Agenten*. Berlin: Edition Q, 1993. The two versions contain somewhat different content.

Tyson, James L. *U.S. International Broadcasting and National Security*. New York: Ramapo Press, 1983.

Wala, Michael. *The Council on Foreign Relations and American Foreign Policy in the Early Cold War*. Providence: Bergham Books, 1994.

Washburn, Philo C. *Broadcasting Propaganda: International Radio Broadcasting and the Construction of Political Reality*. Westport, Conn.: Praeger, 1992.

Weiner, Tim. *Legacy of Ashes: The History of the CIA.* New York: Random House, 2007.

Weiser, Benjamin. *A Secret Life: The Polish Officer, His Covert Mission, and the Price He Paid to Save His Country.* New York: PublicAffairs, 2004.

Whelan, Joseph G. *Radio Liberty: A Study of Its Origins, Structure, Policy, Programming, and Effectiveness.* Washington, D.C.: Congressional Research Service, 1972.

Wilford, Hugh. *The Mighty Wurlitzer: How the CIA Played America.* Cambridge, Mass.: Harvard University Press, 2008.

Wise, David, and Thomas B. Ross. *The Invisible Government.* New York: Random House, 1964.

 Wolf, Markus. *Man Without a Face: The Autobiography of Communism's Greatest Spymaster.* New York: PublicAffairs, 1997. Also in German: *Spionagechef im geheimen Krieg: Erinnerungen.* Berlin: Econ & List Taschenbuch Verlag, 1998. The two editions have somewhat different content.

Zake, Ieva, ed. *Anti-Communist Minorities in the U.S.: Political Activism of Ethnic Refugees.* New York: Palgrave Macmillan, 2009.

Video Materials

 Cold Waves. DVD. Luxembourg: Paul Thiliges Distributors, 2008.

To Russia with Love: The Great Radio War—Radio Free Europe and the Cold War. DVD. Munich: Tangram Films, 2008.

Voice of Hope. DVD. Warsaw: Andrzej Drygas, 1998.

Waves of Liberty. DVD. Girona: Canal Paradis, 2007.

Index

Notes are indicated by n following the page number.

Bede, István, 111
Ben, Philippe, 84
Beneš, Edvard, 69, 164
Benkő, Zoltán, 95–96n55
Berecz, János, 185
Bernard, Noel, 120, 153–54, 154n69, 198, 198n45
Bertrandias, Richard, 174
Béry, László, 97n58, 102, 109
Betrayal at Budapest (documentary), 94n52
Bissell, Richard M., Jr., 128
Board for International Broadcasting (BIB), 3, 218, 221, 224, 226
BOB. *See* Bureau of the Budget
Bohlen, Charles E., 26, 50, 122n134
Bohnsack, Günther, 201n49
Boiter, Albert, 172
bombing of RFE headquarters, 196–97
book program, 76–78, 239
Borbándi, Gyula, 98n60, 109, 111
Borhi, László, 102n71
Borkenau, Franz, 110n105
Borsányi, Julian, 93n42
Bourgin, Simon, 79, 79n1
Bow, Frank, 206n15
Braden, Thomas W., 12n13, 34, 49, 203, 234
Brandt, Willy, 74, 209, 210, 210n31
Brezhnev, Leonid, 166, 192
"bridge-building policy," 24
Briggs, Ellis O., 71
British Broadcasting Service (BBC): central scripting at, 182; and Hungarian Revolution (1956), 113, 114n113; jamming of, 159; and RFE programming policy, 40; RFE/RL differentiation from, 39; and RL operational planning, 174
Broadcast Analysis Department (RFE), 119, 226
Broadcasting Freedom (Puddington), 2, 223
broadcast licenses. *See* licensing agreements
Brown, J. F., 222, 244

Brown, Thomas H., Jr., 118
Brundage, Avery, 214
Brzezinski, Zbigniew, 135nn15–16
Buchan, Alistair, 124n140
Buckley, William F., Jr., 126
Bulgaria, intelligence operations against RFE/RL, 191, 196
Bundesamt für Verfassungsschutz (BfV), 74
Bundy, McGeorge, 135
Bureau of the Budget (BOB), 122, 128, 205. *See also* Office of Management and Budget (OMB)
Burks, R. V., 112, 131, 136
Burnham, James, 48
Bušová-Kasalová, Helena, 195n33

Cancer Ward (Solzhenitsyn), 183
Captive Nations Week, 180
Carlos the Jackal, 197–98, 197n38
Carter, Jimmy, 223
CAS. *See* Covert Action Staff
Case, Clifford, 205, 215, 215n48
Catholic Church, 139–40, 144, 149
Ceauşescu, Nicolae, 152–53, 196–97, 198n45
censorship of mail, 61
Central Intelligence Agency (CIA): and AMCOMLIB, 26–36; and autonomy of RFE/RL, 230; as consumer of RFE/RL research, 43; at creation of RFE/RL, 7–38; and Czechoslovak Service, 160, 160n6; disclosure as funding source, 202–27; and disinformation campaigns, 133n7; and émigré organizations, 30n69, 31–32, 77n128; and evolution of Communism, 82; and FEC, 10–26, 76, 128; and Hungarian Revolution (1956), 88, 90, 118; and leaflet campaigns, 58; and McCarthyism, 60; and Moscow Protocol coverage, 164; and policy goals, 46; and psychological warfare programs, 49–50; and public-private partnership with RFE and RL, 2; records of, 3;